Political Choice in Canada

Political Choice in Canada

Harold D. Clarke
University of Windsor

Lawrence LeDuc
University of Windsor

Jane Jenson
Carleton University

Jon H. Pammett
Carleton University

McGRAW-HILL RYERSON LIMITED

Toronto   Montreal   New York   St. Louis   San Francisco   Auckland
Beirut   Bogotá   Düsseldorf   Johannesburg   Lisbon   London
Lucerne   Madrid   Mexico   New Delhi   Panama   Paris   San Juan
São Paulo   Singapore   Sydney   Tokyo

POLITICAL CHOICE IN CANADA

ISBN 0-07-082783-4

1 2 3 4 5 6 7 8 9 10   D   7 6 5 4 3 2 1 0 9 8

Printed and bound in Canada

Care has been taken to trace ownership of copyright material contained in this text. The publishers will gladly take any information that will enable them to rectify any reference or credit in subsequent editions.

Canadian Cataloguing in Publication Data

Main entry under title:

Political choice in Canada

ISBN 0-07-082783-4

1. Elections — Canada. 2. Political participation — Canada.
3. Voting — Canada.   I. Clarke, Harold D., 1943-

JL193.P65   324'.71   C78-001443-X

To Our Parents and Our Families

Contents

LIST OF TABLES

xi

xiii

LIST OF FIGURES

Preface

For most Canadians political participation is confined to voting in periodic elections. Their voting decisions serve individually as a fundamental symbol of democratic politics, and collectively as an integral part of the process by which Canada is governed. Political leaders' arrival in and departure from office is contingent upon the collective action of the electorate. Recognition that the electoral choices of individual citizens play a significant role in understanding the processes of and prospects for peaceful political change in Canada and other Western democracies provided the basic impetus for this study.

Three major areas of interest form the organizational foci for this volume. The first of these concerns citizens' attitudes toward Canadian politics and society, together with the relationships found between societal cleavages and political behaviour. The latter topic has long been central in discussions and analyses of voting in Canada. The former, however, is less familiar. Political attitudes are investigated on the assumption that an enhanced understanding of the background of political choice may be obtained from an appreciation of how individuals perceive and evaluate their political and social environments, especially the regions of Canada and the federal system. An emphasis on orientations toward regions and the federal system derives from the recognition that, although the concepts *region* and *federalism* have great currency in commentary on Canadian politics, little is known about their subjective reality for individual citizens. Do Canadians see their society in regional terms? If so, to what extent is there a consensus on the definition of regions, and are they similar to those used by social scientists for theoretical and analytic purposes? Providing answers to such questions should significantly expand our comprehension of the context of political choice.

A second major focus of this book involves the psychological components of electoral choice. An appreciation of voters' perceptions of and attitudes towards the elements of electoral politics is crucial for understanding both individual voting behaviour and electoral outcomes, as well as processes of political change. Perhaps most important are voters' links with political parties. Of all the concepts developed in electoral behaviour research, none has received more attention than party identification — a person's sense of attachment to a political party. In addition to ascertaining the direction of partisan attachments, we will be concerned with the intensity of these ties, their stability over time, and their consistency in federal and provincial politics. Intensity and stability of feelings about political parties have been subjects of research in a variety of political settings, but consistency of partisan attachments in federal systems has

1

seldom been investigated. It would seem important to do so in Canada, given the wide divergence between federal and provincial party systems in some provinces and the salience and significance of both levels of government for many citizens.

Images of party leaders and concerns with political issues are also potentially significant influences on electoral choice. Canadian political leaders often have been accorded a prominent role in explanations of voting behaviour and election outcomes, and an examination of party leader images, therefore, is an important preliminary step in evaluating their effects on electoral choice. Although issues are also traditionally assigned a prominent position in the matrix of factors influencing political decision-making, little is known about how they shape either individual voting behaviour or electoral outcomes. Thus, we are concerned with describing voters' issue perceptions and positions and linking these to electoral behaviour at both the individual and aggregate levels of analysis.

Assessing the actual importance of factors influencing voting behaviour and election outcomes constitutes the third major task of this book, particularly with reference to the 1974 federal election. Analyses focus on the impact of party leaders, local candidates, and issues as short-term forces affecting voting choices, as well as the relative importance of long- and short-term factors. In pursuing these analyses, we will examine the ways in which different types of voters (defined in terms of patterns of partisanship and levels of political interest) react to the stimuli of election campaigns. The impact of differing electoral contexts is further examined by performing equivalent analyses using data from earlier national election studies.

The 1974 election outcome and broader processes of political stability and change in Canada are the final topics to be considered. Patterns of voter migration between the 1972 and 1974 elections are traced in conjunction with an examination of the behaviour of those entering the electorate in the latter year to determine which groups were particularly instrumental in producing the Liberal victory in 1974. Also, issue effects on different types of voters are reconsidered to determine the significance of specific issues in the outcome of the 1974 contest. More general processes of political change are analyzed with reference to inter-generational variations in partisanship and changes over time in the composition of the electorate.

The principal data base for this investigation derives from personal interviews (averaging one-and-one-half hours in length), with a national probability sample of 2562 members of the Canadian electorate, conducted in the three months immediately following the 1974 federal election. Field work for the survey was conducted by Canadian Facts Ltd.

under the supervision of the authors as part of the 1974 national election study funded by the Canada Council (grant #S73-0633). The nationwide sample of eligible voters was a multi-stage, stratified, cluster design, weighted by province to permit systematic oversampling of several smaller provinces, including Newfoundland, Prince Edward Island, Nova Scotia, and New Brunswick, and systematic undersampling of Ontario (see Appendix A). Appropriate case weights for respondents in the various provinces yield a valid national sample of 2445 cases.

Included in the interview schedule were a wide range of open- and closed-ended questions dealing with federal and provincial voting behaviour and other forms of political participation, psychological attachments to political parties in federal and provincial politics, party and party leader images, issue perceptions, and a number of social background and demographic items (see Appendix B). Also included were questions designed to solicit perceptions of and attitudes toward regions of Canada, the federal system, and other features of the political system and society. It should be noted that although responses quoted as illustrations in this book derive from actual interviews, fictitious names are employed to preserve anonymity of members of the sample.

Information gathered by Professor John Meisel and his colleagues in previous national election studies conducted in 1965 and 1968 is also employed in a number of our analyses. These data were made available to us by the Inter-University Consortium for Political and Social Research. Of course, neither the original collectors of the data nor the Consortium bear any responsibility for the analyses or interpretations presented here.

Typical of large-scale research projects, the present study required substantial support from a number of sources. We wish to thank those individuals and institutions who have facilitated our efforts. The 1974 election study would not have been possible without the generous financial assistance of the Canada Council. Council personnel, particularly Mireille Badour, Marie Cordeau, Dan O'Hagan, and Jean Van Loon, were especially helpful. Also invaluable to us in the construction of the sample was the assistance of the Chief Electoral Officer, Jean Marc Hamel, and his staff. The highly professional and meticulous work of Mary Auvinen, Marian Malo, and their assistants at Canadian Facts did much to ensure the success of the field work and data preparation. Valuable administrative support and computing facilities were provided by the University of Windsor and Carleton University.

The high quality work and enthusiasm of many student research assistants at the two universities contributed significantly to the success of the project, among whom were:

Windsor	Carleton
Phil Bezaire	Janet Bliss
Steve Brooks	Margaret Buhlman
Jim Bruton	John Campbell
Mike Burke	Anne Castle
Bob DeGregory	Cathy Devlin
Lucien Gava	Peggy Dover
Théo Hoffman	David Drake
Sid Indig	Jennifer Keck
Mike O'Mally	Bruce MacNaughton
David Rees	Brian Mosely
Monica Schouten	Gary Munro
Marianne Stewart	Ghislain Savoie
	Bruce Ziff

A special note of thanks is due to Mrs. Juel White for her skill and patience while typing the present manuscript.

The valuable inputs of several colleagues are gratefully acknowledged. We wish to particularly thank Robert Drummond, Kai Hildebrandt, Barry Kay, Allan Kornberg, and John Zipp for reading the completed manuscript in whole or in part. In the formative stages of the project, helpful advice and suggestions were offered by Sam Barnes, William Irvine, Henry Jacek, John Meisel, Richard Rose, Michael de Salaberry, and John Wilson, and by those who reviewed the project proposal for the Canada Council.

Of paramount importance was the assistance of 2562 Canadians who permitted us to question them at length regarding their political attitudes and behaviour. Without their cooperation, this book would not have been possible.

Harold D. Clarke
Jane Jenson
Lawrence LeDuc
Jon H. Pammett

I.

THE CONTEXT OF
POLITICAL CHOICE

Chapter One

Perceptions Of Canadian Politics

Joe Donnelly is a 63-year-old fisherman from Lunenburg, Nova Scotia. He was born in Newfoundland, where his father and his grandfather before him fished for cod off the Grand Banks. After finishing Grade 7, Joe left school for full-time work on the fishing boats. His life has been a constant struggle for enough money to support his family, and it is only now that his income has reached the six- or seven-thousand dollar mark. But there is some hope for the future — his eldest son has gotten a higher-paying white-collar job.

During the course of an interview for the 1974 National Election Study, the interviewer presented Joe with a blank map of Canada and instructed him to "write in five words or phrases which best describe politics in Canada."[1] The points he chose to write down reveal quite clearly the things Joe associates with politics (Figure 1.1). They were:

1. Fishermen get rough deal.
2. Politicians don't come around enough.
3. Unemployment not fair to fishermen.
4. Crooked.
5. Not fair.

Joe feels that politicians have not done much for him. They are remote figures, looking after their own interests ("crooked"), who ignore the people except when they need them at election time. He is obviously concerned in particular with his own industry, fishing, and feels that politicians are insensitive to the hard conditions and seasonal unemployment that are endemic to fishermen. His remarks are not "placed" on the map, in the sense that the part of the country where he wrote his answer does not seem to be related to the content of the answer. Rather, they are general com-

FIGURE 1.1

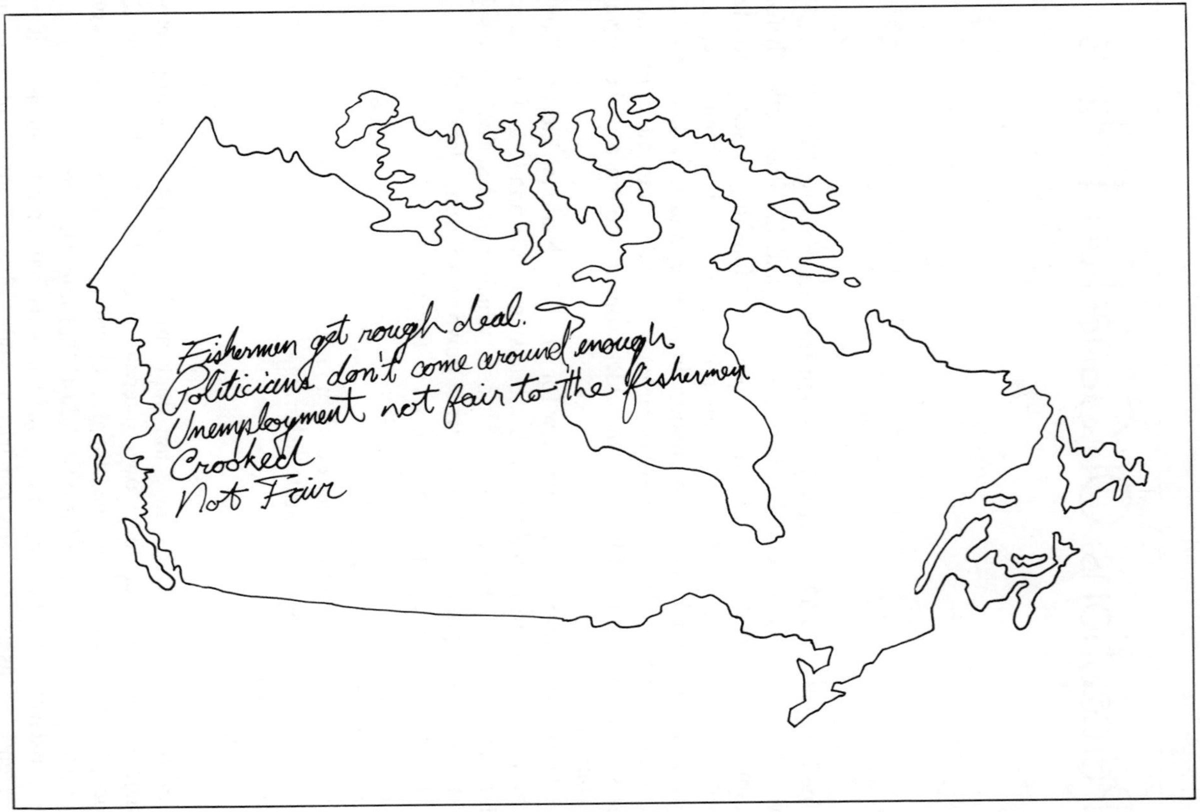

Fisherman get rough deal.
Politicians don't come around enough
Unemployment not fair to the fisherman
Crooked
Not Fair

"Joe Donnelly"

ments about the lack of fair treatment that life in general and politicians in particular have accorded him.

In contrast to Joe Donnelly, Sarah Carbano of Toronto, the wife of a well-to-do wholesale merchant, took the opportunity presented to her to write on the map her optimistic view of Canada's future.

1. God's country.
2. Full of natural resources still unexplored.
3. Land of opportunity.
4. Has the best of the British Isles and United States combined.
5. Has the best chance for a prosperous future if left to private enterprise.

Another Torontonian, Gerald Smith, a 25-year-old who has training as a welder but is now unemployed, places his responses deliberately in different spots on the map (Figure 1.2), and is very conscious of economic conditions prevailing in different parts of Canada. In Newfoundland he has written "economically poor," in New Brunswick "growing slowly," in Quebec "satisfying lifestyle," in Ontario "strong growth," and in the West "general discontent." In the analysis to come, we will be distinguishing between "placed" responses of this type and more general "unplaced" responses. In addition, we will be separating out economic responses such as these from those which are either political or more general sociological descriptions of parts of the country.

Denise Rocher, a young Montrealer, also "places" most of her responses, in the sense that most of them are concerned with the province of Quebec. She writes:

1. Très belle province, Québec.
2. Beaucoup d'organisation avec le maire de Montréal.
3. L'Expo 67 nous a donné beaucoup.
4. Trudeau est un homme merveilleux pour le Canada.
5. Nous sommes libres dans le Québec.

Her satisfaction with living in her province is apparent; it is beautiful and its citizens have their freedoms. An ardent Liberal supporter at both federal and provincial levels, she is enthusiastic about Prime Minister Trudeau, and she also feels that Mayor Drapeau's undertakings in Montreal, particularly Expo 67, have been beneficial to the city.

An interesting mixture of perceptions of Canadian politics is evident in the items written on the map by James Hanna, who teaches elementary school in a suburb of Winnipeg. He has a college education and makes an income of $16 000 per year. He is interested in politics generally, but did

FIGURE 1.2

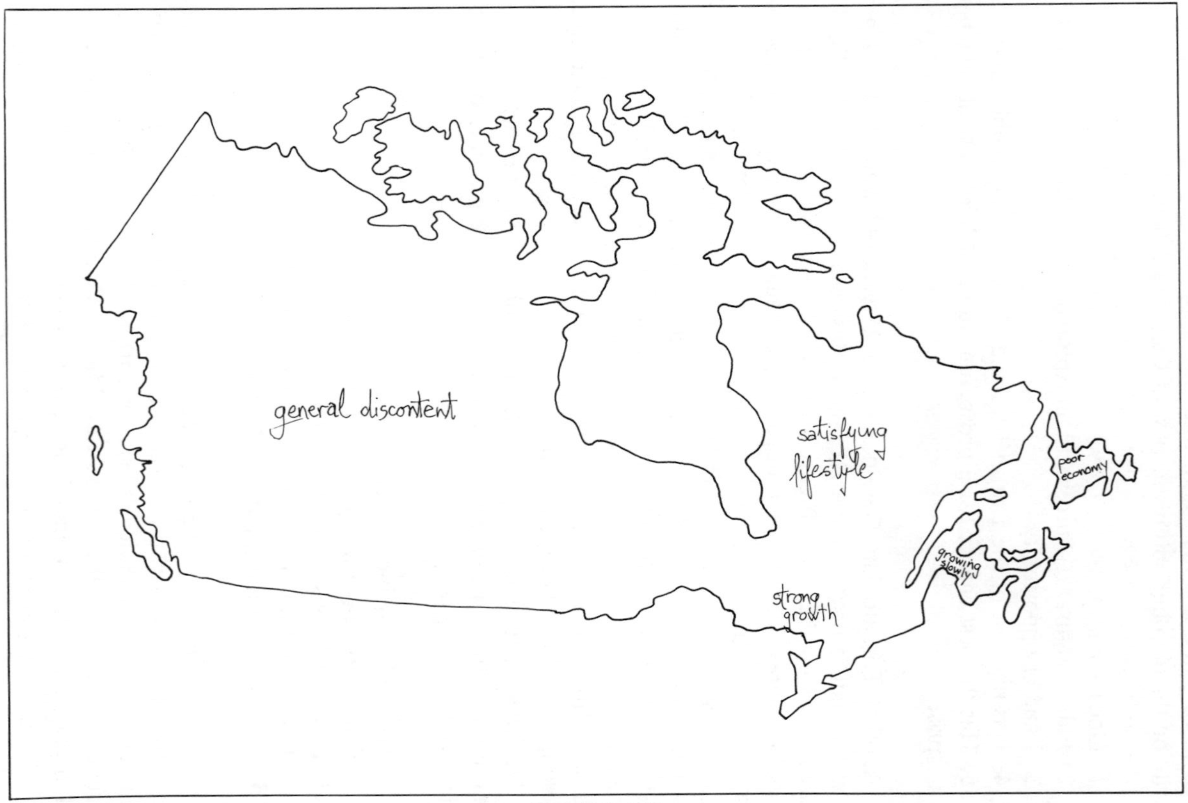

"Gerald Smith"

not vote in 1974 because he was away on holiday and "did not feel there was a contest." Hanna writes:

1. Responsible to the people.
2. Better to have majority government.
3. Cabinet shuffle's good policy.
4. MPs report to constituents.
5. Constituency system gives Eastern Canada more power than Western Canada.

James Hanna's answers are a mixture of democratic principles (the responsibility of elected officials), structural factors (the effects of the constituency system), and current political developments (a Cabinet shuffle). When he is asked to think about the salient aspects of Canadian politics, then, a variety of things come to mind.

This is not so for Mabel Macgregor of Truro. When she is asked to think about Canadian politics, she thinks of specific political issues:

1. Too much for the wealthy person.
2. Not enough pension considering rising prices.
3. Free prescriptions for the elderly a good thing.
4. Family allowances should be adjusted so that those who need it receive more and those who don't need it don't get it at all.
5. Should be free dental service for senior citizens.

Mrs. Macgregor's concern for inadequate pensions and social services for the elderly is doubtless motivated by her personal situation. At age 66, she and her husband, a retired mechanic, are trying to get along on a pension of less than $5000 per year. Her view of Canadian politics, therefore, is coloured by the kind of job government is seen to be doing in providing essential services to people.

Another approach is provided by Heather Concannon, a 20-year-old computer operator from Saskatoon. She wrote:

1. Eastern and Western Canada are out of touch.
2. Parliamentary arrangement protects us from dictatorship type of government.
3. Canadians are apathetic generally with regards to their government.
4. Provincial governments are inclined to alienate one province from another, making "have" and "have not" provinces, when Canada should be *one* country, not ten provinces.
5. English is the universal language of the world, Quebec!

She has an overriding concern with Canadian unity, feeling that the two halves of the country have little contact with each other, that the existence and behaviour of provincial governments exacerbate the matter, and that Quebec's insistence on remaining French also hinders the development of feeling for Canada as a whole. She considers that Canadians are generally politically apathetic, a judgment that might well apply to her also, since she did not vote in 1974 and considers herself "neutral politically."

Heather Concannon's view that English is the "universal language of the world" would hardly appeal to Jean-Pierre Tremblay, though he could well believe that English Canadians feel that way. Jean-Pierre is a 57-year-old artist making a modest living on the north shore of the St. Lawrence from painting and other crafts. He is an enthusiastic separatist, has joined the Parti Québécois, and refers to its leader, René Lévesque, as "mon idole." His views of Canadian politics are:

1. Contre le fédéralisme.
2. Je trouve que le Canada n'exploite pas ses resources naturelles avec des fonds canadiens.
3. Augmente le salaire minimum que chaque personne qui travaille aille un revenu de base pas taxable pour qu'il puisse vivre.
4. Baisser l'âge de la pension de retraite.
5. Etablir une justice sans différence des classes.

Besides the large-scale political change desired with Quebec independence, Jean-Pierre wants specific changes made in the area of foreign investment, to raise the minimum taxable income, and to lower the retirement age for receipt of a pension.

The responses we have quoted above only partially illustrate the diversity of political perceptions prevalent across the country. We could just as well have cited the young mortician's assistant who feels that "Canadian politics are too overshadowed by our American cousins' affairs," the fireman who writes, "It's all Liberal and they are doing as they like," or the elderly news vendor who says, "C'est toujours pareil-jamais le changement." In this chapter we will document a wide range of political perceptions held by Canadians, as revealed by their answers written on the blank maps of Canada. Although we asked respondents to "write in five words or phrases which best describe politics in Canada," it must be noted that by no means everyone referred to *politics* in their answers — in fact, only about half of the responses are political. Specifically, those who wrote their responses in particular places on the map were less likely to refer to the places in political terms than they were to make sociological descriptions of parts of Canada. The unplaced responses were much more likely to be political, with references to politicians, parties, and political issues predominating.

PLACED RESPONSES

Because those responses placed in particular geographical positions on the map were of quite different types than those not referring to geographic areas of Canada, it is useful to separate our analyses of placed and unplaced responses. Considered together in this section are two types of placed responses, those which were actually written on a part of the map and seemed to refer to that place, and those which referred to a geographic location in Canada even though they were not written directly on it. Thus, respondents who wrote "The West is neglected by the federal government" are considered to have placed their response, whether or not that answer was actually written on the Western part of the map.

Classification of the placed responses will enable us to first look at how various provinces and regions of Canada were described by all Canadians in 1974, and then at specific regional or provincial patterns. After that, the responses will be examined on two dimensions, a positive-negative one measuring affect, and a political-economic-sociological one measuring substantive content. Finally, we will look at whether respondents see their own provinces in a different way than they see the rest of the country.

Appendix 1A presents a detailed breakdown of the content of responses placed in Canada's provinces and regions. It is interesting to note first of all that only about 38% of the responses to the question were placed, either directly or indirectly. Considering that the map of Canada on which the respondents answered the question might have been expected to encourage people to write responses referring to specific geographical locations in the country, the total number of such placed responses is somewhat below our expectations. Much of the thinking Canadians do about politics, then, does not seem to be specific to regions or provinces of the country. Rather, it is in terms of more general political objects, leaders, and issues. We will turn to these unplaced responses later in this chapter.

Similarly, even though it was specified in the instruction to the respondent that he or she was to note down items about *politics* in Canada, many responses were not of a specifically political nature. General positive responses, characterizing places as "good" or "well-off" are common, as are the general negative answers denoting poor conditions in many areas. In addition, many Canadians referred to the state of the economy in areas of the country, and also to the nature and abundance or lack of natural resources. Some references to political parties and provincial governments are present, but very few are made to political leaders, either federal or provincial. Many people took the opportunity presented to them via this map question to note down their views about the country in general or its regions, without concentrating on politics. Thus, the content of the placed responses may be seen as an indication of the images that Canadians have of the regions of the country, and not just of political characteristics of those regions.

Quebec is the area of the country in which the largest number of responses is placed, followed by the West (either in general or in reference to individual provinces), the Atlantic region (or its provinces), and Ontario. To some extent the results may be accounted for by the structure of the map drawing, which provided a prominent open space in the Western part of the country and another large space in Quebec. Nonetheless, Quebec is an area of the country about which Canadians have distinct views, and many of these views are negative ones. Many Canadians just do not like Quebec. Some see it as a hotbed of separatism and a proponent of bilingualism, or they do not like the way French is given primacy. Others see Quebec as parochial in its concern for itself, as continually complaining, and as distorting Canadian federalism through the favouritism shown to it by the federal government. Quebeckers themselves, on the other hand, are of course more likely to give positive or neutral connotations to items such as separatism, bilingualism, or "the French homeland," which are perceived more negatively in the rest of the country. It is interesting to note that these negative feelings about Quebec precede by two years the election of the Parti-Québécois government in 1976.

In contrast to Quebec, which many people see in negative and political terms, perceptions of the West show two different themes. The first is alienation and neglect. The West, which is most often seen as a single region and not in terms of its individual provinces, is perceived as disgruntled at its consistent neglect by the East and by the federal government. It is not seen as very powerful in the Canadian federation, but rather as underrepresented in it. The second theme in the common perceptions of the West deals with its natural resources, particularly oil in Alberta and wheat in Saskatchewan. The West feeds the country and provides it with its energy supplies, and in return it is ignored — a theme of alienation. So runs the thinking of many Canadians, particularly Westerners themselves.

In looking at the popular perceptions of British Columbia, at the top of the list we meet two responses which are scarcely present at all anywhere else. The thing people most frequently associate with British Columbia is isolation — a sense of its being cut off from the rest of the country by the mountain barrier. Secondly, people see the province as strike-ridden. It is quite likely, however, that the prominence of this response was a product of the fact that a well-publicized dockers' strike was going on in British

Columbia at the time the questionnaire was being administered. The provincial government of Premier Barrett was also highly visible in 1974, and the number of people expressing negative views of it, the NDP, and socialism in general, perhaps foretold the defeat of that government a year later.

The two other frequently named parts of the country, Ontario and the Atlantic area, are seen largely in economic terms. Ontario and the centre of the country are perceived as wealthy and powerful, as the heartland of industry, and as generally favoured, presumably by both God and government. The Atlantic region, however, suffers in the eyes of Canadians from a shaky economy, caused perhaps by its reliance on fishing, and as a consequence needs government assistance. The references to neglect in perceptions of the area suggest, moreover, that the assistance has not been forthcoming, and that the Maritimes do not have the power to compel it. There are transportation problems in the Maritimes too, and Prince Edward Island needs its long-promised causeway.

The theme of neglect that we have seen with regard to both the West and the Maritimes is encountered once again when we look at perceptions of the North. Canadians' basic view of the North is that not enough has been done to tap its potential. It is rich in resources which should be exploited, but it is thinly populated and needs governmental concentration on its development. Also of concern with regard to the North is the plight of the native Indian and Inuit populations; they are seen to have been badly treated under the white man's regime. The data also reveal that a powerful, favoured, Eastern part of the country is seen by some people, that it was relatively uncommon for cities to be marked on the map (with the exception of Ottawa), and that the few people who placed their responses in the United States did so largely with the purpose of denoting its power or expressing a negative view of its presidential system of government.

In general, the words which respondents chose to describe particular parts of Canada on the map reflect a fairly keen awareness of the political, economic, and sociological differences between parts of the country. In particular, many Canadians are concerned that the peripheral parts of the country have been neglected through a concentration of population, industry, and economic growth in the centre of the country. The federal government is seen as being responsive to these central Canadian interests, whether they be the economic demands of Ontario or the cultural demands of Quebec, at the expense of the West and the Maritimes. These areas are seen as isolated, neglected, and alienated, by their own residents and by others. Central Canadians, as well as Westerners and Easterners, share the perception of the disadvantaged position of the periphery.

Table 1.1 shows where the residents of the various provinces distributed

TABLE 1.1

Location of Placed Responses, by Province of Residence of Respondent
(column percentages)

RESPONSES PLACED BY RESIDENTS OF:

RESPONSES PLACED IN	NFLD.	P.E.I.	N.S.	N.B.	QUE.	ONT.	MAN.	SASK.	ALTA.	B.C.	TOTAL
Newfoundland	41%[a]	3%	3%	7%	1%	4%	2%	2%	1%	2%	3%
Prince Edward Is.	—	19	3	3	—	—	—	—	—	—	—
Nova Scotia	—	2	17	3	—	1	1	1	—	—	2
New Brunswick	—	2	3	15	2	1	1	—	—	—	2
Atlantic Area	9	20	14	13	8	7	3	7	5	4	7
Quebec	6	13	10	14	39	21	12	15	15	13	22
Ontario	3	8	7	10	8	21	9	7	9	9	12
Central Area	13	6	9	2	3	2	5	3	3	7	4
The East	—	1	1	1	1	1	10	10	11	5	3
The West	19	12	12	12	15	16	22	21	23	16	17
Manitoba	—	—	1	—	1	—	6	—	—	1	1
Saskatchewan	—	2	1	—	1	1	3	6	3	3	2
Alberta	—	2	3	1	2	4	5	5	13	5	4
British Columbia	3	5	7	6	5	9	5	15	10	27	10
The North	6	4	4	4	4	6	2	7	2	6	5
Cities	—	1	5	7	4	3	11	1	4	1	4
United States	—	1	1	1	1	2	2	—	—	1	1
Other Specific	—	—	1	1	3	2	3	—	—	—	2
N =	32	109	198	177	660	645	129	147	216	311	2515[b]

a. Percentages in this and subsequent tables may not sum to 100% because of rounding.
b. Italics indicates weighted number of cases. See Appendix A for description of sample weights applied in this and subsequent tables.

their placed answers to the question asking them to write in five things which best characterized Canadian politics. As might be expected, there is some tendency for responses to be placed in the province where the respondent resides, or at least in the general area of the country closest to the place of residence. Placing responses in or writing specific things about the respondents' own province is most noticeable in Newfoundland, Quebec, and to a lesser extent British Columbia. It should be noted, however, that no provincial boundaries were actually supplied on the maps handed to the respondents, so that it was sometimes very difficult, if not impossible, for those coding the question to determine whether a response written in the middle of the western part of the country was actually intended to be specifically related to a province, or to the West in general. In cases of doubt, the response was coded as being placed in the larger entity (e.g., in "the West" rather than in Saskatchewan) and so appears in the "larger" category in these tables. Furthermore, it is likely that the simple geographical structure of the map of Canada encouraged responses on either side (e.g., in Newfoundland or British Columbia) to be made more specific. Nevertheless it seems reasonable to conclude that those in Newfoundland, Quebec, and British Columbia taking the map cue to think of Canadian politics in geographical terms were more concerned than residents of other areas with the characteristics of their own provinces.

When it came to concentrating placed descriptions in one's own area of the country — East, Centre, or West — there was little variation among the residents of the different provinces. Among Western responses, the proportions which were concentrated in either the West in general or in one of the four provinces specifically totalled 52% of the responses placed by British Columbia residents, 49% for Albertans, 47% for Saskatchewanians, and 41% for Manitobans. Forty-four per cent of Ontarians' and 50% of Quebeckers' placed responses occur either in Ontario, Quebec, or the centre of the country generally. Similarly, the percentages of responses placed in either "the East," "the Atlantic area," or one of the four provinces specifically reached 50% in Newfoundland, 47% in Prince Edward Island, 41% in Nova Scotia, and 42% in New Brunswick. In most cases, then, if a response to a request to characterize Canadian politics was going to be related to a particular place in the country, the chances were about 50-50 that it portrayed some aspect of the area the respondent lived in.

The most common places, outside the respondents' own area, for comments to be specified were in Quebec, the West, and to a lesser extent Ontario and British Columbia. The "visibility" of political, economic, and societal conditions of Quebec and the West seems to be quite general throughout Canada and occasions a fairly high degree of specific comment from all sectors. In particular, it can be noted from Table 1.1 that placed responses of Ontario residents were actually just as likely to be specific to Quebec as they were to be specific to their own province.

The responses were further categorized on two additional dimensions,

according to whether they paint a positive, neutral, or negative picture of
the area they are describing (affect), and according to whether they refer
to political, economic, or sociological aspects of a given area (substance).

TABLE 1.2

Affective Content of Placed Map Responses
by Province of Residence
(column percentages)

RESPONSES PLACED BY RESIDENTS OF:

	NFLD.	P.E.I.	N.S.	N.B.	QUE.	ONT.	MAN.	SASK.	ALTA.	B.C.	TOTAL
Positive	47%	15%	13%	12%	18%	14%	12%	8%	14%	21%	16%
Neutral	3	56	56	61	50	41	50	27	40	30	43
Negative	50	29	32	27	32	45	38	65	46	48	42
N =	32	109	200	177	675	648	130	147	216	315	*2511*

TABLE 1.3

Substantive Content of Placed Responses
by Province of Residence
(column percentages)

	NFLD.	P.E.I.	N.S.	N.B.	QUE.	ONT.	MAN.	SASK.	ALTA.	B.C.	TOTAL
Political	28%	42%	35%	14%	24%	38%	32%	27%	35%	41%	32%
Economic	25	11	8	9	11	13	10	29	7	9	12
Socio-logical	47	47	58	78	65	49	59	45	58	51	56
N =	32	109	200	177	675	648	130	147	216	315	*2511*

It can be seen from Appendix 1A that many of the initial coding categories for these responses were constructed with a positive-neutral-negative
dimension to them. Comments on the state or nature of the economy, for
example, can either reflect the respondents' view that it is doing well, that
jobs are plentiful, etc., or that it is suffering, or simply that it is of a
certain type, for example a wheat economy. The area can be described as
powerful, which has a positive tone, or as lacking power, which has a
negative one. Similarly, categories of "general positive responses" and
"general negative responses" show that it was quite common for the
parts of Canada to be called "good," "well off," "rotten," and so on. The
substantive dimension was constructed by classifying as political, responses
dealing with government, politicians, leaders, parties, and the power of
parts of the country; as economic, responses dealing with the state of the
economy, employment, inflation, and the deficiencies of the economy; and

as sociological, responses which were basically descriptions of the kind of life lived in the area, without appreciable political or economic content.

It is clear that by our definitions of positive and negative, many more responses had a negative cast to them than a positive one, by a ratio of better than 2:1 (Table 1.2). There are, in addition, substantial differences between the residents of various provinces in how negatively they view parts of the country. We will shortly be able to locate *which* areas of the country are more damned and pitied than others, but looking here overall, it seems that residents of Saskatchewan, by a wide margin, cast the most jaundiced eye over parts of Canada. Just about two-thirds of all placed responses given by Saskatchewanians are negative in tone. Half the responses of Newfoundlanders are negative, but this is offset by the fact that most of the rest of their responses are positive, by far the largest proportion of any of the provinces. In general, Table 1.2 indicates that residents of the West and Ontario are more likely to describe Canada and Canadian politics in negative terms than are Easterners and Quebeckers.

It becomes apparent from Table 1.3 that even though the question asked for descriptions of Canadian *politics* to be written down on the blank map of Canada, many more people preferred to think in terms of descriptions which we have classified as sociological. This tendency to think in sociological terms was particularly apparent in New Brunswick and Quebec, where three-quarters and two-thirds of the responses, respectively, were of this type. There is, however, no particular East-West difference in the propensity to think politically about areas of the country; in general, about one-third of all placed responses were political, and although there were differences between provinces in this regard (Table 1.3) they were not systematic in nature. Unlike most other provinces, there is also a substantial number of economic responses from Saskatchewan. Although the information in Table 1.2 and 1.3 does not directly show this, it suggests that the main thing differentiating the Saskatchewan placed responses from those of some of the other provinces is the number of negative views of the economy (of both their own province and other areas). We will address this question later on, using the unplaced as well as the placed responses, but it is worth noting here that this possibility is in fact supported by the data.

Two aspects of Tables 1.2 and 1.3 are most interesting to pursue. They involve the distribution of the negative responses noted in Table 1.2 and the political responses in Table 1.3. It is not possible to tell from those preliminary tabulations what areas of the country were the *objects* of the negative and political images noted there. Table 1.4 details how negative the views of the residents of each province were with regard to their own province and other areas of the country, both near and far.

TABLE 1.4

Percentage of Negative Responses Placed by Residents of Each Province in Their Own Province and in Other Areas

RESPONSES PLACED BY RESIDENTS OF: (% NEGATIVE)

PLACE DESCRIBED	NFLD.	P.E.I.	N.S.	N.B.	QUE.	ONT.	MAN.	SASK.	ALTA.	B.C.
Own Province	62	23	47	42	43	37	63	89	17	59
Atlantic (ind. or region)	x	45	38	37	32	74	56	64	54	78
East	x	x	x	x	37	17	23	36	30	40
Quebec	x	38	58	38	—	45	40	55	56	44
Ontario, Centre	40	19	13	5	14	25[a]	18	38	23	25
West (ind. or region)	0	12	15	13	20	36	55	68	70	46
British Columbia	x	40	36	9	31	40	50	95	55	—

x   N less than 5.
[a]   Centre only.

In almost all cases (Prince Edward Island and Alberta being exceptions), people have more negative things to say about their own provinces than they do about other areas of the country.

TABLE 1.5

Percentage of Political Responses Placed by the Residents of Each Province in Their Own Province and in Other Areas

RESPONSES PLACED BY RESIDENTS OF: (% POLITICAL)

PLACE DESCRIBED	NFLD.	P.E.I.	N.S.	N.B.	QUE.	ONT.	MAN.	SASK.	ALTA.	B.C.
Own Province	27	29	26	15	39	36	25	22	31	52
Atlantic (ind. or region)	x	38	26	11	14	24	22	29	14	28
East	x	x	x	x	x	50	33	29	35	40
Quebec	x	43	32	13	—	49	47	32	41	44
Ontario, Centre	20	50	45	19	15	38[a]	28	22	42	48
West (ind. or region)	33	59	36	4	14	42	18	29	28	29
British Columbia	x	40	36	18	25	40	33	14	45	—

x   N less than 5.
[a]   Centre only.

Thus, things that are closer to hand and presumably more familiar seem to have given people more of an opportunity to develop a critical image of them than things which are farther away. Similarly, Table 1.5 shows what parts of the country were given the most political images.

Although there are certain exceptions to every generalization which can be made from the figures in Table 1.4, some patterns appear to be present. By and large, for example, Canadians have negative images of the Atlantic provinces, whether they refer to the individual provinces or to the region as a whole. There are, in contrast, relatively fewer negative perceptions of living conditions in Ontario or of that province in general. Perceptions of the West and of British Columbia show a different pattern. Residents of the Western provinces seem to give a very heavy negative cast to descriptions of the area, but the residents of the rest of the country associate mostly positive or neutral things with the West. Thus, the Western negative self-image does not seem to be reciprocated by other parts of the country at all; rather, they think of positive characteristics of the West. Finally, it should be noted that while descriptions of Quebec are in most cases more negative than average, they rarely reach the extremes of negativity associated with the Atlantic area, or the self-perceptions of Westerners.

The distribution of political responses shows (Table 1.5) that Quebec and British Columbia differ, in that the residents of those provinces view their own provinces more politically than they view the other areas. Thus, Quebec and British Columbia have the most "politicized" sets of self-images, and, of course, we have already detailed a fairly extensive series of politically relevant characteristics generally associated with the two areas. Although there is considerable variation among the provinces, it is evident that substantial numbers of political responses are associated with Quebec, Ontario, and the Centre of the country.

UNPLACED RESPONSES

To this point we have been dealing with descriptions associated with particular places on the map of Canada, whether specific provinces, larger regions, or smaller areas within provinces. It is natural that these placed answers would first attract our attention, since the question format using the map of the country implicitly suggests that such responses would be appropriate. As we noted earlier, however, such placed responses were not the norm; it was about twice as likely for people to associate things with politics in Canada which did *not* relate to particular parts of the country than things which did. Although many of the unplaced responses were written *on* the map as well (since the page handed to respondents was dominated by the map, it was difficult not to write on it) the content of these answers did not relate to the particular area of the country, generally the large open area in the West, which was chosen for the inscription of the response.

The content of the unplaced responses may be conveniently divided into three categories. First, just over 40% of these responses were of a "general political" nature, making comments on the nature of politics in Canada, what government does, the character of politicians, the structures of government, the political parties, and so on. Second, there were many responses, about one-third of the total, which dealt with issues, both political and economic, ranging from inflation to immigration to agricultural policy. A third category, comprising about one-quarter of the responses, contained more general comments on Canada, Canadians, and sociological descriptions of the country. It will be apparent that the unplaced responses are much more political than was the case with those encountered earlier.

A detailed breakdown of the unplaced responses is presented in Appendix 1B. Most common were the general political answers. Politics is seen as benefiting or not benefiting the public: "It stands the public in good stead, *or* it lets us all down; politicians are doing a good job, *or* they are a bunch of dishonest people making things worse; government is doing its best, *or* it's overspending and has lost contact with the people; democracy is the principle our politics is run by, *or* democracy is lacking in the operation of government today; the people are represented well *or* the people are represented poorly; the federal system of government is the solution to Canada's diverse needs, *or* the federal system is not working well and should be replaced by a unitary system; more power should be given either to the federal government *or* to the provincial governments; the Government, or the Liberal Party, is doing a good job for the country, *or* electing them was the biggest mistake we ever made; the Opposition is destructive and uncooperative, *or* doing its best to provide a good alternative government; Pierre Trudeau is a great Prime Minister, *or* a rotten one; thank goodness the 1974 election produced a majority government, *or* we would have been better off in a minority parliament; election campaigns are too long and boring and much too expensive, and furthermore, the media coverage of the 1974 campaign was biased; Canada's political parties are doing a fine job for the country, *or* they're all the same, and generally a bad lot."

It is apparent from inspection of these responses that a high proportion of them are distinctly negative in tone. We have noted the negative nature of many responses placed in particular locations on the map earlier, but here the attitudes of dislike and distrust are much more specifically keyed to politics and politicians. There are no overtones of dislike of other places in the country to distract us here — it is impossible to overlook the fact that a majority of Canadians simply do not like politics or politicians.

Examples of this distaste for politics are numerous. The general comments on politics were 33% positive and 52% negative. The general comments on politicians were a staggering 78% negative in tone. Politicians tend to be seen by Canadians as "terrible," as "crooked," as "doing a bad job," as "out for themselves," as "wasting the money we pay in taxes," as "serving the big interests," and as "generally ineffectual." Government has the same image; attitudes towards it are 75% negative. Similarly, the general comments on parties are 78% negative.

Many Canadians, then, have a negative image of politics, politicians, government, and parties. This does not seem to mean, however, that the political system, specific parties, or individual politicians are all seen in a negative way. Rather, the comments on democracy and representation were 79% positive. Most Canadians feel this is a democratic political system and that the people are genuinely represented. Additionally, those who felt disposed to comment on specific politicians, whether leaders or not, or about specific political parties, whether the Government or the Opposition, gave a negative tone to only 33% of these descriptions.

Comments on Canada and Canadians are also somewhat more positive in nature. For example, attitudes toward the country were dominated by positive comments to the effect that Canada is a good land, a good place to live, and fortunate, compared to the rest of the world. These far outweighed responses portraying Canada as a land full of injustice or "generally in a mess." There are indications, however, that even these types of images of the country may not be so rosy. The category of general comments on Canadians is dominated by responses which characterize Canadians as dull, passive, or unexciting; which cite the lack of citizen interest or involvement in the country; or which call for changes in individual behaviour to set things straight. Furthermore, the data contain a number of rather plaintive cries from respondents who felt "It's all too complicated for me" or "It's very difficult to understand." And, of course, there are those who simply stated that "I'm not interested in politics."

Turning to the numerous issues raised by respondents, not surprisingly we find that the most common national concerns are over economic issues, frequently those which affect individual respondents personally. As we might expect, inflation is the number one problem, and far more people cite their concerns with rising prices — particularly of food, clothing, housing, and fuel — than refer to any other political issue. Next in order of concern come pensions, unemployment, taxes, bilingualism, welfare, foreign investment, foreign affairs and aid, and a whole series of other issues. A good many of these issue responses are complaints that the issues of concern to Canadians are not being adequately dealt with by government. Some examples are: "Inflation is bad, pensions are too low and are not keeping pace with the rise in the cost of living; the unemployment insurance system allows people to cheat; taxes are too high; bilingualism is being forced down our throats; too many bums are on welfare; foreign investment is turning us into Americans; our schools are falling apart; health insurance doesn't work; everybody's on strike; you can't afford to buy a house; the farmers are getting a bad deal; freight rates are too high; they are letting in too many immigrants; women are discriminated against; pollution is rife; the policy on oil prices is discriminatory; family allowances are too low; and they are letting murderers get off." It's a wonder Canadians can face getting up in the morning!

It is worth emphasizing here that the litany of complaint poured out by Canadians and documented in this chapter comes, not in response to a question asking them what is *wrong* with Canada or with Canadian politics, but simply for the things which best *describe* Canadian politics. We had expected that a question worded in this manner, and including the map as a stimulus to comment on differing parts of the country's politics, would produce a preponderance of rather neutrally worded descriptive answers which would allow us to document the objects that were most associated with Canadian politics, the areas of the country thought of most often, and so on. It is somewhat surprising, therefore, to find that most types of response to the question, and particularly those dealing with politics, politicians, and political issues, were not neutral answers, but were very negative. We will comment further on the implications of this basic finding later in this chapter.

Let us pursue the analysis of the unplaced responses further by breaking them down into two dimensions, the affective classification and the substantive one. Tables 1.6 and 1.7 provide these data, arranged by province to show how respondents situated in different parts of the country see its politics. Interestingly enough, the data reveal that they see politics in remarkably similar ways. Table 1.6 indicates a rather minor amount of fluctuation between the provinces in the degree of negativity they assign to the Canadian political, economic, and social systems. The most negative province, as also was the case with the placed responses (Table 1.2), was Saskatchewan, followed closely by British Columbia, Prince Edward Island, New Brunswick, and Newfoundland. The least negative province was Quebec, though this was caused by more of the Quebec responses

TABLE 1.6
Affective Content of Unplaced Map Responses
by Province of Residence
(column percentages)

	NFLD.	P.E.I.	N.S.	N.B.	QUE.	ONT.	MAN.	SASK.	ALTA.	B.C.	TOTAL
Positive	24%	19%	21%	28%	20%	24%	27%	16%	25%	19%	22%
Neutral	17	18	23	12	30	20	18	19	20	17	22
Negative	59	63	56	60	50	56	55	66	55	64	56
N =	96	160	273	198	1241	1249	197	167	220	529	*4219*

TABLE 1.7

**Substantive Content of Unplaced Map Responses
by Province of Residence
(column percentages)**

	NFLD.	P.E.I.	N.S.	N.B.	QUE.	ONT.	MAN.	SASK.	ALTA.	B.C.	TOTAL
Political	52%	69%	66%	62%	55%	63%	61%	57%	59%	68%	61%
Economic	16	15	10	14	18	15	13	25	17	10	16
Socio-logical	32	16	24	25	27	22	25	19	24	22	24
N =	96	160	273	198	1241	1249	197	167	220	529	*4219*

being of a neutral nature than in other areas, not by a preponderance there of positive images. The high negative content of responses goes along in British Columbia and in Prince Edward Island with higher than average totals of political responses, as shown in Table 1.7, indicating that these two areas have particularly soured on politics and politicians. The high negative content of the Saskatchewan responses, however, is once again associated with a higher than average economic content to the answers.

An examination of the Saskatchewan responses reveals the reason for the high economic and negative content noted in Tables 1.6 and 1.7. A total of 15% of unplaced Saskatchewan responses were references to inflation and the high cost of living; this is about twice as high as the normal rate of reference to inflation. Saskatchewanians were also heavily concerned with other political issues as well, with strikes, welfare, pensions, and agricultural policy leading the way. Thus, instead of the one-third of responses being classified as issue-oriented, which is the norm across the country, in Saskatchewan close to half (46%) of the responses dealt with issues, and were highly critical of lack of government action on them.

Inspection of the specific responses from the other provinces reveals few striking differences. There are some examples of particular concerns in specific provinces; for instance, New Brunswick responses are twice the national average on the subjects of high taxes and abuses of the welfare system, and Prince Edward Islanders are especially concerned with pensions and make twice the average number of comments on specific political parties, particularly "the government." Illustrative of the more general pattern, however, are the responses from British Columbia. On the substantive dimension (Table 1.7) these can be seen to be more political than most, but do not concentrate on a few specific political grievances. As measured by both placed and unplaced responses, British Columbians seem to think more politically than do residents of some other areas.

POLITICAL NEGATIVISM

Many images stand out from the data presented so far in this chapter: the contrast of a neglected, economically distressed, isolated periphery of the country with the wealthy, catered-to central provinces; or the general propensity of the respondents to avoid political descriptions of the areas of the country, but to apply general political judgments to politics, politicians, and issues of the day. Perhaps the most striking impression to be gained from the data, however, is one we have commented on several times along the way — the overwhelmingly negative feelings Canadians have toward politics in this country.

As a summary of the amount of such negative feeling, we may look at Table 1.8, which classifies all the responses, placed and unplaced, according to their affective nature, as well as to their substantive characteristics. Both of these classification schemes are the same ones that were used in previous tables.

Overall, half of all the responses to the map question were negative in tone, just as half were political in nature. It is particularly apparent that the political and economic responses were negative. We have noted already the types of negative perceptions prevalent about politics and politicians, and thus the fact that the political responses were more than twice as likely to be negative than positive should not now be surprising. The responses classified economic here are comments about the state of the

TABLE 1.8

Affective Content of Map Responses
(Placed and Unplaced) by Substantive Content
(diagonal percentages)

		POSITIVE	NEUTRAL	NEGATIVE	TOTAL
Political		11	14	25	50
Economic		2	1	12	14
Sociological		7	15	14	36
	Total	20	30	50	100%

N = 6746

economy in various parts of the country, as well as about particular economic issues such as inflation, and it can be seen that these comments are almost totally negative. Finally, it is interesting to note that even the responses which we have classified as sociological, mainly descriptions of characteristics of the country, have more negative than positive content. We would, of course, have expected the neutral responses to predominate here, and they are slightly more common than the negative ones, but the difference is not great. We are forced to conclude that even when Canadians are not talking politics or thinking of economic conditions but are simply describing their country, they are inclined to be negative.[2]

What degree of importance should we attach to these negative responses? This question may be addressed by classifying the *objects* of these positive and negative attitudes. To do so, we will adapt a conceptual scheme designed by Pammett and Whittington to classify the objects in the political world towards which citizens are socialized.[3] This scheme (Figure 1.3) has two dimensions. The first utilizes David Easton's division of the political system into three levels: the political community, the regime, and the authorities.[4] The second classifies the type of attitude as structural, symbolic, or conceptual.

FIGURE 1.3
Objects of Attitudes Toward the Political System in Canada

TYPE

LEVEL OF POLITICAL SYSTEM	STRUCTURAL	SYMBOLIC	CONCEPTUAL
Political Community (Canada)	Territory, geography	Flags, heroes, etc.	Nationhood, nationality, the Canadian identity or way of life
Regime (Government & Constitution)	Constitution, federal system	Monarchy, Parliament Buildings	Democracy, responsible government, ideology, politics
Authorities (people in the system)	Parties, groups, politicians, leadership — all general	Specific parties and politicians, 1974 election	Issues

The political community is the political aspect of the total society, the nation or entity which permits people in one country to identify themselves as separate from the rest of the world.[5] The regime is the set of values, norms, and structures which determine the form of the state. It includes not only the basic values which determine system goals, but also the institutional mechanisms which allow their attainment. The regime includes the federal system, the parliamentary system, and structures such as the Cabinet and the courts. The authorities include the actual politicians, parties, and politically active groups at any particular point in time.

Attitudes toward the Canadian political system, then, may be directed at the level of the community (the country itself), the regime (the type of government), or the authorities (the political actors and issues of the day). By adding to this three-fold division a second dimension of the type of attitude, we may construct the typology in Figure 1.3. The type of attitude may be *structural,* connoting the actual physical or organizational makeup of the community, regime, or authorities; *symbolic,* connoting things or persons which stand for principles relating to the three levels; or *conceptual,* connoting complex generalizations that we make about the nature of the three levels of the system.

Although the classification of our map responses into these different types is bound to be a bit arbitrary, we have settled on the following divisions, as summarized in Figure 1.3. Structural objects relating to the political community are the geography of Canada, conceptions of its territory, and references to the component regions of the country. Regime-level structural objects would include the British North America Act, the federal system, as well as the judicial system and the civil service. Structural objects at the level of the authorities are political parties, groups, politicians, and leadership. We have made a distinction here between general references to parties, politicians, and groups, which we place in the structural category at the authorities level, and references to specific persons in political life or specific parties, which we classify as authorities-symbolic because of their transient nature. Symbolic objects at the community and regime levels, on the other hand, are not transient in nature but enduring, and these include, at the community level, the flag, the beaver, the maple leaf, and any national heroes who may exist; at the regime level, the Crown and the Parliament Buildings. Finally, on the conceptual level, associated with the political community are conceptions of the Canadian identity, nationality, or way of life; with the regime, basic ideas of democracy, responsible government, representation, particular ideologies like socialism or capitalism, as well as general ideas about the nature of politics; and with the authorities, the issues of the day.

Table 1.9 shows the positive or negative content of the responses classified into the nine-fold division suggested by Figure 1.3. The numbers of responses falling in the different categories is suggestive of a relatively even concern of Canadians with the three levels of the political system. About one-third of the responses were related to the political community level, one-quarter to the regime level, and about 40 per cent to the authorities. It will be seen, however, that two of the categories in Figure 1.3 are neglected. First, the community symbolic category, dealing with national symbols such as the flag or heroes, is not present at all. No Canadian made a spontaneous reference to a heroic figure, political or otherwise, out of the past, and none mentioned the flag, either as a political issue or as a symbol. It may be that the question was not particularly suited to symbolic responses, because the regime-symbolic category is also barely present — the only responses coded here were references to Ottawa, the nation's capital, and the site of the Parliament Buildings. It is possible, however, that the lack of references to symbols at the community or regime levels is indicative of a relative lack of such symbols in Canada, a fact which may have important consequences for the nature of Canadian national feeling.

TABLE 1.9

Affective Nature of Attitudes Towards
Objects in the Canadian Political System
(row percentages)

OBJECTS OF ATTITUDES	POSITIVE	NEUTRAL	NEGATIVE	N
Community structural	17%	46	37	1764
Community symbolic	—	—	—	—
Community conceptual	42%	18	41	566
Regime structural	18%	23	59	580
Regime symbolic	—	100%	—	44
Regime conceptual	33%	17	50	987
Authorities structural	15%	11	74	442
Authorities symbolic	23%	40	37	585
Authorities conceptual	9%	26	65	1660
Total	20%	30	50	6628

Attitudes toward various objects within the political system seem to vary with the level of the system. In the first place, feelings for the political *community* are not as negative in tone as are feelings for the regime and the authorities. This is particularly true for conceptual feelings, those having to do with the nation as an abstract entity. As we noted earlier, positive or neutral images of the country generally outweighed negative images. Some concern is expressed for the state of national unity. But we also noted, particularly in the placed responses, the preponderence of negative images Canadians have of other parts of the country, particularly those, like Quebec and British Columbia, which are seen in political terms, and those, like the Atlantic provinces, which are seen as being badly off economically and neglected by government. We also noted the tendency for Westerners to think of themselves as disadvantaged when it comes to treatment of their area by the centrally dominated government.

Thus it was most common, when responding about the structure of the Canadian political community, to simply denote the place or to give some neutral description of what it was like. Very little positive feeling is expressed for the parts of the country, and the negative feeling is primarily directed toward adverse economic climates and neglect, leading in some cases to feelings that areas of the country are alienated. With regard to the conceptual feelings about the community, there is about an even split between those with positive and negative images about the Canadian community. It is, of course, conjectural how positive one would expect such feelings to be about a "healthy" political community. Perhaps the Canadian political system can get along quite well without an overwhelmingly positive public feeling for either the nation as a whole or its component regions and provinces. But we do feel it is necessary to point out that the negative nature of the feelings many Canadians hold about the basic Canadian community may not augur well for the existence of any large-scale spirit of Canadian unity.

If we regard the results in Table 1.9 as indicating a rather mixed set of feelings toward the Canadian political community, attitudes toward the *regime* seem decidedly negative in tone. Close to 60% of the regime-structural attitudes and half of the regime-conceptual ones are classified as negative. This is indicative, with regard to the structural answer, of negative orientations toward government and the federal system in general, and the federal government in particular. This could stem from feelings that the country is overgoverned, or that government is too big, or just that government has lost contact with the people.[6] Some people call for changes in the constitution with regard to the distribution of powers between the federal and provincial governments, but in most cases there is simply a feeling that "government," as a vague, amorphous entity, is remote from the people, spending too much money and not providing adequate services.

Conceptual attitudes at the regime level have to do with the principles of democracy, representation, and ideology, as well as with politics in general. As might be expected from the earlier discussion, the references to democracy account for many of the positive regime-conceptual attitudes noted in Table 1.9 and negative reactions to politics for many of the negative. There are also a number of negative reactions to a perceived lack of citizen involvement in the system and some calls for changes in individual behaviour in this regard.

While some of these may be regarded as hopeful signs for the perpetuation of the democratic values which have been expressed, the general distrust of the political process nevertheless persists. Canadians may well be deferential to political authority, as Lipset has argued,[7] but they certainly do not *trust* it.[8] The political process does not seem to be, in the public's mind, a satisfactory way of resolving the many problems and conflicts that exist in the country today.

Two of the reasons why politics does not seem in high repute in Canada can be found in responses to the objects at the *authorities* level. In general, the parties and politicians who run the political system are regarded with distaste by most of the public. These objects, which are coded in the authorities-structural category in Table 1.9, cause three-quarters of the responses in that category to be negative in tone. Although we must temper our judgment somewhat in the knowledge that when it comes to evaluations of specific politicians and parties, the public attitudes are not as negative (e.g., in the authorities-symbolic category in Table 1.9), we are still struck by the tendency to turn away from the political process, its methods, and its practitioners.

Similarly, the negative nature of the comments on issues included in the authorities-conceptual category adds to the picture. While it is to be expected that, given a forum, many people would air their grievances on particular issues, the overwhelming litany of complaint on virtually every political issue one could think of gives evidence of considerable public dissatisfaction. These calls for the correction of so many social and political ills, taken together with the bad image the public has of government, politics, parties, and politicians, give little indication that Canadians have confidence that the political system will solve any of their problems.

The most direct attempt by political scientists to measure people's feelings about the responsiveness of the political system is found in the concept of political efficacy. Developed originally by researchers on American voting behaviour, measures of political efficacy have been extensively used in comparative research on political attitudes and cultures.[9] By asking respondents a series of questions about the perceived utility of potential political action, the responsiveness of decision-makers to public concerns, and their ability to understand the political process, a tabulation of the level of political efficacy in a society may be made.

Table 1.10 presents the distribution of the answers to five political efficacy questions in the 1974 study. In each of these questions the "low efficacy" response is indicated by agreement with the statement; for example, the answer, "Yes, I don't think that the government cares much what people like me think." Table 1.10 shows how many Canadians *disagreed* with each item; that is, how many gave the politically efficacious response. Overall, except for one item, the feelings of political efficacy held by Canadians are revealed to be quite low. Only 52% of the sample believe that the government cares what they think; 44% feel that they have a say in what the government does; 33% believe that Members of

TABLE 1.10

Per Cent of Respondents Disagreeing with Five "Low Efficacy" Statements About Politics and Government, by Province

	NFLD.	P.E.I.	N.S.	N.B.	QUE.	ONT.	MAN.	SASK.	ALTA.	B.C.	TOTAL
So many other people vote in elections that it doesn't matter very much whether I vote or not.	78	80	81	79	77	89	81	90	85	93	84
I don't think that the government cares much what people like me think.	41	54	61	46	45	54	44	65	53	64	52
People like me don't have any say about what the government does.	29	32	52	50	30	52	31	42	47	60	44
Generally, those elected to Parliament soon lose touch with the people.	20	32	44	32	27	36	37	39	33	36	33
Sometimes politics and government seem so complicated that a person like me can't really understand what's going on.	12	34	41	21	33	36	15	29	24	43	33
Mean score on four-item political efficacy scale.	1.6	2.0	2.3	2.0	1.8	2.3	1.7	2.3	2.1	2.6	2.1 $F=7.3*$
N =	50	48	88	66	341	344	59	52	87	127	1203

	AGE	LANGUAGE	COMM. SIZE	EDUCATION	SES	SEX
Correlations between four-item efficacy scale and . . . (Pearson r)	—.14*	.19*	.07*	.34*	.28*	.02

*Significant at .01 level.

Parliament retain a concern with their electorates; and 33% feel that government and politics are not so complicated as to prevent them from understanding what is going on.

On a four-item political efficacy scale,[10] Canadians average just over two politically efficacious responses. Table 1.10 indicates some significant inter-provincial differences in this regard, with British Columbia being the most politically efficacious province and Newfoundland the least.[11] In addition, the correlations between the efficacy scale and the demographic measures reported in the table indicate that those with higher education and social status are more likely to be efficacious, as are those in younger age groups, and Anglophones. In general, however, the political negativism contained in the responses to the map question, which has formed the major data source for this chapter, is reflected once again in these data on political efficacy, which show that Canadians, by and large, are not very confident that they can understand and affect the political process.[12]

CONCLUSION

There is, however, one subject on which most Canadians do appear to be politically efficacious. A return glance at Table 1.10 shows that 84% of the respondents did *not* agree with the statement "So many other people vote in elections that it doesn't matter very much whether I vote or not." Elections, then, are seen to be important. Despite their dislike for the political process, their distrust of politicians, and their dismay at the activities or the inactivities of government, Canadians put aside these feelings long enough to render an electoral judgment. Their motives for doing so are likely to be very different.

For some, the election is a basic principle of democracy to which they are committed, regardless of other feelings. Such participation takes place out of a sense of civic duty. For another group of people, an election may be a chance to take one more try at remedying some of the injustices which concern them, or at least trying to replace some of the politicians they see as being ineffectual. For still others, an election is a chance to render judgment on the political parties, either for or against change. Whatever the motives, most Canadians participate in electoral politics to the extent of casting a ballot on the appointed day. However, they may well remain skeptical about the ability of the political process to produce a satisfactory resolution of their problems and concerns.

FOOTNOTES

1. See Appendix B, Q. 14, for description of map question and codes. A similar map question was used by John Johnstone in *Young Peoples' Images of Canadian Society* (Ottawa: Queen's Printer, 1969). There is, however, one significant difference between Johnstone's wording of the question and ours. Johnstone asked his respondents to "write in five words or phrases which best describe Canada," while we asked for "five words or phrases which best describe *politics* in Canada."

2. To examine the possibility that the negative or political nature of the responses seen in this chapter might be a function of demographic variables, such as age, education, or language, a series of controls for these variables was undertaken. The result was a complete absence of significant effect on the relationships shown in Chapter One. The demographic characteristics of Canadians do not relate strongly to their conceptions of Canadian politics.

3. Jon H. Pammett and Michael S. Whittington, eds., *Foundations of Political Culture* (Toronto: Macmillan, 1976), p. 15.

4. See David Easton, *A Systems Analysis of Political Life* (New York: Wiley, 1965), pp. 171-219.

5. Pammett and Whittington, *op. cit.*, p. 14. The description of the categories here follows their description closely.

6. On "government overload" see Richard Rose, *The Problem of Party Government* (New York: Free Press, 1974), *passim*, and Gabriel Almond and G. Bingham Powell, *Comparative Politics: A Developmental Approach* (Boston: Little, Brown, 1966), pp. 190-212.

7. Seymour Martin Lipset, *The First New Nation* (New York: Basic Books, 1963). On the nature of Canadian values, see also Tom Truman, "A Critique of Seymour M. Lipset's Article, 'Value Differences, Absolute or Relative: The English-speaking Democracies,'" *Canadian Journal of Political Science*, 4 (1971), pp. 497-525; Gad Horowitz, "Conservatism, Liberalism and Socialism in Canada: An Interpretation," Chapter One in his *Canadian Labour in Politics* (Toronto: University of Toronto Press, 1968); and Milton Rokeach, *The Nature of Human Values* (New York: The Free Press, 1973), pp. 89-93.

8. Other studies have shown that trust in government elsewhere in the world is on the decline. See Arthur H. Miller, "Political Issues and Trust in Government: 1964-1970," and Jack Citrin, "Comment: The Political Relevance of Trust in Government," *American Political Science Review*, 68 (1974), pp. 951-1001.

9. The concept of political efficacy was developed by A. Campbell, G. Gurin and W. Miller, *The Voter Decides* (Evanston, Ill: Row Peterson, 1954). Its most extensive cross-national use has been by G. A. Almond and S. Verba, *The Civic Culture* (Princeton: Princeton University Press, 1963). See also Lawrence LeDuc, "Measuring the Sense of Political Efficacy in Canada," *Comparative Political Studies*, 8 (1976), pp. 490-99.

10. See derivation of Political Efficacy Scale, Appendix B, Q. 9.

11. Note the agreement with data on political efficacy from the 1965 and 1968 National Surveys as presented in Richard Simeon and David Elkins, "Regional Political Cultures in Canada," *Canadian Journal of Political Science*, 7 (1974), pp. 397-437.

12. There is, as might be expected, a modest relationship between the "posi-

tive-negative" classification of the map responses and the political efficacy scale, with respondents scoring high on political efficacy being generally more likely to describe Canadian politics in positive terms. The Pearson correlation between the two measures is .15.

APPENDIX 1A
Content of Placed Responses to Map Question (numbers of responses)

Placed in Newfoundland

12 General positive responses
11 State of the economy negative
11 Neglected
8 References to Joey Smallwood
6 References to fishing
6 Underdeveloped
4 General negative responses
3 References to travel or tourism
3 Provincial government positive
2 Provincial government negative
2 Conservative party neutral
2 Jobs needed
2 Name of province written in
6 Miscellaneous single mentions

Placed in Nova Scotia

5 Name of province written in
4 General positive responses
4 General negative responses
4 References to fishing
3 Neglected
3 Jobs needed
3 Transportation negative
3 Industry lacking
2 Liberal party neutral
2 Natural resources exist
2 Provincial government positive
2 Provincial government negative
12 Miscellaneous single mentions

Placed in Centre of Country

14 Powerful
9 Industrial
9 Region name written in
6 Favoured
6 General negative responses

Placed in Centre of Country (con't)

5 State of economy positive
5 Heavily populated
5 Bilingualism neutral
4 Favoured by federal government
4 Overrepresented
3 Transportation positive
3 Bilingualism negative
3 Does not care about periphery
3 Subsidizes rest of country
2 General positive responses
2 Inflation references
2 Liberal party neutral
2 Nature of government bad
2 Provincial government neutral
9 Miscellaneous single mentions

Placed in Prince Edward Island

10 Miscellaneous responses

Placed in New Brunswick

7 General positive responses
6 Name of province written in
4 Agricultural area
3 State of the economy negative
3 Conservative party neutral
2 Liberal party neutral
2 General negative responses
2 Tourism
2 French-English relations positive
13 Miscellaneous single mentions

Placed in Atlantic Region

34 State of economy negative
31 Neglected

Placed in Atlantic Region (con't)

24 Reference to fishing
12 Needs federal government assistance
12 General negative responses
10 Region name written in
 6 Underdeveloped
 5 Neglected by federal government
 5 Not powerful
 5 Tourism
 4 Maritime Union positive
 2 Nature of government bad
 2 Transportation negative
 2 Industry lacking
 2 Competitive political parties
 2 Reference to Robert Stanfield
 2 Underrepresented
14 Miscellaneous single mentions

Placed in Quebec

45 Name of province written in
45 General negative responses
32 Separatism negative
31 Separatism neutral
26 Homeland of French
25 Liberal party neutral
23 General positive responses
18 Bilingualism negative
18 Bilingualism neutral
18 Impact on federalism negative
17 James Bay project
14 Puts French first, negative
14 Favoured
13 Provincial government negative
12 Complaining
12 Parochial
12 Independent
11 Conflict within Quebec
 9 Separatism positive
 9 English-French conflict
 9 Favoured by federal government

Placed in Quebec (con't)

 8 Puts French first, neutral
 7 Neglected, alienated
 7 Powerful
 7 Natural resources exist
 7 Mining
 7 Puts French first, positive
 7 Other issues neutral
 6 Forestry
 6 Provincial government, positive
 6 Inflation
 6 French too powerful
 5 Provincial government neutral
 5 Foreign investment negative
 5 Underdeveloped
 5 Neglected by federal government
 5 Transportation positive
 4 State of economy negative
 3 Bilingualism positive
 3 Asbestos
 3 Tourism
 2 Jobs lacking
 2 Other issues negative
 2 Agricultural
 2 Lack of agriculture
 2 Parties not competitive
 2 Trudeau neutral
 2 Liberal party positive
 2 Wants special treatment
 2 English-French conflict negative
 2 Impact on federalism positive
 2 Impact on federalism neutral
19 Miscellaneous single mentions

Placed in Ontario

33 Wealthy
30 General negative responses
26 General positive responses
22 Name of province written in
20 Industrial
17 Powerful

Placed in Ontario (con't)

14 Liberal party neutral
13 Conservative party neutral
9 Favoured
9 Population density high
8 Pollution exists
8 William Davis negative
7 Provincial government negative
7 State of economy positive
7 Inflation
5 Reference to Northern Ontario
4 Foreign investment negative
4 Federally oriented
4 Nature of government good
4 Jobs needed
3 Mining
3 Tourism
3 Other issues neutral
3 Transportation negative
3 Housing problem
3 Favoured by federal
   government
3 Neglected
2 Liberal party positive
2 Jobs plentiful
2 Taxes too high
2 Trudeau negative
2 Other federal politician
2 Conservative party positive
2 Conservative party negative
2 Bilingualism negative
2 Immigration neutral
2 Strikes
19 Miscellaneous single mentions

Placed in Manitoba

4 Province name written in
3 General positive responses
2 State of economy positive
2 NDP neutral
2 Provincial government negative
9 Miscellaneous single mentions

Placed in Saskatchewan

5 NDP neutral
4 Wheat
3 Province name written in
3 Transportation negative
3 Neglected
2 General positive responses
2 General negative responses
2 State of economy positive
2 Underdeveloped
2 NDP negative
11 Miscellaneous single mentions

Placed in Alberta

46 Oil
11 Conservative party neutral
8 General negative responses
6 Province name written in
5 State of economy positive
5 Natural resources exist
4 General positive responses
3 Provincial government positive
3 Tourism
2 Underrepresented
2 Provincial government neutral
2 Provincial government negative
12 Miscellaneous single responses

Placed in British Columbia

27 Isolation
25 General positive responses
23 Strikes
22 General negative responses
19 Provincial government negative
12 Provincial government positive
11 NDP neutral
10 Province name written in
8 Tourism
8 Socialism neutral
7 Lumbering
7 NDP negative
5 Socialism negative
5 Natural resourses exist

Placed in British Columbia (con't)

4 Wants autonomy
4 Provincial government neutral
4 Industry exists
3 Liberal party neutral
3 Neglected by federal government
3 Powerful
3 State of economy positive
3 Agricultural
3 Social Credit neutral
3 Underrepresented
3 NDP positive
2 Separatist
2 Other issues positive
2 Other issues negative
2 Troubled
13 Miscellaneous single mentions

Placed in the West

50 Neglected, alienated
33 Wheat
33 Oil
33 Divided from the East
30 Region name written in
27 General positive responses
22 Neglected by federal government
18 General negative responses
18 Conservative party neutral
15 Farm prices too low
14 Underrepresented
11 Wants autonomy
10 Natural Resources
9 Agricultural
8 Transportation negative
6 Favoured
6 State of economy positive
6 Inflation
5 Reference to John Diefenbaker
4 Trudeau negative
4 Underdeveloped

Placed in the West (con't)

4 NDP neutral
3 Favoured by Federal government
3 Not powerful
3 Industry lacking
3 Provincial governments positive
3 Bilingualism neutral
3 Bilingualism negative
3 Liberal
2 Powerful
2 Provincial governments neutral
2 Agricultural policy positive
2 State of economy negative
2 Transportation positive
2 Other issues positive
2 Nature of government good
2 Tourism
15 Miscellaneous single mentions

Placed in the East

16 Divided from the West
14 Region name written in
14 Favoured
10 Powerful
6 Favoured by federal government
6 Overrepresented
3 Industrial
3 General negative responses
2 Bilingualism neutral
2 Agriculture needs aid
9 Miscellaneous single mentions

Placed in Cities

42 Ottawa, home of Parliament
16 Montreal
8 Toronto
3 Vancouver
20 Miscellaneous other mentions

Placed in the U.S.A.

13 Nature of government bad
8 name written in

Placed in the U.S.A. (con't)

4 Powerful
4 General negative responses
3 General positive responses
2 Foreign investment negative

Placed in the North

29 Underdeveloped
21 Indians and Inuit mistreated
18 Neglected
9 General positive responses
8 Under federal government control
4 Rich in natural resources
3 Region name written in
3 Lacks population
3 Pollution threat
3 Tourism
2 Neglected by federal

Placed in the North (con't)

government
2 Not powerful
2 Transportation negative
2 Foreign investment negative
2 Underrepresented
2 Large size
7 Miscellaneous single mentions

Placed in Other Specific Locations

18 Specific name written in
5 General positive responses
5 Neglected
5 Other issue negative
4 General negative responses
2 Transportation negative
2 Underdeveloped
2 Natural resources exist
3 Miscellaneous single mentions

APPENDIX 1B
Content of Unplaced Responses to Map Question
(numbers of responses)

I. Political Comments

1. General comments on politics	466
2. General comments on politicians and leadership	346
3. General comments on government	283
4. Democracy and representation	169
5. The federal system and general comments on federal and provincial governments	156
6. Comments on particular parties and the government and the opposition	134
7. Particular leaders and other specific politicians	98
8. The 1974 election, majority government	83
9. General comments on parties	78
	1813 41.8%

II. Comments on Issues, Political and Economic

1. Inflation, general or specific	375
2. Pensions	101
3. Employment or unemployment; unemployment insurance	100
4. Taxes	96
5. Language and culture, bilingualism and multilingualism	79

6. Welfare	70	
7. Foreign investment	66	
8. Foreign affairs, foreign aid	52	
9. The economy generally	51	
10. Education policy	49	
11. Health or social policy	47	
12. Strikes	39	
13. Housing	36	
14. Agricultural policy	35	
15. Transportation, communication policy	29	
16. Immigration policy	26	
17. Women's rights, abortion	23	
18. Environmental policy, pollution	21	
19. Oil policy	20	
20. Family allowances	19	
21. Capital punishment	5	
22. Other issues	108	
	1447	33.4%

III. Comments on Canada and Canadians

1. General comments on the country	467	
2. General comments on Canadians	115	
3. Complicated nature	68	
4. Natural resources	58	
5. References to social classes	53	
6. Regional, decentralized nature	51	
7. Political disinterest	50	
8. Big business, corporations, capitalism	45	
9. Labour, workers, unions	35	
10. Economic redistribution needed	32	
11. Transportation, communications, travel	27	
12. Socialism	22	
13. Native peoples	17	
14. Agriculture	15	
15. Industry	12	
16. Pressure groups	5	
	1072	24.7%

Total N = *4332*

Chapter Two

Regional Consciousness in Canada

Canada is generally seen as a country with distinct regions. These regions have been particularly important in the political development of the country, since loyalty to regions and not to the nation as a whole was a basic reason for the selection of a federal system of government. Canada, it has been proposed, has several "regional political cultures," containing political orientations so divergent as to rival differences between countries elsewhere in the globe.[1] Some of Canada's regional cultures have been called "disaffected," while others have been styled "citizen" societies.[2] Some have been said to maintain party systems appropriate for pre-industrial societies, and others to have "modern" party systems reflecting the cleavages of the industrial age.[3]

Explanations of Canada's regional differences, moreover, have been thoughtful and imaginative, and have challenged the minds of many of our most prestigious thinkers. Geography has been an important factor, isolating particular segments of Canadian society behind barriers of rock, water, and timber.[4] Sections of the country were settled at different times by groups with varied ancestral homelands and very different cultural origins.[5] These groups brought with them clusters of values and beliefs which reflected their varied national characters. Different languages were, and are, spoken. What some observers have chosen to call Canada's "obsession with national unity"[6] has essentially consisted of attempts to forge communication links between geographically and culturally separate settlements.

In addition to variations in the origin of their inhabitants, factors peculiar to the economic pursuits of regions have accentuated differences among them. Fishing, lumbering, trapping, small-scale agriculture, mining, large-scale agriculture, and manufacturing have all played a part in the development of the Canadian economy, but these activities have never been universally pursued across the land. Rather, several geographically distinct "regional economies" have developed, each emphasizing one or two of these sectors.[7] Thus the geographical separation, different settlement patterns and countries of origin, and lack of commonality in economic pursuits have all contributed to the distinctiveness of the regions of Canada.

While there is general agreement that regions do exist, and that the three factors mentioned above are primarily responsible, there is no consensus as to the exact "boundaries," or even the exact number, of Canada's regions. It is sometimes maintained that Canada has two basic cultures, English and French, and that English Canada has essentially the same set of values and attitudes no matter what geographical part of the country is referenced.[8] Another position holds that Canada has ten political cultures corresponding to the boundaries of the ten provinces, although it is allowed that some of these cultures are similar to each other.[9] More common are divisions of the country into five regions, grouping together the four Atlantic provinces and the three Prairie provinces.[10]

It is partly because the meaning of region as a political variable is so imprecise that all of the divisions cited above (and more) are possible. Region is generally treated as a "system name" variable, as a combination of other characteristics, as an admission, in effect, that we have not been willing or able to ferret out all the real factors that are causing the "regional" differences we see.[11] Richard Simeon refers to regions simply as "containers," not as explanatory variables in themselves, and thus maintains that we, as analysts, can draw the regional boundaries anywhere we find it useful or sensible to do so, either along provincial boundaries (his choice) or in other locations.[12] Similarly, in her extensive analysis of "the sociology of regional persistence in Canada," Mildred Schwartz opts for regional boundaries

> that have political relevance. This means that, for the most part, we concentrate our comparisons on the ten provinces of Canada, excluding the sparsely populated northland. In other words, for our purposes, region and province are often synonymous.[13]

Research proceeding from such regional breakdowns along provincial lines, treating the provinces either singly or in groups, has provided interesting data on Canadian politics, and a rather impressive argument for the existence of differences between the residents of various provinces in political attitudes, values, and behaviour. Nevertheless, such research sidesteps the basic question of whether the particular regional boundaries chosen by the researcher are at all matched by the perceptions of the people living in those areas. The lack of such perceptions of regional consciousness does not necessarily mean that differences are not important; as Schwartz says, "It is possible for an outside observer to describe regional differences based on economic, demographic or political criteria without these being recognized or acknowledged by the respective residents."[14] However, such a lack of regional identity, she goes on to say, could have the serious effect of making it difficult to mobilize the public to press for action in remedying regionally based deficiencies, in promoting regional interests, or even in spreading information about regional problems. Simeon agrees:

> To be politically important, regionalism . . . needs to be more than simply the correlation of certain economic, social or other characteristics with provincial boundaries. It must also include some degree of self-consciousness, some widespread sense of the provincial community as the most relevant political unit or category.[15]

There are thus two reasons why the subject of perceptions of regional differences, or regional consciousness, is important to study. The first, as Simeon and Schwartz outline, is that only if such feeling is present will the differences between regions that the observer can document be effectively politicized. The second is that only if such feeling is present can region itself, aside from particular social or economic characteristics which it may contain, be used as an explanatory variable. It only makes sense to suggest that being a Maritimer might explain why somebody does something if that person feels he is a Maritimer. If region is a "real" variable as opposed to a container or a surrogate for others, then we may be able to better address the question of what the "real" regional boundaries are in Canada. If the analytical boundaries we are accustomed to using match those which exist in people's minds, we can be more confident that we are delineating actual differences between populations. If the people of a "region" form a coherent entity and feel some sort of kinship for those from the same region that they do not feel for those from other regions, we will have more confidence in the utility of studying regionalism as a factor in Canadian politics.

In the course of the 1974 National Election Study, respondents were questioned directly about the nature of Canada's regions. They were asked first whether they thought of the country in terms of regions, and if so, what region they lived in and what the other regions were. Responses were recorded verbatim, and no pre-coding scheme was imposed on the data. This allowed the actual terms used to describe the Canadian regions to be recorded. This chapter, then, is a systematic examination of how Canadians perceive the regions of the nation, both their own and the others they see existing across the land.

REGIONAL CONSCIOUSNESS

What kinds of Canadians think of their country in terms of regions? An influential model of social and political change in countries with strong and persistent regional loyalties is one which hypothesizes a gradual process of "deregionalization" with the evolutionary development of national identity and commitment.[16] Lipset and Rokkan, for example, have seen the process of nation-building as involving a gradual reduction of conflict between regional and national interests.[17] In such a process, political parties and other institutions which initially reflect regional or cultural interests gradually come to represent national divisions, such as social class. If, therefore, such a process of deregionalization is taking place in Canada, if regional consciousness is a vestige of traditional patterns of thought which are on the decline in a developing society, then we would find older Canadians, those dwelling in rural areas and small towns, less educated and less travelled, being *more* likely to think in regional terms. Were we to find these patterns present in the data, we could construct a plausible argument that regional ties are a function of older people's ties with their localities, and that as younger generations come along, these regional patterns will be eroded in favour of some other basis of cleavage in a unified Canada. Further, with increasing migration from rural areas to cities and geographical mobility within the country, the breakdown of regional loyalties would become even more likely.

To test ideas such as these about the present extent of regional consciousness in Canada and its possible future fate, we present in Table 2.1 an Index of Regional Consciousness. Utilizing all the indicators of regional feeling from the data set, this index scores respondents from 0 to 3, adding increments of one if the respondent: (a) thought of Canada in regional terms and described his/her region, (b) described at least one other region, and (c) gave at least one placed response to the map question.[18] As can be seen in Table 2.1, the mean score for all respondents is 1.6, indicating that out of three opportunities to express a regional feeling, the average Canadian took advantage of between one and two. Variation by province places the four Western provinces highest and Newfoundland lowest, reflecting patterns of regional consciousness we will examine in detail later in this chapter. Quebec and Ontario appear here as slightly below the Canadian average in regional consciousness, as does New Brunswick.

Table 2.1 produces no support whatsoever for any argument that deregionalization, or declining regional consciousness, is taking place in Canada. The data is far more consistent with an argument that regional feeling is *increasing*. Regional consciousness is highest among Canadians that are young, more highly educated, better off, English-

TABLE 2.1
Relationships Between Index of Regional Consciousness
and Selected Demographic Variables
(mean scores on three point index)

PROVINCE		AGE	
CANADA	1.6	18-29 years	1.8
Saskatchewan	2.0	30-45 years	1.7
Manitoba	1.9	46-59 years	1.4
British Columbia	1.9	60+ years	1.2
Alberta	1.8	$F = 23.5*$	
Prince Edward Island	1.6		
Nova Scotia	1.6	EDUCATION	
Ontario	1.5	Grade school or less	1.0
Quebec	1.4	Some high school	1.4
New Brunswick	1.4	High school completed	1.7
Newfoundland	0.8	Some post secondary	2.1
$F = 9.8*$		Degree or equivalent	2.1
		$F = 23.5*$	

COMMUNITY SIZE		LANGUAGE (SPOKEN)	
Rural areas	1.4	English	1.7
Towns	1.4	French	1.4
Smaller cities	1.6	Other	0.9
Metropolitan area	1.7	$F = 20.8*$	
$F = 7.4*$			

INTERPROVINCIAL MOBILITY		SOCIO-ECONOMIC STATUS	
Low	1.5	Low	1.2
Medium	1.6	Medium low	1.4
High	2.0	Medium high	1.7
$F = 15.6*$		High	2.0
		$F = 49.9*$	

SUBJECTIVE SOCIAL CLASS			
Working class	1.4		
Middle class	1.7	*Significant at .01.	
Upper middle class	1.9		
$F = 28.0*$			

speaking, from metropolitan areas and smaller cities, upper-middle class in identification, and geographically mobile. The relationship of regional consciousness with age is particularly important, since it indicates that younger Canadians are more conscious of the regional divisions of the country than their elders, and more accustomed to thinking about Canadian politics in regional terms. The additional relationship with education suggests that the age relationship is a generational rather than a life-cycle one, since educational levels have risen significantly in the past decades. Furthermore, it seems unlikely that the aging process would bring about a lessening of awareness of regional diversity, since older people would have had a chance to amass more information about the country.

One important cause of the higher regional consciousness among younger generations may be their higher levels of formal education. As demonstrated by Table 2.2, a control for education diminishes the relationship of regional consciousness with both age and socio-economic status. On the other hand, the control for socio-economic status does not have important effects on any of the zero-order relationships reported in Table 2.2. This pattern would tend to suggest that increasing regional consciousness in Canada is a function of knowledge of and exposure to the political system, rather than of generation per se. Younger people, who are better educated than their parents, have a greater knowledge of Canada's regions than their elders, and are therefore more conscious of the country's regional divisions. So, too, are those who have resided outside their home province and likewise have obtained a greater knowledge of the country. And, of course, as levels of education, mobility, and socio-economic status have increased over time, so too has regional consciousness, thus producing a generational effect.

TABLE 2.2

Correlations Between Index of Regional Consciousness and Selected Demographic Variables
(Pearson r)

	ZERO-ORDER	CONTROLLING FOR EDUCATION	CONTROLLING FOR SOCIO-ECONOMIC STATUS
Education	.32*	—	.25*
Socio-Economic Status	.22*	.07*	—
Age	−.16*	−.04	−.15*
Mobility	.11*	.08*	.08*

*Significant at .01 level.

We may extend our analysis of relationships between demographic variables and a propensity to think regionally by considering the provincial breakdown in Table 2.3. Relationships with education and socio-economic status are strong in many of the provinces. The relationship between socio-economic status and regional consciousness is generally stronger in the Atlantic provinces and Ontario than in Quebec and in the West. Interestingly, New Brunswick, which Table 2.1 showed to have a low incidence of regional feeling, shows fairly weak correlations of that feeling with education. In Newfoundland, however, where the number of people thinking regionally is also low, what regional con-

TABLE 2.3

Correlations Between Index of Regional Consciousness and Selected Demographic Variables, Nationally and by Province

(Pearson r)

	TOTAL	NFLD.	P.E.I.	N.S.	N.B.	QUE.	ONT.	MAN.	SASK.	ALTA.	B.C.
Education (years)	.36*	.32*	.39*	.42*	.18	.30*	.44*	.35*	.22*	.29*	.30*
SES (Blishen score)	.25*	.37*	.25*	.40*	.32*	.17*	.34*	.19	.00	.34*	.19*
Subjective Social Class	.15*	.03	.09	.19*	.28*	.09*	.21*	.04	.09	.32*	.11
Age	-.18*	-.16	-.21	-.16	-.06	-.15*	-.23*	-.22*	-.11	-.16	-.19*
Interprovincial Mobility	.13*	.00	.15	.14	.00	.08	.15*	-.04	.13	.11	-.02
Community Size	.09*	.23	.22*	.19*	.33*	.08	.11*	.15	-.25*	.13	.03

*Significant at .01 level.

sciousness does exist is more concentrated among people of higher status and higher education.

Since we have seen that the four Western provinces express higher degrees of regional awareness, it is reasonable to expect that the pervasiveness of such feeling would reduce the likelihood of there being sharp demographic differences within their populations between people who think of Canada in terms of regions and people who do not. Alberta and British Columbia, however, do show modest relationships between thinking regionally, and education, socio-economic status, subjective class, and age, while Manitoba shows a significant relationship with age and education only. Saskatchewan is unique in that its residents who live in towns and rural areas are more likely to think regionally than city-dwellers, whereas in every other province the reverse is true. In Ontario

FIGURE 2.1
Index of Regional Consciousness by Age and Area of Country

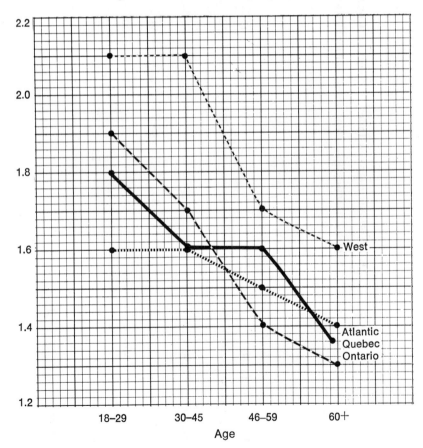

especially there is a modest relationship between having lived in another part of Canada and being aware of regional differences.

Our analysis confirms Schwartz's argument that "regionalism is not a declining force in a country that otherwise bears all of the characteristics of a modern state."[19] As Canadian nationhood has grown to maturity, consciousness of and identification with regional divisions have persisted, and indeed would appear to be increasing as new, better-educated generations socialized into regional thinking assume their places in Canadian political and social life. As Figure 2.1 graphically portrays, younger generations in all areas of the country, people who provide the "replacements" so important to dynamic models of political change,[20] have a set of attitudes more conducive to regional thinking than do their elders. For analyzing political trends in Canada, then, any model providing for the replacement of regional cleavages by national ones does not seem appropriate. We will return to this point in our analysis of the role of social class in voting behaviour in Chapter Four.

CANADIANS' CONCEPTIONS OF THEIR OWN REGIONS

The data in Table 2.4 describe how Canadians view their own regions.[21] It will be seen immediately that any assumption that virtually all Canadians *have* such a perception is open to some dispute. The first two rows of the table, denoting as they do the people who answered "no" or "I don't know" when asked if they thought of Canada as being divided into regions, comprise just over 40% of the sample. Thus, though it is perfectly possible to support the statement that a majority of Canadians think of the country in regional terms, it must be remembered that we are only talking about 59% of Canadians. This would not seem to constitute a consensus. In addition, the distribution of the regional awareness that does exist is not uniform across the provinces. The four provinces west from Manitoba are, as a group, more likely to think of Canada in regional terms, and much more likely to be sure of their thinking in this regard. Regional consciousness in Canada is much more a Western than an Eastern phenomenon.

In the Atlantic provinces, for instance, only two of the four provinces show substantial degrees of regional awareness. Prince Edward Island and Nova Scotia both have close to half of their populations who conceive of themselves as citizens of an Atlantic or Maritime region. The other two provinces, however, have substantially lower degrees of regional feeling, no matter what designation is used to describe the region. Newfoundland's lack of common feeling with an Atlantic region is understandable, given its geographical separation and the separate development of the society; indeed, designations of Canada's regions often classify Newfoundland as a separate region.[22] However, the data in Table 2.4 indicate that Newfoundlanders do not claim to think of them-

TABLE 2.4

Definition of Own Region by Province
(column percentages)

	NFLD.	P.E.I.	N.S.	N.B.	QUE.	ONT.	MAN.	SASK.	ALTA.	B.C.	TOTAL
Does Not Think Regionally	28%	25%	26%	40%	31%	33%	23%	19%	21%	28%	30%
Does Not Know	38	20	15	13	16	8	4	5	12	3	11
Own Province	6	2	3	2	19	19	4	2	7	29	16
East/West*	10	4	6	16	7	3/	36	33	43	35	14
Atlantic/Maritimes	14	45	46	23	—	—	—	—	—	—	3
Central	—	1	—	—	2	13	12	2	1	1	6
Prairies	—	—	—	—	—	—	15	30	10	—	3
General Area of Own Province	—	1	—	2	2	10	1	2	2	—	4
Specific Area of Own Province	—	—	1	2	20	4	—	—	—	—	7
Economic/Linguistic	5	2	4	2	3	10	4	8	5	5	6
N =	102	97	180	134	702	702	113	101	179	252	2445

*Answers refer to East for provinces Newfoundland to Ontario and West for provinces from Manitoba to British Columbia.

selves as such a separate region either. Indeed, the number of Newfound-landers thinking of their own province as their region is less than half the number thinking of themselves as Maritimers.

A puzzling aspect of the Newfoundland results is the extremely large number of people who answered that they did not know whether they thought in regional terms or not. It is difficult to know whether to inter-pret this as a genuine lack of regional thinking, or to put it down to a general unwillingness to answer questions on the part of the Newfound-land respondents. It is tempting to argue the latter, since many of the other open-ended questions on the 1974 survey have much data missing from the Newfoundland interviews. A further possibility is that the relatively low educational level of the Newfoundland respondents may affect answers to a fairly abstract question. Whatever the reason for the Newfoundland results, it is difficult to support the position that New-foundland has much common regional consciousness with an Atlantic region.

While this conclusion is not a particularly surprising one to make for Newfoundland, it *is* surprising that the data suggest the same conclusion applies to New Brunswick. New Brunswickers were, by a substantial margin, more likely to answer "no" when asked if they thought of Canada as being divided into regions than were residents of any other province. Combining the first two rows of Table 2.4, we find that an absolute majority of New Brunswick residents either do not think re-gionally or do not know if they do or not. Fewer than one-quarter of New Brunswickers felt that they lived in an Atlantic or Maritime region; almost as many people felt that they lived in an Eastern region, a much vaguer term which could well include the whole Eastern half of the country.

Quebec and Ontario are commonly considered to be regions of Canada in which a feeling of regional identity corresponds to the provincial boundaries. The data, however, cast at least some doubt on this assump-tion. Fewer than one-fifth of the residents of these two provinces con-sciously think of themselves as residents of a region of Canada called Quebec or Ontario. Quebeckers were, for example, just as likely to name a specific location *inside the province* as their region, as they were to name the province as a whole. These answers, of which the main ones were Montréal, Lac St. Jean, Saguenay, and Gaspésie, indicate a localized consciousness that seems to exist in Quebec to a much higher extent than in other provinces. We are inclined to interpret this finding as a genuine cultural difference between Quebec and the other provinces, despite the fact that the word "region" in French may itself have more localized connotations than it does in English. It seems unlikely to us that the localized consciousness found in Quebec is an artifact of the question wording; indeed, the fact that the word "region" may have a more localized meaning in Quebec is itself an indication of a cultural difference. It will also be remembered that the question asked specifically about the regions into which Canada was divided, not into which Quebec was divided. We conclude, therefore, that when we are classifying Quebec as a region of Canada, we must be aware that a good deal of the regional consciousness which does exist in Quebec centres around particular geographical areas of the province and not the province as a whole, except secondarily.

Ontario also shows considerable consciousness of regions within the province. In contrast to Quebec, however, Ontarians were more likely to employ a general geographic term, such as Southern or Northern Ontario, than they were to employ a specific place name, such as Toronto. It may be that the large and heavily populated land area of Ontario motivates a relatively large number of its residents to think of general areas of the province. In addition, the distinct differences in the economies of various areas of Ontario undoubtedly encourage residents to perceive the areas as individual entities.

Another prevalent pattern in Ontario is the existence of some feeling for a Central region. Thirteen per cent of Ontarians conceive of themselves as dwelling in such a Central region, as do just about the same proportion of Manitobans. Interestingly, the existence of this feeling for a Central region does not seem to apply to Quebeckers to any great extent, though from a strict geographical standpoint it might have seemed a reasonable proposition. Another relatively large category in Ontario is the group of people who think of the country not in geographic terms, but in economic or linguistic ones. In Ontario, about two-thirds of the respondents in this category referred to their region in economic terms such as "industrial," while one-third felt they existed in a language region called English Canada, a conceptualization likely to extend far beyond provincial bounds. Since the number of people thinking of themselves as members of subprovincial, Central, economic, or linguistic regions substantially outweighs those classifying Ontario as their region, we should be very cautious about our use of the province as a whole as a synonym for region.

If the results from the areas of Canada we have been considering up to now give us some reason to doubt the salience and coherence of public conceptions of region, the same cannot be said for the four Western provinces. As was noted earlier, this area has the highest level of regional consciousness in the country. West is the term preferred by residents of Manitoba, Saskatchewan, and Alberta to denote their region. The use of the term Prairies comes close to the total reached by West only in Saskatchewan. Though we might have expected residents of Alberta, because of the economic pre-eminence of the province, to consider the province itself as a region, only 7% did so. Called the West by most, but the Prairies by some, these three provinces provide the best-defined regional unit in Canada.

The question of whether British Columbia should be included in such a Western region or conceptualized as a separate region has long interested students of Canadian political culture.[23] The data here do not give any clear solution to the problem and indeed provide support for both views. On the one hand, British Columbia residents chose their own province as their region at a higher rate than residents of any other province; 30% named the province or used some other term, such as West Coast or West of the Rockies, to denote British Columbia as a separate region. If we are going to regard Quebec and Ontario as "single province" regions, even though they have lower levels of such explicit consciousness, it certainly seems reasonable to do so for British Columbia. On the other hand, Table 2.4 shows that the percentage of people from that province who considered that their region was simply the West is five percentage points higher than those who see the province as a separate region. Thus, it appears to be at least as reasonable to conceive of one four-province Western region of Canada, as to treat British Columbia as a region separate from the other three Western provinces.

The point that emerges most forcefully from this initial examination of Canadians' definitions of their own region is that the phenomenon of regional consciousness is much more complex than the common analytical breakdown of the country into two, five, or ten regions would suggest. Basic questions, such as which provinces to include in an Atlantic or Western grouping, are not subject to unequivocal answers, at least according to the residents of those areas. The status of the so-called "single province" regions is open to some doubt, since many people in them were found to have other conceptions of what their regions were. Finally, the perceptions of region vary between very localized areas and vast territories known as the West, East, or Centre of the country.

CANADIANS' CONCEPTIONS OF OTHER REGIONS

The complexity we have noted with regard to the ways in which Canadians define their own regions is multiplied when we add a second dimension of regional consciousness, perception of the other regions of the country.[24] If we simply look at the number of other regions mentioned in Table 2.5, the total population of the four Western provinces seems to have a somewhat more complex conception of the regional nature of the country. This, of course, would be expected, given their already noted tendency to conceive of Canada in regional terms, and their propensity to agree on the proper designation for their own region.

We must be careful, however, not to make a single East/West generalization, because residents of Nova Scotia and Ontario also tend to name additional regions. Also, once the response rate to the questions on region is removed as a factor by excluding the missing data from the tabulations, the four Eastern provinces show a tendency to name somewhat *more* regions than do Westerners. Thus, to give an accurate summation of the regional conceptions of the provinces, we must make the rather cumbersome statement that when we consider the total provincial populations, Westerners have a more complex conception of the country's regional structure (mention more "other" regions) than do Easterners, but that if we consider that subset of the population that does have such conceptions at all, Easterners have more complex conceptions than do Westerners.

Whether one considers the situation with nonrespondents included in or removed from the analysis, there seems to be no underlying meaning to the way the provinces order themselves on this measure of the number of other regions mentioned. Considering the total group of the population surveyed, there seems to be no reason why one would expect Saskatchewan and British Columbia residents to name a higher number of other regions, and yet Albertans to name fewer. Similarly, considering those who responded to the questions on region, Nova Scotians would appear to have the most complex conceptions of the regional structure of Canada, while residents of New Brunswick rank substantially lower.

The rankings of Newfoundland and Quebec, however, are to be expected. The very low rate of response to the items on region has already been noted for the Newfoundland sample, and this is the factor producing the very low mean number of other regions mentioned. Among those Newfoundlanders who did conceive of the country in terms of regions, however, the number of such regions named is not dissimilar to totals named by Manitobans or Albertans. We must be aware, however, that when we speak of the regional conceptions of Newfoundlanders, we refer only to that one-quarter of the Newfoundland sample who responded to this question, and should treat the Newfoundland results with some caution.

Whether we consider the total sample of Quebec, or simply those mentioning regions, Quebeckers are not disposed to name many other regions they see in Canada. Considering the total population surveyed, the reticence of Quebeckers to name other regions is exceeded only by Newfoundlanders; considering only those who thought of the country in terms of regions, Quebec drops to last place in the number of other regions mentioned. For those Quebeckers who think in regional terms, the modal number of regions named is only one, whereas for all other provinces the mode is greater than one (for example, the mode for Nova

TABLE 2.5

Number of Other Regions Mentioned, by Province

(column percentages)

	NFLD.	P.E.I.	N.S.	N.B.	QUE.	ONT.	MAN.	SASK.	ALTA.	B.C.	TOTAL
None[a]	76%	47%	45%	56%	55%	43%	28%	25%	35%	31%	44%
One	3	4	6	8	17	9	6	5	6	14	11
Two	9	13	8	13	9	10	17	19	20	16	12
Three	7	17	11	11	9	15	48	42	33	15	17
Four	5	13	15	10	6	12	—	8	6	16	9
Five	1	4	11	3	2	6	—	—	—	6	4
Six or more	—	1	5	—	2	5	1	2	1	4	3
Mean Number Mentioned	.66	1.63	1.96	1.20	1.08	1.85	1.89	2.11	1.73	2.09	1.65
Mean Number Excluding Missing Data	2.68	3.10	3.58	2.69	2.39	3.22	2.64	2.80	2.65	3.01	2.93
N =	102	97	180	134	702	702	113	101	179	252	2445

[a]Includes respondents who said they did not think of Canada in terms of regions, respondents who did not know if they did or not, and respondents who did not name any "other regions."

Scotia is four, while for Ontario and most of the Western provinces it is three). Along with the subprovincial nature of many of the "own region" responses in Quebec, this finding begins to indicate the extent of Quebec's conceptions of the country. Many Quebeckers are either unaware of or attach little significance to the regional diversity of areas outside of Quebec. Although we will turn in a moment to an examination of the content of these views of "other regions," it may be noted here that the data give no indication that the low number of Quebec views of other regions comes because the rest of the country is seen as a monolithic entity named English Canada or "the rest of the country." Quebec residents use, by and large, the same terminology to describe other regions that other Canadians use, but they simply use it far less liberally.

Table 2.6 tabulates *which* other regions were mentioned by citizens of each of the provinces; it includes only those who did have such conceptions. The table shows many distinct provincial patterns of reference to the other regions. Most striking, perhaps, is the extent to which the terms East and West are used to denote other regions of the country. Citizens of Manitoba, Saskatchewan, Alberta, and, to a slightly lesser extent, British Columbia are united in seeing the East as another region,

TABLE 2.6

Other Regions Mentioned, by Province
(percentages)

OTHER REGION MENTIONED[a]	NFLD.	P.E.I.	N.S.	N.B.	QUE.	ONT.	MAN.	SASK.	ALTA.	B.C.
Maritime/Atlantic	19	12	1	—	27	37	30	46	41	39
East	4	12	2	5	7	29	69	68	59	45
Quebec, Ontario, both[b]	23	43	71	48	34	44	27	21	32	28
Central	54	47	25	18	7	1	3	7	10	17
West	58	69	46	62	30	44	20	15	4	6
Prairies	15	24	33	28	10	30	—	1	2	46
B.C./West Coast	12	16	41	22	13	29	17	25	14	—
North	23	33	33	20	11	27	16	25	19	26
Subprovincial	—	2	6	5	30	10	1	4	3	3
Economic/ Linguistic	27	6	5	7	5	11	7	8	7	8

[a]Figures in the table are percentages of those answering the question in each province who mentioned each region. Missing data have been excluded.
[b]Most frequently, both were mentioned. For elaboration, see text. This category also includes some mentions of Upper and Lower Canada by Maritime respondents.

and their conceptualization is reciprocated by citizens of Newfoundland, Prince Edward Island, New Brunswick, and to a lesser extent Nova Scotia, who see another region called the West. By and large, residents of the provinces mentioned are likely to choose the large, vague, unspecified terms East and West to describe the divisions of the rest of the country, rather than specific provincial names or names particular to smaller regions, such as Prairies.

Ontario and Quebec, however, are not as likely to employ the terms East and West. Quebec, in particular, seems less inclined to make use of either one of the terms. The low number of mentions of East as another region in Quebec, may, of course, be due to many people not making a distinction between their own area and the East, although Table 2.4 indicates that few Quebeckers employed the East as a descriptive term for their own area. However, it is rather surprising that only 30% of Quebeckers see the West as another region of Canada. Ontarians are somewhat more likely to see a Western region than an Eastern one, but overall usage of the general terms East and West is lower in Ontario than it is in the less geographically central provinces.

Thus, residents of the four Western provinces tend to see a large other region called the East, and vice versa. How is the centre of the country perceived? Upon investigation of this question, the similarities we have noted between the Western and Eastern parts of the country seem to disappear. Citizens of the provinces from Manitoba west are much less likely to mention Ontario, Quebec, or a Central region than are residents of the provinces from New Brunswick east. Indeed, it is tempting to reason that Westerners do not make a distinction between the Central provinces and the East as a whole, conceptualizing the rest of the country in terms of one other region. One finding from Table 2.6, however, must give us some pause in this regard, since a fairly high number of Westerners, especially from Saskatchewan west, point to the existence of an Atlantic or Maritime region. It seems likely that a substantial number of Westerners see the existence of both a Maritime and an Eastern region. It is possible that to Westerners, the Maritimes form a subregion within a larger Eastern region, much as the Prairies and British Columbia might form subregions of a Western region as perceived by Easterners. Speculation along these lines must remain tentative, since the data provide no information on what is included within the boundaries of the terms used. Nevertheless, the normal meaning of terms like East and Maritime would suggest that the East has a larger, more inclusive territory, and that the Maritimes might well be included in the East but retain some separateness for Westerners.

If Westerners seem disinclined to separate the Central provinces of Ontario and Quebec from an Eastern region in their minds, the same cannot be said for Easterners. Very high proportions of those respondents in Newfoundland, Prince Edward Island, New Brunswick, and Nova Scotia who perceived the country in regional terms denoted Quebec, Ontario, or a general Central region as part of their regional perception. In the case of category three in Table 2.6, it was most common for both Ontario and Quebec to be mentioned, but if only one was mentioned it was usually Quebec. Interestingly, the table seems to indicate that Quebec has a higher profile as a separate region of Canada for Easterners than Westerners, a fact that does not jibe well with the current image of Westerners as being particularly resentful of supposed favoured treatment for Quebec.

It is also interesting to note that some residents of the four Eastern provinces used the term Upper Canada, and to a much lesser extent Lower Canada, to describe other regions of Canada. The number of people doing so amounted in Newfoundland and Prince Edward Island to about 4% of those mentioning another region, but the total in New Brunswick reached 8% and in Nova Scotia a fairly substantial 14%. It has, of course, often been pointed out that many residents of those provinces carry on the pre-Confederation terminology, in order to indicate the continued dominance of Upper Canada over Eastern affairs, but survey confirmation of this has been rare. However, it should be pointed out that the number of people using the Upper and Lower Canada terminology to answer the questions on the survey is distinctly in the minority in all provinces concerned.

Forty-four per cent of Ontarians who see the country in terms of regions appear in category three of Table 2.6. Of this total, almost all mention Quebec alone as another region, with only 1% citing Quebec and their own province of Ontario as well. This pattern is not as prevalent in Quebec, however. Five per cent of Quebeckers naming another region named Quebec as that other region, and 6% named both Quebec and Ontario. In addition, also as presented in Table 2.6, 30% of Quebeckers name a subprovincial location, mostly within Quebec, as the other region they see. These answers go together to reinforce strikingly the pattern of introversion noted earlier in the Quebec answers to the "own region" designation. As we will demonstrate shortly, there is a strong correlation between thinking of a specific geographical location within Quebec as one's own region, and denoting other subprovincial regions as the other regions of Canada. When Quebeckers are asked what other regions *of Canada* they see, more name *another part of Quebec or Quebec itself* than name, for example, the West or the Atlantic provinces.

The perception of a Central region of Canada, or of Quebec and Ontario as regions, is much more an Eastern than a Western phenomenon.

In particular, the two island provinces are very much more likely to think of such a Central region than are mainlanders. Table 2.6 indicates that conceptions of such a Central region vary inversely with the actual geographical distance the province is from the centre of the country, suggesting that distance from the centre of Canada does not serve to blur distinctions between regions, but rather encourages people to make such distinctions between a Central region and other regions.

In keeping with this reasoning, one would expect to find residents of the far West provinces postulating the existence of a separate Maritime or Atlantic region moreso than residents of the Central provinces. Table 2.6 shows that indeed this is generally true, with Saskatchewan, Alberta, and British Columbia citizens more likely to name the Maritimes as a region. It is also quite common for Ontarians to do so as well, however, and they trail British Columbians by very little in this regard, so that we do not want to assert the "geographical distance leads to separateness" dictum as more than a general tendency. Interestingly, 19% of Newfoundland respondents and 12% of Prince Edward Islanders also think of a Maritime or Atlantic region as an *other* region. The Newfoundland result gives impetus to any move to classify that island as a separate entity and not merge it into analyses of a Maritime region. Prince Edward Island, however, is probably a different case. We saw from Table 2.4 that a high percentage of Islanders thought of themselves as Maritimers, as opposed to the total from New Brunswick. The results here probably simply show that there would be some resistance to such a classification from the Island, but not from New Brunswick. In other words, people from New Brunswick do not think of the Maritimes as an other region — many are just not used to thinking of themselves as Maritimers. In Prince Edward Island, many people consider themselves Maritimers, but a minority resists that classification and sees the Maritimes as a separate entity not including their island.

The Western side of the problem of which provinces to include in a region, namely the degree of distinctiveness of British Columbia from a Prairie region, can also be addressed from these data. Table 2.6 seems to show that residents of British Columbia itself recognize such distinctiveness more than do respondents from the East. Forty-six per cent of British Columbian residents who think of the country in regional terms see the Prairies as an other region distinct from themselves. This total, unsurpassed in any province, is not mirrored by any large number of British Columbians seeing the West as an other region. Given the data in both Tables 2.4 and 2.6, it seems most probable that British Columbians see themselves as Westerners, but divide the West into two regions — themselves as a single province, and the other three provinces as the Prairies. However, residents of other provinces are not so sure that they see

British Columbia as separate from the West, or that they see a separate Prairie region. The proportion of people seeing either British Columbia or the Prairies as separate regions rises above the 30% mark only in Nova Scotia, approaches it in Ontario, and is far below it in the other provinces. Perhaps most revealingly, the other three Western provinces do not share the tendency of British Columbians to see two subregions in the West. Only 17% of Manitobans, 25% of Saskatchewanians, and 13% of Albertans see British Columbia as a separate region from themselves. A Canada with British Columbia as a separate region, then, fits the self-images of British Columbians far better than it does the regional conceptions of the rest of the country, and especially the rest of the West.

Two final elements of the perceptions by Canadians of the other regions of the country remain to be discussed. The first is the remarkably consistent percentage from each of the provinces which refers to the North as a region of Canada. With the exception of Quebec, and the lower total in Manitoba, between 20% and 30% of Canadians who think of the country in terms of region designate the North as a region. The fact that about one-quarter of Canadians see the North as a region could be interpreted as surprisingly high or surprisingly low, depending on expectations. Those who think of the North as ignored might not have expected so many to be conscious of it. On the other hand, those who see the "northern vision" as a compelling myth for all Canadians may be shocked to note that it springs to so few minds as a distinct region of the country. The lack of geographical concentration of those seeing the North as an other region argues for its nationwide appeal as a reference point, and perhaps as a myth, but the number of mentions of it argues against its centrality in Canadian belief-systems.

The other category in the regional classifications is that of economic or linguistic descriptions of region. In contrast to the economic-linguistic descriptions of own regions (Table 2.4), in which the economic terms such as industrial or agricultural predominate, linguistic terms are predominant in the other region category. Thus, a number of people in the English-speaking provinces see French Canada as another region. Curiously, however, the reverse does not seem to be true, since only about 1% of Quebeckers who think in terms of region (or about one-half of 1% of Quebeckers overall) think Canada has another region called English Canada. The evidence is persuasive that for most Canadians of whatever ethnic group, the term "region" has basically territorial connotations, not those of language or the economy.

PATTERNS OF RESPONSES

Now that we have described in some detail the way Canadians define their own regions and other regions, we may pursue the analysis a step further. It seems likely that the *kind* of answer given to the request to designate one's own region would be consistent with the terms chosen to denote the other regions of the country. We would expect, for example, that someone choosing to classify his own region in economic or linguistic terms would also see other regions in such non-geographic ways. A person seeing an area within the province as his own region would be likely to choose other such sub-provincial areas as additional regions.

As a first step, we will examine something we might call the "East-West phenomenon," which emerges strikingly from the data on these two region variables. We have already seen that a substantial proportion of the population identifies either the East or the West as its own region, and the companion term as another region of Canada. It seems reasonable to hypothesize that the two terms would be used together; that is, that those who identify with the East would be more likely to name the West as another region than those who consider their own province to be their region, or use some other term to denote it.

Table 2.7 shows that this pattern is quite apparent, with about three-quarters of those defining their own regions as the East or the West, identifying the other as another region of Canada. Overall, Easterners and Westerners see fewer other regions existing in the country, and the ones they do see are described in such large terms as East, West, and Centre, and less often in terms of specific provinces or more narrowly defined terms such as Maritimes or Prairies. As Table 2.7 indicates, those using the East-West terminology mention other large regions more than single provinces. Those who define a more specific region as their own are likely to be more balanced in their willingness to name both single provinces and larger areas as other regions of Canada. They are also likely to name more regions. In other words, those people who see the country in East-West terms are not nearly as likely to have diversified conceptions of the regional structure of the country as are those who employ more specific definitional terms.

A few examples will point out the nature of the different perceptions of East-West and other identifiers. The four provinces of Newfoundland, Prince Edward Island, New Brunswick, and Nova Scotia have, for the most part, two types of regional identifiers — Easterners and Maritimers. Those who feel that they are Easterners are highly likely to see another region called the West, and are moderately likely to name another region in the centre of the country, either calling it a Central region, or naming Ontario, Quebec, or both. Thus, Easterners have essentially a three-region conceptual framework, with their own region on one side of the country, the vast West on the other, and some Central unit in between. Maritimers, however, are more varied in their conceptions. They are still quite likely to name a Western "other region," but may see a Prairie or British Columbian region as well. They are also more likely to be specific about the regions they see in the Centre of the country, giving them Ontario or Quebec designations.

Residents of Manitoba, Saskatchewan, Alberta, and British Columbia follow a similar pattern. Those who consider themselves Westerners are highly likely to conceive of another region called the East, but do not concentrate their perceptions on any other region to a great extent. Prairie identifiers, however, resemble Maritimers in their designation of other regions. They are, in fact, quite likely to state that the Maritimes are another region for them, as well as the East, and they also consider British Columbia to be a separate region. British Columbians reciprocate by seeing the Prairies as a separate region of Canada.

TABLE 2.7

Other Regions Mentioned, By Definition of Own Region

OTHER REGIONS MENTIONED	DEFINITION OF OWN REGION							
	MARITIMES	EAST	QUE.	ONT.	CENTRAL	WEST	PRAIRIES	B.C.
Mean number of mentions[a]	3.42	2.47	2.52	3.28	3.07	2.69	3.02	3.38
Mean number of provinces[b] mentioned	1.41	.45	.81	1.05	.65	.43	.92	.82
Mean number of large[c] regions mentioned	1.70	1.84	.80	1.33	1.92	1.61	1.95	1.97
% mentioning Maritimes	—	27	30	58	44	31	71	55
% mentioning East	5	—	5	23	51	74	49	31
% mentioning Ont., Que., both	58	25	45	62	32	23	34	31
% mentioning Centre	33	28	2	0	—	15	11	5
% mentioning West	57	78	22	40	65	—	23	7
% mentioning Prairies	36	17	10	29	31	12	—	65
% mentioning B.C.	33	9	22	36	27	4	42	—

[a]Includes categories of other region not detailed in this table.
[b]Includes mentions of any single provinces.
[c]Includes mentions of East, West, Centre, Maritimes, and Prairies.

Table 2.7 sheds some light on the question of whether British Columbia and the Prairies are perceived as separate regions or not. The data indicate that designations of those two regions as separate come mainly from those who identify themselves as British Columbians and Prairie residents, though there is some support for this position from Maritimers, and Ontario and Central region identifiers. Easterners and Westerners are highly unlikely to note either the Prairies or British Columbia as subregions of the West. Thus, the impetus to divide the West into two subregions of the Prairies and British Columbia comes mainly from a subset of a group that Table 2.4 revealed to be a minority in the area, those who identify with the specific regions involved and not with the West as a whole.

The consistency observed in ways of denoting regions is reinforced when we consider people who define regions in two other ways, either in subprovincial terms (whether general or specific locations), or in economic or linguistic terms. Subprovincial identifiers are, in fact, very likely to describe the other regions they see in subprovincial terms as well. In Quebec and Ontario, the two provinces where usage of subprovincial categories is prevalent enough to provide sufficient cases for analysis, the percentage of such respondents naming another region in subprovincial terms is over 60%. In contrast, the proportion of those who do not identify their own region in subprovincial terms but do so for another region is only 13% in Quebec and 7% in Ontario. Similarly, of those who say they are living in a region economically or linguistically defined, over half name another region in such terms, as opposed to very small numbers of others who do so.

Despite the fact that we have referred to East-West respondents as being an identifiable group of Canadians, differing in their conceptual maps of regions from those having specific cognitions, there are no conspicuous differences between these two groups in terms of demographic characteristics. Those with more complex conceptual maps of Canada's regions are not higher in formal educational training, nor are they better off in material terms. What relationships do exist between conceptions of region and such variables as income, education, mother tongue, age, and size of community are small and inconsistent in direction from one part of the country to another. It seems clear that an inclination to view Canada in East-West-Centre terms or in more specific regional terms is not a manifestation of some set of background characteristics of Canadians, but rather a simple difference in ways of perceiving the political world.

CONCLUSION

We mentioned in introducing this chapter that a strong argument can be made that only if a substantial degree of regional consciousness is found to be present could differences between areas of the country be effectively politicized, or could region itself be used to explain political behaviour in Canada. Since such a substantial degree of regional feeling has been uncovered in this chapter, it seems fair to say that the *potential* exists for both politicization of regional cleavages and for region to be an explanatory variable in itself. Whether this potential is realized, however, depends on a number of other factors.

The politicization of regional feeling is dependent essentially on two things: whether that consciousness is accompanied by deep-set feelings of injustice to people's own regions, and whether major actors or institutions, such as provincial governments, political parties, and other groups, are seen as defenders of the region's interests within the Canadian political system. In simple affective terms, liking one's own region does not seem to be a deterrent to liking Canada as a whole — the two feelings are correlated positively.[25] The amount of perceived regional injustice, however, is difficult to gauge.[26] A certain amount emerges from the spontaneous descriptions of Canadian politics in Chapter One, but much of the discontent evident from that data does not have a regional referent and seems rather general in scope. And while we will see in the next chapter that substantial numbers of Canadians, in answer to direct questions on the subject, believe that some *provinces* bear more than their fair share of the costs of governing Canada, we have already seen that the correspondence between regional and provincial boundaries is very far from being exact. In no province does even one-third of the population agree that their own region corresponds with the boundaries of their province. Thus, actors, such as provincial governments, may experience difficulties in being perceived as defenders of regional interests.

The status of region as an analytic variable, rather than just a "container" designated by the analyst, is also left in some doubt by the findings reported in this chapter. In no province does a majority of the population agree on what the boundaries of their own region are, and the diversity of responses in many areas is very wide. This lack of agreement on regional boundaries makes it unlikely that regional consciousness will provide a major explanatory variable in the definition of Canadian party politics and in the explanation of Canadian electoral behaviour,[27] although its potential in other areas of investigation, such as system support, would seem to be somewhat higher. In the analysis of voting behaviour to be undertaken in this book, regional consciousness remains a variable which helps only to define the context of electoral choice.

FOOTNOTES

1. Richard Simeon and David Elkins, "Regional Political Cultures in Canada," *Canadian Journal of Political Science*, 7 (1974), p. 405.

2. *Ibid.*, p. 415.
3. John Wilson, "The Canadian Political Cultures: Towards a Redefinition of the Nature of the Canadian Political System," *Canadian Journal of Political Science*, 7 (1974), pp. 438-83; Jane Jenson, "Party Systems," in David J. Bellamy, Jon H. Pammett, and Donald Rowat, eds., *The Provincial Political Systems: Comparative Essays* (Toronto: Methuen, 1976), pp. 118-31.
4. Donald F. Putnam and Donald P. Kerr, *A Regional Geography of Canada* (Toronto: Dent, 1964).
5. Daniel Kubat and David Thornton, *A Statistical Profile of Canadian Society* (Toronto: McGraw-Hill Ryerson, 1974); Stewart Crysdale and Christopher Beattie, *Sociology Canada* (Toronto: Butterworth, 1973), pp. 144-49. Arthur Lower, *Colony to Nation*, 4th ed. (Toronto: Longmans, 1964).
6. John Porter, *The Vertical Mosaic* (Toronto: University of Toronto Press, 1965), pp. 368-69.
7. S. D. Clark, *The Developing Canadian Community*, 2nd ed. (Toronto: University of Toronto Press, 1968); Donald Creighton, *The Commercial Empire of the St. Lawrence* (Toronto: Ryerson, 1937); W. T. Easterbrook and H. G. Aitken, *An Economic History of Canada* (Toronto: Macmillan, 1956).
8. Kenneth McRae, "The Structure of Canadian History," in Louis Hartz, *The Founding of New Societies* (New York: Harcourt, Brace & World, 1964), pp. 219-74; Gad Horowitz, "Conservatism, Liberalism, and Socialism in Canada: an Interpretation," *Canadian Journal of Economics and Political Science*, 32 (1966), pp. 143-71; Seymour Martin Lipset, *The First New Nation* (New York: Basic Books, 1963).
9. John Wilson, *op. cit.*, p. 440.
10. Mildred A. Schwartz, *Politics and Territory* (Montreal: McGill-Queen's Press, 1974), pp. 5-6.
11. Adam Przeworski and Henry Teune, *The Logic of Comparative Social Inquiry* (New York: Wiley, 1970), chap. 1.
12. Richard Simeon, "Regionalism and Canadian Political Institutions," *Queen's Quarterly*, 82 (1975), p. 499.
13. Mildred Schwartz, *op. cit.*, p. 5.
14. *Ibid.*, p. 17.
15. Richard Simeon, *op. cit.*, p. 504.
16. See Schwartz, *op. cit.*, pp. 312-15 for a discussion of such a model; see also Robert Alford, *Party and Society* (Chicago: Rand McNally, 1963).
17. Seymour M. Lipset and Stein Rokkan, "Cleavage Structures, Party Systems and Voter Alignments: An Introduction," in Lipset and Rokkan, eds., *Party Systems and Voter Alignments* (New York: Free Press, 1967). See also the application to Norway by Rokkan, "Geography, Religion, and Social Class: Cross-cutting Cleavages in Norwegian Politics," in the same volume, pp. 367-444.
18. See Appendix B, Q. 14-15. The map question is discussed in Chapter One.
19. Schwartz, *op. cit.*, p. 313. This conclusion is also reached by Donald Blake, "The Measurement of Regionalism in Canadian Voting Patterns," *Canadian Journal of Political Science*, 5 (1972), pp. 55-81.
20. See, for example, the discussion relating to long-term patterns of political change, in David Butler and Donald Stokes, *Political Change in Britain* (New York: St. Martin's, 1969), chap. 3.

66   *Political Choice in Canada*

21. See Appendix B, Q. 15.
22. See the argument by David Bellamy, "The Atlantic Provinces," in Bellamy, Pammett, and Rowat, *op. cit.*, pp. 3-10.
23. The arguments have mostly been in favour of considering British Columbia a separate political culture. See Martin Robin, "British Columbia," in Martin Robin, ed., *Canadian Provincial Politics* (Toronto: Prentice-Hall, 1972), pp. 27-68; Gordon Galbraith, "British Columbia," in Bellamy, Pammett, and Rowat, *op. cit.*, pp. 62-75.
24. Respondents who said they thought of Canada in regional terms and designated a region as their own were then asked, "What are the other regions of Canada?" See Appendix B, Q. 15.
25. Affect for Canada and for the respondent's own region correlate at a Pearson r of .13. The measure used was the standardized "feeling thermometer," which is employed extensively in the next chapter. See Appendix B, Q. 18, for a description of this measure.
26. On the subject of perceived injustice see David Bell, "Regionalism in the Canadian Community," in Paul Fox, ed., *Politics: Canada*, 4th ed. (Toronto: McGraw-Hill Ryerson, 1977).
27. Mean scores on the regional consciousness index by 1974 vote are:
    1.6 Liberal
    1.8 Progressive Conservative
    1.8 NDP.
    1.4 Social Credit
    $F = 6.5*$
    While statistically significant, this result does not show a strong enough relationship to vote to be a promising analytical variable in explaining it.

Chapter Three

Orientations To The Federal System

Federal institutions and their effects pervade Canadian politics. They affect, to varying degrees, all political phenomena in this country. Over the years since Confederation the control by the federal government in Ottawa has alternatively tightened and loosened, with the most recent swing, in the post-World-War-II years, being toward a greater decentralization of federal power in favour of provincial control.[1] This trend has been most visible in recent years in the demands made and the successes achieved by the province of Quebec in gaining a large degree of mastery of its own affairs. However, Quebec has by no means been the only province to make demands for greater provincial autonomy. Throughout Canadian history, Ontario has often led the fight for provincial power, and that province has been joined in the 1960s and the 1970s by newly wealthy Western provinces, particularly Alberta, in the fight for augmented provincial control and financing.[2]

An important reason for the growth of provincial power lies in the fact that the provincial governments have had an increasingly large impact on people's lives, since it was that level of government which, by the British North America Act, was given responsibility for areas of jurisdiction like education, most social services, and municipal and local affairs.[3] Therefore, the provincial governments have seemed to impinge increasingly on the daily lives of Canadians and have become much more visible to citizens in doing so. With all that, however, the federal government performs many important functions, and is, in fact, operating in many of the areas reserved in the constitution for provincial jurisdiction.

Although the federal and provincial levels of government have come to share relatively equally the powers of the Canadian federation, they have retained and even enhanced their status as distinctly *separate* levels.

Of particular concern to this book is the separate status of the provincial and federal party systems. Political parties, particularly in the Central and Western parts of the country, take great pains to maintain independent existences at the two levels, even when they bear the same name as a party at the other level of government. Thus, the federal and provincial Liberal parties in Quebec and Saskatchewan — two obvious examples — take very different positions on many issues, and maintain separate organizations and personnel. Frequently the provincial level of government contains distinctive parties, like the Social Credit party of British Columbia or the Parti Québécois of Quebec, which have no equivalents at the federal level in those provinces.[4]

With the separate status and reasonably equal power of the two levels of the Canadian federal system, the potential for conflict is high, and even a cursory glance at Canadian history provides a large number of instances where it has broken out. Federal and provincial governments have hurled invective at each other in the public press, waged election campaigns "against" the other level, battled each other in the courts, and bargained bitterly in federal-provincial conferences.[5] While it would be inaccurate to describe the history of federal-provincial relations solely in terms of such conflict, the fact that both levels of government are oftentimes competing for scarce financial resources in order to advance ambitious programs of legislation, inevitably means that the governments are frequently placed in the position of adversaries.

While conflict seems endemic to the relations between Canadian governments, its effects on the political perceptions of citizens are by no means clear. It is at least reasonable to speculate that the constant infighting between governments contributes to the negative image most Canadians have of the whole political process, as documented in Chapter One. If politicians are seen as primarily engaged in argument rather than in the improvement of the lot of their constituents, it may be natural that they develop a negative image. Perhaps a politically negative and cynical population is an outgrowth of a federation in which disputes over the division of authority frequently occur.

Of direct concern to us in this chapter are the effects of the existence of a federal system on the political attitudes and behaviour of the population. Specifically, we are interested in establishing whether the existence of two levels of government means that Canadians direct their attention to only one of these systems, or whether the majority is able to accommodate reasonably high levels of understanding, attention, and activity at *both* levels in the federal system. In particular, since we are primarily interested in this volume in analyzing electoral behaviour at the federal level, we might ask whether individuals' loyalty to their province may, at least partially, diminish their loyalty to the nation, and whether participation in politics at the provincial level may inhibit such activity at the federal level. In his address to the nation following the Parti Québécois victory in the 1976 Quebec provincial election, Prime Minister Trudeau stated that it was not impossible to be a good Canadian *and* a good Québécois, Nova Scotian, or British Columbian at the same time.[6] It is by no means obvious that this statement reflects the political reality.

The investigation of this question requires us to look at the affective, cognitive, and evaluative attitudes Canadians have toward the two levels of government, and the political behaviour they demonstrate toward each.[7] Affective attitudes are feelings about objects in the real world — emotional ties, which are expressed in the current study by likes and dislikes for various political objects. We will be looking shortly at people's degrees of affect for the constituent units of the Canadian federation. Cognitive attitudes, or cognitions, consist of beliefs about and knowledge about objects. They are beliefs about what exists, and constitute raw political information. To look at the cognitive attitudes of Canadians, we will investigate their knowledge of the actual functioning of the two levels of government. Evaluative attitudes are value judgments about the rightness or wrongness, worth or worthlessness, of particular phenomena. They are preferences between alternative political objects, and are expressed in the form of statements about what "should" or "ought to" be. We will later see how Canadians evaluate federal and provincial governments.

It is, of course, the case that the three types of attitudes described above are not independent of one another. The things one believes to be true can be coloured by one's values; the things one believes ought to be done are related to the things that are liked; the things one likes are affected by the things believed to be true. Nevertheless, it is convenient for the purposes of analysis to separate attitudes which seem to be predominantly of one type or another, in order to examine them closely. We will be able to see whether people feel closer to one part of the system, whether they have a reasonably accurate grasp of the functions of both levels, and whether they evaluate one as more important to their lives. Finally, and most crucially, we will examine frequency of voting and participation in federal and provincial politics to determine whether, despite feelings of attachment to one or the other level of government, people are used to participating at both levels of the federal system.

AFFECTIVE ORIENTATIONS TO THE FEDERAL SYSTEM

There are quite large differences in the degree of affect felt by the residents of the provinces toward nation and province. While most people are willing to grant a high level of affective support to Canada, that support is provincially differentiated. In the 1974 National Election Study, one measure of attachments to several political institutions, groupings, and actors was developed by presenting the respondents with a thermometer on which they were asked to mark a score from 0 to 100, indicating their feelings about the specific object. Scores above 50 on the thermometer indicate feelings of warmth toward the objects, while scores below this neutral point indicate feelings of coolness.[8] Respondents were asked to rank Canada and their own province in this way.[9] The mean score for Canada is 84, indicating a very warm feeling, but as Table 3.1 shows, provincial differences are immediately apparent. The residents of Ontario score the country highest, while those in Newfoundland, New Brunswick, and Quebec score it substantially lower.

TABLE 3.1

Affective Support for the Country and Own Province
(mean thermometer score, rank in parentheses)

		CANADA	OWN PROVINCE	CANADA MINUS OWN PROVINCE[a]
Total	(N=*2413*)	84	78	+ 6
Newfoundland	(N=96)	76 (9)	82 (5)	− 7 (10)
Prince Edward Island	(N=96)	86 (6)	86 (1)	0 (9)
Nova Scotia	(N=170)	89 (2)	83 (4)	+ 7 (4)
New Brunswick	(N=132)	82 (8)	70 (10)	+12 (1)
Quebec	(N=687)	75 (10)	71 (9)	+ 4 (6)
Ontario	(N=688)	91 (1)	80 (7)	+11 (2)
Manitoba	(N=111)	87 (4)	79 (8)	+ 8 (3)
Saskatchewan	(N=99)	87 (5)	81 (6)	+ 4 (5)
Alberta	(N=176)	85 (7)	85 (2)	0 (8)
British Columbia	(N=250)	87 (3)	85 (3)	+ 2 (7)
		F=42.4*	F=23.1*	F=11.7*

*Significant at .01 level.
[a]Individual scores.

There are also observable provincial differences when the support for the province is measured. Overall, respondents demonstrated considerable affect for their provinces, but the overall level is somewhat lower than that for the nation. The data presented in Table 3.1 demonstrate that residents of the provinces most distant from the centre of the country tend to give the province a high score, while New Brunswick, Quebec, Ontario, and Manitoba are the lowest-ranked provinces. Newfoundland is the one province that would seem to present a possible instance of conflicting or competing loyalties, since Newfoundland ranks very high on the measure of provincial affect and low on the national measure.

Because Newfoundland was the last province to enter Confederation, and also because opinion on that union was sharply divided, this relationship is not surprising.[10] In the case of Quebec, where the historical expression of conflict between national and provincial loyalties has been persistent, there seems to be a weakening of affection for both levels.

When individuals' provincial affect is subtracted from their federal score, the tendency for the more geographically peripheral provinces is to have a higher provincial than Canadian affect, as Table 3.1 shows. Residents of the island provinces are most likely to rank the province above Canada, with Newfoundland's case being quite striking. The far Western provinces are relatively equal in their provincial and national scores, whereas the more Central provinces rank country well above province. The one break in a pattern based solely on geography is Quebec, which, in rating the country only slightly above the province, does not show the characteristics of other Central provinces.

TABLE 3.2

**Correlations Between Standardized Thermometer Score
for the Country and Own Province, by Province
(Pearson r)**

Total	−.05*
Newfoundland	.02
Prince Edward Island	.12
Nova Scotia	.08
New Brunswick	.00
Quebec	−.10*
Ontario	−.09*
Manitoba	.19
Saskatchewan	.14
Alberta	−.14*
British Columbia	−.15*

*Significant at .01.

When we look at individual relationships rather than provincial aggregates, there is, in fact, a very small (though statistically significant) correlation between the national and provincial scores (Table 3.2). The Pearson r equals only −.05. To construct this table the thermometer scores of individuals have been standardized, removing the effect of variation in the range of the scale as used by individual respondents.[11] It may be seen that the correlation between attitudes toward the nation and those toward the respondents' own provinces are positive in some instances and negative in others. They are, however, weakly negative for the nation as a whole, indicating that high levels of affect for the province are associated with a lower score for Canada. Interestingly, it is in the largest and most economically viable provinces that this negative relationship is found. It may not be impossible to be a good Canadian and a good Québécois, Albertan, British Columbian, or Ontarian at the same time, but the data presented here would tend to suggest that in some provinces these loyalties are in conflict with one another more often than they are mutually reinforcing. However, the correlations are small and it is possible, in looking at provinces as a whole, to speak only of tendencies toward conflict. These tendencies within important sub-groups of provincial populations will be further examined later in the chapter.

TABLE 3.3

Affect for Level of Government by Province
(row percentages)

| | LEVEL TO WHICH RESPONDENT FEELS CLOSER | | | |
	FEDERAL	PROVINCIAL	BOTH	N=
Newfoundland	18%	67	15	(94)
Prince Edward Island	14%	77	10	(94)
Nova Scotia	25%	55	20	(154)
New Brunswick	21%	60	20	(111)
Quebec	31%	45	23	(621)
Ontario	51%	34	16	(628)
Manitoba	22%	60	18	(105)
Saskatchewan	25%	65	11	(93)
Alberta	13%	78	9	(166)
British Columbia	20%	71	9	(233)
Total	34%	49	17	(*2175*)

A measure of the attachments of Canadians toward the *governments* in the federal system is provided by a question which asked the respondents to indicate the level of government to which they felt closer.[12] Table 3.3 reports the results by province, and once again quite strong provincial differences emerge. The first observation of note is that fewer Canadians in each province, except Ontario, felt closer to the federal government than to the provincial, and that everywhere, except in Ontario and Quebec, this preference was by a substantial margin. We may further observe that despite the events of recent years, residents of the province of Quebec gave the second lowest number of "provincial" answers. Almost one-quarter of the Quebec respondents indicated the importance of *both* levels of government, despite the fact that the question did not include that category as a response option. Further, another third mentioned that they felt closer to the federal government, which is the highest rate of "federal" answers in any province except Ontario.

Once again, the overall impression given by these data is that the farther away the respondent is from Ottawa or Central Canada, the greater the attachment to the province. The residents of the two Ceneral provinces, Ontario and Quebec, feel closest to the federal level, and they provide the fewest reports of closeness to the provincial government. The drop-off in federal mentions and the increase in provincial ones is quite marked in both the East and the West. Residence in a geographically peripheral province is clearly associated with greater support of the provincial level, whereas residence in the centre of the country is tied to greater affect for the federal level.

It may, of course, be that simple geographical distance is the factor affecting the reports of "closeness" examined above. However, as noted in Chapter Two, a discovery of regional or provincial differences does not produce an immediate explanation of the reason for those differences. Further analysis is necessary to specify more thoroughly the variables which lie behind the statistically observable differences related to geography. One obvious strategy is to ask whether the affective attitudes noted here are related to the characteristics of the individuals who hold them. We will concentrate our attention here on language and age, the two variables most directly related to affect for levels in the system.

TABLE 3.4

Feelings About Country and Own Province
(mean thermometer scores)

		N	COUNTRY	PROVINCE
Age	18-29 years	(706)	81	76
	30-45 years	(668)	84	78
	46-59 years	(590)	87	79
	60+	(409)	88	79
			F=21.8*	F=3.8*
Language	French	(645)	73	73
	English	(1593)	88	80
	Other	(167)	94	89
			F=217.7*	F=35.7*

*Significant at .01 level.

Looking first at the affective orientation measured by the thermometer scores and language, the pattern of these relationships is quite clear (Table 3.4). Language has a statistically significant effect on all of the measures, but particularly on the score for Canada. Francophone Canadians exhibit a lower absolute level of affect for the nation than do English-speaking Canadians, but the data also show a lower francophone score for province. Indeed, it may be seen that the scores for franco-

TABLE 3.5

Feelings About Country and Own Province, by Language, for Quebec and Rest of Canada

(mean thermometer scores)

		N	COUNTRY	PROVINCE
Quebec	Anglophone	(79)	91	62
	Francophone	(591)	72	72
			F=76.6*	F=17.5*
Rest of Canada	Anglophone	(1516)	88	81
	Francophone	(57)	82	77
			F= 7.3*	F= 1.6*

*Significant at .01 level.

phones are quite close together, while those of anglophone and other language backgrounds vary substantially.

It is appropriate to distinguish the effects of language and province at this point, because it might be expected that the large non-francophone minority in Quebec will show a separate pattern on these measures, as may francophone Canadians living in provinces other than Quebec. As is seen in Table 3.5, English-speaking residents of Quebec are similar to anglophone residents of other provinces in their level of affect for Canada, but differ more substantially in their orientaton to the province. This very large relative difference is seen clearly if the thermometer score for the province is subtracted from that of Canada for these groups. The strong national orientation of English-speaking Quebeckers is shown by the gap of 29 degrees between affect scores given to country and province. This large relative difference is due both to the high degree of affect for the nation and the relatively low orientation to province, which combine to produce the large positive result. The comparable value for non-Quebec residents is a rating approximately 7 degrees higher for country than province. Quebec francophones disclose virtually identical (and quite low) affective feelings toward both province and nation.

After language, the most interesting socio-demographic correlate of affective orientation is age. The pattern observed with respect to age is particularly important, because of the possibility that relationships due to age may suggest elements of social and political change. Age is clearly not a perfect surrogate for other measures of change across time, but it may potentially serve in the present instance as a kind of window on large scale processes of political and social change which might otherwise not be measurable in a single survey.

In Table 3.4, it was seen that affect for Canada tends to be significantly lower in the younger age groups, while the province scores show little

TABLE 3.6

Correlations Between Age and Thermometer Scores for Country and Own Province, by Province

(Pearson r)

	COUNTRY	PROVINCE
Newfoundland	.02	−.03
Prince Edward Island	.06	−.03
Nova Scotia	.15	.04
New Brunswick	−.03	−.08
Quebec	.23*	−.06
Ontario	.08	.12*
Manitoba	.19	.20
Saskatchewan	.16	.07
Alberta	.22*	.29*
British Columbia	.23*	.21*
Total	.16*	.06

*Significant at .01.

difference. This pattern was not uniform across the nation, however. A summary measure of the relationship between age and affect for country and province, shown in Table 3.6, discloses that the relationship between age and affect for Canada is fairly strong in several provinces, notably Quebec, Alberta, and British Columbia, but is not statistically significant in most others. Whether these trends are representative of a growing "alienation" of young people from the nation in certain parts of the country is difficult to say, in the absence of more definitive measures examined over a longer period of time. In Quebec, the patterns are clearest, and the younger respondents are substantially lower in affect for Canada. Figure 3.1 graphically portrays the great differences which exist between Quebec and the other provinces, and also between older and younger citizens of Quebec.

Similar differences between individuals emerge when we examine the closed-ended question asking to which level of government people "feel closer." Once again, language and age are the two demographic correlates which most influence the affect for the two levels of the system. It could be hypothesized that the relationships between the affect measures and the two variables of language and age might be due, at least in part, to the effects of other variables, such as education and socio-economic status. Controls introduced for such factors, however, do not appreciably diminish the results reported here. The fact that younger people and francophones, particularly in Quebec, demonstrate lower levels of affect for the nation and the federal government persists, despite differences in education and socio-economic status.[13]

FIGURE 3.1
Affect for Canada by Age and Region

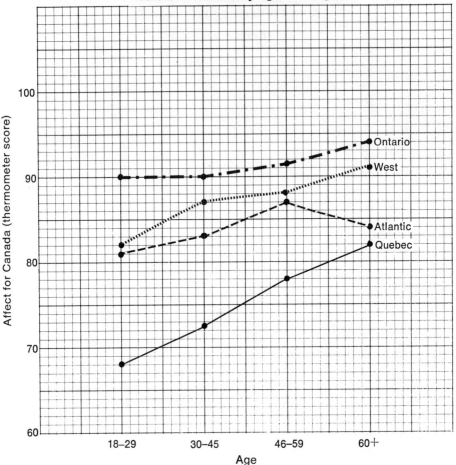

Our examination of affective orientations to the federal system has established that Canadians feel somewhat warmer, on the average, toward Canada than toward their provinces, but that they feel substantially closer to their provincial governments than to the federal government in Ottawa. There are also important differences among Canadians of varying ages, languages, and provinces of residence in levels of affect, with provincial feelings being highest among francophones and residents of geographically peripheral provinces. Although these results might suggest the potential for a division in the population, with some people nationally oriented and some provincially oriented, there is scant evidence that such a division has occurred. Affect for both the country and the province are relatively high, and the negative correlation between the two feelings, while present, is very low (Table 3.2). In the provinces of Alberta, British Columbia, and Quebec, the negative correlations are somewhat higher, however, and these three provinces bear watching for additional signs of conflict. In Quebec, the younger citizens are heavily provincially oriented, but this is offset to some extent by Quebec's relatively low feeling of affect for the provincial government (Table 3.3). (We should, of course, note that this situation may have changed since 1974.) In Alberta and British Columbia, respondents are much more likely to report feeling close to the provincial government than they are to the federal, but the association with age, noted in Quebec, is not present. None of these relationships, however, appears to be strong enough to support any statement that affect for the federal and for the provincial levels of the Canadian political system are necessarily in conflict.

COGNITIVE ORIENTATIONS TO THE FEDERAL SYSTEM

The existence of a federal system means that responsibilities for governmental services and programs are divided between two levels, according to the provisions of the constitution. In Canada, the British North America Act in 1867 provided for a basic division of responsibility, according to the principle that "that which is local" would belong to the province, and "that which is national" to the federal government. However, in the last 110 years this line of simple division has become blurred, as a result of changes in judicial interpretation by the Judicial Committee of the Privy Council in Britain and by the Canadian Supreme Court, as well as by changes in this century in the kinds of activities undertaken by governments.[14] These two factors have produced substantial alterations in Canadian federalism, resulting in a system which has been characterized "cooperative federalism." In essence, a cooperative federal system is one in which new programs and policies are often jointly negotiated by both levels of government in order to allocate responsibility and expenditure.[15] In such a complex atmosphere it might be expected that the Canadian population would exhibit some difficulty in understanding the nature of the federal system and its constitutional boundaries.

The opportunities for cognitive confusion in such a system, which combines an elaborate formal designation of powers in the constitution with an informal process of negotiation and sharing of responsibilities in many areas, are such as to possibly affect political behaviour. If people are not reasonably clear which government is responsible for particular areas of legislation and administration, they may have difficulty differentiating the levels in general. On the other hand, if we find reasonably accurate knowledge about what the different governments do in the federal system, we may conclude that the basis for independent action at each level is indeed present.

The data indicate that the majority of respondents does have a basic understanding of the division of responsibilities within the Canadian federation, scoring an average of only approximately one incorrect answer out of six. The question, reported in Table 3.7, asked which government had primary responsibility in a number of policy areas: education, foreign affairs, local government, hospital insurance, unemployment insurance, and the economy. In each case the formally correct answer was picked by a majority of respondents. Constitutionally, the provinces were given control over education, local government, and hospital insurance, while the federal government controls foreign affairs, the economy generally, and, through a wartime amendment to the B.N.A. Act, unemployment insurance.

TABLE 3.7

Cognitive Orientations — Perceptions of the Division of Responsibility Between the Federal and Provincial Levels of Government (row percentages)

POLICY AREA	GOVERNMENT WITH PRIMARY RESPONSIBILITY			
	FEDERAL	PROVINCIAL	BOTH	N=
Education	16%	69	16	(2383)
Foreign Affairs	89%	3	8	(2318)
Local Government	8%	80	12	(2296)
Hospital Insurance	27%	62	11	(2421)
Unemployment Insurance	63%	26	11	(2377)
The Economy	69%	8	23	(2370)

We would, of course, expect that the answers to such a "knowledge" question would vary with the degree of education received. The amount of information available and the amount of exposure to the "facts" of federalism might alter the patterns found in Table 3.7. It is not, however, immediately clear how the more highly educated respondents would be expected to respond. Two possibilities would seem to exist. The first is that the more highly educated will better understand the formal constitutional allocation of responsibilities. The second is that they might better perceive the complexity of cooperative federalism and see a sharing of responsibilities in many areas.

TABLE 3.8

**Cognitive Orientations — Perceptions of the Division of Responsibility
Between the Federal and Provincial Levels of Government,
Controlling for Educational Level
(row percentages)**

EDUCATION — TEN YEARS OR LESS

POLICY AREA	FEDERAL	PROVINCIAL	BOTH	N=
Education	19%	59	22	(*1062*)
Foreign Affairs	82%	5	13	(*1006*)
Local Government	12%	71	17	(*1009*)
Hospital Insurance	27%	59	14	(*1099*)
Unemployment Insurance	59%	27	14	(*1072*)
The Economy	63%	11	26	(*1051*)

EDUCATION — MORE THAN TEN YEARS

POLICY AREA	FEDERAL	PROVINCIAL	BOTH	N=
Education	13%	77	11	(*1312*)
Foreign Affairs	94%	2	4	(*1303*)
Local Government	5%	87	8	(*1278*)
Hospital Insurance	27%	65	8	(*1313*)
Unemployment Insurance	66%	26	8	(*1297*)
The Economy	74%	5	21	(*1311*)

Table 3.8 seems to indicate that the first of these possibilities is more prevalent. The effect of education, used as a surrogate indicator of information, is to more tightly compartmentalize the answers so that one level is seen as responsible for the specific policy area. There are, of course, policy areas which remain somewhat problematic even for the better informed respondents. The areas of hospital insurance, unemployment insurance, and control over the economy are ones in which many joint programs do exist, and the effects of cooperative federalism in blurring constitutional boundaries are most likely to be experienced. This is particularly the case in the area of control of the economy, where 21% of those with higher education and 26% of those with low education assign joint federal-provincial responsibility. By contrast, foreign affairs is initially seen as a federal responsibility by 89% of the population, and this rises to 94% of those with education above the mean level.

We may conclude that most Canadians understand in a reasonably accurate way the workings of the federal political system, at least in terms of its formal division of powers. Thus, even though they might "feel closer" to one level or another, Canadians have the basic information to allow them to operate effectively at both. Therefore, the affect shown for provincial governments in Table 3.3 is not likely to mean that Canadians have a highly inaccurate grasp of what the federal government does.

EVALUATIVE ORIENTATIONS TO THE FEDERAL SYSTEM

The third type of attitude manifested toward the federal system is the evaluative. These attitudes reflect the judgments made by citizens about the impact of federal institutions on themselves, their families, and their place of residence. We will examine here how people rate the importance of the two governments to their daily lives. We will want to know whether these judgments of the importance of the levels of government approximate the relatively even distribution of actual governmental power that we have asserted exists at the present time. Should Canadians feel, for example, that the provincial governments are much more important, we might well have grounds for considering political behaviour at the federal level to be engaged in on a relatively casual basis. We would, at the very least, need to keep the lesser importance assigned to federal politics in mind as a contextual feature of federal political behaviour.

TABLE 3.9

Evaluative Orientations — Level of Government Most Important By Province
(row percentages)

| | LEVEL | | | |
	FEDERAL	PROVINCIAL	BOTH	N=
Newfoundland	41%	36	22	(85)
Prince Edward Island	29%	43	29	(87)
Nova Scotia	36%	33	31	(151)
New Brunswick	38%	41	20	(107)
Quebec	33%	38	29	(581)
Ontario	52%	28	20	(580)
Manitoba	32%	44	24	(97)
Saskatchewan	32%	47	22	(88)
Alberta	36%	50	15	(151)
British Columbia	28%	50	23	(232)
Total	40%	37	23	(2056)

V=.15*

*Significant at .01.

The responses of the 1974 sample to the question of which level of government was most important "to the way you and your family get on" are presented in Table 3.9.[16] It can be seen that, while the federal level is rated as being slightly more important overall, respondents divide fairly evenly on the question.[17] Furthermore, a substantial percentage of respondents refused to make a judgment on this question, and stipulated an answer indicating the importance of both levels to their daily lives. Ontario is, as we would expect from previous data, the most strongly federal of the provinces, with a majority there considering the federal government most important to the way they and their families live. The Eastern provinces (excepting Prince Edward Island) and Quebec divide relatively equally, while the four Western provinces are united in feeling that the provincial governments are more important to them.

The imposition of a control for level of education on this relationship (data not shown) has the effect that as the amount of information available increases, the evaluation of federalism alters. Low levels of education are associated with more mentions of the joint effects of both levels of government. We observed this same pattern with the cognitive attitudes — as level of education increases, so does the willingness to make an evaluation of impact. The choice of level varies in the following way: For the better educated, in all provinces except Alberta the proportion mentioning the provincial government as more important is greater than that for those with less education; thus, the making of a choice between levels, which the more educated are more willing to do, means that the provincial level is more likely to be chosen. Evaluations of the federal level do not follow a similarly consistent pattern. In the peripheral provinces, except British Columbia, the evaluation of the importance of the federal government increases with education, whereas in Quebec it is reduced and Ontario undergoes no change.

In evaluating the importance of levels of government, then, Canadians give reasonably equal weight to each, a judgment which matches that of most impartial observers. Another evaluative attitude has to do not with importance of the governments, but with the justice or injustice of the distribution of costs and benefits of the federal system. We have seen at numerous points in the first two chapters how different parts of the country air grievances about their treatment. The periphery sees the centre as dominating the federation (often with good reason), and the centre sees itself as financing the periphery (often with similar good reason). We will want to see whether Canadians are aware of the various inequalities and redistributive effects of federalism.

1974 respondents were asked whether they saw some provinces paying more than their fair share of the costs of federalism, and whether they saw some provinces gaining more than their fair share of the benefits of federalism. The first result which emerges from Table 3.10 is that about two-thirds of the respondents see both that some provinces gain more than others and that some pay more than others for the existence

TABLE 3.10

Evaluations of Federalism

		PER CENT SEEING SOME PROVINCES AS BEARING MORE THAN FAIR SHARE	PER CENT SEEING SOME PROVINCES AS GAINING MORE THAN FAIR SHARE
Newfoundland	(N=50)	52	54
Prince Edward Island	(N=68)	61	65
Nova Scotia	(N=120)	41	58
New Brunswick	(N=90)	56	63
Quebec	(N=473)	65	64
Ontario	(N=532)	62	59
Manitoba	(N=86)	70	80
Saskatchewan	(N=75)	53	71
Alberta	(N=130)	79	72
British Columbia	(N=205)	59	63
Total	(N=*1794*)	63	63
	V=	.14*	.10*

*Significant at .01 level.

of federalism. Alberta is high on both counts; 79% of Albertans see some provinces bearing more than a fair share, and 72% feel that some provinces gain more than their fair share. Manitoba is also high on these two evaluative indicators. In contrast, the Atlantic provinces tend to be less dissatisfied with the federal arrangements and to see a more equal sharing of costs and benefits.

Specification was also made of *which* provinces gained and lost as a result of federalism. Looking first at the evaluation of costs in Table 3.11, it is obvious that the residents of each province are very likely to see their own province as being unfairly assessed for the costs of federalism. With the exception of Nova Scotia, the pattern is clear and strong; each province is mentioned more by its own residents than by anyone else, and in many cases the gaps are quite large. Residents of other provinces do not share such perceptions of unequal treatment. For example, almost one-quarter of the residents of New Brunswick claim that that province bears more than its fair share of the cost of federalism; this value is three times higher than the assessment of the New Brunswick contribution reported anywhere else. Two-thirds of Albertans feel unfairly treated, but this value is more than twice as great as that granted by their nearest neighbours. This position is the same as that of Quebec, although the residents of Quebec are less willing than those of Alberta to report that they pay an unusually high share. Ontario is the only province for which many residents of other provinces are willing to

TABLE 3.11

Per Cent of Respondents Mentioning Each Province as One Which Bears More Than Its Fair Share of Costs of Federalism
(multiple responses)

PROVINCE OF RESPONDENT

PROVINCE MENTIONED:	NFLD.	P.E.I.	N.S.	N.B.	QUE.	ONT.	MAN.	SASK.	ALTA.	B.C.
Newfoundland	13	—	—	3	1	1	2	—	—	1
Prince Edward Island	4	9	3	7	1	1	1	—	1	2
Nova Scotia	4	3	8	11	—	1	2	—	—	2
New Brunswick	4	9	4	25	2	1	2	—	—	2
Quebec	15	22	7	12	50	14	8	7	3	3
Ontario	35	42	19	19	30	55	17	17	26	23
Manitoba	6	3	2	2	2	3	26	17	3	6
Saskatchewan	6	—	3	—	1	2	15	25	15	8
Alberta	4	7	6	8	6	11	23	31	64	31
British Columbia	15	16	8	5	6	16	14	11	32	48
Per Cent Mentioning: Only Quebec	2	2	1	4	22	2	1	1	2	—
Only Ontario	6	9	8	3	4	25	2	3	—	1
N =	(55)	(69)	(120)	(93)	(478)	(542)	(86)	(75)	(130)	(205)

share the assessment of Ontario residents that the province pays a dis-proportionate cost for federalism, although there is also some national sympathy for the other two "have" provinces, Alberta and British Columbia. Even in the case of Ontario, however, the residents of that province are much more likely to feel unfairly treated than are those residing elsewhere.

Respondents who mentioned Ontario or Quebec were aggregated in another way as well. The last two rows of Table 3.11 report the per-centage in each province mentioning Quebec or Ontario alone as the province most unfairly treated by the conditions of federalism. The pattern described above reappears here, with the residents of Quebec or Ontario being much more convinced that their province bears more than its share of the costs of Confederation. Findings such as these would seem to imply that there is a generalized evaluation of inequity in the distribution of costs, an evaluation which is made in all provinces in a similar way. It may be just such a generalized feeling of injustice that underlies the contribution of federalism to the negative political feel-ings expressed by much of the population, as described in Chapter One.

The evaluations of the benefits of federalism are quite different. There is general agreement that the Central provinces, Ontario and Quebec, gain disproportionately from the federal arrangements (Table 3.12). The rate of mention of any other province is quite low; residents of all the other provinces are agreed that neither themselves nor anybody, other than the "big two" Central provinces, gains unduly. With regard to Quebec and Ontario, everyone is agreed, *except* the residents of those provinces, that they are the unseemly beneficiaries. In addition, there are some differences between the way Ontario and Quebec are evaluated; residents of the Western provinces are somewhat more likely to see Quebec as gaining from Confederation than are residents of either Ontario or the Eastern provinces.

The Canadian federal system is evaluated, then, as an unjust one by most people. There is a general dissatisfaction with its operation, at least with regard to its distribution of costs and benefits. Most people feel their areas pay the costs, and that other areas get the benefits. There is no evidence, however, that the evaluative attitudes of Canadians serve to hamper their normal political behaviour at both provincial and federal levels. Indeed, they may well make it more likely that opportunities to act in the federal arena will be grasped, since the chances of other areas gaining even more than they do now would be enhanced if vigi-lance is relaxed.

TABLE 3.12

Per Cent of Respondents Mentioning Each Province as One Which Receives More Than Its Fair Share of Benefits from Federalism
(multiple responses)

PROVINCE OF RESPONDENT

PROVINCE MENTIONED:	NFLD.	P.E.I.	N.S.	N.B.	QUE.	ONT.	MAN.	SASK.	ALTA.	B.C.
Newfoundland	6	4	2	1	4	4	—	1	2	2
Prince Edward Island	—	7	2	1	2	2	—	—	1	1
Nova Scotia	2	3	4	2	2	3	—	—	2	2
New Brunswick	2	4	2	4	2	3	—	—	—	1
Quebec	26	38	40	32	18	37	58	49	62	51
Ontario	28	27	29	34	27	15	47	53	29	25
Manitoba	4	—	2	1	5	2	—	—	2	2
Saskatchewan	6	—	2	1	4	2	3	—	2	3
Alberta	12	7	6	7	8	7	9	6	3	2
British Columbia	10	9	4	6	5	6	10	7	4	5
Per Cent Mentioning: Only Quebec	4	15	16	12	9	23	17	8	25	26
Only Ontario	10	3	7	11	13	7	5	12	4	5
N =	(50)	(68)	(131)	(90)	(473)	(532)	(97)	(83)	(130)	(214)

PARTICIPATION IN FEDERAL AND PROVINCIAL POLITICS

Voters in Canada are confronted with an electoral process which separates the acts of participation at the two levels of government.[18] Federal and provincial elections are held at different times, and it is not customary for more than one provincial election to be held at the same time. We will be interested in knowing whether participation takes place at one level more than another, or whether, despite affect directed toward the nation or the province, it is the norm for individuals to engage in the same sort of political activity at both levels of the political system. A finding that the latter is true would allow us to conclude that Canadians determine what political activities they will undertake in provincial and federal election campaigns, without much regard for a preference between levels.[19]

The 1974 Election Study explored in some detail the participation habits of the Canadian electorate. Information was collected on participation in the 1974 election itself, as well as in federal, provincial, and

TABLE 3.13

**Frequency of Different Modes of Political Participation —
Federal and Provincial Elections**

(row percentages)[a]

		OFTEN	SOMETIMES	SELDOM	NEVER
Vote frequency[b]	Federal	60%	28	8	5
	Provincial	53%	28	10	10
Read newspapers	Federal	41%	29	18	13
	Provincial	42%	29	16	13
Discuss politics	Federal	24%	37	22	17
	Provincial	26%	37	20	17
Convince friends	Federal	8%	13	10	69
	Provincial	9%	14	9	68
Work in community	Federal	5%	15	12	67
	Provincial	6%	15	11	68
Attend meetings	Federal	10%	15	12	69
	Provincial	5%	15	11	69
Contact officials	Federal	3%	11	14	72
	Provincial	3%	12	11	74
Sign, sticker	Federal	5%	9	4	82
	Provincial	5%	9	4	82
Campaign activity	Federal	4%	7	6	83
	Provincial	4%	7	6	84

[a]N=*1184*

[b]For vote frequency only, the categories are: "voted in all elections," "most,"
"some," "none."

local politics generally, although we will confine the analysis here to reports of general participation in federal and provincial politics.[20] Table 3.13 displays the frequency of different types of participatory acts for both federal and provincial politics. The range of participation is wide — from the mere act of voting, which only 5% and 10% report *never* doing in federal and provincial elections respectively, to working in a campaign, which only 17% report *ever* doing at either level. This table shows, most obviously, that there are very few differences between rates of participation for different acts across levels. The number of people who report participating in each way is almost identical at the two levels. The largest difference which emerges is in rates of voting, where 60% of the respondents report that they often vote in federal elections, and 53% that they often vote provincially. That difference of 7% is not very large, however, and the correspondence of values in all other cells is very high.

TABLE 3.14

Distribution of Respondents on Federal and Provincial Participation Scales

(column percentages)

PARTICIPATION	FEDERAL	PROVINCIAL
Low (Inactive)	11%	17%
(Vote)	29	25
(Discuss politics)	30	27
(Convince friends/Attend meetings)	21	22
High (Campaign Activity)	9	10
N =	(*1203*)	(*1203*)
Coefficient of Reproducibility =	.95	.93
Coefficient of Scalability =	.77	.70

Two summary measures (Guttman scales) have been constructed using a subset of information on participation, one for provincial electoral activity and one for federal. The items used are voting in elections at the respective levels, discussing politics, convincing friends how to vote or attending meetings, and working for a party during an election campaign. The distribution of respondents on these scales is shown in Table 3.14. The mode for participation in both federal and provincial politics is voting plus "something else," in this case discussing politics. Sixty per cent report discussing politics often or sometimes during federal elections, and 59% during elections at the provincial level. Only a small proportion of the electorate can be classified as "inactive" — 11% for federal politics and 17% for provincial. Once again the correspondence in the distributions for the two levels of government is very high. The portion of the electorate found at each point on the scale is very close, with the largest gap being the 6% difference at the lowest point. Thus, the important factor influencing the decision to participate in politics would seem to be the *type of act* involved, and not the *level of government* at which the act is performed. The "fall-off" rate for each type of participation, whether discussing politics, convincing friends how to vote, or displaying a sign or sticker for a preferred candidate is essentially the same for both provincial and federal politics.

TABLE 3.15

Federal Participation by Provincial Participation
(column percentages)

PROVINCIAL PARTICIPATION SCALE

FEDERAL PARTICIPATION SCALE	INACTIVE	VOTE	DISCUSS POLITICS	CONVINCE FRIENDS OR ATTEND MEETINGS	CAMPAIGN ACTIVITY
Inactive	52%	4%	1%	3%	4%
Vote	22	78	11	10	4
Discuss politics	19	9	81	11	4
Convince friends or attend meetings	6	7	6	72	12
Campaign activity	2	2	2	4	77
N =	(202)	(303)	(321)	(263)	(114)

r = .72*
*Significant at .01 level.

The next question of interest is whether these aggregate results are produced by individuals who select different rates of participation depending on the level of government, or whether individuals are consistent in their rates of participation at both levels.[21] In other words, is there a situation where individuals choose some types of activities in federal politics, perhaps voting and putting up signs, while they confine their provincial electoral activity to discussing politics with their friends, or is the situation one in which people who put up signs for provincial candidates tend to also have signs on their lawns in federal elections? Table 3.15 indicates that the latter interpretation is the more valid one to describe the findings of the 1974 data. This table, showing a cross-tabulation of the federal participation scale with the provincial one, reports a very strong relationship between ways of participation in politics at the two levels. The great majority of the respondents are found on the diagonal of this table, the major exception being in the first column, where there is an observable tendency for those people who are inactive in provincial politics to report a somewhat higher rate of activity in federal politics. However, the overall relationship, as measured by Pearson's r, is strong (.72).

TABLE 3.16

Distribution of Federal and Provincial Political Participation Scale Means by Province

	FEDERAL SCALE MEAN	PROVINCIAL SCALE MEAN	T	CORRELATION (PEARSON R)	(N)
Canada	1.89	1.82	2.64*	.72*	(*1203*)
Newfoundland	1.80	1.76	0.50	.89*	(49)
Prince Edward Island	2.10	2.00	1.00	.84*	(50)
Nova Scotia	2.03	2.18	−2.07*	.86*	(87)
New Brunswick	1.91	1.82	0.80	.68*	(66)
Quebec	1.92	1.99	−1.54	.69*	(341)
Ontario	1.90	1.67	5.04*	.73*	(344)
Manitoba	1.85	1.73	0.98	.65*	(59)
Saskatchewan	1.90	1.85	0.55	.84*	(52)
Alberta	1.74	1.61	1.37	.77*	(87)
British Columbia	1.83	1.92	−1.10	.63*	(127)
F =	0.62	2.63*			

*Significant at .01 level.

When differences across provinces in federal and provincial participation are examined (Table 3.16), the conclusions emerging from the above discussion are supported. Differences in rates of participation are due more to the location of the province than to the governmental level. While there is a statistically significant difference in national mean rates of participation at the two levels, the difference in mean values is very small (.07 on a 5 point scale). The statistical significance is due more to the large number of cases than to any meaningful difference in rates of participation. When these differences are examined within provinces, in only two cases are the mean values large enough to produce a statistically significant difference. These cases are Nova Scotia, where provincial participation is higher than federal (difference of .15), and Ontario, where federal participation is higher than provincial (difference of .23). The result for Ontario is not surprising, in light of the distribution of orientations toward the two levels discussed in the first part of the chapter. For the other eight provinces, the aggregate rates of participation are very close; the provinces differ in their rates of participation, but their citizens tend to be almost equally active at both levels.

CONCLUSION

Important for an understanding of Canadian federalism is the recognition that the two levels of government are perceived by the population as jointly important and having positive characteristics. Canadian politics has always been characterized by a great deal of separation, if not independence, between federal and provincial politics. Many studies have pointed out the organizational and programmatic separation that exists between federal and provincial party systems, but the independence of electoral choice at the two levels and the willingness of Canadians to maintain different partisan links to federal and provincial parties requires further explanation.

As federalism has come to be characterized more and more as a form of diplomatic interchange and modelled on international negotiations,[22] the question of the allegiance of citizens to one level or another becomes increasingly problematic. Diplomacy is most workable when it is characterized by flexibility of stances and positions, by the possibility for negotiators to move back and forth in seeking a compromise, and by a willingness to accept compromises reached. Thus, federal-provincial diplomacy works best in a situation where the population is not polarized into opposing camps, as federalists or provincial rightists, but rather where for some purposes they look to the federal actors, and for others they turn to their provincial governments.

Our examination of attitudes toward the federal system and behaviour within it has led to the conclusion that such a polarization has not taken place in Canada. The examination of affect, using the thermometer measures, was inconclusive about the complete absence of conflicting loyalties, but found no persuasive evidence that they were strongly present. The positive affect for both the nation and the province of residence supports this finding. Cognitive attitudes, when examined, proved to show that a strong majority of Canadians have little difficulty distinguishing between the functions performed by the two governments within the system, and allow the conclusion that there is substantial information on which to base behaviour at both levels. In terms of evaluation, the overall impression is that for the country as a whole, both levels retain importance in the eyes of the public, though there is some provincial variation in this regard. Finally, our examination of participation shows that Canadians have little inclination to favour one level of the system or the other when it comes to degree of political activity.

Thus, based on indications from both individual level and aggregate patterns, it is probably unwise to look for a separation or polarization of the population into "federalists" or "provincialists." Rather, a natural outgrowth of a federalized political culture may be that some involvement, attitudinally and behaviourally, at both federal and provincial levels is the norm for Canadians.

FOOTNOTES

1. General descriptions of the development of Canadian federalism may be found in Donald V. Smiley, *Canada in Question: Federalism in the Seventies*, 2nd ed. (Toronto: McGraw-Hill Ryerson, 1976); J. Peter Meekison, ed., *Canadian Federalism: Myth or Reality*, 2nd ed. (Toronto: Methuen, 1971); Richard J. Van Loon and Michael S. Whittington, *The Canadian Political System: Environment, Structure and Process*, 2nd ed. (Toronto: McGraw-Hill Ryerson, 1976), Part 3; R. MacGregor Dawson, *The Government of Canada*, 5th rev. ed. (Toronto: University of Toronto Press, 1970), Parts I and II; Edwin Black, *Divided Loyalties* (Montreal: McGill-Queens Press, 1975); and A.R.M. Lower et al., *Evolving Canadian Federalism* (Durham, North Carolina: Duke University Press, 1958).

2. See Donald Swainson, ed., *Oliver Mowat's Ontario* (Toronto: Macmillan, 1972); Larry Pratt, "The State and Province Building: Alberta's Development Strategy," and Garth Stevenson, "Federalism and the Political Economy of the Canadian State," both in Leo Panitch, ed., *The Canadian State: Political Economy and Political Power* (Toronto: University of Toronto Press, 1977), pp. 133-62 and pp. 77-100.

3. See David J. Bellamy, Jon H. Pammett, and Donald C. Rowat, eds., *The Provincial Political Systems* (Toronto: Methuen, 1976).

4. See, for example, David Smith, *Prairie Liberalism* (Toronto: University of Toronto Press, 1975); Michael Stein, *The Dynamics of Right Wing Protest* (Toronto: University of Toronto Press, 1973); and Maurice Pinard, *The Rise of a Third Party* (Toronto: Prentice-Hall, 1975).

5. See Donald Smiley, *op. cit.*, chap. 4; and Neil McKenty, *Mitch Hepburn* (Toronto: McClelland and Stewart, 1967).

6. *Toronto Globe and Mail*, November 25, 1976, p. 7.

7. See the discussion of these terms in Gabriel Almond and Sidney Verba, *The Civic Culture* (Princeton: Princeton University Press, 1963) chap. 1, and Jon H. Pammett and Michael S. Whittington, eds., *Foundations of Political Culture* (Toronto: Macmillan, 1976), chap. 1.

8. See Appendix B, Q. 18, for a description of the thermometer measures.

9. The questions read: "We would like to know how you feel *in general* about this province of _____?" and "How do you feel *in general* about Canada?"

10. See Appendix B, Q. 18a and 18f.

11. See Appendix B, Q. 18.

12. See Appendix B, Q. 16.

13. *Correlations Between Age, Language, and Affect for Canada, Controlling for Education and Socio-economic Status*

(partial r)
Controlling for

	Zero Order	Education	Socio-economic Status (Blishen Score)
Language	.29*	.29*	.28*
Age	.16*	.15*	.13*

*Significant at .01 level.

14. A good review of constitutional interpretation is given in Alan Cairns, "The Judicial Committee and Its Critics," *Canadian Journal of Political Science*, IV (September 1971), pp. 301-45; and in Ronald Cheffins and Ronald Tucker, *The Constitutional Process in Canada*, 2nd ed. (Toronto: McGraw-Hill, 1976).
15. Shared cost programs are described in Van Loon and Whittington, *op. cit.*, chap. 8. The most recent listing appears in Federal-Provincial Relations Office, *Federal-Provincial Programs and Activities* (Ottawa: Government of Canada, 1977).
16. See Appendix B, Q. 4.
17. The gap between evaluations of the federal and provincial levels has narrowed since 1965. The identical question, asked of a national sample that year, revealed 30% federal, 40% provincial, 21% both, 5% neither, and 4% don't know. This is reported in Mildred Schwartz, *Politics and Territory*, p. 217.
18. See Rick Van Loon, "Political Participation in Canada: The 1965 Election," *Canadian Journal of Political Science*, 3 (1970), pp. 376-99; Mark Sproule-Jones and Kenneth D. Hart, "A Public Choice Model of Political Participation," *Canadian Journal of Political Science*, 6 (1973), pp. 175-94; Susan Welch, "Dimensions of Political Participation in a Canadian Sample," *Canadian Journal of Political Science*, 8 (1975), pp. 553-59; Harold D. Clarke *et al.*, "Motivational Patterns and Differential Participation in a Canadian Party: The Ontario Liberals," *American Journal of Political Science*, 22 (1978), pp. 130-51; and Jon H. Pammett, "Adolescent Political Activity as a Learning Experience: The Action-Trudeau Campaign of 1968," in Jon H. Pammett and Michael S. Whittington, eds., *Foundations of Political Culture* (Toronto: Macmillan, 1976), pp. 160-94.
19. Previous studies of participation in federal as opposed to provincial politics have focused exclusively on the act of voting. See Howard A. Scarrow, "Patterns of Voter Turnout in Canada," *Midwest Journal of Political Science*, 5 (1961), pp. 351-65; and also Van Loon, *op. cit.*, p. 388.
20. See Appendix B, Q. 9-12.
21. No attempt is made here to analyze the determinants of participation rates in federal and provincial politics. Such an analysis using the 1974 election study is contained in Mike Burke, Harold D. Clarke, and Lawrence LeDuc, "Federal and Provincial Political Participation in Canada: Some Methodological and Substantive Considerations," *Canadian Review of Sociology and Anthropology*, 15 (1978), pp. 61-75.
22. See Richard Simeon, *Federal-Provincial Diplomacy* (Toronto: University of Toronto Press, 1972), chaps. 9-10.

Chapter Four

Societal Cleavages and Canadian Voting Behaviour

Students of Canadian politics traditionally have placed great stress on the significance of societal cleavages. Specifically, the importance of regional, religious, and ethnic divisions for understanding both the history and present-day operation of the Canadian polity has been articulated so frequently that it has become conventional wisdom among political scientists and laymen alike.[1] Using data from the 1974, 1968, and 1965 national election studies, this chapter will investigate relationships between several societal cleavages and voting in three federal elections. Such an investigation is an important preliminary step in developing an explanation of electoral choice in Canada.

Although specific evidence is required to demonstrate the impact of societal divisions on voting or other forms of political behaviour, even a cursory inspection of socio-demographic data suggests the potential political significance of these cleavages. If by cleavages one means those "criteria which divide the members of a community or subcommunity into groups,"[2] it is obvious that Canadian society is highly fragmented. Perhaps the most obvious division is territorial. Canada is the second-largest state in the world, with a relatively small population living in several widely separated and distinct regions. Although nearly two-thirds of the population reside in the two provinces of Quebec and Ontario, the political significance of smaller populations in other regions is enhanced by a federal system of government. Then, too, as many scholars have noted, the significance of region in social and political life is exacerbated by sharp and persistent economic disparities of various kinds.[3] Regional economic disparities are associated with wide divergences in per capita income, and more broadly, of standards of living in different regions. In 1973, for example, per capita incomes ranged from $2760 in Newfoundland to $4840 in Ontario.[4]

Closely associated with regional economic disparities are differences in levels of urbanization and industrialization. Thus, while 82%, 81%, and 76% of the populations of Ontario, Quebec, and British Columbia, respectively, resided in urban areas at the time of the 1971 census, comparable figures for the Atlantic provinces ranged from a low of 38% for Prince Edward Island to a high of 57% for Newfoundland.[5] Again, basic geographic differences between regions mean that not only *levels* of industrialization but also *types* of industrial and related forms of economic activity vary from one region or province to the next. Thus, occupational profiles differ across provinces and regions in complex ways not fully revealed by simple statistics regarding the percentage of population engaged in agricultural, industrial, or professional pursuits.

Canadian society is also highly fragmented along ethnic and religious lines. As noted in Chapter Two, these cleavages have their roots in the patterns of settlement established in North America by the British and the French in the seventeenth and eighteenth centuries. Subsequent historical events ensured that the country would be composed of large numbers of citizens with differing ethnic-linguistic and religious characteristics. The extent of ethnic and religious fragmentation is indicated by 1971 census data. This census revealed that 45% of the population were of Anglo-Celtic origin, while 29% claimed French ancestry.[6] A great variety of other ethnic groups comprised the remaining 26% of the population, with the next two largest categories being German (6%) and Italian (3%). Patterns of immigration, especially in the post World War II period, have produced a set of ethnic groups for which the "ethnic mosaic" metaphor is both familiar and apt.

Religious affiliation constitutes yet another line of social cleavage. In 1971, Roman Catholics comprised the single largest religious group, with 46% of the population claiming affiliation with this church. The census of the same year revealed that nearly 40% of Canadians were members of one of several Protestant churches, with the largest two denominations being United (18%) and Anglican (12%). The remaining 14% of the population claimed at least nominal membership in a wide variety of churches or sects, or professed no religious affiliation whatsoever.[7]

Similar to many other societies, Canada is divided along class lines. Although social class membership may be based on a number of criteria, in Canada, as in other advanced industrial nations, occupation, income, and education play important roles in determining social class. Although Canada is one of the most affluent countries in the world, census data indicate that there are sharp inequalities in the distribution income and education. In 1971, for those aged 21 and over, 52% of the population had formal education beyond the grade school level, and merely 8% had attended college or university.[8] Regarding the distribution of income, it can be noted that on a cumulative scale the bottom 20% of the population received 6% of the total income, whereas the top 20% received fully 39%.[9]

In terms of occupation, Canadian society resembles most other industrialized and urbanized countries. In the labour force, the proportion of those engaged in non-farm manual occupations is quite large (36%), while the percentage of farmers is only 7%, according to the 1971 census. A substantial minority (24%) hold professional or managerial positions, and 33% are engaged in various clerical, commercial, or service occupations.[10] Although the manual-non-manual occupational distinction is usually considered critical in terms of assigning individuals to social class categories, the significance of this distinction is mitigated to some extent at the present time by the relatively large incomes earned by skilled labourers and some other unionized manual workers. On the other hand, different occupational groups with the same income tend to dispose of their incomes in varying ways, the result being "lifestyle" differences with social class connotations.

Some or all of these societal divisions exist in many other societies, including most, if not all, contemporary Western democracies. Particularly noteworthy in the Canadian case, however, is the "reinforcing" structure of these cleavages. Conceptually, the extent to which societal divisions "reinforce," as opposed to "cross-cut," one another can be thought of as the likelihood that individuals who are in the same group on one cleavage are in the same group on others.[11] In Canada, the most salient example of reinforcing societal cleavages involves region, religion, and ethnicity, with French-Canadians tending overwhelmingly to be at least nominal members of the Roman Catholic church and to reside in the province of Quebec.

The reinforcing structure of social forces is, however, more general than the Quebec-French-Catholic example might suggest. Patterns of settlement by various ethnic and religious groups in different regions, with persistent disparities in levels of economic well-being and types of economic activity, have produced a societal cleavage structure which may be among the most strongly reinforcing of any contemporary Western democracy. For example, using data on social class, ethnic-linguistic, racial, regional, religious, and urban-rural cleavages, Clarke and Kornberg found that the tendencies for cleavages to reinforce one another is greater in Canada than in Australia, the United States, Great Britain, Italy, or West Germany.[12]

There are, however, potentially important cross-cutting features in Canadian society. In particular, social-class differences can be found in all regional, religious, and ethnic categories. Cognizant of this fact,

TABLE 4.1
Percentage of Popular Vote by Province and Region
(row percentages)

1974	LIBERAL	P.C.	N.D.P.	S.C.	OTHER
Newfoundland	47%	44	9	x	x
Prince Edward Is.	46%	49	5	x	x
Nova Scotia	41%	48	11	x	x
New Brunswick	47%	33	9	3	8
Atlantic Region	(44%)	(42)	(10)	(1)	(3)
Quebec	54%	21	7	17	1
Ontario	45%	35	19	x	1
Manitoba	27%	48	24	1	x
Saskatchewan	31%	36	32	1	x
Alberta	25%	61	9	3	2
Prairie Region	(27%)	(51)	(19)	(2)	(1)
British Columbia	33%	42	23	1	1
Canada	43%	35	15	5	1
Range:a	29	40	27	17	8

1972	LIBERAL	P.C.	N.D.P.	S.C.	OTHER
Newfoundland	45%	49	5	x	1
Prince Edward Is.	41%	52	8	x	x
Nova Scotia	34%	53	12	x	x
New Brunswick	43%	45	6	6	1
Atlantic Region	(39%)	(50)	(8)	(2)	(1)
Quebec	49%	17	6	24	3
Ontario	38%	39	22	x	1
Manitoba	31%	42	26	1	1
Saskatchewan	25%	37	36	2	x
Alberta	25%	58	13	5	x
Prairie Region	(27%)	(48)	(23)	(2)	x
British Columbia	29%	33	35	3	x
Canada	39%	35	18	8	1
Range:	24	41	31	24	3

xLess than 1%

aRange in percentage of popular vote across provinces

1968

1968	LIBERAL	P.C.	N.D.P.	S.C.	OTHER
Newfoundland	43%	53	4	x	x
Prince Edward Is.	45%	52	3	x	x
Nova Scotia	38%	55	7	x	x
New Brunswick	44%	50	5	1	x
Atlantic Region	(41%)	(53)	(6)	x	x
Quebec	54%	21	8	16	1
Ontario	47%	32	21	x	1
Manitoba	42%	31	25	x	2
Saskatchewan	27%	37	36	x	x
Alberta	36%	50	9	x	5
Prairie Region	(35%)	(41)	(22)	x	(3)
British Columbia	42%	19	33	x	6
Canada:	46%	31	17	4	2
Range:	27	36	33	16	6

1965

1965	LIBERAL	P.C.	N.D.P.	S.C.	OTHER
Newfoundland	64%	32	1	2	1
Prince Edward Is.	44%	54	2	x	x
Nova Scotia	42%	49	9	x	x
New Brunswick	48%	43	9	1	x
Atlantic Region	(47%)	(45)	(7)	x	x
Quebec	46%	21	12	17	4
Ontario	44%	34	22	x	x
Manitoba	31%	41	24	4	x
Saskatchewan	24%	48	26	2	x
Alberta	22%	47	8	22	x
Prairie Region	(25%)	45	18	11	x
British Columbia	30%	19	33	17	1
Canada:	40%	32	18	8	2
Range:	42	35	32	22	4

Mean Percentage Vote for Various Parties in Last Four Elections

Liberals	PC	NDP	SC	Other
42%	34%	17%	6%	1%

some scholars, such as Horowitz and Wilson, have suggested that the increasing political importance of social class would serve to mitigate the severity of persistent political conflicts centering on regional, ethnic, or religious differences.[13] Implicit in this suggestion is a more general assumption that the political significance of societal cleavages is, in part at least, a function of the extent to which such cleavages reinforce or cross-cut one another. Age and sex are two additional examples of potential cross-cutting cleavages. In some political systems, age and sex differences in political behaviour have been extensively documented,[14] but in Canada, the political significance of these cleavages has seldom been investigated. Given that age and sex differences exist within all ethnic, religious, regional, or social-class groups, the potential political import of such cleavages would appear considerable. This is, perhaps, particularly true at present, given recent social and political events in Canada such as the enfranchisement of 18-to-20 year olds and a growing awareness that women have been subject to a variety of forms of economic, social, political, and legal discrimination.

It can also be hypothesized that the political significance of social patterns is at least partially a function of how individual citizens view their society, their political system, and the relationships between society and polity. It will be recalled that the previous chapters have documented considerable diversity in perceptions of the Canadian political and social systems. For example, many respondents, when presented with a blank map of Canada, indicated some awareness of political cleavages related to region, religion, ethnicity, or social class, although the range of comments was quite broad. Further, Chapter Three has shown that affective, cognitive, and evaluative orientations to Canadian federalism vary both among and within provinces, age groups, and linguistic groups in the population. On the other hand, when respondents were queried regarding perceptions of regions, a substantial proportion of answers diverged markedly from the traditional division of the country into five regions used by scholars and journalists, and 41% stated that they "did not know" or did not think of Canada in regional terms. Diverse patterns such as these suggest that the manner in which societal cleavages influence political behaviour is potentially very complex.

A description of the types and structure of societal cleavages, however detailed, tells one nothing about their relationships with political behaviour. In the past, however, considerable weight has conventionally been placed on such cleavages in explanations of Canadian voting behaviour.[15] Indeed, the significance attributed to socio-demographic variables for understanding electoral choice in Canada is so great that it warrants an extensive analysis of their relationships with voting behaviour. Such a study will provide valuable descriptive information about the basic patterns of variance in electoral behaviour and should help to establish a framework for the construction of explanations of this behaviour.

PROVINCE AND REGION

One of the most evident cleavages in Canadian electoral behaviour is geographic. Fresh documentation of inter-provincial and inter-regional heterogeneity in party-support patterns is provided by each set of federal election returns. The magnitude and persistence of these provincial and regional differences can be appreciated by an inspection of Table 4.1, which summarizes voting choice by province and region for the 1965, 1968, 1972, and 1974 federal elections.

If one considers the 1974 election as an example, the range of the Liberal vote is 29%, from a high of 54% in Quebec to a low of 25% in Alberta. Similar or even greater variability is observable in inter-provincial differences in the vote for the Progressive Conservative, New Democratic, and Social Credit parties, the relevant percentages being 40%, 27%, and 17% respectively. These figures are not atypical, in that inter-provincial variations in support for various parties are of comparable magnitude in 1972, 1968, and 1965. Overall, for the last four federal elections, the mean range in the popular vote across the provinces has been 30% for the Liberals, 38% for the Conservatives, 31% for the New Democrats, and 21% for the Social Credit. The magnitude of these variations can perhaps be placed in better perspective when one realizes that, for the country as a whole, the Liberal vote has varied by only 7% in these four elections. Variations in the national vote for the Progressive Conservatives, New Democrats, and Social Credit are even smaller — 4%, 3%, and 3% respectively.

The finding that there have been consistently strong inter-provincial and inter-regional differences in levels of electoral support for various parties should not lead one to infer that such support levels are constant for particular provinces over even relatively restricted time spans. That such an inference is not warranted can be easily documented by computing the range of popular vote for different parties within provinces for the 1965-74 set of elections (data not shown in tabular form). Such data confirm the reality of intra-provincial, over-time variability in electoral support in federal elections. Perhaps more importantly, these data reveal that the magnitude of intra-provincial variations from one election to the next are generally considerably smaller than inter-provincial differences for a given election. Thus, the mean range of *intra*-provincial variation in party support is 4%, while the mean range of *inter*-provincial variation is 30%. Also, intra-provincial variations are themselves sharply variable in magnitude both by province and by party. A good example of this variability concerns support levels for the Progressive Conservative party in British Columbia and Quebec. In British Columbia the Conservative percentage of the popular vote varied by 23% in the 1965-74 period. The comparable Quebec figure is merely 4%. Similar examples could be cited for each of the other parties. The data also document that provinces diverge markedly in levels of inter-party competition in a particular election.[16] If one focuses on competition between the two leading parties in a given province, Alberta and Quebec have consistently been less competitive than several other provinces. In contrast, although there is some variance from one election to the next, the Atlantic provinces manifest relatively high levels of two-party competition.

Despite these differences in the levels of party competition between provinces, it is important to observe that in every province at least two parties garner a considerable percentage of the popular vote. Consider, for example, the Quebec situation. Persistent Liberal pre-eminence in federal elections in this province is one of the most basic pieces of conventional wisdom on contemporary Canadian politics, a fact confirmed by the large number of Liberal MPs from Quebec returned in virtually every federal election. Yet, as Cairns has argued, Canada's single-member plurality electoral system obscures the true electoral strength of the Liberals in this province.[17] In the four federal elections from 1965 through 1974, the average Liberal vote in Quebec was 51%, an impressive figure, but certainly far less than the Liberal percentage of seats (79%). The Conservatives, on the contrary, traditionally win few seats in Quebec, but nevertheless have averaged 20% of the Quebec vote. This percentage is much smaller than that for the Liberals, but still represents the voting preferences of several hundred thousand Canadians in each election. A parallel commentary could be offered regarding Conservative dominance of Alberta federal elections. The general point that parliamentary representation is an imperfect guide to the voting behaviour of individual Canadians in various provinces is a fundamental one that cannot be neglected in any analysis of electoral choice in Canada.

RELIGIOUS AFFILIATION

With the possible exception of ethnicity, no socio-economic or demographic correlate of Canadian voting behaviour has been commented on more frequently than religion. The simple proposition that Catholics tend to vote Liberal while Protestants support the Progressive Conservatives is a common observation about Canadian politics. Although the volume of scholarly literature on the topic is surprisingly small, existing analyses of statistical relationships between religious affiliation and electoral choice consistently have provided empirical support for this proposi-

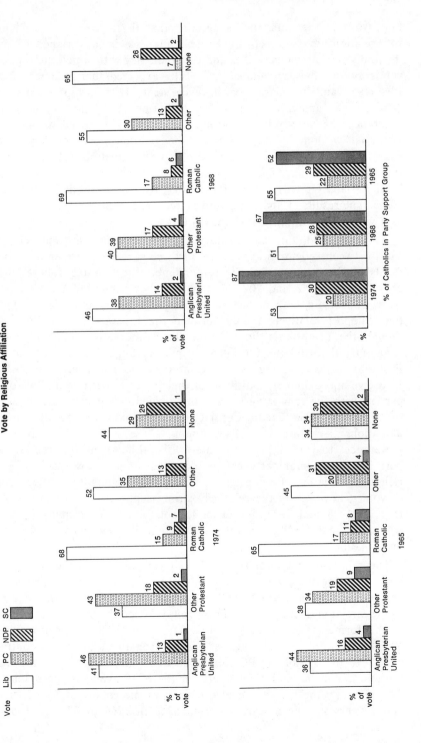

FIGURE 4.1
Vote by Religious Affiliation

tion, while at the same time suggesting that the nature of the religion-vote relationship is subject to noticeable inter-provincial variance.[18] Given the findings of previous studies and the frequency with which the religion-vote proposition is articulated, it is fully expected that analyses of the 1965, 1968, and 1974 data sets will reveal strong relationships when voting behaviour is analyzed by religious affiliation. Furthermore, if voting differences between religious groups are as deeply rooted as the conventional wisdom would suggest, these relationships should manifest considerable stability over time. For purposes of analysis, religious affiliation is grouped into five categories: high-status Protestant (Anglican, Presbyterian, United), other Protestant, Roman Catholic, Other, and None. The results of analyzing vote by religious affiliation for the country as a whole are contained in Figure 4.1.

As anticipated, the data demonstrate strong and consistent relationships between religion and vote. In all three surveys, approximately two-thirds of the Roman Catholic respondents report voting Liberal, with only between 15% and 20% stating that they supported the Conservatives. Conversely, both high-status and other Protestants tended to divide their support relatively evenly between the Liberals and the PCs. Although the Protestants did vote for the Conservatives relatively more frequently than did the Catholics, in no election did a majority of the Protestants report voting for the Conservatives. The Protestant pattern is to give approximately two-fifths of their votes to each of the two older parties, with the remaining votes being divided, albeit unevenly, between the NDP and Social Credit. Considering additional categories of religious affiliation, there are tendencies among those with "other" religious preferences to vote disproportionately Liberal.[19] Again, differential support for the Liberal party can be detected among those professing no religious affiliation. Perhaps most noteworthy among this latter group of voters, however, is the relatively strong support offered to the NDP. In both 1968 and 1974, for example, roughly twice as many of those with no religious affiliation voted NDP than did any of those with such an affiliation.

The relationship between religion and vote can be further elucidated by considering the data in terms of the proportion of each party's support coming *from* various religious groups rather than with reference to the direction of the vote *by* these groups. When the data are considered in the former fashion, analyses reveal that in all three elections, over 50% of the total Liberal vote was cast by Roman Catholics. In contrast, only 20% to 25% of the PC support in these three elections came from Catholics, and the equivalent figure for the NDP averages approximately 29%. Finally, the proportion of Catholics in the cohort of Social Credit voters veers sharply upward — from 52% in 1965 to 67% in 1968 to fully 87% in 1974. This variance is undoubtedly attributable to the precipitous decline of the fortunes of the federal Social Credit party outside of Quebec in this period.

The findings outlined above are based on analyses of data drawn from national samples of the Canadian electorate. Given the results of previous research, which suggest that the religion-vote relationship is subject to significant regional and even sub-regional variance, it will be useful to examine this relationship at the regional level. The results of such analyses are summarized in Table 4.2.

These data strongly confirm that the *strength* and even the *direction* of the relationship between religious affiliation and voting behaviour varies by region. In all three elections, the survey data indicate that the tendencies for Catholics to offer more support to the Liberals than do Protestants are particularly strong in Ontario and the Atlantic provinces. Similar, although considerably weaker, relationships obtained in all three surveys in the Prairies and British Columbia. Most interesting, however, are the Quebec data, which document that in both 1968 and 1974, the proportion of Quebec Protestants voting Liberal actually equalled or exceeded levels of Catholic support for the Liberal party in this province. In 1965, the Quebec pattern followed national trends, but the percentage of Catholics voting Liberal was greater than the comparable figure for high-status Protestants by only 5%. In summary, the data taken from the three national surveys of Canadian voting behaviour convincingly illustrate a substantial degree of variance in the religion-vote correlation

TABLE 4.2

Percentage of Group Voting Liberal Controlling for Region

1974	ATLANTIC	QUEBEC	ONTARIO	PRAIRIES	BRITISH COLUMBIA
Anglican, Presbyterian, United	49	71	43	31	36
Roman Catholic	64	71	73	54	45
1968					
Anglican, Presbyterian, United	31	78	47	40	56
Roman Catholic	67	66	80	57	76
1965					
Anglican, Presbyterian, United	46	56	37	27	31
Roman Catholic	65	61	80	46	46

by region. Thus, while inter-provincial analyses would serve to document this variance more precisely, the data in Table 4.2 are sufficient to suggest the necessity of caveats regarding generalizations about religion and Canadian electoral behaviour from national trends alone.[20]

ETHNICITY

Similar to religion, ethnicity is widely assumed to be one of the most significant correlates of electoral choice in Canada. It is a virtually undisputed assumption that ethnic cleavages are a salient and persistent factor in Canadian politics generally and in voting behaviour in particular.[21] Again, as with religion, systematic, empirical research concerning the ethnicity-vote relationship has been quite limited, and the existence of three national election surveys provides the opportunity to map various facets of this relationship in some detail.

The basic proposition regarding ethnicity and voting in Canada is well known. Inspection of electoral returns on a province and/or constituency basis has suggested to many commentators that the normal voting pattern in federal elections in the 20th century is for French-Canadians to support strongly the Liberal party, and for Canadians of British descent to support, albeit to a somewhat lesser extent, the Progressive Conservatives. Voting patterns among other ethnic groups have been noted with considerably less frequency, but the prevailing consensus seems to be that these Canadians, especially those settling in Central Canada in the post World War II era, manifest strong proclivities to vote Liberal.[22] Similarly, the body of commentary on patterns of ethnic support for the NDP and Social Credit is quite limited, with available electoral data suggesting distinct tendencies for NDP support to be confined primarily to non-French Canadians. Social Credit voting has seldom been discussed with reference to ethnicity, except to note the rapid growth and persistence of strong support for the party among French-Canadians in Quebec during the 1960s.

For each survey, responses to questions on ethnic origin are categorized so that the two largest ethnic groups (Anglo-Celtic, French) can be considered separately. Other categories employed include Northern and Western Europe, Eastern Europe, and a residual "other" category.[23] The data on ethnicity and vote in Figure 4.2 basically confirm widely held assumptions about the electoral behaviour of different Canadian ethnic groups. In all three elections, those reporting French ethnicity tended to vote heavily Liberal, with relevant percentages ranging from a low of 63% in 1965 to a high of 72% in 1974. Those of Anglo-Celtic origin, on the other hand, divided their vote quite evenly between the two older parties, giving approximately 40% to both the Liberals and the Conservatives. While a detailed report of the voting choices of other ethnic groups would be tedious, generally the data indicate that those belonging to neither of the two "charter" ethnic groups disproportionately supported the Liberals. Particularly noteworthy in this regard are the Italian-Canadians, whose Liberal voting percentages ranged from 82% in 1965 to 76% in 1974.

FIGURE 4.2
Vote by Ethnicity

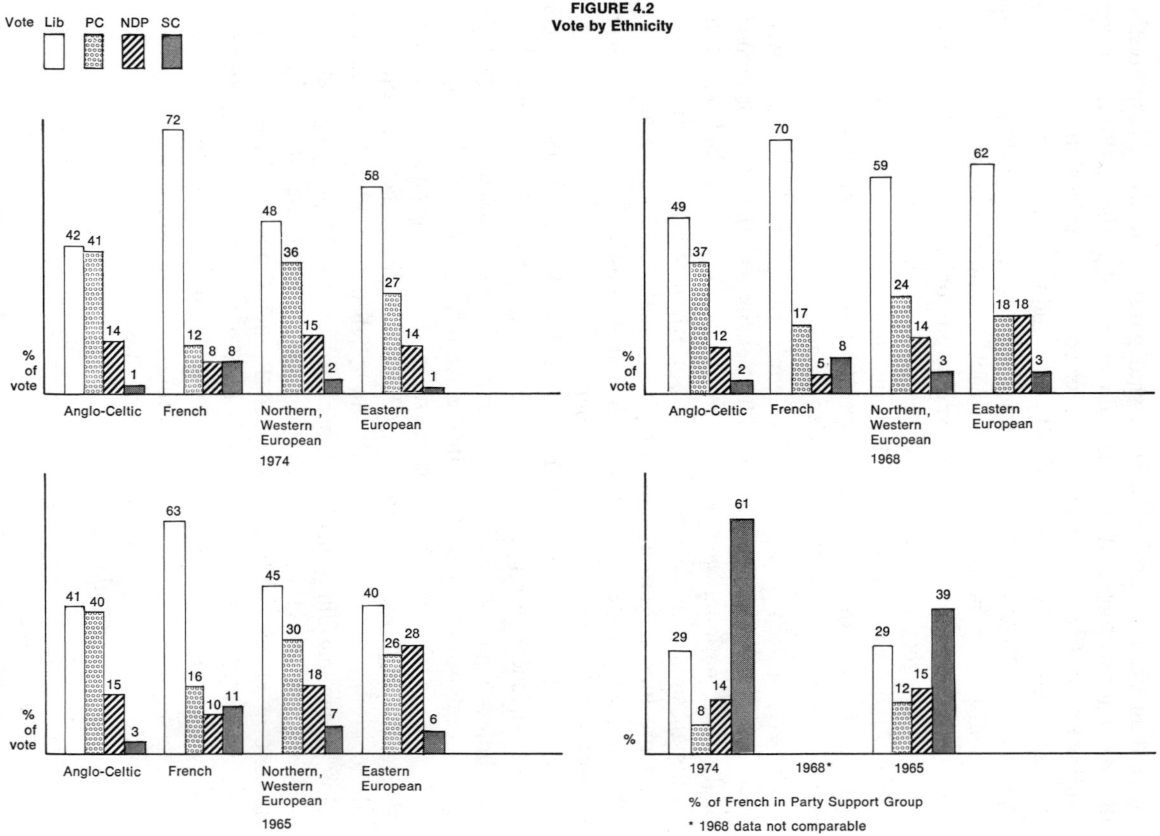

Vote Lib ☐ PC ▦ NDP ▨ SC ■

% of French in Party Support Group

* 1968 data not comparable

The data also confirm expectations regarding patterns of ethnic voting for the NDP and Social Credit parties. With regard to the NDP, there are discernible tendencies for New Democratic support to come from other than French-Canadians. Somewhat parenthetically, it is interesting to note that the 1965 and 1974 data do suggest that the NDP has a larger contingent of French-Canadians in its cohort of voters than does the PC party (eg., 14% versus 8% in 1974). Additionally, the analyses indicate that the NDP draws votes from a wide range of ethnic groups, but is in a distinct minority position in each instance. Similarly, for Social Credit, the data document the prevailing minority position of this party in every category of ethnicity. At the same time, however, the fact that Social Credit votes in federal elections now come predominantly from those of French ancestry is indicated by the fact that in 1974 61% of all Social Credit voters were French-Canadians.

The electoral choices of different ethnic groups in Canada as a whole have been documented in Figure 4.2. Yet, as was the case for religion, analyses of national samples may mask significant regional variations. Although small sample sizes for certain ethnic groups in particular regions preclude a thoroughgoing regional analysis of voting patterns by ethnicity, some differences in French and Anglo-Celtic voting in various regions can be reported with confidence. If one considers only Quebec, Ontario, and the Atlantic provinces, the data document strong and persistent tendencies for French-Canadians to vote Liberal (data not shown in tabular form). In 1974, for example, French Canadian support for the Liberals ranged from 69% in the Atlantic region to 72% in Quebec and 70% in Ontario. What is more interesting, however, is that the differential in levels of support for the Liberal party between these two ethnic groups is markedly smaller in Quebec than elsewhere. In 1974 their percentage differences in Liberal voting in Quebec were only 4%, and in 1968 and 1965, Liberal strength among those of Anglo-Celtic descent in Quebec actually exceeded French-Canadian Liberal support by 10% and 3% respectively. By way of contrast, in the Atlantic provinces and Ontario, French-Canadians voted for the Liberals in far heavier numbers, with percentage differences between the French and Anglo-Celtic groups voting Liberal in these two regions averaging 31% across the three election studies.

Overall, then, similar to earlier work by Meisel, Blake, and others,[24] these analyses suggest that regional and provincial level investigations are required to produce an accurate portrait of the voting habits of different ethnic groups in Canada. Although, as noted previously, the problem of diminishing sample sizes limits the utility of national survey data for producing such portraits, the documentation of high levels of Anglo-Celtic support for the Liberals in Quebec is a particularly salient example of inter-regional variance in the voting behaviour of a major ethnic group. This finding, by itself, constitutes eloquent testimony on the point that even some of the most familiar generalizations about the voting habits of different groups in the Canadian electorate are subject to important qualifications regarding inter-regional differences.

SOCIAL CLASS

In most contemporary Western democracies, social class is widely expected to be one of, if not *the,* major basis of political cleavage.[25] Those hypothesizing the political importance of social class have frequently predicated their arguments on the growth of industrialization and urbanization. These social and economic developments, characteristic features of many societies in the 20th century, will, according to this argument, both sharpen social class cleavages and erode traditional regional, religious, and ethnic bases of political conflict. Data presented in Chapter Two on the persistence of regional consciousness among younger Canadians would seem to conflict with such a model of socio-political change in Canada. Also, as noted earlier in the present chapter, there is considerable evidence suggesting the continuing relevance of region, religion, and ethnicity in Canadian political life. With regard to voting behaviour specifically, the presence and persistence of correlations between these variables and electoral choice in Canadian federal elections has been documented. However, the other side of the industrialization-political change argument, namely the importance of social class for understanding voting behaviour in contemporary Canada, remains to be examined.

A systematic examination of social class-voting relationships in Canada was first provided by Robert Alford in his seminal study of voting behaviour in four Anglo-American democracies.[26] Analyzing public opinon data over a 20 year period, Alford concluded that in comparison with Great Britain, Australia, and the United States, levels of class voting in Canada were very low.[27] Adhering to the general developmental model described above, however, Alford predicted that the importance of social class would increase in Canada concomitant with further industrialization and urbanization of Canadian society.[28]

Over the past decade, both Alford's findings and his prognosis regarding the future significance of social class in Canadian electoral politics have been disputed. Some scholars, most notably John Wilson and N. H. Chi, have argued that already there is an important "class dimension" to Canadian voting behaviour and Canadian politics more generally. Analyzing data from selected locales, Wilson has demonstrated the significance of measures of socio-economic status as predictors of the vote in federal elections.[29] Such variables can be stronger correlates of voting than are either ethnicity or religion.[30] Chi, examining the 1965 national election study data, has concluded that several of the "conditions for class politics" already exist in Canada, and in particular has argued that the NDP already has a distinctive working-class electoral base.[31]

Students of Canadian voting behaviour have also debated the developmental hypothesis. On the one hand, Wilson has argued and attempted to demonstrate, through analyses of political trends within provinces, that this hypothesis is correct. Wilson has illustrated his argument regarding the growing importance of social class by thorough examinations of the weakening minority position of the provincial Liberal party in provinces such as Ontario and Manitoba.[32] Wilson's basic expectation would seem to be that the developing class cleavages will eventually produce fundamental changes in the Canadian party system. Essentially, Canada will recapitulate the British experience, with the "centrist" Liberal party being "pulled apart" — its working and middle class support gravitating to the NDP and Progressive Conservatives respectively.

The empirical basis for the arguments of Alford and Wilson cannot, however, be said to be firmly established. Using aggregate data for several Canadian elections in the 20th century, Donald Blake has argued that there is no secular trend towards an increase in class voting in Canada, and that ethnic, religious, and regional effects on voting are persistently strong.[33] Blake's analyses would appear to be particularly damaging to any simple version of the industrialization-class voting hypothesis, in that the period covered in his study is one which has witnessed massive transformations in Canadian society in the direction of greater urbanization and industrialization.

Pertinent also is the analysis of class voting in Quebec by Maurice Pinard. Pinard's examination of provincial voting patterns in Quebec in the late 1950s and early 1960s shows that working-class support for the conservative Union Nationale actually exceeded this party's strength in the middle class.[34] More significantly, Pinard's analyses led him to explain his findings not in terms of traditional cultural factors operative in Quebec society as a whole, but rather in terms of the belief systems and political behaviour of elite groups. If Pinard's argument that the potential for class voting can be "deflected" by the alternatives being supplied by elites and counter-elites is correct, then the growth of class cleavages in Canadian politics would appear to be conditioned by more than simply general societal trends towards urbanization and industrialization.

The role of social class as a correlate of Canadian voting behaviour can be examined in detail, with data available in the 1965, 1968, and 1974 national surveys. Here, objective indicators of social class, such as occupation, socio-economic status scores, and education, as well as a subjective measure of social class will be employed to determine levels of

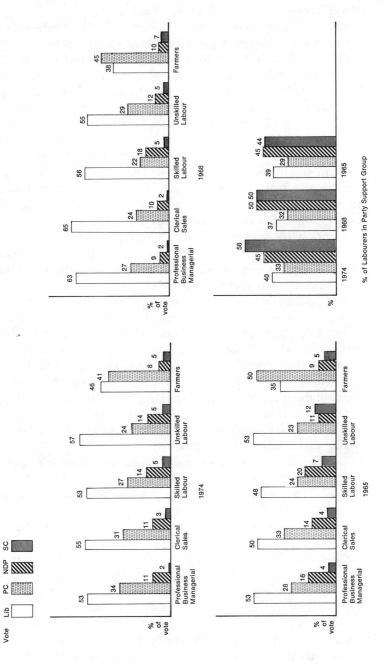

FIGURE 4.3
Vote by Occupation

class voting. Data gathered in the context of three federal elections over a nine year period make it possible to detect variance in the strength of the class-vote relationship over time.

The overall relationship between occupation and vote documented in Figure 4.3 is relatively weak in all three studies. Particularly striking is the ability of the Liberals to draw large percentages of votes from every occupational group, and with minor exceptions, percentage differences in the Liberal vote across occupational categories are not large. In 1974, for example, the range of the Liberal vote is only 11%. Percentage differences in the Liberal vote across all occupations are somewhat larger in 1965 and 1968 primarily because of the popularity of the PCs among farmers, but the overall picture remains one of generalized Liberal strength in all occupational groups. The Conservatives are also able to draw considerable electoral support from all occupational groups. They do particularly well among farmers, but not among upper-status business, managerial, and professional people. This pattern is consistent with the observations of Regenstreif and others that during the "Diefenbaker Interlude" in Canadian politics, upper and upper-middle status groups that traditionally aligned with the Conservative party tended to abandon the Tories in favour of the Liberals.[35]

The relationship between occupation and NDP voting is consonant with the results of previous research. The NDP fails to capture a majority of the votes from any occupational category, but does consistently well within the "skilled" segment of the working class.[36] At the same time, however, there are no detectable trends that the New Democrats are broadening their base of support within the working class. Although minor differences in the categorization of particular occupations in the three studies renders precise comparisons impossible, the finding that the New Democrats' share of the vote those categorized as skilled among labour varies from 20% in 1965 to 18% in 1968 to 14% in 1974 offers little comfort to those who would argue that there has been a net increase in New Democratic strength among the working class in the last decade. The data suggest that the relative importance of working class support for the NDP should not be exaggerated. Although New Democrats do draw a larger proportion of their votes from the skilled and unskilled labour categories than do either the Liberal or Conservative parties, only in 1968 was 50% of the NDP vote found in these two occupational groups. Again, illustrating the weakness of the correlation between occupation and vote in Canada is the fact that, on the average, 39% of Liberal and fully 51% of Social Credit voting strength came from the skilled and unskilled labourers. Conservative strength is derived from a somewhat differently balanced occupational coalition, but the mean percentage of the Conservative vote from the skilled and unskilled labour categories is nevertheless 32%.

In advanced industrial societies, where individual achievement tends to replace or at least co-exist with traditional ascriptive criteria as the basis of social status, education is considered to be an important indicator of social class. While millionaire grade-school dropouts may be the subject of personality profiles in *Weekend Magazine,* and some blue collar workers with only a few years of formal education may earn more than college professors, formal education would seem to be a key avenue of social mobility in contemporary Canadian society.[37] Although different measures of formal education can be constructed, number of years of school attended is utilized here because this variable is available in all three election studies. The relationships between years of schooling and electoral choice in 1965, 1968, and 1974 are depicted in Figure 4.4.

Similar to the analyses discussed previously involving occupation, level of formal education is but a weak correlate of the direction of the vote in federal elections, as evidenced by the small percentage differences in the data in all four panels of Figure 4.4. There are, however, some interesting differences across the three elections. Particularly noteworthy are the NDP percentages. In 1965 and 1974, the NDP received its strongest support from those with 17 or more years of education, with 25% of these respondents voting New Democratic in 1965, and 18% in 1974. In contrast, in 1968 only 8% of the most highly educated Canadians cast an NDP ballot, but 69% voted Liberal — fully 24% and 17% more than comparable Liberal percentages in this educational group in 1965 and 1974. Speculatively, these data may reflect the special attractiveness of Mr. Trudeau's candidacy among better-educated Canadians in 1968. Indeed, in that year, the relationship between education and Liberal vote shows a monotonic increase from 53% among those with grade school education, to the previously mentioned figure of 69% for respondents with 17 or more years of formal schooling. This pattern is atypical of the 1965 and 1974 results, where Liberal voting was proportionately stronger among those with 0 to 8 and 13 to 16 years of education respectively.

Comments on the patterning of Conservative and Social Credit data are also in order. The PC vote in different educational categories is almost invariant across all three elections, the relevant ranges being only 5% in 1965, 6% in 1968, and 5% in 1974. As for Social Credit, all percentages are relatively small, a not unexpected result given the party's relatively poor performance in these elections. More interesting is the finding that Social Credit vote percentages decline monotonically across the four educational categories in each election. In 1974, for example, the Social Credit vote totals ranged from 6% to 4% to 2% to 0% across the four education categories. The weakness of Social Credit among those with 13 or more years of formal schooling is especially

FIGURE 4.4
Vote by Number of Years of Formal Education

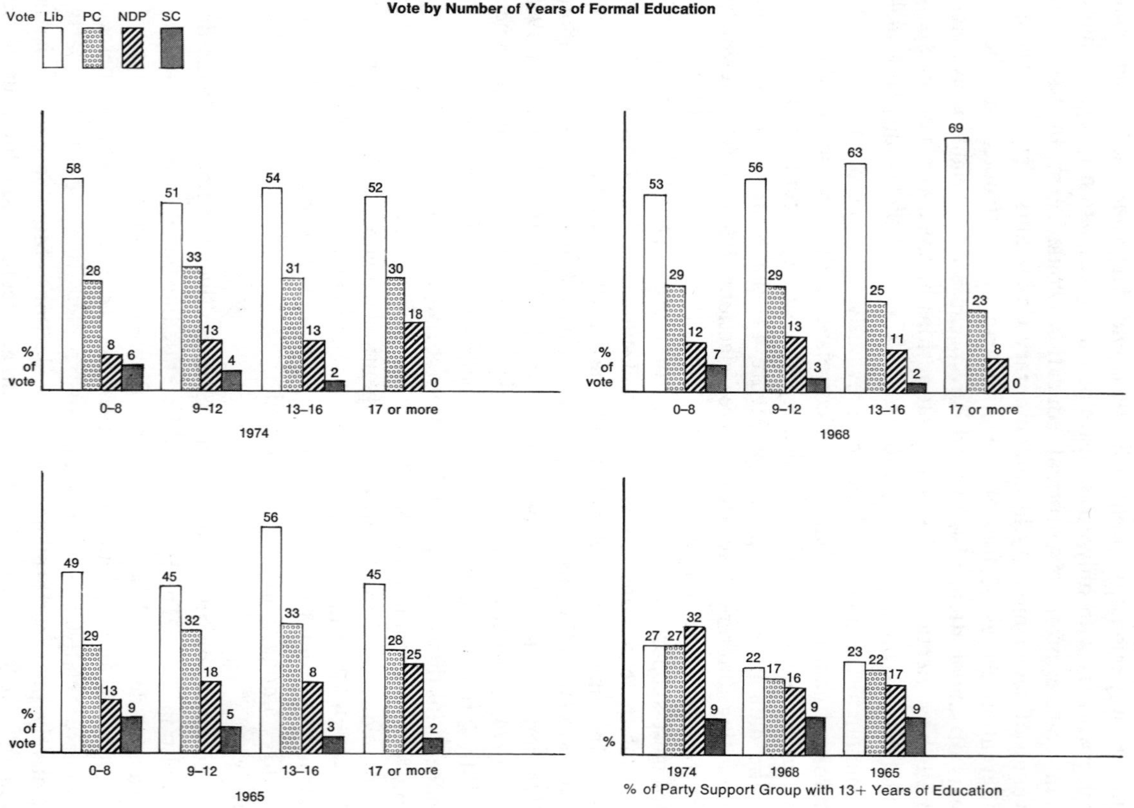

Vote: Lib (PC), NDP, SC

1974

Education	Lib	PC	NDP	SC
0–8	58	28	8	6
9–12	51	33	13	4
13–16	54	31	13	2
17 or more	52	30	18	0

1968

Education	Lib	PC	NDP	SC
0–8	53	29	12	7
9–12	56	29	13	3
13–16	63	25	11	2
17 or more	69	23	8	0

1965

Education	Lib	PC	NDP	SC
0–8	49	29	13	9
9–12	45	32	18	5
13–16	56	33	8	3
17 or more	45	28	25	2

% of Party Support Group with 13+ Years of Education

Year			
1974	27	27	32	9
1968	22	17	22	16	9
1965	23	22	17	9

noticeable. Of 1410 respondents in this educational group in the three surveys, only 27 (2%) report a Social Credit vote.

The relative strength of region, religion, and ethnicity as correlates of voting choice documented above suggests that an analysis of class voting within different regional, religious, and ethnic groups would be in order. For these purposes, the Blishen measure of socio-economic status will be employed.[38] Blishen scores are correlated with voting for the Liberal, Conservative, and NDP parties separately, and for all four parties arrayed along a hypothesized left-right continuum.[39] These analyses (Table 4.3) document once again the weakness of the social class-voting linkage in Canada. All 1974 correlations are very small (the maximum absolute value being only .17), thereby indicating that social class can explain only a very small portion of the variance in electoral choice. Some of the correlations are statistically significant, but this result is not difficult to achieve, given the relatively large sample sizes. Table 4.3 documents that weak correlations were obtained in 1974, not only for the country as a whole, but also within each region and both major religious and ethnic groups. Similar analyses performed using the 1965 and 1968 data yield comparable results. Thus, there is no evidence in any of the data employed in this study to support the proposition that socio-economic status has strong relationships with voting behaviour.

TABLE 4.3

Vote by Socio-Economic Status (Blishen Scores)
(Pearson r)

1974	VOTE (L–R)	VOTE LIB.	VOTE PC	VOTE NDP
Whole Sample	−.01	−.03	.07*	.003
Region:				
Atlantic	.09	−.15	.15	.03
Quebec	−.17*	.06	.01	.09*
Ontario	.09*	−.09*	.11*	−.02
Prairies	.03	.11*	−.002	−.12*
British Columbia	.08	−.08	.10	−.03
Religion:				
Protestant	.11*	−.04	.10*	−.09*
Catholic	−.15*	.05	−.05	.09*
Ethnicity:				
Anglo-Celtic	.08*	−.02	.08*	−.07*
French	−.16*	.01	−.03	.14*

1968

Whole Sample	-.05	.11*	-.04	-.06*
Region:				
Atlantic	.02	-.02	.02	-.01
Quebec	-.22*	.16*	-.10*	.07
Ontario	.11*	.03	.06	-.11*
Prairies	-.07	.18*	-.08	-.08
British Columbia	.07	.13	.09	-.18*
Religion:				
Protestant	.01	.12*	-.03	-.10*
Catholic	-.14*	.10*	-.07	.03
Ethnicity:				
Anglo-Celtic	-.02	.12	-.06	-.08*
French	.01	-.02	.04	-.004

1965

Whole Sample	-.09*	.05*	-.03	.03
Region:				
Atlantic	.02	-.10	.07	.09
Quebec	-.28*	.08	-.13*	.19*
Ontario	.06	.05	.02	-.09*
Prairies	-.10	.08	-.01	.03
British Columbia	-.02	.14	.15	-.13
Religion:				
Protestant	-.03	.12*	-.03	-.07*
Catholic	-.18*	.04	-.09*	.13*
Ethnicity:				
Anglo-Celtic	-.03	.09*	-.03	-.04
French	-.23*	.05	-.11	.19*

*Significant at the .01 level.

The small magnitude of the several correlation coefficients makes it unnecessary to comment extensively on the results of the Blishen score-vote analyses. One might note, however, the statistically significant and *relatively* large *negative* r (-.17) for Quebec in 1974 when the four parties are arrayed on a left-right continuum. This result is also obtained in 1965 (-.28) and 1968 (-.22). The negative signs on these coefficients indicate an inverse relationship between socio-economic status and voting in Quebec, a finding anticipated in previous commentary on the relative strength of the Social Credit party among poorly educated respondents and among skilled and especially unskilled labourers. That negative class voting in Quebec federal elections cannot be accounted for strictly in terms of these patterns of Social Credit support, however, is evidenced

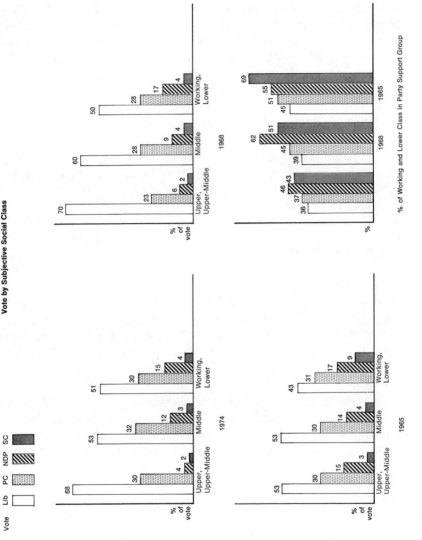

FIGURE 4.5
Vote by Subjective Social Class

by the fact that the Progressive Conservative vote-Blishen score correlations in this province are negative in 1965 (−.13) and in 1968 (−.10) also.

Social class has a *subjective* as well as an *objective* dimension. One might thereby attempt to explain the weakness of the class-vote linkages outlined above by arguing that for whatever reason, the fit between objective classifications of respondents into socio-economic status groups on the basis of occupation, education, or even the Blishen scoring system fails to correspond with the subjective social classes into which Canadians place themselves. If this argument is valid, then the failure of previous analyses to uncover class-vote correlations is an artifact of the measures used, rather than descriptive of class-related political tendencies in the Canadian electorate. To investigate this possibility, an analysis of the fit between subjective social class and voting is necessary.

Combining the data obtained from an appropriate sequence of questions,[40] it is possible to classify a large proportion of the Canadian electorate (94%) into three subjective social class categories. The results of analyzing this variable with vote in 1974, 1968, 1965 are shown in Figure 4.5. These data reveal monotonic relationships between subjective social class and vote for the Liberal and NDP parties in 1974 and 1968 and for Social Credit in all three elections. Liberal percentages, for example, range from 68% in the upper and upper-middle class, to 53% in the middle and 51% in the working and lower classes in 1974. Conversely, moving down the subjective social class hierarchy, NDP voting rises from 4% to 12% to 15%. Conservative percentages are virtually invariant across each of the three categories. Overall, the relationship between subjective social class and vote appears very modest. This conclusion is buttressed by a summary measure of association, Cramer's V, which equals 0.7, .10, and .09 in 1974, 1968, and 1965, respectively.

The conclusion that subjective social class is not a powerful correlate of voting choice is further supported by the analyses summarized in Figures 4.6 and 4.7. In these analyses, the relationship between subjective social class and vote is examined for the country as a whole as well as by region. Analyses are structured similar to earlier research on class voting by Alford. Respondents are dichotomized as either: (a) upper, upper-middle, or middle class, or (b) working or lower class. Respondents who declined to place themselves in a social class are eliminated from the analyses. To measure the strength of class-vote relationships, indices of class voting analogous to Alford's are computed. One index is obtained by subtracting the percentage of upper, upper-middle, and middle class respondents voting for the Liberal or NDP parties (the "left of centre" parties, according to Alford) from the percentage of working and lower class persons choosing these parties. Recognizing that some scholars are unwilling to categorize the Liberals as "left of centre"

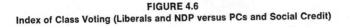

FIGURE 4.6
Index of Class Voting (Liberals and NDP versus PCs and Social Credit)

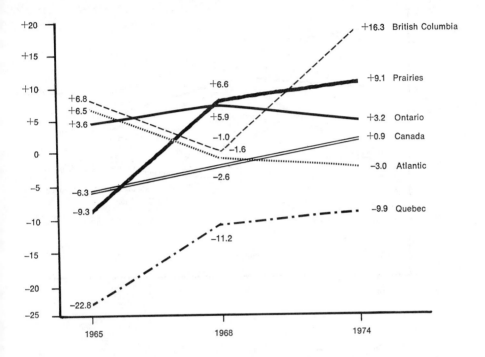

on the Canadian ideological continuum, a second index of class voting is computed using NDP vote as the only "left" option.[41] When computed, both indices of class voting confirm previous conclusions. The measure obtained by aggregating NDP and Liberal vote has a value of +0.9 in 1974 and is actually negative in 1968 (−2.6) and 1965 (−6.3). If NDP vote only is used in building the index, values are positive for all three surveys, but the magnitudes are small: +4.4 in 1974, +8.7 in 1968, and +3.1 in 1965.

Regionally, the data are somewhat more interesting, in that there is some evidence of modest levels of class voting in British Columbia, Ontario, and Quebec. In the latter province, the indices are consistently negative, indicating again the inverse relationship between class and vote among the Quebec electorate. Furthermore, the values for the index using both Liberal and NDP vote are always larger than that for the NDP vote only, indicating the very strong position of the federal Liberal party among the upper and middle classes in Quebec. Indeed, the data

FIGURE 4.7
Index of Class Voting (NDP versus Liberals, PCs, Social Credit)

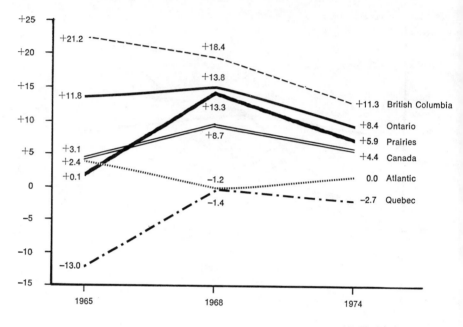

show that in the three elections for which surveys were conducted, the Liberals drew from 66% (1965) to 73% (1974) of the votes of those subjectively placing themselves in these classes.

British Columbia and Ontario emerge as the two regions having the highest levels of *positive* class voting. The strength of the class-vote linkage is especially salient for the measure of class voting which categorizes the NDP as the sole "left" party. This finding indicates the importance of working class support for the NDP in these two regions. In contrast, in all three surveys, levels of class voting in the Atlantic provinces are consistently very weak, regardless of which index is used.

Finally, the graphic displays of the regional coefficients of class voting contained in Figures 4.6 and 4.7 illustrate that the *relative* strength of class-vote relationships between different regions is subject to little variance from one election to the next. As further documentation of this point, the Spearman's rank-order correlations for the relative strength of class voting in all three pairs of elections (1965-68, 1965-74, and 1968-74) in different regions have large positive values (+1.0, +.6, and

+.7 respectively). The data also indicate that there are no obvious trends across all regions towards increasing levels of class voting over time. This is especially true if one considers the NDP as the only valid "left of centre" option in Canadian federal politics.

Analyses of class voting within major religious (Protestant, Catholic) and ethnic (Anglo-Celtic, French) groups can also be performed. Such analyses are not particularly revealing. Class voting coefficients for Protestants and those of Anglo-Celtic origins tend to be weak but positive across the three surveys (average values equal +.1 and +2.5 respectively), while those for Catholics, and especially French Canadians, tend to be somewhat larger and negative (−7.5 and −11.0 respectively). The latter finding is not surprising, given the persistently negative correlations obtained for Quebec in the regional analyses discussed above.

In summary, the analyses of the relationships between social class and vote indicate weakness of socio-economic status as a politically relevant societal cleavage in Canada. Confidence in this conclusion is buttressed by the fact that several measures of social class, including occupation, education, Blishen scores, and subjective assessments of social class position, all failed to yield strong correlations with voting behaviour in any of the three national surveys. Further, although analyses by region did document interesting inter-regional differences in the direction and magnitude of the class-vote relationship, in all instances the relationships were modest and there were no clear-cut trends towards an increase in class voting. More generally, these findings, taken in conjunction with data demonstrating the continuing existence of relationships between region, religion, ethnicity, and voting, and the relatively high levels of regional consciousness among younger voters, do not support the developmental model espoused by Alford and others. If processes of industrialization and urbanization do generate forces tending to increase the significance of social class while diminishing the political relevance of regional, religious, and ethnic characteristics, such forces have yet to make their effects apparent in any large-scale fashion in Canada.

AGE, SEX, AND COMMUNITY SIZE

In the existing literature on Canadian voting behaviour, scholarly attention has been focused primarily on regional, religious, ethnic, and class differences in electoral choice, with other social cleavages such as age, sex, or urban-rural differences being largely neglected. Yet, in some political systems, these latter variables repeatedly have been found to correlate with voting behaviour. With regard to age, for example, the proposition that older people tend to vote for more conservative parties is a common finding in European political sociology.[42] Again, studies in Western European democracies have frequently documented that women prefer parties further to the right on the ideological continuum, while the votes of men, particularly younger men, constitute the bulk of the electoral support gained by socialist and Communist parties.[43] Finally, a number of studies have examined differences in voting behaviour in urban and rural settings. In some instances, the focus of this research simply has been to describe voting in particular types of geographic areas with no apparent overarching, theoretical concerns. In other cases, employing the developmental model discussed previously, urban-rural differences in voting behaviour have been investigated over time in an attempt to trace the historical development of cleavages concomittant with the emergence of class politics under conditions of industrialization and urbanization.[44]

The first variable to be examined here is age. As noted, little research on age differences in the political behaviour of the Canadian electorate has been conducted to date. Still, one can find scattered references to age differences in electoral choice in the scholarly literature. In her study of NDP voting in Niagara Falls and Peterborough, Pauline Jewett, for example, concluded that the New Democrats were likely to be especially attractive to young, urban males.[45] Perhaps particularly noteworthy is Peter Regenstreif's analysis of voting by age in *The Diefenbaker Inter-lude*. Regenstreif's work is interesting in the context of Canadian electoral research because he explicitly sets forth and discusses briefly the notion of a "political generation."[46] The idea that various cohorts of Canadian voters behave differently because of differences in crucial socialization experiences is important, albeit difficult to test empirically within the confines of survey data gathered at one point in time. Without panel data gathered over lengthy time intervals, it is impossible to foreclose the possibility that observed variance between age groups does not reflect generational differences in crucial political socialization experiences, but rather life-cycle differences in political behaviour common to all generations.[47] Sorting out generational versus life-cycle effects, however important an analytical exercise, remains a second stage in age-vote analysis. Providing evidence of age differences is the "first step," a task which can be addressed with the present data.

Using the 1965, 1968, and 1974 election data, there is no evidence of pronounced differences in the voting behaviour of different age groups in Canadian federal elections. Indeed, age-vote correlations are even weaker than those for social class and vote documented previously.[48] Not even in 1968, an election in which Mr. Trudeau, at least according to the popular commentary of the time, had an especially strong attraction for younger voters, is there any evidence of strong age-related differences in electoral choice. This is not to say that an inspection of the data does not reveal any variance whatsoever. In all three studies,

FIGURE 4.8
Vote by Age

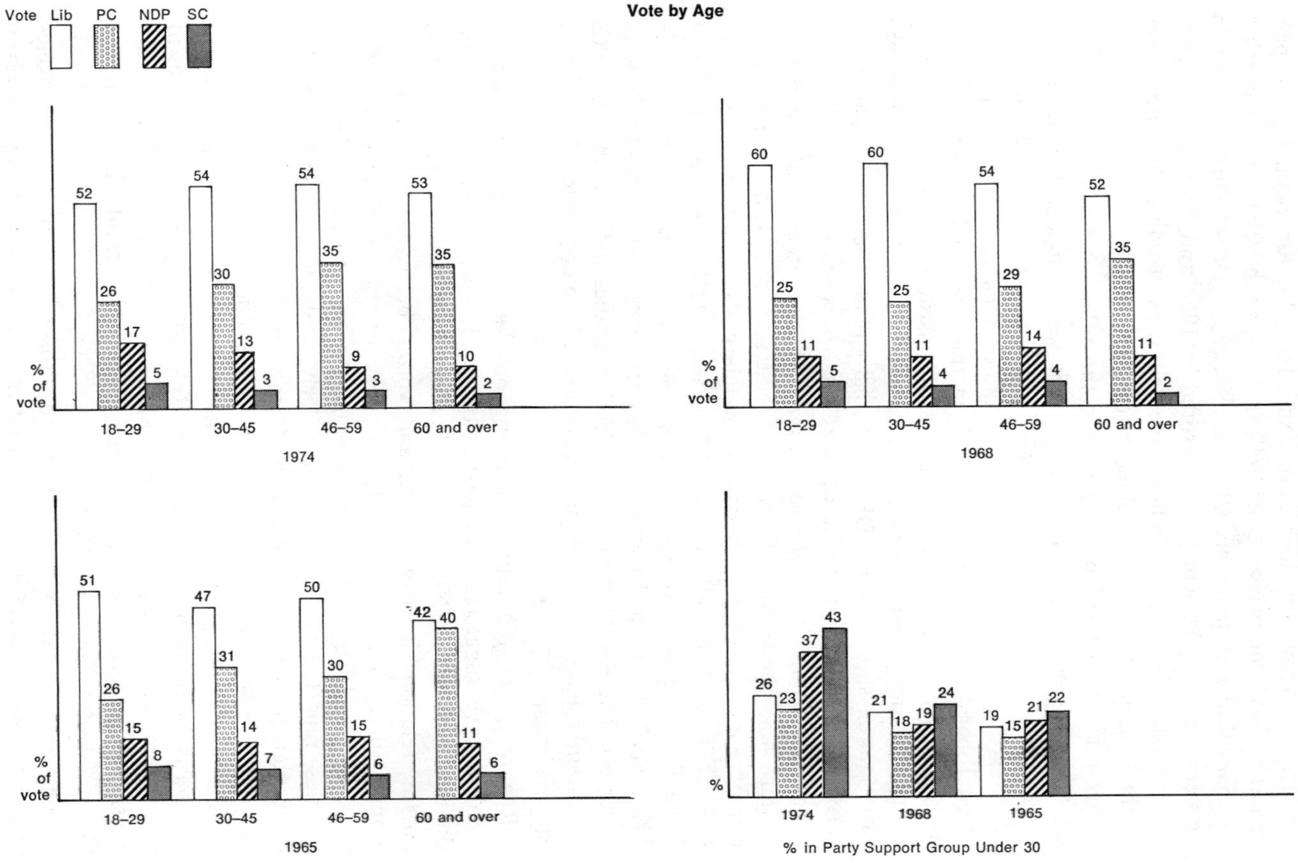

there is evidence to suggest that the Progressive Conservatives are particularly attractive to older Canadians. In 1974, for example, the percentage of PC voters rises from 26% of those in the 21 to 29 age bracket to 35% of the respondents 60 years of age or older. This relationship between age and PC voting is mirrored in 1968 and 1965, and in both instances the data clearly indicate the relatively stronger drawing power of the Conservatives among older voters.

Age-related patterns of support for the other three parties are considerably less clear. Basically, however, it would appear that over time the Liberals have been able to capture larger proportions of the votes of older Canadians. In 1965, 42% of those of 60 years of age and over voted Liberal, whereas by 1974 53% in this age bracket cast a Liberal ballot. Generally, however, the Liberals consistently manifest relatively strong drawing power among all age categories. Also, although there are variations in support for NDP and Social Credit, the weakness of these parties in each age group in all three studies is quite evident.

The age composition of those groups voting for each of the parties (Figure 4.8) shows that the Social Credit and, to a lesser extent, New Democratic support groups contain the largest proportions of younger voters. This is especially true in 1974, when 43% of the Social Credit and 37% of the NDP voters were under 30 years of age. In contrast, only 26% and 23% of the Liberal and Conservative voters respectively were under 30. The data for the three election studies indicate that the PCs consistently have the smallest proportion of voters under 30 in their support group.

Regarding sex differences in voting behaviour, as stated previously, scholars have suggested that parties on the left of the ideological continuum, such as the NDP, are particularly attractive to men. The data on the relationship between sex and voting behaviour (not shown in graphic form) offers some modest support for this proposition. In 1974, for example, 15% of the male respondents, as opposed to 10% of the females, reported an NDP vote. Similarly, in both 1968 and 1965, 4% more men than women voted New Democrat. More generally, sex-vote linkages are very weak. In addition to the findings regarding support for the NDP, perhaps the clearest trend in the data is for women to vote Liberal more frequently than do men. Relevant percentage differences in this regard are not large, but persist across all three studies. There is no consistent tendency for either of the sexes to differentially favour the Conservative or Social Credit parties.

The final correlate of voting to be examined is community size. Relevant data (see Figure 4.9) indicate that in each election voting behaviour varies fairly sharply by size of community. Cramer's V's for the three cross tabulations (average value = .14), while not large in an absolute

FIGURE 4.9
Vote by Community Size

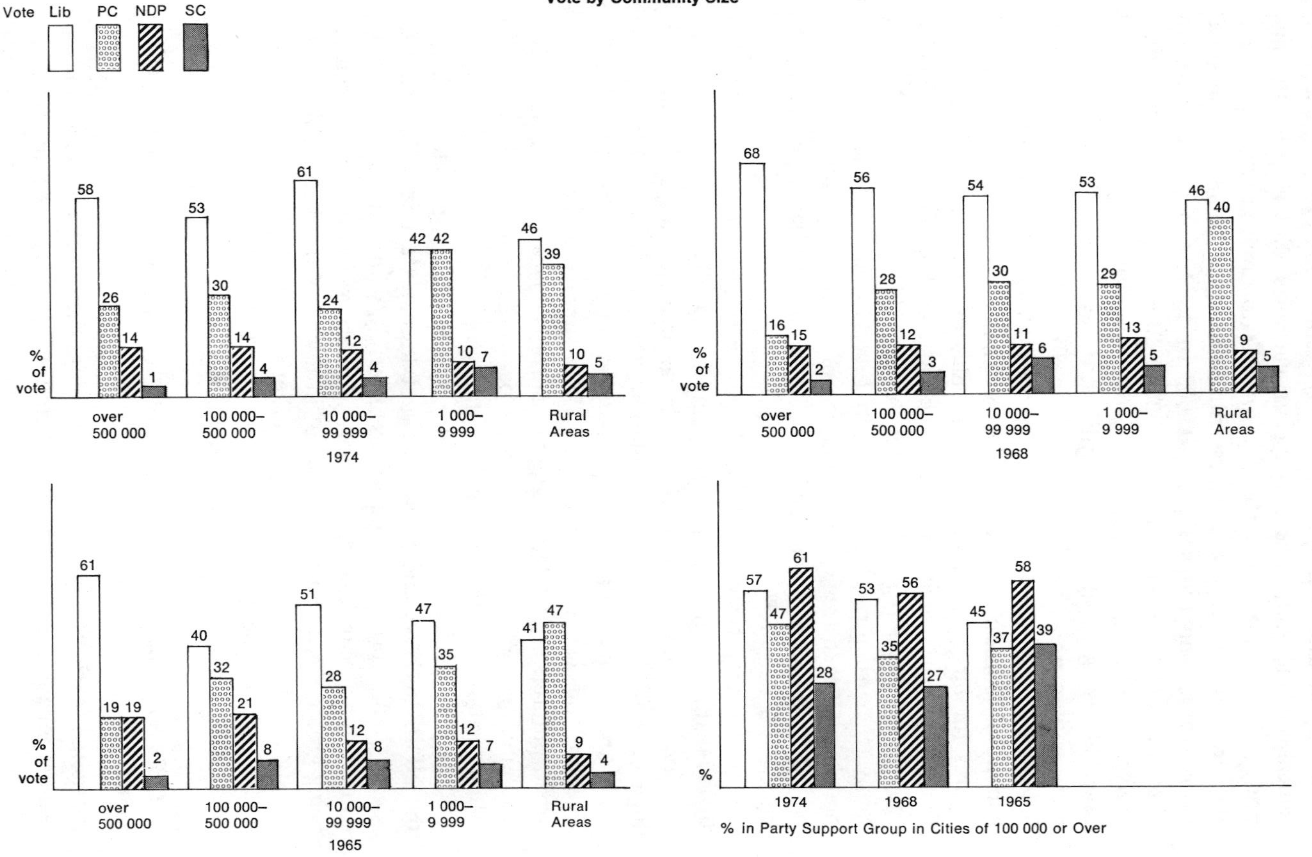

sense, are greater than those for analyses involving age, sex, occupation, education, and subjective social class variables. Not surprisingly, given previously documented tendencies for PCs to draw heavy support from farmers, Conservative voting percentages are greatest in rural areas and towns with populations under 10 000. In 1974, the Conservative vote percentage in rural areas is 39%, but in cities over 500 000 the Conservatives received only 26% of the vote. The Liberal pattern is sharply reversed. In general, the Liberals' strongest electoral base is in the metropolitan areas — for example, in 1974 they received 58% of the vote in cities with populations over 500 000. Liberal support in smaller communities and rural areas runs approximately 15% to 20% behind the figures for larger cities. This pattern obtains in all three elections, and thereby supports suggestions that the basis of Liberal and Conservative support has been realigned during the late 1950s and early 1960s. Certainly, the urban-rural differences in Liberal and Conservative strength noted by Regenstreif in his analyses of federal elections held in this period have been maintained with undiminished strength during the intervening decade.[49]

New Democratic voting bulks largest in major urban areas. Indeed, in 1974, the percentage of respondents voting NDP increases with community size, from a low of 10% in rural areas, towns, and villages to a high of 14% in cities with populations greater than 500 000. Although the patterns in the data are not quite as simple for the 1968 and 1965 elections, the general picture in all three surveys is similar. That rural-urban differences in NDP voting are not greater can at least partially be attributed to the deep roots which the party and its predecessor, the CCF, established among farmers in Saskatchewan.

Regarding Social Credit, the pattern is basically opposite to that for the NDP. In 1974, and to a somewhat lesser extent in 1968 and 1965, Social Credit voting strength varies inversely with community size. The relationship is curvilinear, however, with Social Credit vote percentages being greatest not in rural areas, but in towns or small cities. Again, this finding is congruent with those of earlier studies which have documented in some detail the popularity during the 1960s and early 1970s of the Créditistes in the smaller urban areas of Quebec.[50]

SOCIETAL CLEAVAGES AND VOTING — A MULTIVARIATE ANALYSIS

As noted earlier, arguments concerning the electoral importance of region, religion, and ethnicity are routinely made in commentaries on Canadian voting behaviour. Either explicitly or implicitly, it is a corollary of such arguments that these variables manifest strong statistical relationships with the direction of the vote. Analyses conducted above have dealt with each cleavage variable in turn, and thus the total predictive power of the several variables acting together remains unknown. Moreover, the relative strength of the relationships between each of the several cleavage variables and voting behaviour in the presence of controls for all of the other variables has not been ascertained. To measure the independent and overall statistical effects of the societal cleavages discussed in this chapter, multivariate analytic techniques are required. Use of such techniques will permit a more comprehensive assessment of the strength of the socio-demographic variables considered previously in this chapter, and hence yield valuable information regarding the validity of statements about the significance of regional, religious, and ethnic effects on voting in Canadian federal elections.

Although a variety of statistical tools might be utilized for the purposes outlined above, multiple regression analysis is employed here. In the regression analyses, the dependent variables are Liberal, Progressive Conservative, and NDP voting, each variable being measured in terms of simple "yes-no" dichotomies. Independent variables entered in each regression analysis include region, religion, ethnicity, subjective social class, age, sex, and community size.[51] The results of the multiple regression analyses for 1974 are contained in Table 4.4.

Inspection of the results displayed in this table and those obtained in comparable analyses of the 1968 and 1965 data (not shown in tabular form) yields a number of interesting findings. Perhaps most strikingly, the multiple R^2 for each analysis documents that the overall predictive power of the societal cleavage variables is quite low. The proportion of variance explained ranges from a low of 5% for each analysis of NDP voting to a high of 11% for the analysis of Conservative voting in 1974. Regarding the independent effects of *individual* variables, the Beta-weights indicate that in all three elections, the Catholic-non-Catholic dichotomy has significant relationships with both Liberal and Progressive Conservative voting. Other relatively good predictors of the likelihood of voting for the two older parties are region- and community-size variables. Regional effects in the Liberal and Conservative analyses are particularly evident in 1974. Subjective social class and sex, which were weak predictors of Liberal and Conservative voting in the tabular analyses reported previously, are again shown to have extremely modest effects.[52]

Turning to the analyses of NDP voting, none of the independent variables has a strong effect. Taken together, all variables can explain only 5% of the variance in each analysis. However, similar to the PC and Liberal analyses, there is no single variable such as religion which can account for most of the explained variance. Social class, for example, has statistically significant independent effects on NDP voting (as

TABLE 4.4

Results of Multiple Regression Analyses of 1974 Voting Behaviour

	LIBERAL		PC		NDP	
	r	BETA	r	BETA	r	BETA
REGION						
Atlantic	.01	.03	.05*	.02	-.06*	-.06
Quebec	.20*	.12*	-.25*	-.17*	-.11*	-.10*
Prairies	-.14*	-.10*	.16*	.11*	.02	.00
B.C.	-.12*	-.11*	.07*	.06*	.10*	.05
RELIGIOUS AFFILIATION						
Catholic	.19*	.13*	-.20*	-.13*	-.08*	-.04
Other Non-Protestant	.00	.05	.02	-.03	.01	-.03
None	-.05*	.02	-.01	-.06*	.10*	.06
ETHNICITY						
Other Non-Anglo						
Celtic, Non French	.02	.07*	-.01	-.07*	.03	-.02
SOCIAL CLASS						
Upper &						
Upper-Middle	.07*	.04	-.01	.01	-.08*	-.06*
Working & Lower	-.03	.00	-.02	-.05	.07*	.06*
COMMUNITY SIZE						
over 500 000	.08*	-.01	-.08*	.05	.05*	.01
100 000-500 000	.00	-.02	-.02	.02	.02	-.00
1000-10 000	-.08*	-.09*	.08*	.10*	-.03	-.00
Rural Non-Farm						
& Farm	-.08*	-.09*	.10*	.11*	-.04*	-.05
SEX	-.06*	-.06*	.02	.02	.08*	.07*
AGE	.01	.03	.09*	.07*	-.10*	-.09*
	$R^2=.10$		$R^2=.11$		$R^2=.05$	

*Significant at the .01 level.

measured by the regression coefficients only in 1974, and even in this instance the magnitude of the class effect is weak. In 1974, age has a significant Beta, as does sex and the Quebec region variable. More generally, statistically significant regional effects on NDP voting are evident in analyses of all three elections.

All of the regression analyses discussed thus far are what statisticians call "main effects only" models, that is, these analyses do not take into account possible interaction effects. Given that the effects of variables such as religion and social class have been shown in the tabular analyses to have different effects in different regions, one might expect to improve, perhaps markedly, the percentage of variance explained in voting behaviour by the several societal cleavage variables by incorporating regional interaction terms in the several regression analyses.[53] To test this notion, the 1974 data, which on balance showed the strongest regional main effects, were re-analysed, incorporating region-religion, region-ethnicity, and region-class interaction terms. When these analyses are performed the results are disappointing, in that the total proportion of variance explained in Liberal, Conservative, and NDP voting changes only very little (data not shown in tabular form). The regional interaction terms Quebec-Catholic and Ontario-Catholic emerge as significant predictors of Liberal and PC voting. These findings are consonant with those for the main effects models of Liberal and Conservative voting, which documented the significance of the Catholic–non-Catholic variable. More interesting is the NDP interaction effects analysis. Although the total percentage in NDP vote explained increases by only 2%, the Ontario working class and the B.C. working class interaction variables emerge as significant predictors, as does age. It will be recalled that the latter variable was a significant predictor in the "main effects" analysis of NDP vote.

CONCLUSION

The purpose of this chapter has been to utilize data from the 1965, 1968, and 1974 national election studies to map some of the basic relationships between societal cleavages and voting in recent Canadian federal elections. For the most part, the terrain sketched here will be familiar to one who is acquainted with previous research on voting behaviour in Canada. As anticipated, region, religion, and ethnicity manifested persistent correlations with electoral choice. Particularly noteworthy in all three surveys were the pronounced preferences of Roman Catholics and French-Canadians for the Liberal party. Consistent national level patterns in the voting preferences of other ethnic groups were also in evidence. As a caveat, however, it is important to note that the strength and, in some cases, even the direction of the electoral choices of different religious and ethnic groups varied considerably across regions. Also consistent with the results of previous research, several measures of social class were but weakly related to voting behaviour, and no clear trends towards an increase in class voting could be detected. Finally, community size, age, and sex variables had only very modest correlations with voting. The clearest tendencies involved the attractiveness of the Conservatives to older voters and those in rural areas, and the strength of the Liberals in larger metropolitan areas.

The combined effects of several societal cleavages (region, religion, ethnicity, subjective social class, community size, age, and sex) on voting behaviour was also assessed through the use of multiple regression analyses. These analyses documented that none of these variables nor all of them taken together can explain a large proportion of the variance in individual voting behaviour. This finding is understandable, given the strength of the Liberal party in all major socio-demographic categories and its drawing power in the two most heavily populated regions, Ontario and Quebec. More generally, the results of the regression analyses indicate the limitations of an approach to explaining electoral choice in Canada cast strictly in terms of societal cleavages and, in turn, strongly suggests that an adequate explanation of Canadian voting patterns will require a detailed investigation of the beliefs, attitudes, and perceptions of voters eligible to cast their ballots in any particular election. Specifically, it is necessary to examine voters' psychological attachments to salient political objects, such as parties and party leaders. Perceptions and evaluations of these objects and other significant political phenomena — most notably, the issues associated with particular electoral campaigns — also deserve close scutiny. An investigation of these topics constitutes the focus of the next section of this book.

FOOTNOTES

1. This view is set forth in most textbooks on Canadian politics. See, for example, Richard J. Van Loon and Michael S. Whittington, *The Canadian Political System,* 2nd ed. (Toronto: McGraw-Hill, 1976), chap. 2.
2. Douglas W. Rae and Michael Taylor, *The Analysis of Political Cleavages* (New Haven: Yale University Press, 1970), p.1.
3. See, for example, John Wilson, "The Canadian Political Cultures: Toward a Redefinition of the Nature of the Canadian Political System," *Canadian Journal of Political Science,* 7 (1974), pp. 438-83; Richard Simeon and David J. Elkins, "Regional Political Cultures in Canada," *Canadian Journal of Political Science,* 7 (1974), pp. 433-34; Mildred Schwartz, *Politics and Territory* (Montreal: McGill-Queen's University Press, 1974), pp. 319-22.
4. Van Loon and Whittington, *op. cit.,* p. 47, Table 2-4.
5. Daniel Kubat and David Thornton, *A Statistical Profile of Canadian Society* (Toronto: McGraw-Hill Ryerson, 1974), pp. 12-14, Table P-1.
6. *Ibid.,* p. 25, Table P-10.
7. *Ibid.,* p. 29, Table P-12.
8. *Census of Canada, 1971,* Statistics Canada, Bulletins, 1.1-3.3.
9. Van Loon and Whittington, *op. cit.,* p. 53.
10. Kubat and Thornton, *op. cit.,* pp. 153-54, Table J-3.
11. Rae and Taylor, *op. cit.,* p. 92.
12. Harold D. Clarke and Allan Kornberg, "A Note on Social Cleavages and Democratic Performance," *Comparative Political Studies,* 4 (1971), pp. 349-50.
13. Gad Horowitz, "Conservatism, Liberalism, and Socialism in Canada: An Interpretation," *Canadian Journal of Economics and Political Science,* 32 (1966), pp. 144-71; John Wilson, "Politics and Social Class in Canada: The Case of Waterloo South," *Canadian Journal of Political Science,* 1 (1968), pp. 307-309.
14. See, for example, Mattei Dogan, "Political Cleavage and Social Stratification in France and Italy," in S. M. Lipset and S. Rokkan, eds., *Party*

Systems and Voter Alignments (New York: The Free Press, 1967), pp. 129-96; David Butler and Donald Stokes, *Political Change in Britain* (New York: St. Martin's, 1969), chap. 5; Norman H. Nie, Sidney Verba, and John R. Petrocik, *The Changing American Voter* (Cambridge: Harvard University Press, 1976), chap. 4.

15. See, for example, Robert R. Alford, *Party and Society* (Chicago: Rand McNally, 1963), chap. 9; John Meisel, ed., *Papers on the 1962 Election* (Toronto: University of Toronto Press, 1964); Peter Regenstreif, *The Diefenbaker Interlude* (Toronto: Longmans Canada, 1965), chaps. 5-9; John Wilson, "Politics and Social Class in Canada: The Case of Waterloo South"; Donald E. Blake, "The Measurement of Regionalism in Canadian Voting Patterns," *Canadian Journal of Political Science*, 5 (1972), pp. 55-81; Mildred Schwartz, "Canadian Voting Behaviour," in R. Rose, ed., *Electoral Behaviour: A Comparative Handbook* (New York: The Free Press, 1974), pp. 543-618; John Meisel, *Working Papers on Canadian Politics*, 2nd enlarged ed. (Montreal: McGill-Queens University Press, 1975).

16. For data on patterns of inter-party competition in Canada see J. A. A. Lovink, "Is Canadian Politics too Competitive?" *Canadian Journal of Political Science*, 6 (1973), pp. 341-79; Frederick C. Englemann and Mildred A. Schwartz, *Canadian Political Parties: Origin, Character, Impact* (Scarborough: Prentice-Hall, 1975), chap. 15.

17. Alan C. Cairns, "The Electoral System and the Party System in Canada, 1921–1965," *Canadian Journal of Political Science*, 1 (1968), pp. 55-80.

18. The relationship between religious affiliation and voting behaviour in Canada has been documented in a number of studies. For a listing of several pertinent analyses see William P. Irvine, "Explaining the Religious Basis of the Canadian Partisan Identity: Success on the Third Try," *Canadian Journal of Political Science*, 7 (1974), p. 560. For another recent discussion of religion and Canadian politics see John Meisel, *Working Papers on Canadian Politics*, chap. 6.

19. Regarding specific groups in the "other" category, Jewish support for the Liberal party is particularly strong. In the three surveys, an average of 77% of Jewish voters cast a Liberal ballot.

20. Blake, *op. cit.*, pp. 65-75; Meisel, *op. cit.*, p. 5.

21. See, for example, Van Loon and Whittington, *op. cit.*, pp. 58-64.

22. Regenstreif, *op. cit.*, p. 91; Blake, *op. cit.*, pp. 65-72; Schwartz, "Canadian Voting Behaviour," p. 578.

23. See Appendix B, Q. 90 for a description of the question employed in the 1974 survey.

24. Regenstreif, *op. cit.*, chaps. 5-9; Blake, *op. cit.*, *passim*; Meisel, *Working Papers*, chap. 7.

25. Alford, *op. cit.*, chaps. 2, 11; Lipset and Rokkan, *op. cit.*, pp. 1-64.

26. Alford, *op. cit.*, chap. 9.

27. *Ibid.*, chaps. 2 and 9.

28. *Ibid.*, pp. 284-85.

29. Wilson, *op. cit.*, *passim*.

30. *Ibid.*, pp. 300-307.

31. N. H. Chi, "Class Voting in Canadian Politics," in O. Kruhlak et al., eds., *The Canadian Political Process*, 2nd ed. (Toronto: Holt, Rinehart and Winston, 1973), pp. 226-47.

130   *Political Choice in Canada*

32. John Wilson and David Hoffman, "Ontario: A Three-Party System in Transition," in M. Robin, ed., *Canadian Provincial Politics* (Scarborough: Prentice-Hall, 1972), p. 198-239; John Wilson, "The Decline of the Liberal Party in Manitoba," *Journal of Canadian Studies,* 10 (1975), pp. 24-41.
33. Blake, *op. cit.,* p. 79.
34. Maurice Pinard, "Working Class Politics: An Interpretation of the Quebec Case," *Canadian Review of Sociology and Anthropology,* 7 (1970), pp. 87-109.
35. Regenstreif, *op. cit.,* p. 39; John Meisel, "The Party System and the 1974 Election," in H. R. Penniman, ed., *Canada at the Polls: The General Election of 1974* (Washington, D.C.: American Enterprise Institute for Public Policy Research, 1975), p. 12; Jane Jenson, "Party Strategy and Party Identification: Some Patterns of Partisan Allegiance," *Canadian Journal of Political Science,* 9 (1976), pp. 1-27.
36. See, for example, Wallace Gagne and Peter Regenstreif, "Some Aspects of New Democratic Party Urban Support in 1965," *Canadian Journal of Economics and Political Science,* 32 (1967), p. 537; Wilson, "Politics and Social Class," p. 297.
37. On class-related inequalities in educational opportunities in Canada see Ronald Manzer, *Canada: A Socio-Political Report* (Toronto: McGraw-Hill, 1974), pp. 188-206.
38. Bernard R. Blishen and Hugh A. McRoberts, "A Revised Socioeconomic Index for Occupations in Canada," *Canadian Review of Sociology and Anthropology,* 12 (1976), pp. 71-9. See the discussion of this measure in Appendix B, Q. 76.
39. For this purpose the left-right ordering of parties employed is NDP, Liberal, Progressive Conservative, Social Credit. In arraying the parties in such a fashion, it is recognized that the ideological position of Canadian parties on a left-right continuum has been subject to considerable debate. Concerning this debate, see H. D. Clarke, "The Ideological Self-Perceptions of Canadian Provincial Legislators," *Canadian Journal of Political Science* (forthcoming).
40. See Appendix B, Q. 87.
41. Both indices range from −100 to +100, with values greater than 0 indicating the extent to which members of the working and lower classes cast proportionately more votes for left parties than do middle and upper class individuals. Values less than 0 document that the latter group give proportionately more support to left parties than does the former.
42. In the European context, the strength of the age-vote relationship varies both between political systems and over time. See, for example, the several chapters on voting behaviour in Western Europe in Rose, *Electoral Behaviour: A Comparative Handbook, op. cit.*
43. The relationship between sex and vote varies in strength from one system to the next and in terms of variables such as religiosity. Compare, for example, the chapters on Italy by Barnes and the Netherlands by Lijphart in Rose, *Electoral Behaviour,* chaps. 4 and 5 respectively.
44. Lipset and Rokkan, "Cleavage Structures, Party Systems, and Voter Alignments: An Introduction," *Party Systems and Voter Alignments,* pp. 1-64.
45. Pauline Jewett, "Voting in the 1960 Federal By-Elections at Peterborough and Niagara Falls: Who Voted New Party and Why?" *Canadian Journal of Economics and Political Science,* 28 (1962), pp. 35-53.

46. Regenstreif, *op. cit.*, pp. 85-9. For a recent attempt to use age cohort analysis in the study of Canadian voting behaviour see David Rees, "An Age Cohort Analysis of Religious Voting in Canada," unpublished M.A. thesis (Dept. of Political Science, University of Windsor, 1976). Rees documents changes in the relationship between religion and vote, showing that this relationship is weaker among younger age cohorts.
47. See, for example, Butler and Stokes, *op. cit.*, chap. 5.
48. The mean Cramer's V for the age-vote relationship for the three studies is .07. The equivalent value for the subjective social class X vote relationship is .09.
49. Regenstreif, *op. cit.*, pp. 94-5.
50. See, for example, William Irvine, "An Analysis of Voting Shifts in Quebec," *Papers on the 1962 Election*, p. 134; Michael B. Stein, *The Dynamics of Right-Wing Protest: A Political Analysis of Social Credit in Quebec* (Toronto: University of Toronto Press, 1973), p. 5.
51. On the use of "dummy" variables in regression analysis, see Gordon Hilton, *Intermediate Politometrics* (New York: Columbia University Press, 1976), pp. 187-92. In performing the regression analyses, it is recognized that the use of dummy variables places restrictions on the possible percentage of variance which can be explained. See Jim C. Nunnally, *Psychometric Theory* (New York: McGraw-Hill, 1967), pp. 128-33.
52. Social class remains a very weak predictor of voting if Blishen scores are substituted for the subjective social class variable.
53. For an example of the use of interaction terms in an analysis of Canadian voting behaviour see Blake, "The Measurement of Regionalism in Canadian Voting Patterns," *passim*. For a somewhat different statistical approach with the same aim in mind see Rose, *Electoral Behaviour*, p. 15. Using an A.I.D. analysis, Rose is able to explain 15% of the variance in the 1965 data. The weakness of interaction effects in voting behaviour at the provincial level has been documented in Drummond's analysis of electoral choice in Ontario. See Robert J. Drummond, "Party Choice in a Canadian Province: The Case of Ontario" (unpublished Ph.D. dissertation, Northwestern University, 1975).

II.
THE COMPONENTS OF POLITICAL CHOICE

Chapter Five

Partisanship in Canada

The significance of political parties in shaping and directing the preferences of the electorate has long been recognized by political scientists.[1]
It is frequently argued that political parties are of crucial importance in
Western democracies because they provide a major link between the
individual and the state. More specifically, parties are sometimes viewed
as major institutions of national integration, aggregating individual
preferences within or across societal cleavages. Also, in at least some
political systems, parties are judged to perform significant political
socialization and recruitment functions, as well as being widely recognized
as significant forces structuring individual voting choices.[2] Given these
theoretical perspectives on political parties and their ubiquitous presence
in democratic societies, it is clearly necessary to understand how people
relate to these salient political objects.

A number of explanations of the relationship between citizens and
parties have been fashionable at different points in time. For example,
it has been suggested by some democratic theorists as well as by those
interested in constructing rational choice models of political decision-
making, that voters resemble consumers in the market place who weigh
and assess the alternatives and vote for the party which they judge most
likely to defend and advance their interests.[3] However, an alternative
theoretical construction which has been of crucial importance is a model
of voting choice which incorporates a concept of partisanship as a tie to a
political party different and distinct from a decision to vote for that party.
A survey of the literature on voting behaviour indicates that, of the several
concepts developed to explain electoral choice in the last thirty years,
none has received as much attention as party identification.[4] The notion
that voters develop partisan attachments and that these self-perceptions
serve as a powerful influence on voting choice has provided the basis

for much of the theoretical and empirical literature on voting behaviour in Western democracies.[5] This chapter will examine partisan attachments and perceptions as they were manifested by the Canadian electorate in 1974. Of particular concern are the effects of a federalized party system and changes in partisanship over time. In addition, a new measure of partisanship will be developed, which is designed to capture significant characteristics of the Canadian electorate's links to the party system.

The concept of party identification was introduced by Angus Campbell and his colleagues in analyses of electoral behaviour in the United States conducted in the late 1940s and early 1950s. In *The Voter Decides,* Campbell *et al.* offered the first detailed discussion of party identification:

> The sense of personal attachment which the individual feels toward the group of his choice is referred to . . . as identification, and, with respect to parties as groups, as *party identification.* Strong identification is equated with high significance of the groups as an influential standard.[6]

This analysis stresses the *affective* component of party identification, which is closely related to the conceptualization of parties as reference groups: "[t]he present analysis of party identification is based on the assumption that the two parties serve as standard-setting groups for a significant proportion of people. . . ."[7] In *The American Voter,* the origins of the concept in reference group theory are again made explicit:

> Both reference group theory and small-group studies of influence have converged upon the attracting or repelling quality of the group as the generalized dimension most critical in defining the individual-group relationship, and it is this dimension that we will call identification. . . . [T]he political party serves as the group toward which the individual may develop an identification, positive or negative, of some degree of intensity.[8]

In the last twenty-five years many scholars have focussed their electoral research on the relationship between party identification and individual political behaviour in mass publics and, to a lesser extent, on an explication of the significance of party identification for understanding macro-processes of political stability and change. The assumptions that party identifications (a) are acquired early in life, (b) tend to be stable over time for most individuals, and (c) tend to influence perceptions and judgments of various political objects, have led many analysts to view party identification as a key long-term, stabilizing force on political behaviour.[9]

Recently these assumptions and inferences have been reconsidered in the United States and elsewhere. In the United States, continuing surveys of the American electorate have documented that greater instability of party identification and a weakening of the intensity and incidence of partisan attachments have characterized American voters, especially younger voters, in the period since 1964.[10] In Western Europe also, studies conducted over the past decade have revealed considerable variance between countries, both in the proportion of electorates reporting an identification and in the intensity and stability of these identifications.[11]

In Canada, there has been a continuing dispute over the utility of the concept of party identification. Specifically, it has been argued that many voters do not have stable ties to political parties and that this has important implications for understanding Canadian electoral behaviour and raises broader questions relating to political change.[12] Empirically, analyses of Canadian data reveal patterns of party identification which resemble the British or American situations in some respects, and the smaller European democracies in others. Available evidence documents that Canadians are not reluctant to express partisan attachments. In response to the sequence of questions on party identification, 89% of the 1974 national sample of the Canadian electorate indicated that they either identified with or "leaned toward" a party at the federal level.[13] However, while the incidence of party identification is relatively high, the strength of these attachments is weaker, with 28% of 1974 respondents reporting a strong federal party identification. A similar pattern was found by Irvine in comparing Canada with several other countries, including Great Britain, Australia, and the United States.[14] Using 1965 data, he reported that Canada ranked eighth in a list of ten political systems in terms of the proportion of identifiers reporting strong identifications.

Equally significant are data on the relationship of party identification to the vote and the stability of identifications over time. In a given election, the relationship between direction of party identification and reported voting behaviour is very strong.[15] Further, the correlation between direction of the vote and party identification varies directly with intensity of identification. For example, in 1974, fully 97% of the strong Liberal identifiers voted Liberal, whereas 74% of those with weak Liberal identifications cast a Liberal ballot (see Chapter 11, Table 11.2).[16] These relationships are similar to those reported in other countries, with the correlation between identification and reported vote being very strong, although not quite as large as comparable figures reported in some European studies. However, and of potential import for understanding the nature and significance of party identification in Canada, there is also evidence of considerable instability in the party identification of sizable segments of the Canadian electorate. In 1974, for example, 36% of those reporting a federal party identification recalled having changed this identification at some point in their lives.[17] This figure is somewhat lower than that reported in some countries, but it is notably higher than that for several others.[18] The relatively high levels of instability of party identifications in Canada suggest that a detailed investigation of the partisan attachments of Canadian voters is in order.

Regarding the conduct of such an investigation, it is important to recognize that Canada is a federal system, with widely varying party systems in its ten provinces.[19] To date, existing studies of party identification in Canada have usually ignored this most salient feature of the Canadian political system. This would seem unwarranted, in that provincial party systems vary not only in terms of the electoral strength of the several parties present in the system, but even more fundamentally with reference to the actual presence or absence of certain parties in some provinces. Moreover, in certain provinces there are acute differences in the electoral strength of the "same" parties in provincial as opposed to federal politics, and some provincial party systems have been subject to sharp discontinuities over relatively short time periods. The theme of the "meteoric" rise and fall of "third" parties in Canadian politics is perhaps the most familiar example of this phenomenon. In sum, there is not one Canadian party system but several, and these party systems have historically been characterized by significant inter-system (i.e., inter-provincial and federal-provincial) as well as temporal variation. In addition to documenting the incidence, content, and stability of party identification in Canada, charting the complexity of federal-provincial patterns will be a major task of the present chapter.

CROSS-LEVEL VARIATION: THE SPLIT PARTY IDENTIFIER

It is clear from the preceding discussion that cross-level differences in partisanship represent an important potential source of variation and require more careful scrutiny than they have received to date. While investigations of cross-level variation, or split party identifications, in the United States and Australia have tended to document a relatively low incidence of such variation,[20] there is good reason to infer that the marked differences between the federal and provincial party systems in Canada might lead to significantly greater variability in federal and provincial patterns of identification. Cross-level variation in partisanship is not a contradiction of the conception of the political party as a reference group. Within the context of Canadian federalism, the structural potential exists for the maintenance of two parallel reference groups in the voter's mind. Whether such potential is realized depends upon the inclination and ability of voters to differentiate between the two levels of government.

The differing provincial party alignments of the ten Canadian provinces are basically of three types. The first type is characterized by strong provincial parties which either do not exist or fail to compete successfully for support at the federal level. The Union Nationale and Parti Québécois are confined exclusively to the provincial arena in Quebec, while the Social Credit party in Alberta and British Columbia has been highly successful at the provincial level but has been characterized by electoral weakness federally. In all three cases the provincial party alignments are fundamentally different from the federal. In the second type, parties of the same name compete at the federal and provincial levels, but often with substantial variations in electoral strength and party platforms. Manitoba, Saskatchewan, and Ontario would be included in this group, since certain parties in these provinces cannot be easily recognized in successive federal and provincial elections as being the same thing. Third, there are provincial party alignments, such as those of the Maritimes, which historically have been quite similar at both the federal and provincial levels.

In order to empirically demonstrate the difference between federal and provincial party alignments, Table 5.1 presents a ranking of the ten provinces on a measure of these differences. It is obtained by subtracting the percentage of the vote obtained by each party in the nearest *provincial* election (which may be zero if the party fielded no candidates in that election) from the percentage of vote obtained by that party in the 1974 *federal* election (which may likewise be zero). The provinces are arranged in the table according to the sum of absolute differences of these percentages.[21]

TABLE 5.1

Relative Electoral Strength of Federal and Provincial Parties, by Province (percentage of the vote in 1974 federal election minus percentage of the vote in nearest provincial election)

PROVINCIAL ELECTION	PROVINCE	LIBERAL	PC	NDP	SC	SUM OF ABSOLUTE DIFFERENCES
1972	British Columbia	17	29	−17	−29	92
1973	Quebec	0	21	7	7	70a
1975	Alberta	19	−2	−4	−13	38
1973	Manitoba	8	10	−17	—	35
1972	Newfoundland	9	−17	9	—	35
1975	Ontario	13	−4	−8	—	25
1975	Saskatchewan	−1	9	−10	—	20
1974	Nova Scotia	−7	9	−3	—	19
1974	Prince Edward Island	−7	9	−3	—	19
1974	New Brunswick	0	−13	5	—	18

aIncludes − 30 Parti Québécois and − 5 Union Nationale.

These rather substantial observed differences between federal and provincial party alignments within provinces may, to be sure, be both cause and effect of individual variations within provinces. Putting this question aside for the time being, these aggregate differences imply the possible existence of individual variations in party identifications across levels. However, the assessment of the magnitude of this phenomenon is a problem both of measurement and interpretation.

The importance of this phenomenon has been recognized in earlier Canadian and Australian research where standard party identification questions have been followed by probes designed to determine the level(s) of government originally referenced and to establish the pattern of variation across levels.[22] The 1965 post-election survey in Canada found 11% of all party identifiers in a national sample maintained *different* party identifications at the federal and provincial levels, and a further 13% indicated identification with one level of government only.[23] These two groups, reporting one of two particular types of variability across level, together constituted more than a fifth of the total national sample of that year. The limitation imposed on any sequence about partisanship contained exclusively within the context of a *federal* election survey is obvious, particularly given hypotheses about the possible variability of party identification over time. But, even within these limitations, this finding of a 24% difference is large.

With this in mind, we opted in the 1974 post-election survey to further investigate the variability of partisanship across level by including in the survey instrument completely parallel sequences of items on federal and provincial party identification. This included material on direction, intensity, and change at both levels of government. Although one cannot completely escape the possible contamination by the federal election context, the two sequences were widely separated in the questionnaire and the provincial sequence was grouped with other items specific to provincial politics.[24]

Table 5.2 shows 14% of party identifiers maintaining an identification at *only one level of government*. This is comparable to the findings of other Canadian studies.[25] However, the proportion of split identifiers (those persons maintaining a *different* party identification at each level) is 18%, significantly larger than previous findings. Taken together, these two groups of inconsistent partisans constitute nearly one-third of all party identifiers and 30% of the total national sample. The phenomenon of cross-level variation in party identification is a sufficiently evident feature of the Canadian electoral landscape to make an appreciation of it crucial to our utilization of the party identification concept.

The sequence of questions used in the 1974 national election study also permits detailed examination of those individuals who support the same party federally and provincially but who report differences in the *intensity* of that support. Nearly two-thirds of all party identifiers in Canada sup-

TABLE 5.2

Variations in Patterns of Party Identification in Canada, by Province, 1974
(row percentages; party identifiers only)

PROVINCE	aFULLY CONSISTENT	PARTIALLY CONSISTENT	SPLIT IDENTIFIERS	SINGLE-LEVEL IDENTIFIERS	N
British Columbia	34%	15	35	16	234
Quebec	39%	22	23	16	654
Manitoba	39%	30	21	10	103
Alberta	41%	24	24	12	165
Saskatchewan	44%	23	21	12	89
Ontario	49%	25	11	15	649
New Brunswick	62%	23	5	10	120
Newfoundland	63%	26	6	5	96
Nova Scotia	63%	23	9	6	167
Prince Edward Island	64%	23	4	10	84
Total	44%	23	18	14	*2258*

aFully consistent — consistent in both direction *and* intensity. Partially consistent — consistent in direction but not in intensity. Split identifiers — identification with two different parties at the federal and provincial levels. Single level — a party identification at one level but no identification at the other.

port a single party at both levels, but approximately one-quarter of these (23% of all party identifiers or 21% of the national sample) indicate variations in the *intensity* of attachment to their party between the two levels.[26] These respondents are labelled "partially consistent" in Table 5.2, and are distinguished from those who are fully consistent in both intensity and direction and from those who are split or single-level identifiers.[27]

A national distribution of types of party identifiers by variation across level is found in the bottom row of Table 5.2. Forty-four per cent of all party identifiers (41% of the national sample) are fully consistent across level. Comparable distributions are shown in the table for each of the provinces. There are considerable inter-provincial differences in the degree of cross-level consistency. Five provinces have large numbers of split identifiers (the four Western provinces and Quebec), while Quebec and British Columbia show the highest incidence of single-level identification. However, almost all provinces show substantial variations in intensity among respondents who are at least nominally consistent in direction of party identification. The degree of full consistency across level ranges from a low of 34% of all party identifiers in British Columbia to a high of 64% of all party identifiers in Prince Edward Island. The Maritime provinces show considerably higher levels of full consistency than do the other provinces.

It should be noticed that the ordering of provinces by degree of inconsistency in Table 5.2 corresponds closely to the ordering by dissimilarity of party systems in Table 5.1. A Spearman R of .84 exists between these two rankings. It is reasonable to expect that the systems showing the greatest dissimilarity between provincial and federal party systems will also show the highest levels of inconsistency of party identification. In British Columbia and Quebec, for example, which maintain fundamentally different party systems at the provincial and federal levels, one might expect to find high proportions of split and single-level party identifiers. Manitoba and Ontario, which have party systems of the second type, might be expected to exhibit higher levels of variation in intensity as opposed to direction of partisanship, since the same parties compete at the federal and provincial levels, but with significant variation in electoral strength. The Maritimes predictably show much lower incidence of split and single level identification. Nevertheless, all party systems of this third type exhibit substantial variation in intensity between the levels. The data suggest that this variation in intensity may be less directly related to the nature of the party system than is the case with the relationship between variations in direction represented by split or single-level identification.

Appendix 5A documents the wide range of combinations which are found in the ten party systems and suggests their relative importance. Varying combinations of party identifiers appear as percentages by province. While the entries appear small in absolute terms, cumulatively their effect might be considerable in particular provinces. Certain variations in federal-provincial electoral results can be brought about by relatively small proportions of voters if party cross-over is involved.[28] In Ontario, for example, the longstanding weakness of the provincial Liberal party, in contrast to its strong federal performance, might be partially explained by considering the aggregation of the 6.0% provincial Conservative-federal Liberal cell, the 6.3% who identify only with the federal Liberal party, and the 2.2% identifying exclusively with the provincial Conservative party. Similarly, patterns of split identification in favour of the NDP in Manitoba and Saskatchewan might account for the ability of that party to form provincial governments in those provinces while remaining much weaker federally.

Thus far, we have concentrated on variations in the direction of party identification at the federal and provincial levels, and we have introduced the question of intensity only to distinguish partially consistent identifiers from those who are fully consistent at both levels. It can be argued,

however, that some of these variations in intensity have electoral implications that are as significant conceptually and politically as directional
variations. Table 5.3 and Appendix 5B show breakdowns of directionally
consistent party identifiers for each province, again given as a percentage
of all party identifiers in that province. In many instances, groups of
partially consistent identifiers who indicate higher levels of support for a
party at one level over the other are as large or larger than comparable
groups of split or single-level identifiers. Our tentative suggestions regarding the electoral implications of variation in the direction of provincial and federal party identifications are buttressed by the addition of
these groups. In Ontario, for example, the chronic weakness of the provincial Liberal party might be partially explained by the existence of a
rather large group of consistent Liberals (7.4% of all party identifiers;
17.9% of all provincial Liberal identifiers) who indicate that their Liberal
partisanship is weaker at the provincial level. Similarly, in Manitoba and
Saskatchewan, the provincial strength of the NDP is enhanced by the
existence of substantial groups of partisans (6.8% and 6.7% respectively)
with a stronger provincial than federal party identification.

What is noteworthy in the above figures, in addition to the variations
shown by supporters of particular parties in particular provinces, is the
relative strength of provincial identification. The fully consistent partisans,
as we have called them, constitute the largest single group of party
identifiers in each province. This designation signifies, for those respon-

TABLE 5.3

**Variations in Intensity of Partisanship for Consistent Party Identifiers,
by Province
(row percentages; party identifiers only)**

INTENSITY

PROVINCE	FULLY CONSISTENT	STRONGER FEDERAL	STRONGER PROVINCIAL	N
British Columbia	34%	6	9	234
Quebec	39%	10	11	654
Manitoba	39%	13	18	103
Alberta	41%	10	13	165
Saskatchewan	44%	12	10	89
Ontario	49%	13	12	649
New Brunswick	62%	8	15	120
Newfoundland	63%	16	10	96
Nova Scotia	63%	9	14	167
Prince-Edward Island	64%	10	13	84
Total	44%	11	12	*2258*

dents, that provincial identification is as strong as federal identification. Beyond this are groups of respondents whose intensity of partisanship varies between the levels. But in nearly every case, the number of those with a stronger provincial identification is equal to or greater than the proportion with a stronger federal identification. The inference is clear that provincial party identification in Canada is not a secondary form of identification, but an attachment in every sense equal to federal identification. Such a conclusion is further supported by the distribution of the 14% of all party identifiers in the national sample who identify with a party at only one level (i.e., single-level identifiers). These, too, divide almost equally between the provincial level and the federal.

Assessing the role of provincial identification relative to federal party identification in this manner requires a slightly more detailed examination of the intensity distributions for certain groups of identifiers. The meaning of partisanship for the fully consistent identifiers is fairly clear, as it is for the single-level identifiers. However, the partially consistent

TABLE 5.4

Variations in Intensity of Party Identification at the Federal and Provincial Levels for Consistent and Split Identifiers (diagonal percentages)

CONSISTENT IDENTIFIERS

PROVINCIAL INTENSITY

FEDERAL INTENSITY	VERY STRONG	FAIRLY STRONG	WEAK
Very Strong	27	9	2
Fairly Strong	10	31	5
Weak	2	6	8
$Tau_c=.47*$			100% (N=*1519*)

SPLIT IDENTIFIERS

PROVINCIAL INTENSITY

FEDERAL INTENSITY	VERY STRONG	FAIRLY STRONG	WEAK
Very Strong	5	6	3
Fairly Strong	11	29	9
Weak	8	15	13
$Tau_c=.11*$			100% (N=*414*)

*Significant at .01.

and split identifiers warrant further examination because of the potential complexity of some of the combinations which may exist. For the partially consistent identifiers, the variation in intensity may range across three degrees of relative strength and run in one of two possible directions. Similarly, for split identifiers, the two identifications may be equal in strength, or may favour one level over the other. Table 5.4 shows a cross-tabulation of federal and provincial intensities for these two groups of consistent and split identifiers.[29] It is clear from the tables that for consistent identifiers, the variations between levels are approximately equal in each direction, and that they tend toward overall strength rather than weakness. For split identifiers, however, the distribution more definitely favours the provincial identification, and there are more cases to be found in the "weak" cells for each level.[30] Interestingly, the proportion of split identifiers maintaining a "very strong" identification at each level is quite small, although the total proportion of split identifiers maintaining truly co-equal identifications (in the table, the sum of the three diagonal cells) is nevertheless impressive (47% of the split identifiers and 9% of all party identifiers). Still, there is a hint that split identification incorporates a somewhat greater degree of weakness at one or both levels than is the case for the consistents.

So far our discussion of party identification has focussed on variation across levels of the political system rather than across time. Of course, *any* of the conditions that we have thus far identified — partial consistency, split identification, single level identification — may be stable or variable over time.

CROSS-TIME VARIATION: THE UNSTABLE IDENTIFIER

The documentation of variations over time in patterns of party identification has been a major factor leading to the re-thinking of traditional concepts of individual ties to parties. We will now examine in some depth this phenomenon of instability of party identification across time, concentrating on the extent of, the reasons for, and the timing of these changes. Consideration of these factors will reveal an electorate containing some types of partisans for whom the tie to party seems to represent a lasting commitment, shaping the political world, and others for whom a party tie may be one of several possible short-run considerations influencing the vote. This, in turn, suggests that some modification of traditional measures of partisanship is needed if the concept is to retain its analytical utility in explanations of political behaviour.

Canadian voters exhibit considerable instability in party identification. Table 5.5 shows the proportions of several electorates that have been stable in their partisanship.[31] Federally, 64% of the party identifiers have

TABLE 5.5

Stability of Party Identifications at the Federal and Provincial Levels
(row percentages; party identifiers only)

	STABLE	UNSTABLE	N=
Federal Politics	64%	36	*2062*
Provincial Politics			
Newfoundland	82%	18	90
Prince Edward Island	71%	29	80
Nova Scotia	77%	24	160
New Brunswick	83%	17	106
Quebec	69%	31	609
Ontario	80%	20	560
Manitoba	59%	41	97
Saskatchewan	73%	27	89
Alberta	66%	34	153
British Columbia	67%	33	220
Total	74%	26	*2126*

kept the same party tie throughout their political lifetimes. This percentage is very similar in magnitude to that found in 1965, when 62% of Canadian party identifiers reported never changing their partisan affiliation. For provincial parties, stability is somewhat higher, with three-quarters of the respondents reporting no change in party ties. However, important differences emerge when these figures are examined by province. Several provinces have rates of stability in provincial politics which are very high.[32] In both federal and provincial politics, the incidence of instability for the country as a whole is substantial, even among the most highly partisan in the electorate[33] (see Table 5.6). For all categories of intensity, levels of stability in provincial politics are somewhat higher than those observed federally. The 1974 findings for federal partisanship are quite similar to those observed in 1965.[34]

A final point about the overall incidence of instability should be considered here. Canada, as a multi-party system, has experienced the development of new parties and the eclipse of existing parties within the political lifetime of many respondents. One might infer therefore that some of the instability of party ties is due to the availability of new choices and the disappearance of old options. However, on closer examination, this does not account for the observed instability. First, there is little difference between the new and old parties in the rates of instability among their supporters. Second, the new parties still attract relatively small proportions of the electorate, with the exception of the Parti

Québécois. Thus, their contribution to instability is minor. At the federal level the NDP, which first contested federal elections under that name

TABLE 5.6

Stability of Party Identification by Intensity
(column percentages)

FEDERAL STABILITY	VERY STRONG	INTENSITY FAIRLY STRONG	WEAK
Not Stable	26%	38%	42%
Stable	74	62	58
N=	643	947	472

Tau$_c$ = −.13*

PROVINCIAL STABILITY	VERY STRONG	INTENSITY FAIRLY STRONG	WEAK
Not Stable	19%	31%	32%
Stable	80	69	68
N=	764	988	412

Tau$_c$ = −.12*

*Significant at .01.

in 1962, has a higher rate of reported change than do the other parties. However, it is only slightly higher than that for the most stable party, the Liberals. Provincially, the difference between the NDP and the two older parties is even less (data not shown). A large proportion of those identifying with the Parti Québécois (45%) report that they have changed their party identification. It is this finding that partially explains the relatively high rate of overall instability in Quebec shown in Table 5.5. Overall, however, the pattern is one of continuing interchange of support among all parties — from new to old and between old parties, as well as from old to new. With the exception of the Parti Québécois, the reason for the instability of party affiliations must be sought elsewhere than in the introduction of new parties.

The incidence of changing party identification is high in Canada. It is high for partisans of all parties, no matter the strength of their tie. Therefore, questions arise as to the meaning of the acceptance of a party label by a respondent. For more than one-third of our sample the possibility exists of a tie to party that is no more enduring than current preferences. This possibility becomes even more compelling when the data dealing with the time at which the change in party identification occurred are examined. Table 5.7 shows that an overwhelming proportion of the reported changes have occurred very recently. Of those party

148   *Political Choice in Canada*

identifiers who have changed their federal partisanship (36% of all federal partisans), fully 31% report that they changed their party identification at the *time of the last election.* A further 21% changed at the time of or *after the 1972 federal election.* This means that in less than a two year period, 18% of all partisans changed their affiliation.[35] Since the 1968 election, when the present configuration of politics was set by the choice

TABLE 5.7

Time of Change of Party Identifications
(column percentages; unstable party identifiers only)

	FEDERAL	PROVINCIAL
At the time of the last election — 1974	31%	21%
1971–1973	21	26
1967–1970	20	30
Before 1967; "a long time ago"	28	23
N=	567	396

of new leaders for both the major parties, one-quarter of all partisans have changed their party identifications.[36] The provincial patterns are quite comparable. Partisan instability in Canada has not been associated with major political upheavals of the sort that occurred in the United States in the sixties. Rather, these changes took place during a period of relative calm in Canadian politics, and are better seen as responses to changes in day-to-day political conditions.

Not only is instability in party identifications not directly related to major political upheavals, but it is also only weakly related to the intensity of individuals' partisanship. Table 5.8 indicates this quite clearly. Very strong partisans who changed are more likely to have done so

TABLE 5.8

Time of Change of Party Identification by Intensity of Present Federal Party Identification
(column percentages; unstable party identifiers only)

	INTENSITY		
TIME OF CHANGE	VERY STRONG	FAIRLY STRONG	WEAK
At the time of the last election — 1974	27%	31%	35%
1971–1973	15	22	22
1967–1970	20	20	20
Before 1967; "a long time ago"	38	27	23
N=	123	296	148

$Tau_c = -.09$

before 1967, but there are 62% of them who moved in the period since the 1968 election. Of those people who changed and now consider themselves to be fairly strong federal partisans, 73% made the interparty move since that election.

Since many of the changers describe themselves as strong partisans (Table 5.6) and have come upon their new attachments only recently, one might question the meaning of self-confessed party identification for a proportion of the electorate. The willingness of many respondents to define themselves as "generally speaking" a party supporter may indicate for them little more than a highly mutable tie subject to change for short-run political reasons. As Table 5.9 indicates, the most frequently mentioned reasons for change of federal party identification are in the policy/issue category, demonstrating a reaction to specific policy questions.

TABLE 5.9

Reason Given for Change of Party Identification
(column percentages, multiple responses)

	FEDERAL	PROVINCIAL
Leadership	25%	19%
Local candidate	13	15
Policy/issue	31	30
Party performance	16	22
Local reasons	10	4
Majority government	6	2
Personal reasons	7	8
N=	*668*	*499*

The second most frequently cited reason is leadership or the activities of the party leaders. Only 7% of the voters mention personal reasons as having motivated their choice. This distribution indicates that the reasons for inter-party movement are clearly related to those aspects of the political process which are most changeable — leaders, local candidates, and particular political issues, like inflation and the cost of living. As the judgments about the performance of individuals or parties change, so do the party identifications of many Canadians. This can be more clearly seen when the time at which the change occurred is correlated with the reason given (data not shown). There are very frequent mentions of issues or policy in the most recent time periods. For both the 1974 and 1971-73 periods these are mentioned by 43% of all people giving a reason for their inter-party move. The concentration of attention in the 1967-70 period is on leadership reasons, with a rate of mention at 50%. It was at that time that the leaders of both major parties changed and 1968 was the time of "Trudeaumania." This phenomenon is further reflected in the reasons given by Liberals who moved into the party at that time, 64% of whom gave leadership as the reason for the change. Those categories which could be expected to vary less systematically with time, for example, local candidate and party performance, show no clear time-related patterns. Thus, not only do many Canadians move between parties, but they have done so recently and for relatively short-run reasons. They seem to respond willingly to the strategic manoeuvres as the parties attempt to alter the patterns of support by means of the selection of a new leader or the alteration of a party position on a specific policy or issue.

It is interesting to note that the motivations for change often are based on antipathy to the other parties rather than on attraction by the new party. When reasons for change are classified as positive or negative, the frequency of negative mentions is much greater than positive explanations. For many, the motive force is repulsion more than attraction. The implication may be that for some voters the present tie could be changed easily, since it is based less on affection for the party than on dislike of the alternatives. Volatility of support seems inherent in the attitudes of many partisans, even the strongest. Less than a majority (45%) of even the strongest partisans give positive reasons for their personal instability and their inter-party move. Similarly, only slightly more than one-third (38%) of the self-described fairly strong partisans claim to have developed support for their present party because of its attractive features. There are interesting cross-party differences in these patterns, with the Progressive Conservatives being much lower in positive mentions (23%). In no party does a majority of its supporters who have shifted give clearly positive reasons for the inter-party move.

A review of the findings thus far indicates the need to reconsider the meaning of the report by many Canadians that they are partisans of a particular party. There are significant theoretical implications to the observation that more than one-third of the self-defined partisans claim to have changed their party affiliation, many of them very recently for short-run reasons, and because of antipathy to the other possible choices. Yet, at the same time, they are willing to distribute themselves along the intensity measure with almost the same pattern as those partisans who have never changed or who changed long ago. Simple correlations between party identification, even taking into account intensity, and other variables mix together in the analysis both long-run, affectively tied supporters and those who exhibit volatility in their attachments as they respond to altered political conditions.

The implication of this mixing might be clearer if a brief reconsideration is undertaken of the voting choice. The vote is sometimes described as the convergence between long-run influences, especially party identification, and short-run factors, represented by responses to leaders, candidates, and issues. Sometimes, one set of influences predominates, whereas under different conditions the other is more important for understanding the vote. However, this view of the vote decision is dependent upon the existence of a party affiliation *separate* from the vote and based on a different pattern of development. The source of partisanship may be the family, it may be past experiences with one party, or it may be an effort to conform to the perceived norms of a social group. Whatever the source, this partisanship must exist *prior* to vote if long-run factors or a "normal" vote are to exist.

The concept of the normal vote is founded on the existence of both short-term and long-term forces in the vote decision. Originally it was developed to explain aggregate patterns of choice.[37] However, it has also been applied to the individual level of analysis:

> If citizens approached each new election tabula rasa, then there would be no point in analyzing long-term components of the vote. The stability of party identifications, along with the apparent functional autonomy they gain for many individuals over time, however, has been amply documented. On the other hand, if all chanels of political communication were to be shut off, so that citizens were obliged to go to the polls with no new political information to evaluate, there would be no short-term component to analyse. In reality, voting decisions involve a blend of these components. . . .[38]

The same authors argue that "fluctuations in turnout and partisanship of the vote in the national elections are primarily determined by short-term political forces which become important to the voter at election time."[39] But underneath all of this, both for the electorate and for the individual, is the assumption that "the basic element in the long-term trend of the vote is the underlying division of party loyalties."[40]

However, it might be that for some voters in some electorates a long-run partisanship does not exist. Their tie to party is a fleeting one, little different from their commitment to a particular leader or concern about an important issue. It is important to distinguish such short-run partisans from those who display the recognized characteristics of the party identifier. Shortly, we will present a typology which partitions the Canadian electorate, taking into account the phenomenon of short-run partisans who may use the party as a cue in a significantly different way than does the more traditional identifier.

Short-run partisans should be distinguished by their patterns of behaviour. The search here will concentrate on their behaviour in the vote decision, and will focus on partisans who are self-described deviants from the traditional party identification because they have a history of unstable party ties. We would expect that such partisans will rely less directly on party and past experience as a cue to choice and will instead turn to short-term factors as the reason for their decision. Unstable partisans would not be expected to use the party itself as the reason for their vote. Instead, they should indicate that more immediate and changeable factors are the motive for their decision, just as such factors have been seen above to be the reason for their present party identification. To the extent that voters are willing to assign to the party itself, without further qualification, the motivating role, it seems that they are providing different information about the combination of forces composing their vote decisions.

There are two ways in which this proposition might be empirically examined. The first is to look at the self-report of the most important component of the vote decision for stable and unstable party identifiers.[41] When the reports of these two groups are examined, there is no difference between the stable and unstable party identifiers. Both are equally likely to mention a party as most important for their decision. Two-fifths of each group give a "party" answer, and they are equally likely to mention more short-run influences.[42] However, there is a follow-up to this initial explanation of voting choice, and it is a question asking for a characterization of the "party" response, for those who selected that option. The respondents were asked to distinguish between a "party" answer based on the "party's general approach to government," and "its position on certain issues." When this response is examined it becomes clear that stable and unstable party identifiers mean quite different things by a "party" answer; there is a relationship between stability of partisanship and the meaning of a party answer. For the stable identifiers, "party" means a long-run, general characterization of its performance. For more than half the unstable group, however, the "party" answer cloaks a short-run issue answer.

It is useful to examine this same relationship within categories of intensity of party identification. In Table 5.10 it is the strongest identifiers who are most differentiated in their understanding of the "party" cue. Although many unstable identifiers characterize themselves as strong party identifiers, they see that party as an amalgam of issue positions more than do stable party identifiers, while among the weak identifiers the differences disappear. In the first case, the effect of intense party identification is to separate the two groups, whereas as intensity declines they come to resemble each other.

TABLE 5.10

Meaning of Party for Stable and Unstable Partisans, within Categories of
Strength of Party Identification (for Those Who Mentioned "Party" as
the Most Important Reason for the Vote)
(column percentages)

	STRONG IDENTIFIERS	
PARTY MEANS	STABLE	UNSTABLE
Issue Position	32%	51%
General Approach	68	49
N=	203	64

V=.11*

	FAIRLY STRONG IDENTIFIERS	
PARTY MEANS	STABLE	UNSTABLE
Issue Position	37%	50%
General Approach	64	50
N=	222	137

V=.08

	WEAK IDENTIFIERS	
PARTY MEANS	STABLE	UNSTABLE
Issue Position	45%	53%
General Approach	55	47
N=	95	68

V=.02

*Significant at .01.

A similar conclusion emerges from an examination of responses to a
question asking for the reason for the vote in 1974.[43] Once again the
stable party identifiers are much more likely to give an unadorned and
unqualified "party" answer, whereas unstable identifiers list leaders, candidates, and particularly short-run issues as their reasons (data not
shown). The pattern exists within all categories of intensity. Forty-one
per cent of the very strong and stable party identifiers give the party as
the real reason for their vote, whereas only 25% of the equally strong
but unstable group give that answer. In contrast, 36% of the first group
list short-run issues as their reason, and 52% of the very strong and
unstable group do so.[44]

The same pattern emerges when a second choice of party is analyzed.
Respondents were asked to indicate which party they would vote for if
they were ". . . unable to vote for the federal party that [they] most
preferred in the recent election." While the primary intent of this question is to establish a second-choice party, one of the options coded was

not voting at all. Therefore, it can be hypothesized that there should be a difference between the short-run and long-run partisans in their willingness to make, or indicate hypothetically, a second choice. Partisans for whom party is an imporant and long-term cue should have greater difficulty in deciding on another party. Their view of politics in party terms constitutes a rejection of the other parties and, therefore, greater antipathy toward the idea of supporting one of the opposition. However, for the short-run partisans, party is little different from the other components of the vote; if the party which is currently favoured is for some reason unavailable, another choice would be substituted.

Table 5.11 shows that this expectation is confirmed and in exactly the same pattern within categories of intensity of identification. For all party identifiers, 30% of the stable identifiers would not vote if they were unable to vote for their own party. Less than half that number of the unstable identifiers refuse to make another choice. When the relationship is controlled by intensity of party identification, the pattern is maintained at almost the same magnitude. No matter the intensity with which the current party identification is held, the willingness to vote for another party is between two and three times higher for the unstable identifiers than it is for the stable group.[45]

TABLE 5.11

Hypothetical Response If First Choice Party Not Available, for Stable and Unstable Party Identifiers (column percentages)

Response:	STABILITY	
	STABLE	UNSTABLE
Would not vote	30%	14%
Made a second choice	70	86
N=	*1181*	*677*

V=.17*

*Significant at .01.

Within Categories of Intensity, the Per Cent Who Would Not Vote, for Stable and Unstable Party Identifiers (N shown in parentheses)

Intensity:	STABILITY	
	STABLE	UNSTABLE
Very Strong*	39	21
	(397)	*(47)*
Fairly Strong*	24	14
	(460)	*(319)*
Weak*	25	9
	(187)	*(162)*

*Differences significant at .01.

Thus, the unstable party identifiers indicate, as one would expect, that their party attachments tend to be based on short-run considerations of party performance and position in the current political configuration. Such observations are completely consistent with those cited above as the explanations provided for the move from one party to another and the usual timing of that move. There, as well, the emphasis was on short-run considerations. These findings, taken together, indicate that for some proportion of the electorate, the answer given to the usual party identification sequence does not measure partisan attachment as well as it might. For those people, the answer tends to indicate a current partisanship based on short-run considerations, one of which might be performance and/or activity of a party. However, the party does not occupy a position of primacy different in kind from other potential influences. If understanding the role of partisanship as a correlate of both behaviour and attitudes is the goal, these people must be found and reclassified toward the weaker end of the partisan dimension.

A MEASURE OF PARTISANSHIP IN CANADA

The preceding discussion provides evidence that commitments to party in Canada vary widely both between the levels of government in the federal system and over time within each of these levels. It is clear that any assumption that most individuals have a commitment to a party which has remained stable over time, and that can be easily captured in one summary measure on a survey instrument is invalid. We propose, therefore, to refine the concept of "party identification" by introducing a measure, which we will call "partisanship," that takes account of these potential variations in commitment. This is done because it is necessary to be very clear about the different *types* of partisanship in Canada before using that variable to predict and explain attitudes or behaviour.

In order to group individuals according to their commitment to a party, several pieces of information are required in addition to the party they felt closest to at the time the interview was conducted. These are: the consistency or inconsistency of feelings for a party across the federal and provincial levels; and the intensity and stability over time of these feelings at both levels. The interaction of these three "qualifiers" of the basic party identification responses (consistency, intensity, stability) can be used to form a new measure of partisanship. Employing them, we are able to better describe partisanship in Canada, and the detailed categorization in Table 5.12 provides an illustration of the complexity in number and types of Canadian partisans.

TABLE 5.12

A Categorization of Partisanship in Canada, 1974
(column percentages)

CONSISTENT				
(Same Party at Federal & Provincial Level)	stable both levels, over time	intensity same	26%	
		[a]intensity $F>P$	5	
		intensity $P>F$	6	
			37	
	stable F, has varied P	intensity same	4	
		intensity $F>P$	2	
		intensity $P>F$	1	
			7	
	stable P, has varied F	intensity same	7	
		intensity $P>F$	2	
		intensity $F>P$	2	
			11	
	has varied at both levels	intensity same	5	
		intensity $F>P$	2	
		intensity $P>F$	2	
			9	64%
SPLIT				
(Different Federal and Provincial Parties)	stable, both levels	intensity same	3	
		intensity $F>P$	1	
		intensity $P>F$	2	
			6	
	stable F, has varied P	intensity same	1	
		intensity $F>P$	1	
		intensity $P>F$	1	
			3	
	stable P, has varied F	intensity same	2	
		intensity $P>F$	2	
		intensity $F>P$	1	
			5	
	has varied at both levels	intensity same	2	
		intensity $F>P$	1	
		intensity $P>F$	1	
			4	18

FEDERAL PARTY ONLY	stable	4	
	variable	2	
		6	

PROVINCIAL PARTY ONLY	stable	5	
	variable	2	
		7	13

INDEPENDENTS (No Party At Either Level)		6	6
			(N=*2417*)

[a]$F > P$ — federal intensity greater than provincial intensity.

$P > F$ — provincial intensity greater than federal intensity.

Table 5.12 shows that both stability and complete consistency across levels is achieved by just over one-quarter of the electorate (26%). A further 11% have been consistent across levels and stable over time, but vary in the intensity with which they identify with federal and provincial parties. Examination of the remaining categories of consistents (those who support the same party at federal and provincial levels) reveals that there is a total of another quarter of the electorate (27%) who have various combinations of stability and intensity of feelings for their party at the two levels of government. Similar breakdowns and calculations can be made for those who identify with different parties at the two levels and for those who support a party at only one level.

As we have pointed out earlier in this chapter, the relationship between party affiliation and the vote has been at the heart of the debate over the usefulness of party identification as an explanatory variable in voting research in Canada and elsewhere. Thus, as an initial test of the analytic power of the constructed partisanship measure, we will examine the relationship between two different forms of this variable and the reported vote histories of the respondents to the 1974 study. If individuals' relationship to party is truly independent of current vote, and therefore useful as a predictor of it (and this assumption, of course, is the basis of the models constructed around party identification), then we should find that individuals with different types of partisanship have different voting patterns. Specifically, we should find that the likelihood of having voted for the same party is higher for individuals who are strong, stable, and consistent partisans. We should find also that *each* of the three components of partisanship contributes to this relationship, and we should be able to identify those individuals for whom the 1974 federal vote (and last provincial vote) are reflections of long-term ties to "their party," as well as those for whom that behaviour was more the product of short-term factors. For these latter individuals, those who deviate significantly from strong, stable, consistent partisanship, the correspondence of current party identification with vote may only reflect the fact of those votes. By showing what *types* of partisans are likely to have supported only their party at the polls and what types are more likely to have voted for different parties, we will illustrate how this refinement of the party identification concept improves our understanding of Canadian voting behaviour.

The categorizations of partisanship that we have advanced so far are too unwieldly for concise data analysis. The value of such a categorization, however, is that it permits several analytical groupings according to the behaviour under investigation. Two such groupings will be presented here, both of which substantially improve our ability to predict the past voting behaviour of respondents. As a benchmark against which to measure this improvement, Table 5.13 presents the relationship between federal and provincial voting history and the most commonly used "qualifier" of party identification, intensity of identification. Table 5.13 shows that there is indeed a relationship between vote history and intensity of party identification. A Tau_c measure of .18 and .19 exists with past federal and provincial vote consistency respectively. Intensity is, however, only *one* component of the proposed measure, and we expect this new measure to substantially improve the correlations.

TABLE 5.13

Past Vote History by Intensity of Party Identification (Federal and Provincial)

INTENSITY	% ALWAYS VOTED FOR SAME PARTY(N) FEDERALLY	PROVINCIALLY
Very strong	70 (*614*)	70 (*660*)
Fairly strong	55 (*897*)	56 (*847*)
Not very strong	42 (*409*)	40 (*307*)
	Tau_c=.18*	Tau_c=.19*

*Significant at .01.

The first variable developed by regrouping partisan types is one which summarizes the characteristics of consistency, stability, and intensity. This is accomplished by simply summing the number of deviations an individual has from strong, stable, consistent partisanship at either level. Thus, an individual is given one point on the index for being a split identifier or otherwise differing across level, one for having a weak intensity or being an independent at a given level, and one for having changed identification at some time in the past. This index, then, is a test of the reasoning that the several elements of partisanship, acting together, can have a reinforcing effect on commitment to a particular party, and hence to voting for that party consistently over time. The number of deviations from that standard should be related to inconsistent voting behaviour.

This preliminary effort at creating a composite partisanship variable, which appears in Table 5.14, is an improvement over the simple intensity measure used in Table 5.13. Eighty-two per cent of those with no deviations from stable consistent federal partisanship have always voted for the same federal party, compared with only 14% of those with three deviations. Statistically, the Tau_c rises to .53 for the federal and .51 for the provincial relationship.

TABLE 5.14

Past Vote History by Deviations from Consistency in Partisanship (Federal and Provincial)

NUMBER OF DEVIATIONS FROM STRONG, STABLE, CONSISTENT PARTISANSHIP	% ALWAYS VOTED FOR SAME PARTY(N) FEDERALLY	PROVINCIALLY
none	82 (*823*)	81 (*878*)
one	43 (*768*)	41 (*691*)
two	26 (*445*)	26 (*363*)
three	14 (*141*)	14 (*81*)
	Tau_c=.53*	Tau_c=.51*

*Significant at .01.

With regard to the latter point, we compared the single-level identifiers with both consistent and split identifiers on the dimensions of intensity and stability. While the intensity breakdowns were rather erratic for these single-level identifiers, the pattern on stability was clear. The single-level group resembled the split identifiers much more than the consistents. In constructing the final partisanship variable for this analysis, therefore, we have combined the several types of single-level and split identifiers. The variable thus formed appears in Table 5.15 and represents a combination into twelve basic categories of these types of partisans in Canada.

Table 5.15 shows clearly that all three "qualifiers" — consistency, stability, and intensity — have independent effects on past vote history at the federal and provincial levels. For every degree of stability and intensity, the consistent identifiers are more likely than the split and single-level identifiers to have voted for only one party. Among both consistent and split identifiers, those who have been stable over time are much more likely to have voted for one party than are unstable identifiers. Finally, intensity makes a difference in producing higher voting consistency in most cases, the only major exception being among stable, split identifiers. In comparing the two factors of intensity and stability, however, the conclusion is inescapable that stability seems to be a more important variable in producing consistency of voting patterns. The differences in Table 5.15 between stable and variable identifiers are substantial, while those between identifiers of differing intensities are smaller and more erratic.

A summary index does, however, make certain assumptions which might be questioned. First, it is not at all clear that the three components of this index should have the same weight in its construction. In particular, the question of whether stability over time is a more important component of partisanship for a particular analysis than intensity needs further investigation. Another consideration arises from the various types of cross-level inconsistency which are possible within our measure — single level partisanship, for example, or split partisanship.

The partisanship variable set out in Table 5.15 shows a stronger relationship with consistency of past voting than does the deviations index in the previous table. In the case of both federal and provincial voting history, 86% of those who have a stable, consistent, and very strong partisanship report always having voted for the same party. This total declines through the twelve categories, with very few reversals in the ordering, to those with variable, split or single, and weak partisanship, who report consistent voting at levels close to or below those who report no party affiliation at all. The Tau$_c$ measures of .57 in the federal case and .59 in the provincial case are very strong, and indicate a significant improvement in our ability to relate partisan ties to vote history.

This demonstration of the improved predictive capacity of a modified partisanship variable has a number of implications for electoral behaviour that we will discuss in subsequent chapters. It is perhaps not surprising that past vote history is closely related to partisan history, particularly when stability of partisanship is considered. However, by taking into account explicitly some other empirically observable characteristics of partisanship, the analysis indicates that a refinement of existing measures is both possible and desirable.

If there are substantial numbers of non-traditional partisans in Canada as we have argued here, and if they react differently to political stimuli, then an understanding of this relationship is essential for further investigation of patterns of electoral behaviour. This is a strong justification for further attention to the development of new and different ways of measuring partisanship or party identification. Several variations of the improved measures of partisanship developed in this chapter will be employed in our subsequent analyses of electoral behaviour and in an examination of the formation of images of political parties and their leaders, as well as orientations to the issues of the 1974 election. In

TABLE 5.15

Types of Partisans by Past Vote History
(Federal and Provincial)

% ALWAYS VOTING FOR SAME
PARTY (N)

TYPES OF PARTISANSHIP	STABLE FEDERAL VOTE HISTORY[a]	STABLE PROVINCIAL VOTE HISTORY[b]
stable, consistent, very strong	86 *(413)*	86 *(440)*
stable, consistent, fairly strong	78 *(415)*	71 *(429)*
stable, consistent, weak	69 *(134)*	64 *(115)*
stable, split/single, very strong	54 *(43)*	57 *(88)*
stable, split/single, fairly strong	62 *(127)*	58 *(149)*
stable, split/single, weak	44 *(91)*	41 *(85)*
variable, consistent, very strong	34 *(138)*	27 *(87)*
variable, consistent, fairly strong	31 *(238)*	21 *(177)*
variable, consistent, weak	25 *(83)*	20 *(60)*
variable, split/single, very strong	33 *(27)*	19 *(48)*
variable, split/single, fairly strong	13 *(118)*	21 *(78)*
variable, split/single, weak	18 *(103)*	6 *(52)*
variable, split/single, fairly strong	$Tau_c=.57*$	$Tau_c=.59*$

[a] — Includes only those respondents with a federal partisanship.
[b] — Includes only those respondents with a provincial partisanship.
*Significant at .01.

subsequent chapters we will make use of the dimensions of partisanship discussed here in the construction of a more elaborate typology of voters, based both on partisanship and level of political interest.

The importance of political parties to voters is something which is little disputed. The concept of party identification, based in the theory of reference groups and characterized as a stable tie, usually learned in childhood, has traditionally been measured by a single, simple question on surveys. It is this concept, thus measured, that we have attempted to refine in this chapter.

It is to be expected that the relevant dimensions of partisanship will vary between countries. Canada, for example, has been shown to have a good deal of variation in individuals' ties to parties across the two levels of the political system, as well as substantial instability over time. While we have isolated three components of partisanship in Canada, it is quite reasonable to expect that other factors might appear relevant in other polities. It is important for meaningful analysis to identify those dimensions which are most relevant, and to make use of them in developing a categorization of partisans for any particular political system.

FOOTNOTES

1. For a concise exposition of major scholarly perspectives on political parties, see Leon D. Epstein, "Political Parties," in Fred I. Greenstein and Nelson W. Polsby, eds., *Handbook of Political Science*, 4 (Reading, Mass.: Addison – Wesley, 1975), pp. 234-38.
2. On the functions of parties in various political systems see Epstein, *op. cit.*, p. 236. For a more extended discussion by the same author, see Epstein, *Political Parties in Western Democracies* (New York: Praeger, 1967). The functions of Canadian parties are discussed in Frederick C. Engelmann and Mildred A. Schwartz, *Canadian Political Parties: Origin, Character, Impact* (Scarborough: Prentice-Hall, 1975) chaps. 8-14.
3. See, for example, Joseph Schumpeter, *Capitalism, Socialism and Democracy* (New York: Harper and Row, 1950); Anthony Downs, *An Economic Theory of Democracy* (New York: Harper and Row, 1957).
4. On this point see Warren Miller, "The Cross-national Use of Party Identification as a Stimulus to Political Inquiry," in Ian Budge, Ivor Crewe, and Dennis Farlie, eds., *Party Identification and Beyond* (New York: Wiley, 1976), chap. 2.
5. Classic studies include Angus Campbell et al., *The American Voter* (New York: Wiley, 1960); Angus Campbell et al., *Elections and the Political Order* (New York: Wiley, 1966); and David Butler and Donald Stokes, *Political Change in Britain* (New York: St. Martin's, 1969). Many of the relevant studies are cited in Philip Converse, "Public Opinion and Voting Behaviour," *Handbook of Political Science*, 4, pp. 163-69.
6. Angus Campbell et al., *The Voter Decides* (Evanston, Ill.: Row, Peterson, 1954), pp. 88-9.
7. *Ibid.*, p. 90.
8. Campbell et al., *The American Voter*, pp. 121-22.
9. See Campbell et al., *The American Voter*, chap. 6; Campbell et al., *Elections and the Political Order, passim.*; M. Kent Jennings and Richard G. Niemi, "The Transmission of Political Values From Parent to Child," *American Political Science Review*, 62 (1968), pp. 172-74; and Philip Converse, "Of Time and Partisan Stability," *Comparative Political Studies*, 2 (1969), pp. 139-72.
10. See, for example, Norman H. Nie, Sidney Verba, and John R. Petrocik, *The Changing American Voter* (Cambridge: Harvard University Press, 1976), chap. 4; Warren E. Miller and Teresa E. Levitin, *Leadership and Change: The New Politics and the American Electorate* (Cambridge: Winthrop, 1976), chap. 7.
11. The incidence of party identification ranges from a low of 45% in France in the late 1950s and the Netherlands in the 1970s, to a high of 90% for Britain in the 1960s. Regarding the intensity of party identification, the number of strong identifiers varies from 32% in Britain to 18% in the Netherlands. See Philip Converse and Georges Dupeux, "Politicization of the Electorate in France and the United States," *Elections and the Political Order*, p. 277; M. K. Jennings, "Partisan Commitment and Electoral Behaviour in the Netherlands," *Acta Politica*, 7 (1972), p. 447; Butler and Stokes, *op. cit.*, pp. 38, 469. For Norwegian data see A. Campbell and H. Valen, "Party Identification in Norway and the United States," *Elections and the Political Order*, p. 251. Danish data are contained in Ole Borre and Daniel Katz, "Party Identification and

Its Motivational Base in a Multiparty System: A Study of the Danish General Election of 1971," *Scandinavian Political Studies*, 8 (1973), p. 74. For relevant data on party identification in West Germany, see Max Kaase, "Party Identification and Voting Behaviour in the West German Election of 1969," in Budge et al., *Party Identification and Beyond*, pp. 81-102.

That party ties are loosening in Britain is argued at length in Ivor Crewe et al., "Partisan Dealignment in Britain 1964-1974," *British Journal of Political Science*, 7 (1977), pp. 129-90.

12. See, for example, John Meisel, *Working Papers on Canadian Politics*, 2nd ed. (Montreal: McGill-Queen's University Press, 1975), p. 67; Paul M. Sniderman, Hugh D. Forbes, and Ian Melzer, "Party Loyalty and Electoral Volatility: A Study of the Canadian Party System," *Canadian Journal of Political Science*, 7 (1974), pp. 268-88; Jane Jenson, "Party Loyalty in Canada: The Question of Party Identification," *Canadian Journal of Political Science*, 8 (1975), pp. 543-53. Other materials on the nature and functions of party identification in Canada can be found scattered in the reports of a variety of provincial or local level studies of voting behaviour in Canadian federal elections. See, for example, Lynn McDonald, "Party Identification, Stability and Change in Voting Behaviour: A Study of the 1968 Canadian Federal Election in Ontario," in O. Kruhlak et al., eds., *The Canadian Political Process* (Toronto: Holt, Rinehard and Winston, 1970), pp. 267-83; George Perlin and Patti Peppin, "Variations in Party Support in Federal and Provincial Elections: Some Hypotheses," *Canadian Journal of Political Science*, 4 (June 1971), pp. 280-86; G. R. Winham and R. B. Cunningham, "Party Leader Images in the 1968 Federal Election," *Canadian Journal of Political Science*, 3 (March 1970), pp. 31-55. See also Joel Smith, Allan Kornberg, and David Bromley, "Patterns of Early Political Socialization and Adult Party Affiliation," *Canadian Review of Sociology and Anthropology*, 5 (November 1968), pp. 123-55; Jon H. Pammett, "The Development of Political Orientations in Canadian School Children," *Canadian Journal of Political Science*, 4 (March 1971), pp. 132-41.

13. See Appendix B, Q. 30-32.

14. William P. Irvine, "Explaining the Brittleness of Partisanship in Canada," unpublished paper presented at the Annual Meeting of the Canadian Political Science Association, Edmonton, June 1975, p. 4.

15. In the 1974 study, a Cramer's V of .84 is obtained.

16. A similar pattern is reported by Sniderman et al., *op. cit.*, p. 278.

17. Irvine reports that 39% of the 1965 sample reported a change of partisanship. See Irvine, *op. cit.*, p. 4. See also Jane Jenson, *op. cit.*, pp. 547-48.

18. Comparable figures for the number of unstable identifiers in Britain, the United States, and Australia are 17%, 8%, and 21% respectively. The British and American data are reported in Sniderman et al., *op. cit.*, p. 279. The Australian data are reported in Donald Aitkin and Michael Kahan, "Australia: Class Politics in the New World," in Richard Rose, ed., *Electoral Behaviour: A Comparative Handbook* (New York: The Free Press, 1974), p. 452.

19. On party systems in the Canadian provinces, see Engelmann and Schwartz, *op. cit.*, *passim*. See also John Wilson, "The Canadian Political Cultures," *Canadian Journal of Political Science*, 7 (1974), pp. 438-83;

Jane Jenson, "Party Systems," in David Bellamy, Jon H. Pammett, and Donald C. Rowat, eds., *The Provincial Political Systems* (Toronto: Methuen, 1976), chap. 9.

20. M. K. Jennings and R. G. Niemi, "Party Identification at Multiple Levels of Government," *American Journal of Sociology*, LXXII (1966), p. 100; The Australian data are reported in Donald Aitkin and Michael Kahan, "Australia: Class Politics in the New World," in Richard Rose, ed., *op. cit.,* p. 446.

21. Basing our statistics on the nearest provincial election in each instance does produce some significant deviations from persistent historical patterns in several provinces, notably Saskatchewan and Newfoundland. In both instances, a recently resurgent provincial Conservative party affects considerably the ranking of the province on these measures, but the choice of the most recent election has the advantage of being the point in time nearest the 1974 federal election when our data were collected. The volatility of some provincial party systems in recent years necessarily complicates our analysis, but is itself a phenomenon to be considered in interpreting data reported in this chapter.

22. The sequence employed in the 1965 and 1968 Canadian studies was: "Generally speaking, do you usually think of yourself as Conservative, Liberal, Social Credit, Créditiste, NDP, Union Nationale, or what? . . . When you say that you are a _____, are you thinking of national politics, politics here in this province, or both? . . . (If "national") Well, how about politics here in _____? How do you think of yourself? (If "provincial") Well, how about national politics? How do you think of yourself?" The 1967 Australian sequence was similar to this.

23. Of the 13% who indicated that they identified or leaned toward a party at only one level, 11% stated that their reference was to the federal level, while only 2% named the provincial level.

24. See Appendix B, Q. 30-31 and Q. 60-62.

25. However, our distribution of these split identifiers contains more provincial identifiers than did the previous study. We find 7.0% federal-only and 7.4% provincial-only identifiers.

26. We have retained the three-point intensity measure (strong-medium-weak) in preference to the simpler (strong-weak) dichotomy because it can be shown empirically that the differences between the "very strong" and "fairly strong" respondents are, when measured by a number of other attitudinal items, at least as great as are the differences between the "fairly strong" and "weak" groupings.

27. Our treatment of cross-level variations in intensity is conceptually similar to a recent longitudinal investigation of "intraparty" variations in intensity of partisanship in the United States for waves of the 1956-1960 panel study. See Douglas Dobson and Douglas St. Angelo, "Party Identification and the Floating Vote," *American Political Science Review*, 69 (1975), pp. 481-90.

28. Because we are working here with relatively small percentages, considerations of sampling error are particularly important. However, the fact that the percentages are based on all party identifiers provides a large enough group to lend a reasonable degree of accuracy and reliability to the figures for all but the smallest provinces. See Appendix A for appropriate confidence limits.

29. The percentages in this table are based on the total "N" of consistent identifiers (*1519*) and split identifiers (*414*). For comparison with other tables, the percentages can be re-computed on the base of all party identifiers by dividing any cell frequency by the total "N" of *2258*.

30. Because a disproportionate number of the split identifiers are in Quebec and in the Western provinces, the salience of provincial as opposed to federal politics and government is undoubtedly a factor here. In response to a question asking respondents whether they "felt closer" to the federal government or to the provincial government, a majority of Westerners and a plurality of Quebeckers mentioned their provincial government. (See discussion of this item in Chapter 3). Only in Ontario did a majority mention the federal government in response to this item.

31. Throughout this section "stability" and "instability" are measured by the answer to a question asking respondents to remember past partisanship. (See Appendix B, Q. 32 and Q. 62.)

32. These are, in fact, comparable to the high rates of stability reported for the American electorate of the 1950s. See Campbell et al., *The American Voter, op. cit.*, Table 7.2, p. 148.

33. This is quite different from the past U.S. patterns. In 1956, 90% of strong American party identifiers reported they had never changed their party. *Ibid.*

34. See Jane Jenson, *op. cit.*, pp. 543-55.

35. This is more than three times higher than the rate of change reported for a comparable time period in American politics. See Dobson & St. Angelo, *op. cit.*, Table 1, p. 484.

36. It is interesting to note that there is little relationship between age and either stability or the time at which the change occurred. The age/stability relationship in 1974 was statistically insignificant.

37. Philip E. Converse, "The Concept of the Normal Vote," in Campbell et al., *Elections and the Political Order*, pp. 9-40.

38. *Ibid.*, p. 33.

39. *Ibid.*, p. 41.

40. *Ibid.*, pp. 76-7.

41. See Appendix B, Q. 44.

42. The N for the stable group is *1439* and *766* for the unstable group.

43. See Appendix B, Q. 49.

44. The N for the very strong group equals *193* and for the very strong unstable groups it is *71*.

45. A very similar pattern emerges from a comparable analysis of the 1965 election data. Respondents were asked their hypothetical reaction if their own party adopted a policy position which they did not like. Within all categories of intensity of party identification, the unstable partisans were much more likely to say they would vote for another party under those conditions. The stable partisans were much more equivocal and would either abstain or say "it depends." The largest differences were for the very strong identifiers. See Jane Jenson, *Party Identification in Canada: A Rationally Limited Allegiance*, unpublished Ph.D. dissertation, University of Rochester, 1974, p. 163.

APPENDIX 5A

Concentrations of Some Groups of Split and Single-Level Party Identifiers,
By Province (as percentage of all party identifiers in province)
The provincial party is named first.

British Columbia (N = 234)

Social Credit–Conservative (11.1)
Social Credit–Liberal (8.5)
NDP–Liberal (8.5)
Fed. Liberal only (4.7)
Prov. NDP only (4.7)
Prov. Social Credit only (3.5)
NDP–Conservative (3.0)
Fed. Conservative only (1.7)
NDP–Social Credit (0.9)
Prov. Conservative only (0.9)
Conservative–Liberal (0.9)
Liberal–Conservative (0.9)
Conservative–NDP (0.4)
Liberal–NDP (0.4)
Fed. NDP only (0.4)

Saskatchewan (N = 89)

NDP–Conservative (7.9)
NDP–Liberal (7.9)
Prov. NDP only (5.6)
Liberal–Conservative (4.5)
Fed. Liberal only (3.4)
Prov. Liberal only (2.2)
Prov. Conservative only (2.2)

Ontario (N = 649)

Fed. Liberal only (6.3)
Conservative–Liberal (6.0)
Fed. Conservative only (2.3)
Prov. Conservative only (2.2)
Prov. Liberal only (2.2)
Fed. NDP only (1.9)
NDP–Liberal (1.4)
Liberal–Conservative (1.2)
Liberal–NDP (1.1)
Prov. NDP only (0.6)
Conservative–NDP (0.5)
Other (0.3)

New Brunswick (N = 120)

Prov. Conservative only (4.2)
Fed. Liberal only (4.2)
Conservative–Liberal (2.5)
Liberal–Conservative (1.7)
Federal Conservative only (1.7)
Conservative–NDP (0.8)

Alberta (N = 165)

Conservative–Liberal (15.8)
Prov. Conservative only (6.1)
Social Credit–Conservative (4.8)
Fed. Liberal only (2.4)
Fed. Conservative only (1.2)
Fed. NDP only (1.2)
Prov. Social Credit only (1.2)
Liberal–Conservative (0.6)
Conservative–NDP (0.6)
NDP–Liberal (0.6)
Social Credit–Liberal (0.6)
Social Credit–NDP (0.6)

Manitoba (N = 103)

NDP–Liberal (9.7)
NDP–Conservative (5.8)
Conservative–Liberal (2.9)
Prov. NDP only (2.9)
Fed. Conservative only (2.9)
Prov. Conservative only (2.9)
Liberal–Conservative (1.9)
Fed. NDP only (1.0)
Other (1.0)

Quebec (N = 654)

Parti Québécois–Liberal (6.4)
Parti Québécois only (4.6)
Parti Québécois–NDP (4.4)

Quebec (con't)

Prov. Liberal only (3.8)
Fed. Liberal only (2.6)
Union Nationale–Conservative (2.2)
Liberal–Social Credit (1.7)
Social Credit–Liberal (1.5)
Union Nationale–Liberal (1.5)
Parti Québécois–Conservative (1.4)
Parti Québécois–Social Credit (1.4)
Fed. Conservative only (1.2)
Liberal–Conservative (1.2)
Prov. Social Credit only (1.1)
Fed. Social Credit only (0.9)
Social Credit–Conservative (0.6)
Liberal–NDP (0.6)
Union Nationale only (0.5)
Social Credit–NDP (0.2)

Nova Scotia (N = 167)

Liberal–Conservative (3.6)
Conservative–Liberal (2.4)

Nova Scotia (con't)

Prov. Conservative only (2.4)
Conservative–NDP (1.2)
Liberal–NDP (1.2)
Prov. Liberal only (1.2)
Fed. Conservative only (1.2)
Fed. Liberal only (0.6)
Other (0.6)

Prince Edward Island (N = 84)

Fed. Liberal only (4.8)
Prov. Liberal only (3.6)
Liberal–Conservative (2.4)
Conservative–Liberal (1.2)
Prov. Conservative only (1.2)

Newfoundland (N = 96)

Conservative–Liberal (4.2)
Fed. NDP only (2.1)
Conservative–NDP (2.1)
Prov. Conservative only (1.0)
Fed. Conservative only (1.0)
Fed. Liberal only (1.0)

APPENDIX 5B

Variations in Intensity of Party Identification for Consistent Party Identifiers, by Province (as percentage of all party identifiers in province)

N=	Province	Fully Consistent	Stronger Federal	Strong Provincial
234	British Columbia	33.8	6.4	9.0
	Liberals	13.2	3.4	4.3
	Conservatives	4.7	2.6	2.1
	NDP	14.5	0.4	2.1
	Social Credit	1.3	—	0.4
654	Quebec	38.5	10.4	11.3
	Liberal	33.9	9.5	9.5
	Conservative	0.9	0.2	—
	NDP	0.3	—	—
	Social Credit	0.4	0.8	1.5

N =	Province	Fully Consistent	Stronger Federal	Strong Provincial
103	Manitoba	38.8	12.6	17.5
	Liberal	10.7	4.9	3.9
	Conservative	18.4	5.8	6.8
	NDP	9.7	1.9	6.8
165	Alberta	40.6	10.3	13.3
	Liberal	10.9	3.0	2.4
	Conservative	24.8	6.1	9.1
	NDP	3.0	—	1.2
	Social Credit	1.8	1.2	0.6
89	Saskatchewan	43.8	12.4	10.1
	Liberal	20.2	2.2	3.4
	Conservative	9.0	5.6	—
	NDP	14.6	4.5	6.7
649	Ontario	49.0	12.8	12.2
	Liberal	23.7	7.4	5.9
	Conservative	18.3	3.5	4.6
	NDP	6.9	1.8	1.5
120	New Brunswick	61.7	8.3	15.0
	Liberal	38.3	4.2	10.0
	Conservative	21.7	4.2	3.3
	NDP	1.7	—	0.8
96	Newfoundland	62.5	15.6	10.4
	Liberal	47.9	9.4	4.2
	Conservative	13.5	6.3	5.2
	NDP	1.0	—	1.0
167	Nova Scotia	62.9	9.0	13.8
	Liberal	34.1	4.8	4.8
	Conservative	24.0	3.6	7.8
	NDP	4.8	0.6	1.2
84	Prince Edward Island	64.3	9.5	13.1
	Liberal	41.7	3.6	9.5
	Conservative	20.2	6.0	3.6
	NDP	2.4	—	—
2258	Total CANADA	44.3	11.0	11.9
	Liberal	25.3	6.8	6.4
	Conservative	12.2	2.9	3.4
	NDP	5.6	1.0	1.5
	Social Credit	1.2	0.3	0.6

APPENDIX 5C
Direction, Intensity, and Stability of Federal Partisanship

(as per cent of total national sample[a])

Direction of Partisanship

	None	Liberal	Progressive Conservative	NDP	Social Credit	Total
Intensity						
Very Strong	—	16	7	4	1	28
Fairly Strong	—	23	11	5	1	40
Weak	—	11	6	2	1	20
—	12	—	—	—	—	12
						100%
Stability						
Stable	9	33	15	6	2	64
Unstable	3	17	9	5	1	36
						100%
Consistency						
Fully Consistent	5	24	12	6	1	48
Partly Consistent	—	13	6	2	1	22
Inconsistent	7	13	6	3	1	30
						100%
Deviations Index						
0	—	23	9	4	1	37
1	4	16	10	4	1	35
2	6	8	4	2	1	21
3	2	3	1	1	0	7
						100%

[a]Missing data excluded. N = *2343*

Chapter Six

Images of Political Parties

Canadian political scientists have long felt that understanding the "images" which individuals hold of political parties and other political objects can contribute significantly to our ability to comprehend the fundamental elements of electoral behaviour in Canada. In his work on the 1968 election, John Meisel argued that party images might provide the key to separating out the long-term, more stable components of the vote in federal elections, akin to the contribution of party identification to voting research in the United States.[1] Employing a semantic differential technique,[2] Meisel measured the positions of the four political parties and of an "ideal" party on a number of specific image dimensions in 1965 and 1968 (see Figure 6.1).[3] Instead of finding that party images were relatively stable and enduring, however, Meisel's scales reflected the surge of the Liberal party in 1968, registering statistically significant changes on eight of the ten dimensions shown in Figure 6.1.[4] His findings, coupled with our analysis of the nature and content of party images which we will present in this chapter, are suggestive of greater volatility and sensitivity to short-term fluctuations than may previously have been supposed. Similarly, the relationship of individuals' images of political parties to the characteristics of partisanship discussed in the preceding chapter is consistent with some of our findings regarding the nature of Canadians' ties to political parties.

While it has been argued that the concept of party image is useful in electoral research, there is little agreement on specifics of measurement and analysis. Most measures of party images which might be employed suffer from one or more limitations, which may cause the concept to fall short of its theoretical and empirical promise. But the several types of data now available on the subject of political party images are capable of providing a greater understanding of the nature of the images

172   *Political Choice in Canada*

which Canadians hold of their political parties, and of the linkages between such images and the several components of partisanship discussed in the preceding chapter.

While there is no reason to believe that Canadians are any more politicized or politically articulate than are citizens of other Western democracies, the extent to which our survey respondents were able to articulate an image of *some* political party, either at the federal or provincial level, was impressive.[5] To be sure, the proportion of our respondents holding or able to describe a specific image of a *particular* party was predictably low in many instances. Nevertheless, fully 91% of the national sample were able to provide our interviewers with a spontaneous description of the basis for their feelings about at least one party at one of the two levels of government. Eighty-six per cent of the sample held an image of some kind of at least one of the federal political parties, with a slightly smaller percentage (81%) articulating an image of one or more provincial parties.

The images that Canadians hold of their political parties are, in their own way, rich and varied, and can yield much data on the public's conceptualization of the party system and its underpinnings. The national sample had a mean of 6.8 images per respondent — more than 17 000

FIGURE 6.1
Mean Scores of Three Federal Political Parties and an "Ideal" Party on Ten Semantic Differential Scales, 1965

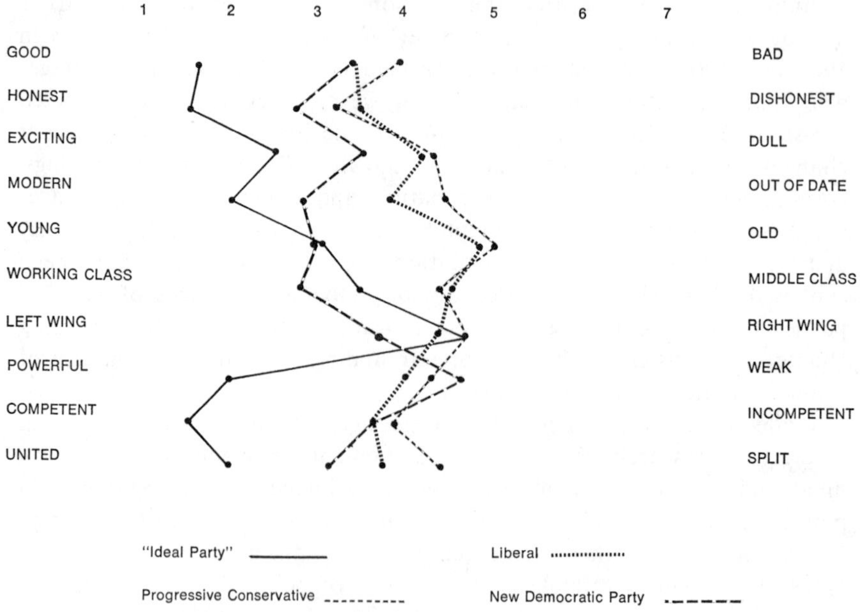

"Ideal Party" ————   Liberal ....

Progressive Conservative _____   New Democratic Party .— — — —

Source: Meisel, *Working Papers in Canadian Politics*, pp. 64-71.

individual bits of data.[6] For illustration, let us consider the responses of four "typical" members of our sample. There are, of course, some dangers in singling out particular sets of responses as "typical," but illustrative responses can often provide considerable insight into the statistics presented. One of our respondents, Agnes Woolhaven of Toronto, is, in many ways, such a typical respondent. She is 44 years old, has a Grade 11 education, is married to a draughtsman employed by the provincial government, and has two children. Although not highly articulate in discussing politics, Mrs. Woolhaven's images of political parties are well formed and she is "very interested" in politics. She is a moderately partisan Liberal, and her partisanship is to a certain extent reflected in her perceptions of the parties. She voted Liberal in the 1974 election. Here is how Mrs. Woolhaven responded to our queries concerning party images:

Now I would like to ask you what you personally think are the good and bad points about political parties at the federal level in Canada. Is there anything in particular that you like about the federal Liberal party?
"Oh, there are a number of things — the leader, their policies, the way they are running the country."
Anything else?
"No, those are the main things."
Is there anything in particular that you dislike about the federal Liberal party?
"I do think they tend to lean toward the French and bilingualism, but I don't think it is that major an issue."
Anything else?
"No."
Is there anything in particular that you like about the federal Progressive Conservative party?
"Not really, no."
Is there anything in particular that you dislike about the federal Progressive Conservative party?
"They are always cutting up the Liberals, and they don't seem to come up with any better solutions of their own."
Anything else?
"No."
Is there anything in particular that you like about the federal New Democratic Party?
"They are a lot for the working man."
Anything else?
"They are trying to give working people a fair deal."
Is there anything in particular that you dislike about the federal NDP?
"I don't like their leader too much."
Anything else?
"They are not a strong enough party yet to get things across."

Is there anything in particular that you like about the federal Social Credit party?
"No."
Is there anything in particular that you dislike about the federal Social Credit party?
"Well, they are a lot for the French-speaking people of the country too."
Anything else?
"No."
. . . Now I would like to ask you what you personally think are the good and bad points about political parties at the provincial level here in Ontario. Let's start with the provincial Progressive Conservative party. Is there anything in particular that you like about the provincial Progressive Conservative party here in Ontario?
"Nothing."
Is there anything in particular that you dislike about the provincial Progressive Conservative party?
"Just about everything. Spending too much money — Ontario Place, for example. It should go more for education and housing."
Anything else?
"I didn't think the Spadina Expressway should be stopped. Toronto needs better transportation.'
Is there anything in particular that you like about the provincial Liberal party here in Ontario?
"Nothing. It's been Conservative for so long that we really don't know much about them."
Is there anything in particular that you dislike about the provincial Liberal party?
"No."
Is there anything in particular that you like about the New Democratic Party here in Ontario?
"Nothing."
Is there anything in particular that you dislike about the provincial NDP?
"No. I don't know encugh about them."

Another of our "typical" respondents whose answers to the extended series of party-image questions can provide some useful illustrations is Mike Borchak, a 38-year-old machinist who lives in Dartmouth, Nova Scotia. Mr. Borchak is married, has a family, and completed high school. Like Mrs. Woolhaven, he is a Liberal, but his partisanship is weak and unstable and he says that he does not follow politics very closely. Mr. Borchak also voted Liberal in 1974.

Now I would like to ask you what you personally think are the good and bad points about political parties at the federal level in Canada. Is there anything in particular that you like about the federal Liberal party?
"They never seem to get going. They have good ideas but can't seem to get going on them."
Anything else?

"They do have a fairly decent foreign policy."
"They could be doing a lot more about the cost of living."
Anything else?
"No."
Is there anything in particular that you like about the federal Progressive Conservative party?
"I liked the idea of wage and price controls that they had in the election."
Anything else?
"No."
Is there anything in particular that you dislike about the federal Progressive Conservative party?
"No."
[MR. BORCHAK GAVE NO RESPONSES TO QUESTIONS ON THE FEDERAL NDP AND SOCIAL CREDIT PARTIES.]
. . . Now I would like to ask you what you personally think are the good and bad points about political parties at the provincial level here in Nova Scotia. Let's start with the provincial Progressive Conservative party. Is there anything in particular that you like about the provincial Progressive Conservative party here in Nova Scotia?
"No."
Is there anything in particular that you dislike about the provincial Progressive Conservative party?
"John Buchanan just doesn't do anything for me. I just don't like the man."
Anything else?
"No."
Is there anything in particular that you like about the provincial Liberal party here in Nova Scotia?
"In the last election they did stop oil and gas prices from going up."
Anything else?
"No."
Is there anything in particular that you dislike about the provincial Liberal party?
"No, I can't say there's anything in particular."
[MR. BORCHAK HAD NO OPINIONS REGARDING THE PROVINCIAL NEW DEMOCRATIC PARTY.]

Joan Miller, a young registered nurse in Prince George, British Columbia, differs from Mrs. Woolhaven and Mr. Borchak in several important ways, but her responses to the party image questions also fall within a range that might be considered "typical." She is "fairly interested" in politics, but considers herself an "Independent." She voted for the first time in 1972, and voted Conservative in the 1974 federal election.

Now I would like to ask you what you personally think are the good and bad points about political parties at the federal level in Canada. Is there anything

in particular that you like about the federal Progressive Conservative party?
"Well, they've been a good opposition party."
Anything else?
"No."
Is there anything in particular that you dislike about the federal Progressive Conservative party?
"No."
Is there anything in particular that you like about the federal Liberal party?
"Can't think of anything."
Is there anything in particular that you dislike about the federal Liberal party?
"I'm not too stuck on LIP grants. Too much of it. A lot of waste."
Anything else?
"No."
Is there anything in particular that you like about the federal New Democratic Party?
"No, I can't think of anything at the moment."
Is there anything in particular that you dislike about the federal NDP?
"No."
Is there anything in particular that you like about the federal Social Credit party?
"No."
Is there anything in particular that you dislike about the federal Social Credit party?
"Don't think they're that strong. Not really in the running."
. . . Now I would like to ask you what you personally think are the good and bad points about political parties at the provincial level here in British Columbia. Let's start with the provincial New Democratic Party. Is there anything in particular that you like about the provincial New Democratic Party here in British Columbia?
"I like their Auto plan."
Anything else?
"Our resources — like mining. I liked the way they looked after them."
Is there anything in particular that you dislike about the provincial NDP?
"They're getting a bit out of touch with the people."
Anything else?
"No."
Is there anything in particular that you like about the provincial Social Credit party here in British Columbia?
"No."
Is there anything in particular that you dislike about the provincial Social Credit party?
"They were really out of touch with the people."
Anything else?
"No."
Is there anything in particular that you like about the provincial Liberal party here in British Columbia?
"Well, Anderson isn't too bad a guy."

Anything else?
"No."
Is there anything in particular that you dislike about the provincial Liberal party?
"No."
Is there anything in particular that you like about the provincial Progressive Conservative party here in British Columbia?
"No, we don't really have them out here, so I don't have any comment about them."
Is there anything in particular that you dislike about the provincial Progressive Conservative party?
"No, they didn't run in this riding."

Our fourth illustrative respondent is, in many respects, quite atypical of the national sample as a whole, but his responses are nevertheless useful in portraying the nature of the party image data and its interaction with partisanship at both levels of the federal system. Gérard Bujold is a young high school teacher in Sherbrooke, Quebec, who until recently had supported the Union Nationale in provincial elections and the Liberal party federally. He is now a strong supporter of the Parti Québécois in provincial politics, and identifies himself as an "Independent" at the federal level. Mr. Bujold was one of a small number of respondents in our Quebec sample who reported deliberately spoiling a ballot in the 1974 federal election as a form of protest. Although articulate and knowledgeable in his discussion of both federal and provincial parties, Mr. Bujold professes to have little interest in politics generally and "no interest whatever" in the 1974 federal election. His attitudes toward parties are closely related to his partisanship, and they reflect both his present and past party ties. He differentiates clearly between the federal and provincial levels with respect to all of the parties.

[translation]
Now I would like to ask you what you personally think are the good and bad points about political parties at the federal level in Canada. Is there anything in particular that you like about the federal Liberal party?
"The way they try to give a fair share to each province, to treat each one equally and with justice."
Anything else?
"Their efforts to bring about bilingualism. They have to be given credit."
Is there anything in particular that you dislike about the federal Liberal party?
"There are some provinces that are more equal than the others, and it seems to be getting that way more all the time."
Anything else?
"No."
Is there anything in particular that you like about the federal Progressive Conservative party?

"The way they have gone after the government on the subject of inflation. They are more likely to take action when there is pressure from the Opposition."
Anything else?
"No."
Is there anything in particular that you dislike about the federal Progressive Conservative party?
"No."
Is there anything in particular that you like about the federal New Democratic Party?
"Their strategy, and the positions that they have taken with regard to the government. They are the ones who have been in a position to decide whether the government would continue or not."
Anything else?
"No."
Is there anything in particular that you dislike about the federal NDP?
"No."
Is there anything in particular that you like about the federal Social Credit party?
"No."
Is there anything in particular that you dislike about the federal Social Credit party?
"Sometimes they like to try and speak for all of Quebec, but they are not really very representative."
Anything else?
"No."
. . . Now I would like to ask you what you personally think are the good and bad points about political parties at the provincial level here in Quebec. Let's start with the Liberal party. Is there anything in particular that you like about the provincial Liberal party here in Quebec?
"No."
Is there anything in particular that you dislike about the provincial Liberal party?
"Yes, I don't like their policies on language, and on foreign investment."
Anything else?
"The way they always bend before the federal government. And it's a bad electoral system that gives them so many seats when they don't have a very big percentage of the vote. It should be changed."
Is there anything in particular that you like about the provincial Social Credit party?
"Their members are close to the people of their communities. That is a good thing."
Anything else?
"No."
Is their anything in particular that you dislike about the provincial Social Credit party?
"There is a lot of disunity in the party."

Anything else?
"No."
Is there anything in particular that you like about the Parti Québécois here in Quebec?
"I am in favour of independence, so I like their position on that."
Anything else?
"Their nationalist position, their positions vis-à-vis the economy of Quebec and on the sovereignty of the language. Everything."
Is there anything in particular that you dislike about the Parti Québécois?
"No."
Is there anything in particular that you like about the Union Nationale here in Quebec?
"No."
Is there anything in particular that you dislike about the Union Nationale?
"The ambiguity of their policies. And I don't like some of the political tendencies of the party."
Anything else?
"No."

Two essential characteristics of the party image data are evident from both Tables 6.1 and 6.2 and the illustrative responses cited above. First, respondents' images of provincial parties are nearly as strong and fully developed as are their images of federal parties. The percentages of the national sample holding an image of *both* provincial and federal parties ranges from a high of 85% in British Columbia to a low of 45%

TABLE 6.1

Distribution of Images of the Federal and Provincial Parties

	%	MEAN NUMBER OF IMAGES
Have an image of a political party	91	6.8
Have an image of a federal party	86	3.8
Have an image of a provincial party	81	3.0
Have an image of one's own party[a]	81	1.6
Have an image of a party other than one' own	77	2.5
Have a positive image of one's own party	74	1.1
Have a negative image of a party other than one's own	69	1.6
Have a positive image of a party other than one's own	54	1.0
Have a negative image of one's own party	42	0.5
	N = *2445*	

[a]"Own" party and "other" party here refer to federal parties only. Percentages based on federal identifiers only. (N = *2088*).

TABLE 6.2

Federal and Provincial Party Images, by Province
(row percentages)

	NONE	FEDERAL ONLY	PROVINCIAL ONLY	BOTH	MEAN NUMBER OF IMAGES FEDERAL	PROVINCIAL	N
NATIONAL	9%	11	5	76	3.8	3.0	*2445*
New-foundland	28%	12	15	45	1.4	1.3	102
P.E.I.	20%	9	6	65	2.5	1.8	97
Nova Scotia	9%	16	8	67	3.2	2.2	180
New Brunswick	3%	10	4	84	3.6	2.5	134
Quebec	5%	5	5	85	3.9	3.9	702
Ontario	9%	17	3	71	4.2	2.5	702
Manitoba	8%	10	6	76	3.8	2.6	113
Saskatche-wan	17%	10	4	69	3.6	2.2	101
Alberta	12%	10	6	73	3.5	2.7	179
B.C.	5%	5	5	85	4.5	4.4	252

in Newfoundland, while the percentage of respondents holding provincial party images (independently of federal) similarly ranges from 90% in British Columbia to 60% in Newfoundland (see Table 6.2). The same figures for the entire national sample are 76% and 81% respectively. This finding is not unexpected in view of the observation made in Chapter Five regarding the strength and salience of provincial partisanship, and our earlier discussion of orientations toward the federal system. The party image data provide further documentation of the significance of the provincial level of politics for many Canadians, and of their ability to distinguish between and relate to each of the two levels of government. All four of our illustrative respondents converse as easily about provincial parties as about federal ones, and three of them exhibit somewhat sharper and more articulate images of the provincial parties. Although not all of our respondents distinguish as clearly between federal and provincial parties as do Mr. Bujold or Miss Miller, a substantial number of them do. There are many respondents who, like Mr. Borchak, sustain a positive image of a federal party, together with a negative image of the party of the same name at the provincial level, separating them along clearly different dimensions. There are also many respondents like Mrs. Woolhaven who, in spite of her Liberal partisanship, is unable to articulate any image of the provincial Liberal party in Ontario. It is not surprising, then, to find, as we shall argue later, that federal and provincial parties are capable of establishing quite independent and often very different images of themselves in the voters' minds.

All four of our illustrative respondents showed considerable sophistication in distinguishing between federal and provincial parties. The overall effect of this is a clear separation of both the strength and content of the images projected by political parties at different levels. Thus, although 77% of the national sample held *some* type of image of the federal Liberal party, the proportion of respondents in the various provinces able to articulate an image (positive *or* negative) of their provincial Liberal party ranges from a high of 77% in Quebec to a low of 27% in Alberta. Many provincial parties hold stronger images than do their federal counterparts in the same provinces. No fewer than 12 provincial parties yield a higher percentage of respondents holding an image of them than do the three federal opposition parties (see Table 6.3). In short, the party image data, like our analyses of partisanship and orientations to federalism, demonstrate clearly the salience of provincial politics. The images projected by various provincial parties are as rich and developed as are those at the federal level.

It may be seen in Table 6.3 that each province, except Newfoundland, has at least one of its provincial political parties in that group of 12 whose images we have classified here as "strong." Three provinces -- Quebec, New Brunswick, and British Columbia — have two provincial parties which project strong images. But, with the exceptions of the Parti Québécois, the Liberal Party in New Brunswick, and the Social Credit Party in British Columbia, all of the parties in this group were the governing parties of their respective provinces at the time of the 1974 survey. On the surface this may suggest nothing more than the greater visibility and impact of the governing party on everyday life — true at

TABLE 6.3

Distribution of Images of Specific Federal and Provincial Parties

PER CENT OF RESPONDENTS HAVING AT LEAST ONE IMAGE (POSITIVE OR
NEGATIVE) OF THE FEDERAL PARTIES

	%	MEAN NO. OF IMAGES
LIBERAL	77	1.5
P.C.	59	1.0
NDP	52	0.8
S.C.	33	0.5

PROVINCIAL PARTIES WITH STRONG IMAGES (MENTIONED BY OVER 50%
OF THE RESPONDENTS)

	%	MEAN
NDP (British Columbia)	89	2.1
LIBERAL (Quebec)	77	1.5
NDP (Manitoba)	76	1.5
P.C. (New Brunswick)	76	1.4
PARTI QUEBECOIS	74	1.3
P.C. (Alberta)	72	1.3
LIBERAL (Nova Scotia)	67	1.2
SOCIAL CREDIT (British Columbia)	67	1.3
NDP (Saskatchewan)	65	1.2
LIBERAL (New Brunswick)	65	1.0
P.C. (Ontario)	64	1.2
LIBERAL (P.E.I.)	62	1.0

PROVINCIAL PARTIES WITH RELATIVELY WEAK IMAGES
(MENTIONED BY 50% OR LESS OF THE RESPONDENTS)

	%	MEAN
P.C. (Nova Scotia)	48	0.7
P.C. (Newfoundland)	46	0.7
P.C. (P.E.I.)	45	0.6
LIBERAL (Saskatchewan)	45	0.7
SOCIAL CREDIT (Quebec)	44	0.6
LIBERAL (Ontario)	43	0.7
LIBERAL (B.C.)	43	0.6
SOCIAL CREDIT (Alberta)	40	0.7
LIBERAL (Newfoundland)	39	0.6
P.C. (Manitoba)	39	0.6
UNION NATIONALE	38	0.6
NDP (Ontario)	37	0.6
LIBERAL (Manitoba)	35	0.5
P.C. (British Columbia)	31	0.5
NDP (Alberta)	27	0.4
LIBERAL (Alberta)	27	0.3
P.C. (Saskatchewan)	23	0.3
NDP (Nova Scotia)	23	0.3
NDP (P.E.I.)	20	0.2
NDP (New Brunswick)	14	0.2
NDP (Newfoundland)	10	0.1

N = Nfld. — 102; P.E.I. — 97; N.S. — 180; N.B. — 134; Que. — 702;
Ont. — 702; Man. — 113; Sask. — 101; Alta. — 179; B.C. — 252;
Total N = *2445.*

both the provincial and federal levels. But close inspection of the rankings in Table 6.3 may give pause to this easy interpretation. In several provinces, parties not long *out* of power stand far down the list — the Liberal Party in Saskatchewan, for example, or the Social Credit Party in Alberta, or the Union Nationale. This may be suggestive of a quality of political party images heretofore not considered: their potential variability across time. Certainly our survey, timebound as are most studies of this type, cannot shed a great deal of light on the question of changes in the image projected by a given party. But the question is sufficiently intriguing to warrant further investigation and even some speculation, particularly in view of our hypothesized linkage betweeen party images and the nature of partisanship. Let us examine the characteristics of the party image data further, bearing in mind the potential significance of this point.

PARTY IMAGES AND PARTISANSHIP

A significant characteristic that stands out in an examination of the summaries of the party image responses is the extent to which the pattern of responses transcends the respondents' own partisanship. Certainly, our respondents were more likely to hold an image of that party with which they identified themselves than of any other, with 81% of federal party identifiers in the national sample articulating an image of their own party. But the proportion holding an image of another party (at the same level) is a nearly equal 77%, and the absolute number of images of other parties is greater on average than of one's own party (Table 6.1).[7] This in itself might not be thought surprising, for the probability of holding images of parties other than one's own is enhanced by the existence of three additional federal parties. What is important, however, is the rather large proportion of respondents who do not conform to the pattern of images that might be associated with the concept of party as a reference group for most voters. Strong, stable, and consistent psychological ties to one political party, for example, might be expected to operate in such a way as to produce a predominance of *positive* images of one's own party and *negative* or blank images of competing parties at the same level.[8] This selective perception or "screening" of information may cause conflicting information (e.g., negative images of one's own party) to be ignored and/or already existing positive attitudes to be reinforced.[9] An impressive 54% and 42% respectively of our sample hold an *opposite* pattern — that is, one or more positive images of parties other than one's own and/or negative images of one's own party. Like our two partisan respondents, Mrs. Woolhaven and Mr. Borchak, a large proportion of partisans have no apparent difficulty in identifying characteristics of their own parties that they tend to dislike, or, conversely, in singling out characteristics of competing parties to which they react positively. This has, in our view, considerable significance for the understanding of the basis of partisanship in Canada and of its importance in electoral behaviour.

A preliminary assessment of the linkages between party images and partisanship can be made by examining the number of federal and pro-vincial party images cited by various types of partisans (see Table 6.4).

TABLE 6.4

Partisanship and Party Images

Deviations from fully consistent, stable partisanship		% WITH FED. PARTY IMAGES	MEAN NO. OF FED. PARTY IMAGES	NO. OF MEAN % WITH PROV. PARTY IMAGES	MEAN NO. OF PROV. PARTY IMAGES	
	N					N
0	(850)	91	3.8	83	2.9	(974)
1	(797)	86	3.9	81	3.3	(765)
2	(459)	92	4.4	85	3.5	(424)
3	(142)	90	5.5	94	4.1	(86)

$F=17.8*$ $\qquad$ $F=10.8*$

Federal[a] $\qquad\qquad$ Provincial[b]

	%	Mean	N	%	Mean	N
Components of Partisanship						
Consistency						
Inconsistent	89	4.4	(1568)	86	3.6	(1568)
Consistent	86	3.6	(680)	79	2.9	(680)

$F=25.9*$ $\qquad\qquad$ $F=24.6*$

Stability						
Stable	85	3.6	(1474)	77	3.6	(1664)
Unstable	92	4.7	(775)	92	3.9	(584)

$F=80.9*$ $\qquad\qquad$ $F=87.2*$

Intensity						
Weak	83	4.1	(423)	77	2.9	(351)
Fairly strong	90	4.1	(927)	84	3.1	(930)
Very strong	93	4.2	(629)	90	3.5	(708)

$F=1.1$ $\qquad\qquad$ $F=30.3*$

*Significant at .01 level.
[a]Federal images and federal partisanship.
[b]Provincial images and provincial partisanship.

Analysis reveals that respondents whose pattern of partisanship involves instability and/or cross-level inconsistencies in intensity or direction have more party images than do those with stable, fully consistent, partisan allegiances. When the data are examined in terms of separate components of partisanship (Table 6.4), inconsistent and unstable partisans are again shown to have more federal and provincial party images. Interestingly, however, partisan intensity correlates positively with the number of party images — that is, those with strong partisan ties tend to have more federal and provincial party images than do those with weaker ties to parties at both levels.

Certain characteristics of partisanship and party images appear to fit neatly together. Our previous discussion in Chapter Five has documented the extent to which there exist in Canada individuals whose partisanship does not fit a stable, consistent model — that is, persons whose partisanship varies across level and/or across time. Regarding the relationship between variations in partisanship and party images, it would be tempting to offer a causal explanation, but it seems likely that the linkage between party images and partisanship is closer to an interactive one. Certainly, split partisans, or those whose partisanship relates only to one level, might be expected to exhibit a different pattern of images from those individuals whose partisanship is fully consistent across levels. On the other hand, there are also those whose images of parties would appear to be more susceptible to conditioning by their partisanship. Within the methodological constraints inherent in the use of cross-sectional data alone, it is possible to pursue somewhat further the linkages between partisanship and party images. Particularly relevant is a more intensive examination of party images with reference to patterns of response in terms of their own party/other party, and positive/negative distinctions. Patterning of these features of party images will be considered in terms of the three specific dimensions of partisanship discussed previously — that is, stability across time, intensity, and cross-level consistency.

Table 6.5 presents the results of a series of one-way analyses of variance, with the several party image variables analysed in terms of a summary measure of partisanship incorporating these three basic dimensions. Also included in the table are the percentages of respondents within each category of the partisanship variable with a particular type of party image. Inspection of the data reveals a pattern consistent with our expectations regarding the effects of partisanship on the formation of party images. While the percentage of respondents with images of other parties increases monotonically with increases in partisan deviations, an opposite pattern obtains for images (particularly positive images) of one's own party.

TABLE 6.5

Federal Party Image Variables by Deviations from Strong, Consistent, Stable Federal Partisanship

DEVIATIONS

		0	1	2	3	F
Own Party	Mean	1.6	1.6	1.7	1.8	3.9
	%	82	79	82	78	
Own Party Positive	Mean	1.1	1.0	1.0	1.0	1.7
	%	78	71	73	65	
Own Party Negative	Mean	0.5	0.5	0.6	0.9	14.6*
	%	37	43	48	64	
Other Party	Mean	2.2	2.5	2.7	3.7	20.0*
	%	74	78	83	87	
Other Party Positive	Mean	0.8	1.0	1.1	1.5	15.3*
	%	46	57	62	71	
Other Party Negative	Mean	1.4	1.5	1.8	2.2	14.5*
	%	65	68	75	82	
N=		*(850)*	*(797)*	*(459)*	*(142)*	

*Significant at .01 level.

Considering the intensity dimension of partisanship separately, the data reveal that intensity of partisanship has significant relationships with some, but not all, of the party image variables (Table 6.6). Particularly noteworthy are those relationships involving images of one's *own* party. Respondents with a strong sense of partisanship are both more likely to have an image of their own party generally, and a positive image in particular. In contrast, weak partisanship is positively associated with negative images of one's own party. Regarding images of other parties, the relationships are not significant, but one does find that, in percentage terms at least, there is a slight tendency for those wth strong party attachments to have more negative and fewer positive images of other parties. Overall, the observed pattern is basically consistent with at least part of the familiar argument regarding the flow of information — that is, strong partisans tend to have party images which emphasize the positive features of their party, with negative images of one's own party being found more frequently among weak partisans. By the same token, the inability of intensity to discriminate the richness of images of *other* parties is at odds with a hypothetical screening function of partisanship for many Canadians.

The idea that partisanship and party images are related is further strengthened when the party images are analysed in terms of the stability of partisanship. The data in Table 6.7 reveal a consistent pattern: respondents with unstable partisanship have richer images, both positive and

TABLE 6.6

Federal Party Image Variables by Intensity of Federal Partisanship

INTENSITY

		VERY STRONG	FAIRLY STRONG	WEAK	F
Own Party	Mean	1.7	1.6	1.5	5.9*
	%	86	81	73	
Own Party Positive	Mean	1.2	1.1	0.9	18.7*
	%	83	74	62	
Own Party Negative	Mean	0.5	0.6	0.6	6.7*
	%	38	43	48	
Other Party	Mean	2.5	2.5	2.6	1.8
	%	80	78	73	
Other Party Positive	Mean	1.0	1.0	1.0	0.9
	%	53	55	54	
Other Party Negative	Mean	1.6	1.5	1.6	2.1
	%	71	69	65	
N=		(*629*)	(*927*)	(*423*)	

*Significant at .01 level.

negative, of their own *and* other parties. While interpretations of this finding, in terms of the possible effects of partisanship on party images or vice versa, are somewhat speculative, the reason why some respondents have unstable party attachments may well be linked to the richness and diversity of their party images. For example, one could well imagine such respondents having been "pulled" across party lines by strong positive images of another party or, alternatively, being "pushed" away from a former partisan allegiance by negative images of that party.

This interpretation of the linkage between partisanship and party images is buttressed by our analysis of the party image data in terms of consistency of partisanship (Table 6.8). Inconsistent partisans — that is, those individuals whose partisanship differs in intensity or direction between the provincial and federal levels — tend to have richer party images than those respondents with consistent partisanship. Particularly

TABLE 6.7

Federal Party Image Variables by Stability of Federal Partisanship

		STABILITY		
		STABLE	UNSTABLE	F
Own Party	Mean	1.5	1.8	25.8*
	%	79	84	
Own Party Positive	Mean	1.0	1.1	6.2
	%	73	76	
Own Party Negative	Mean	0.5	0.7	29.9*
	%	38	50	
Other Party	Mean	2.3	3.0	51.5*
	%	73	86	
Other Party Positive	Mean	0.9	1.2	46.2*
	%	48	65	
Other Party Negative	Mean	1.4	1.8	25.6*
	%	64	77	
N=		(1474)	(775)	

*Significant at .01 level.

striking differences are evident with regard to both positive and negative images of one's own party. It may be suggested that a "screening" function of partisanship is partially or wholly obviated by the co-existence in Canada of separate federal and provincial party attachments. An alternate explanation, however, might be that, for reasons unrelated to the perceptual functions of partisanship, the inconsistent partisans simply have a larger amount of information about parties and, hence, a greater number of party images. Such individuals would make finer distinctions between parties at different levels of government and, hence, might manifest tendencies toward the development of variable federal and provincial partisan allegiances. In all likelihood, both processes outlined above are operative, or have operated in the past, for at least some of the inconsistent partisans in our sample.

Thus far, relationships between dimensions of partisanship and various aspects of federal party images have been examined by considering these one at a time. To better appreciate the linkages between partisanship and party images, however, it will be useful to see if respondents having particular types of partisanship have distinctive patterns of images of *both* their own and other parties. Specifically, if partisanship functions in varying degrees as a perceptual screen, distorting and/or tending to

TABLE 6.8

Federal Party Image Variables by Consistency of Federal Partisanship

CONSISTENCY

		CONSISTENT	INCONSISTENT	F
Own Party	Mean	1.5	1.7	4.4
	%	81	80	
Own Party Positive	Mean	1.0	1.0	0.4
	%	75	72	
Own Party Negative	Mean	0.5	0.6	16.6*
	%	40	48	
Other Party	Mean	2.3	3.0	36.3*
	%	76	83	
Other Party Positive	Mean	0.9	1.2	29.5*
	%	51	62	
Other Party Negative	Mean	1.5	1.8	22.9*
	%	67	74	
N=		*(1568)*	*(680)*	

*Significant at .01 level.

block out information about parties, one might expect that those with weak, unstable, or inconsistent partisan orientations would have a more detailed set of party images than respondents with strong, stable, and consistent partisanship. Moreover, in terms of patterns of party images held, one would expect the latter type of partisan to cite the positive aspects of their own party and negative features of other parties. Extending this same line of reasoning, the former group (the weak, unstable, inconsistents) might be more apt to mention negative qualities of their own party and positive aspects of other parties. Cross-tabulating various combinations of the party image variables, while controlling for specific types of partisanship, makes it possible to examine these expectations empirically.

Table 6.9 presents the percentages of respondents with images of *both* their own and other parties. Considering first the overall measure of deviations from fully consistent, strong, stable partisanship, it can be seen that the more deviations from such partisanship a respondent has, the more likely it is that the respondent will hold some images of *both* his/her own and other parties. The proposition that deviations from a pattern of strong, stable, consistent partisanship are associated with an increasing likelihood of having images of one's own and other parties is

TABLE 6.9

Images of Own and Other Parties by Partisanship (federal)

PERCENTAGES OF RESPONDENTS WITH IMAGES OF BOTH OWN AND OTHER PARTIES
BY VARIOUS MEASURES OF PARTISANSHIP

Number of Deviations*

0	1	2	3
66	69	73	77

Intensity*

Very Strong	Fairly Strong	Weak
73	69	63

Stability*

Stable	Unstable
64	78

Consistency*

Consistent	Inconsistent
67	73

PERCENTAGES OF RESPONDENTS WITH POSITIVE IMAGE(S) OF OWN PARTY AND
NEGATIVE IMAGE(S) OF OTHER PARTIES, BY VARIOUS MEASURES OF PARTISANSHIP

Number of Deviations*

0	1	2	3
60	57	56	55

Intensity*

Very Strong	Fairly Strong	Weak
63	57	49

Stability*

Stable	Unstable
54	64

Consistency*

Consistent	Inconsistent
56	61

PERCENTAGES OF RESPONDENTS WITH NEGATIVE IMAGE(S) OF OWN PARTY AND
POSITIVE IMAGE(S) OF OTHER PARTIES BY VARIOUS MEASURES OF PARTISANSHIP

Number of Deviations*

0	1	2	3
22	32	35	51

Intensity*

Very Strong	Fairly Strong	Weak
24	29	36

Stability*

Stable	Unstable
24	39

Consistency*

Consistent	Inconsistent
27	35

*Between group differences significant at .01 level.

clarified by further examination of each component of partisanship separately. Unstable and inconsistent partisans exhibit more images of their own and other parties, while strong rather than weak party attachments are associated with an increase in the probability of images of own and other parties. This finding is perhaps not unexpected, but it does serve to underscore that the intensity dimension of partisanship is related to party images in a fashion different from that of stability or consistency.

Looking at the own positive/other negative combination (Table 6.9), the data reveal that those with a "very strong" sense of partisanship are more likely (63% versus 49%) to have this particular combination of party images than are other groups, a pattern consistent with the hypothesized "screening" and "distortion" effects of partisanship for those respondents. However, respondents with unstable and/or inconsistent partisanship are also somewhat more likely to have the "own positive/other negative" party image combination.

The converse combination of types of party images — that is, own negative/other positive — shows that intensity of partisanship operates in a fashion consistent with the presumed perceptual screening and distortion functions of partisanship and opposite to the description above (Table 6.9). Specifically, weak partisans are more likely (36% versus 24%) to have a negative image of their own party in conjunction with a positive image of other parties, than are those with "very strong" partisan attachments. Additionally, unstable and inconsistent partisans tend to manifest the own negative/other positive combination more frequenty than do those with stable and consistent partisanship (39% versus 24% and 35% versus 27%, respectively). The summary measure of deviations from strong, stable, consistent partisanship likewise exhibits exactly opposite patterns for the two image combinations.

POLITICAL INTEREST

Party images of all types are also strongly correlated with the several measures of political interest and involvement which were included in the 1974 study. In particular, respondents were questioned regarding their interest in politics generally ("when there isn't a big election campaign going on") and also specifically with reference to the 1974 election. A composite measure[10] of political interest was then constructed from both variables, taking into account the fact that levels of political interest tend to be higher with reference to the election than with respect to "politics generally," and also that levels of interest vary between an election and other political events for many respondents. Most respondents in the survey differentiate between interest in the election and interest in politics, although the two sets of responses are, of course, strongly related.[11] The composite measure employed here is particularly appropriate to our examination of party images, because it takes into account both the long- and short-term characteristics of such images. As we will subsequently see, a substantial number of the party-image responses are distinctively short term in character, many of them related to specific elements of the election campaign. But the images projected by political parties may transcend a single event, such as an election, and thus may remain for a much longer period of time.[12] The images of parties developed by an individual during a period of relatively high political interest (e.g., an election) may well persist beyond that time into one of lower political interest and involvement. It is the level of an individual's interest at the time that the image is first developed, then, that is most likely to account for its formation. Or, as Converse has noted, the flow of information is partially a function of the voter's own motivation.[13]

As is seen in Table 6.10, party images of all types are strongly related to self-expressed levels of political interest. Voters with a high level of political interest are considerably more likely to hold a larger number of party images, particularly images of parties other than their own. This is, of course, not of itself a particularly surprising finding, and there are a number of intervening variables — in particular, education— which partly account for the strength of the relationship.[14] But it nevertheless indicates that highly involved (interested) voters are operating on a larger and more diversified sample of political information than are their less involved, less interested counterparts.[15]

It is important to the present analysis to discover that the level of information available to the voter in the form of the nature and content of party images is strongly related *both* to partisanship and to level of political interest. Political interest does not *explain* the characteristics of partisanship in Canada discussed earlier, but it accounts in part for the assemblage of the kind of political information which is meaningful for certain types of voters, and which may be at least a catalyst in accounting for processes of partisan and electoral change, a point that we shall explore further in a subsequent chapter.

TABLE 6.10

Party Images and Political Interest

COMPOSITE POLITICAL INTEREST[a]

		LOW	MODERATE	HIGH	F
All Federal Parties	Mean	3.0	4.2	5.1	126.1*
	%	81	90	94	
All Provincial Parties	Mean	2.4	3.3	3.9	75.9*
	%	73	84	90	
Own Party[b]	Mean	1.3	1.7	1.9	58.6*
	%	74	82	90	
Own Party Positive[b]	Mean	0.9	1.1	1.2	31.6*
	%	67	76	83	
Own Party Negative[b]	Mean	0.4	0.6	0.7	36.9*
	%	33	45	54	
Other Party[b]	Mean	1.9	2.8	3.3	88.9*
	%	69	81	87	
Other Party Positive[b]	Mean	0.8	1.1	1.3	31.9*
	%	47	58	65	
Other Party Negative[b]	Mean	1.1	1.7	2.1	94.5*
	%	57	74	81	
N =		(1117)	(632)	(696)	

*Significant at .01 level.
[a]Politics generally *and* 1974 federal election.
[b]Federal identifiers only (N = 2088).

CONTENT OF PARTY IMAGES

In addition to assessing the richness of party images, their variation across levels of government, and the linkages between party images, partisanship, and political interest, we wish to categorize the *content* of images that Canadians hold of political parties. Some suggestion of a typology emerges from our illustrative respondents. Mrs. Woolhaven, for example, tended to discuss parties largely in terms of group alignments, and to a certain extent in terms of specific policies. Mr. Borchak and Miss Miller both categorized parties mainly in terms of policies and leaders, and Mr. Bujold's responses, although they also were heavily policy oriented, included references to the relative performance of various parties and their political strengths and weaknesses. While these, of course, represent only a fraction of the possible patterns of response to these open-ended questions, they do provide a reasonably good illustration of several of the main categories of responses that were encountered in the data.

Being guided by the data themselves, rather than by any particular theoretical schema, we attempted to classify *responses* rather than *respondents,* recognizing the probability that many of our respondents hold images which would fit several types.[16] Our regrouping of the 1974 party image data into a basic typology is shown in Table 6.11, together with the percentage of the national sample who gave responses which fit each category. Certainly, there were many individual responses that do not fit our categories perfectly, or that might be subdivided into specific types within each. Nevertheless, this categorization presents a reasonably accurate picture of the images articulated by respondents, with respect to parties at both the federal and provincial levels.

TABLE 6.11

Percentages of 1974 National Sample Associating Political Parties with One or More Specific Image Dimensions[a]

	FEDERAL		PROVINCIAL	
	%	MEAN	%	MEAN
Policy/Issue	61	1.3	55	1.1
Style/Performance	47	0.8	44	0.8
Leadership/Leader	38	0.7	36	0.6
General	35	0.5	27	0.4
Area/Group	28	0.4	15	0.2
Ideology	14	0.2	7	0.1

[a]Multiple response. Each percentage is independent of all others, and is based on total weighted sample N of *2445.*

Several features of the categorization immediately stand out. Few Canadians are ideologues, "ideology" representing the smallest of our six main categories. Those who did give ideological responses were most likely to do so in reference to the NDP, either at the federal level or, to some extent, at the provincial level, especially in Manitoba or British Columbia. "Socialism" or "Communism" were terms that crept into these responses with some frequency, particularly on the negative side. For the small proportion of respondents who did give ideological responses to the party image items, such references were often applied to several parties. For example, one British Columbia respondent indicated his dislike of the British Columbia NDP thusly:

Is there anything in particular that you dislike about the provincial NDP?
"Yes. I don't like their ideas of power and the workers. Socialism doesn't have much standing in the Western world. They try to take over everything, but it doesn't work for the real benefit of the people."

Of the provincial Social Credit party, he said:

Is there anything in particular that you like about the provincial Social Credit party here in British Columbia?
"Well, they're a bit more to the right, more in favour of the free enterprise system."

Much more numerous were the respondents who characterized parties in issue or policy terms, with over 60% of the sample describing one or more federal parties in these terms, and a comparable 55% making policy references to provincial parties. Certainly, these policy references run the full gamut, from the most general to the most specific, and we have already encountered several of each type. Mrs. Woolhaven made a vague reference to the Liberals' "policies" as one basis for her liking of that federal party, and several more specific references to Ontario Place, education, housing, and the Spadina Expressway, with regard to the provincial Conservatives. Mr. Borchak referred to "foreign policy" and the "cost of living" when describing the federal Liberals, and made rather more specific references to "wage and price controls" and "oil and gas prices" in describing other parties. Miss Miller singled out federal LIP Grants and the British Columbia Auto Insurance Plan, even though her responses overall were quite general. Mr. Bujold mentioned a number of specific issues — bilingualism, inflation, separatism — in his discussion of the federal Liberal and Consevative parties, and also in his discussion of the Parti Québécois. There were also several less specific issue/policy references in his responses, such as his characterization of the Union Nationale as "ambiguous" in their policies. In short, the party image data are replete with issue and policy mentions, many of them quite specific in nature. Among those occurring more frequently

— inflation, wage and price controls, family allowances, pensions, welfare programs, unemployment insurance, and foreign policy were mentioned. Perhaps typical of some of the most issue-oriented respondents was the Alberta Conservative who described his own party, as well as several others, almost completely in issue/policy terms.

Is there anything in particular that you like about the federal Progressive Conservative party?
"I liked their stand on wage and price controls and also their position on bilingualism."
Anything else?
"Well, their stand on separatism. That's an important issue."
Is there anything in particular that you dislike about the federal Progressive Conservative party?
"Their stand on American investment. I don't approve of that."
Anything else?
"No."

The second largest number of responses fell into the category that we term "style" or "performance." Many of these responses were quite general in nature, phrases like "doing a good job," "capable," and "trying hard" being common. Some named more specific attributes: "progressive," "united," "inefficient," "incompetent." Mr. Bujold's characterization of the role played by the NDP in the minority Parliament would have been coded in this category, as would Miss Miller's somewhat more vague reference to the British Columbia Social Credit and NDP parties as "out of touch." Perhaps more typical of the type of response which most often fell into this category was that of the New Brunswick woman who said of the federal Liberals:

Is there anything in particular that you like about the federal Liberal party?
"No, I don't like the way they're running things in this country. They've run out of ideas and it's about time to give someone else a chance now."

While she expressed a liking for Mr. Stanfield, this respondent also said of the Conservatives:

Is there anything in particular that you dislike about the federal Progressive Conservative party?
"Yes. Their defeatist attitude."

About a third of the respondents mentioned leadership, the proportion in this group being about the same at both the federal and provincial levels. Most of these responses are quite straightforward, and three of our four illustrative respondents made at least one such reference. Some like Mrs. Woolhaven made very general references to "the leader" or "leadership," while others like Mr. Borchak or Miss Miller singled out specific individuals. Some members of the sample viewed politics almost entirely in terms of leaders, like the following rather agreeable respondent from Ontario:

Is there anything in particular that you like about the federal Liberal party?
"The whole group is pretty good — Trudeau — and most of the Cabinet ministers are high on the list, too."
Anything else?
"Trudeau represents us well in other countries."
Is there anything in particular that you dislike about the federal Liberal party?
"No, I don't think so."
Is there anything in particular that you like about the federal Progressive Conservative party?
"I like their leader, Mr. Stanfield."
Anything else?
"No, I don't think so."
Is there anything in particular that you dislike about the federal Progressive Conservative party?
"Well, I'm just not too sure about the Cabinet that he would have had."
Anything else?
"No, that's about it."
Is there anything in particular that you like about the federal New Democratic party?
"I rather like Mr. Lewis."
Anything else?
"No."
Is there anything in particular that you like about the federal Social Credit party?
"No, nothing in particular."
Is there anything in particular that you dislike about the federal Social Credit party?
"Their leader, Mr. Caouette."
Anything else?
"No."

Some responses to the party image questions are very general, and defy coding into clearly interpretable categories. These are grouped here under the heading "general," and taken together, they account for a significant proportion of all responses to the party image questions in the survey. Many of these are pure affect, or total like-dislike types of responses — "everything," "a lot of things," "not very much," and so forth. A slightly more specific grouping within this category mentioned the campaign, with frequently occurring references to "promises" or a tendency to be "unrealistic." A few of these come close to the "style" category. Still, another group within this category mentions the overall weakness of a party, or lumps it together with another party — "Well, they don't have much chance," or "They're just like the Liberals." In short, this "general" category contains a number of codeable responses which do not fit the five main categories, but which together exhibit the tendency on the part of the respondent to summarily express a liking or disliking for a particular party, based either on one's own partisanship or on the perception of the party system itself. Often, the probe would elicit at least one response in addition to the "general" one. Mr. Bujold, for example, stated that he liked "everything" about the Parti Québécois, but he also mentioned three specific characteristics of the party to which he was favourably disposed. While illustrative responses from this group tend to be potentially misleading, the following Nova Scotia respondent is fairly typical of at least one type of response that occurs with some frequency in the group. One of her responses would also have been coded in the style/performance category, but the overall level of conceptualization of political parties is generally low.

Is there anything in particular that you like about the federal Liberal party?
"Quite a bit. They've done a lot of good things for the country."
Is there anything in particular that you dislike about the federal Liberal party?
"Sometimes they evade critical issues, but I always thought that they were still the best party."
Anything else?
"No."
Is there anything in particular that you like about the federal Progressive Conservative party?
"No, they're too much like the Liberals in a lot of ways."

Yet another major category of responses were those that we have characterized as "area/group" responses — that is, those identifying a party with the interests of a particular group or a section of the country. This is the only category in which the federal and provincial responses sharply diverge, with more respondents associating federal parties with regional or group interests. Many of the responses in the federal group mention Quebec, or "the East," "the West," or various other regional designations such as those delineated in Chapter Two. Others associate a party with the interests of a particular ethnic, social, or economic group — the French, organized labour, big business, and farmers. Still other references were somewhat more general in nature — the "working class," "the people," and the "ordinary man."

It may be recalled that Mrs. Woolhaven gave several responses that were clearly of the area/group type when she identified the federal Liberal Party and Social Credit Party with the interests of French Canadians, and the federal NDP with "the workingman." Mr. Bujold felt that "some provinces were more equal than others" when it came to dealing with the federal government. Some respondents, such as the following man from Saskatchewan, tended to see politics almost exclusively in such terms, often combining regional and group references, particularly in their descriptions of federal parties.

Is there anything in particular that you like about the federal Liberal party?
"No."
Is there anything in particular that you dislike about the federal Liberal party?
"Yes. They're strictly for the East. They don't give a damn about Western Canada and they don't seem to care much about the average citizen."
Is there anything in particular that you like about the federal Progressive Conservative party?
"Well, they're a lot more of a people's party."
Anything else?
"I think they care about all of Canada."
Is there anything in particular that you dislike about the federal Progressive Conservative party?
"No."
Is there anything in particular that you like about the federal New Democratic Party?
"They seem to be a people's party also."
Anything else?
"No."
Is there anything in particular that you dislike about the federal NDP?
"I don't really know them well enough."

Only 28% of the respondents in the federal set and 15% in the provincial set gave responses that fell in this area/group category, making it, in each instance, the fifth of the six main categories, and surpassing only ideology among our six dimensions. The failure of area/group references to bulk large in the party image responses, particularly those dealing with federal parties, is perhaps surprising, given the historic importance of ethnic, religious, and regional cleavages in Canadian political life, and the presumed salience of inter-regional and inter-group differences in rates of support for various parties. Why the area/group responses are not more prominent is not immediately obvious. One might hypothesize that the area/group features of party images are largely subsumed in the policy/issue category — that is, Canadians do have strong area/group components in their party images, but that such images are cast in terms of the differential benefits and costs conferred on regions or groups by the policies pursued by various parties. A close examination of the content and frequency of mention of responses coded in the policy/issue category, however, does not sustain this proposition. An alternative interpretation, consistent with the tenor of much of the party image data, is that area/group responses are not particularly salient features of party images because such images tend to be tied to the more short-term aspects of Canadian politics. It is not logically necessary that area/group responses be conceptualized by the voters with reference to longer-term features of politics. However, the persistence over time of significant regional and inter-group cleavages in the Canadian polity does suggest that if, indeed, party images are geared to shorter-term, more ephemeral political phenomena, area/group responses would not be offered with any great frequency in response to queries about party images.

The inference that party images in Canada tend to be articulated in terms of the short-run, more variable aspects of politics is supported by an over-view of the party image data. In the distribution of our six main categories, the three highest (policy/issue, style/performance, and leadership) are all more likely to be subject to short-term fluctuations than are the types of responses found in the area/group and ideology categories. It is not our intent to argue that *all* policy, leadership, and like references are necessarily of a short-term variety, or, conversely, that area-group responses are by definition long-term. Certainly, it is possible to find the Newfoundland respondent who opposed Confederation in 1949 or an occasional Conservative mentioning the pipeline debate of 1956. But the orientation of these first three categories is overwhelmingly toward the present, our four illustrative respondents again being very typical in this regard. The issues that they mention are most often campaign issues, or issues which have received substantial recent exposure. The leaders are almost always the current party leaders, not the "great" leaders of a party's past. Performance is most often the performance of the governing party, not a party's long past record or events associated with previous times.[17]

To a large extent, this observation links up with our finding that the federal Liberal Party and the governing parties of each of the provinces tend to have sharper and more clearly focussed images. For these parties especially, policy mentions dwarf all other categories (Table 6.12). Once out of power, the image projected by a party appears capable of fading very rapidly or of being reshaped in a variety of ways, either by events or by the conscious design of new leaders.

While our cross-sectional data do not allow us to address directly the question of change over time in the nature and content of party images, the data are highly suggestive of considerable potential variability. It may be recalled that Meisel found significant changes occurring in his fixed image dimensions between 1965 and 1968, perhaps reflecting the changes in party leadership and the strength of the Liberals which occurred during that relatively short period.[18] It seems reasonable, then, to argue, both on the basis of the content of party images discerned in our open-ended measures and the explicit cross-time comparisons available in pre-

TABLE 6.12

Dimensions of Party Images for Federal Parties and Provincial Parties with Strong Images (as percentages of total national and provincial samples)[a]

FEDERAL	LEADERSHIP	IDEOLOGY	POLICY	AREA/GROUP	STYLE	GENERAL
Liberal	17	3	42	14	32	14
P.C.	24	3	24	8	17	13
NDP	10	10	24	13	13	12
Social Credit	9	3	12	3	8	10
PROVINCIAL						
B.C. NDP	10	7	67	12	39	7
Quebec Liberal	14	1	46	8	30	15
Manitoba NDP	10	7	58	12	20	8
New Brunswick P.C.	26	2	36	15	18	13
Parti Québécois	14	5	53	6	20	10
Alberta P.C.	33	1	41	8	17	16
Nova Scotia Liberal	18	1	38	4	22	11
B.C. Social Credit	22	3	33	37	35	11
Saskatchewan NDP	5	3	55	15	11	8
New Brunswick Liberal	30	1	18	5	20	8
Ontario P.C.	20	2	33	6	29	10
P.E.I. Liberal	20	1	30	5	21	10

[a]Multiple response. Percentages may total to more than 100%

N = Nfld. — 102; P.E.I. — 97; N.S. — 180; N.B. — 134; Que. — 702; Ont. — 702; Man. — 113; Sask. — 101; Alta. — 179; B.C. — 252; Total N = *2445*.

vious studies, that the images projected by political parties both at the federal and provincial levels may well be reflective of short-term phenomena associated with a party's policies, leadership, or governing position. If so, they may well be more sensitive to change than would otherwise be suspected. Certainly, the possibility of change in support for parties over relatively short periods of time is enhanced by findings which document the salience of leadership, issue, policy, and performance components in party images — components which are, by their very nature, apt to fluctuate over time. Moreover, our analysis of the relationship between party images and partisanship has implications for the previous discussion of the nature of partisanship in Canada. The analysis has shown that party images at both the federal and provincial levels are

associated with deviations from a model of stable and consistent partisanship, as well as with political interest. Respondents with high levels of
political interest, and those whose partisanship has been unstable across
time or inconsistent in either intensity or direction across level tend
to have more images of political parties, particularly of parties other
than their own, than do those with lower levels of interest or those whose
partisanship is stable and consistent. With regard to the specific components of partisanship, the number of party images is *negatively* associated with both stability and consistency, and positively associated with
intensity only with respect to a respondent's *own* party (Table 6.13).
Moreover, although party images are related to *both* partisanship and
political interest, the two relationships are quite independent of one
another, as the introduction of a control for political interest on the
partisanship variables demonstrates (Table 6.13). As we shall see subsequently, this is largely because political interest and partisanship are
independent, with persons of both high and low levels of political interest
being distributed among a number of partisan types.

The set of relationships between partisanship, political interest, and
party images is a highly suggestive one, and should be explored further
with respect to voting, the nature of election campaigns, and processes
of political change. As Converse has noted, "In a system where partisan
loyalties are fully developed, the volume of information flow may be
seen as an important governor upon the magnitude of oscillations in
party fortunes."[19] The question, however, as to whether these "interested"
voters, and those whose partisanship deviates from a model of stable
consistency, in holding higher levels of information about political parties,
will also be those who account for changes in electoral outcomes is a
more complex one that we will leave for subsequent discussion. Our
analysis in the past two chapters would clearly tend to suggest that neither
partisanship nor party images in Canada uniformly represent the kind
of long-term, stable forces in the political system that some may have
expected they should be, an expectation sometimes derived by implication from some of the now classic voting studies conducted in the United
States in the mid-1950s.[20] A model based on these assumptions would
predict the widespread existence of stable and consistent party attachments coupled with generalized and persistent images of parties, both
of which may have had their genesis in the events, personalities, and
issues of earlier time periods. We have, of course, found that there are
such individuals in the Canadian political system, and that they constitute a significant proportion of the electorate, a point to which we shall
return more fully in our discussion of electoral behaviour. But there
appear to exist a larger contingent of persons with less stable, less consistent party ties, whose images of parties are rooted in relatively short-

TABLE 6.13

Summary of Relationships Between Partisanship, Political Interest, and Party Image Variables

(PEARSON r. FIRST ORDER PARTIAL CONTROLLING FOR POLITICAL INTEREST SHOWN IN PARENTHESES FOR PARTISANSHIP VARIABLES)

NUMBER OF PARTY IMAGES OF:	COMPOSITE POLITICAL INTEREST	DEVIATIONS FROM STRONG STABLE, CONSISTENT PARTISANSHIP	COMPONENTS OF PARTISANSHIP		
			INTENSITY	STABILITY	CONSISTENCY
Federal	.30*	.21* (.19*)	.01 (−.03)	−.15* (−.13*)	−.14* (−.14*)
Provincial	.24*	.19* (.16*)	.02 (−.01)	−.09* (−.07*)	−.14* (−.11*)
Own Party	.24*	.12* (.10*)	.05 (.01)	−.11* (−.08*)	−.05 (−.05)
Own Party Positive	.19*	.05 (.03)	.15* (.12*)	−.05 (−.03)	.00 (.00)
Own Party Negative	.19*	.14* (.12*)	−.08* (−.11*)	−.12* (−.10*)	−.09* (−.09*)
Other Party	.27*	.22* (.20*)	−.02 (−.05)	−.15* (−.13*)	−.15* (−.15*)
Other Party Positive	.16*	.19* (.18*)	−.02 (−.03)	−.14* (−.13*)	−.13* (−.13*)
Other Party Negative	.29*	.18* (.16*)	−.01 (−.04)	−.12* (−.12*)	−.12* (−.13*)

*Significant at .01 level.

term party characteristics, and who may sustain a high enough level of political interest and involvement to maintain a flow of information about two or more political parties. If party images are an important element in the linkage of partisanship, political interest, and electoral behaviour in Canada, it is not because they constitute a stable, long-term element of the Canadian political psyche, but rather precisely because they do not.

FOOTNOTES

1. John Meisel, *Working Papers in Canadian Politics* (Montreal: McGill-Queen's University Press, 1972), p. 63.
2. The most important single work on the semantical differential technique of attitude measurement is Charles Osgood, George Suci, and Percy Tannenbaum, *The Measurement of Meaning* (University of Illinois Press, 1957). See also Osgood and Suci, "Factor Analysis of Meanings," *Journal of Experimental Psychology*, 50 (1955), pp. 325-38; Lawrence LeDuc, "Semantic Differential Measures of British Party Images," *British Journal of Political Science*, 6 (1976), pp. 115-28.
3. Meisel, *op. cit.,* pp. 68-75.
4. *Ibid.,* pp. 76-83.
5. See Appendix B, Q. 55-58 and Q. 66-71, for a description of the questions used in this study.
6. Out of a maximum possible total of 32 mentions per respondent. Up to two mentions were coded for each "like" and "dislike" question for each party. In Ontario, Saskatchewan, and the Atlantic provinces, only three provincial parties were included in the sequence. The maximum possible total for these provinces is therefore 28.
7. The absolute number of images of other parties and, later, the number of negative images of such parties is not a particularly meaningful statistic, since there are three other parties. However, the percentage holding such an image and the proportion holding particular combinations (own/positive—other/negative, for example) is more revealing.
8. See, for example, the arguments regarding sources of consonance and dissonance in Lane and Sears, *Public Opinion* (New York: Prentice-Hall, 1964). The conceptualization of party as a reference group and its attendant effects on the formation and "screening" of images of parties is most fully developed in Campbell et al., *The American Voter*, chaps. 6-7. See also Philip E. Converse, "Information Flow and the Stability of Party Attitudes," in Campbell et al., *Elections and the Political Order* (New York: Wiley, 1966), pp. 136-57.
9. Lane and Sears, *Public Opinion*, pp. 73-75. See also the classic study by Muzafer Sherif, *The Psychology of Social Norms* (New York: Harper, 1936).
10. See Appendix B, Q. 1-3.
11. The correlation (gamma) between interest in politics generally and in the 1974 federal election was .71. More respondents, however, report a high level of interest in the 1974 election (31%) than in politics generally (14%).
12. A number of examples of the stability of party images over time are cited in the United States studies. Converse, for example, quotes the in-

stance of the Nebraska woman who, although a regular voter and a strong partisan, could mention only "prohibition" as a basis for differentiating between the parties. Converse, *op. cit.*, p. 144.

13. *Ibid.*

14. The correlation (Pearson r) between education and the number of federal party images is .27, and between socio-economic status (as measured by the Blishen scale) and federal party images is .26. When the relationship between federal party images and political interest (r = .30) is controlled for education, a partial correlation of .26 is obtained. Similar patterns exist for the other party image variables.

15. Compare with Converse, *op. cit.*, p. 144.

16. This contrasts somewhat with the approach employed by the authors of *The American Voter* in analysing a similar set of responses. While they also arrayed responses to the questions along a set of key dimensions, they attempted to categorize their respondents in terms of "levels of conceptualization." See *The American Voter*, pp. 216-65.

17. A clear contrast is evident here with the distribution found in the work cited above. In particular, the "nature of the times" category, which was found to account for 24% of the total American sample, tended to contain many references to past wars, depressions, and so forth. See *The American Voter*, pp. 44-63 and pp. 240-44.

18. Meisel, *op. cit.*, pp. 68-77.

19. Converse, *op. cit.*, p. 148.

20. Angus Campbell et al., *The Voter Decides* (Evanston, Ill.: Row, Peterson, 1954); Campbell et al., *The American Voter*; Campbell et al., *Elections and the Political Order*. Recently, considerable evidence has been produced pointing to a decline in partisanship in the United States. See, for example, Norman H. Nie et al., *The Changing American Voter* (Cambridge: Harvard University Press, 1976), chap. 4.

Chapter Seven

Party Leaders and Canadian Electoral Politics

The significance of party leaders in Canadian electoral politics is seldom disputed. Indeed, conventional interpretations of Canadian elections and voting behaviour have elevated party leaders to a position not dissimilar to that occupied by societal cleavages such as religion, region, and ethnicity as influences on electoral choice.[1] At present, however, relatively little is known either about individuals' perceptions of and affect for party leaders, or the actual impact of these political figures on voting behaviour. Using data from the 1974 and 1968 national surveys of the electorate, this chapter will describe how voters reacted to the party leaders occupying the electoral stage at these points in time.

A detailed analysis of Canadian voters' perceptions of and affect for party leaders is valuable for several reasons. As noted, political scientists have traditionally attributed considerable importance to party leaders. In a polity rent by deep-seated and persistent ethnic, religious, linguistic, and regional conflicts, electoral campaigns focussing on the personalities and "styles" of party leaders provide a means by which parties can build broadly based coalitions while avoiding the potentially divisive and hence electorally unattractive consequences of discussions of these fundamental conflicts.[2] Relatedly, it has been suggested that the organizational disunity of Canadian parties, a consequence of the fragmentation of Canadian society and the Canadian political system, has operated to enhance the role of leaders both within these organizations and as spokesmen for their parties.[3] Other factors adduced to explain the significance of party leaders include the necessity for contemporary leaders to project an appealing "image" to the electorate via television,[4] and the cultural diffusion effects of Canada's proximity to the United States, where the office and person of the president has bulked increasingly large in the post-World War II period.[5]

Research conducted to date suggests the impact of party leader images on electoral behaviour in Canada. For example, when confronted with a forced choice question concerning which factor — party leader, party as a whole, or local candidate — was most important in their voting choice, 30%, 42%, and 33% of the respondents to the 1965, 1968, and 1974 national election studies respectively selected party leaders.[6] Similarly, upon being presented with an open-ended question regarding the "real reason" for their vote in 1974, 25% responded with reference to one or more of the party leaders.[7] The impact of party leader images is also documented in national surveys conducted during the early 1960s, and in analyses of voting choice in three Hamilton ridings in the 1968 federal election.[8] These studies are important not only for demonstrating party leader effects on the direction of the vote, but also because they indicate that particular party leaders may play significant roles in stimulating voter interest in an election, and thereby boost electoral participation rates.[9] Democratic norms aside, the significance of increased voter turnout lies in the extent to which previously unmobilized segments of the electorate opt disproportionately for a given party, either at a specific time or over a longer period.[10]

The influence of party leader images on voting choice also has been indicated in studies conducted in other Western democracies. In the United States, the electoral significance of attitudes towards presidential candidates has frequently been demonstrated.[11] Recently, it has also been suggested that presidential candidates have played important roles in the development of "issue voting" in American elections in the past decade.[12] In non-American settings, the relevance of party leaders for understanding voting choice has been documented extensively in Great Britain, and is strongly indicated in analyses of German and French electoral data.[13]

With regard to the possible electoral relevance of party leaders, there are a number of analytically distinct topics. For example, as the previous discussion has suggested, one can distinguish between the effects of party leaders on the direction of the vote, as opposed to their role as agents stimulating electoral participation. Also, the variability of party leader effects across political systems and within systems over time are significant subjects for empirical inquiry. Finally, as Stokes has argued, the impact of party leaders on individual voting behaviour is logically distinct from the effects of leaders on electoral outcomes in specific elections.[14]

Preparatory to these types of inquiry, however, is an assessment of the party leader images held by Canadian voters. In the present chapter, data from the 1974 and 1968 national election studies will be used to investigate several aspects of these images including: (a) the extent to which Canadians have party leader images and the affective and cognitive components of these images; (b) the degree of variability of party leader images over time in various segments of the electorate; and (c) relationships between party leader images and voters' partisan predispositions.

PARTY LEADER AFFECT

Perhaps the most fundamental aspect of the relationship between voters and party leaders concerns the level of positive or negative affect, or feelings of "like" or "dislike," that individuals develop toward such political figures. The idea that citizens may develop powerful feelings about political leaders and that such feelings can have potentially great impact is evident from recent political history. Moreover, the power of leaders to generate reservoirs of affect (both positive and negative) is not confined to dictators fostering "cults of personality." In the context of democratic political systems, the capacity of certain prominent political figures to generate intense affective reactions in electorates is a commonplace theme of political discourse.[15] Not every political leader has the ability to stimulate these intense feelings, but the propostion that perceptions and evaluations of leaders' behaviour will be, in part at least, a function of the "likes" and "dislikes" voters have for given leaders suggests that levels of party leader affect are potentially significant elements in the electoral decision of many voters.

Although a variety of approaches to measuring voters' levels of affect for specific party leaders might be considered, respondents in the 1974 national survey were asked to indicate how much they liked or disliked Messrs. Trudeau, Stanfield, Lewis, and Caouette, using the 100 point

TABLE 7.1

Mean Party Leader Thermometer Scores by Province, 1974 and 1968

	TRUDEAU		STANFIELD		LEWIS/DOUGLAS		CAOUETTE	
	1974	1968	1974	1968	1974	1968	1974	1968[a]
Newfoundland	66	67	48	70	51	54	36	—
P.E.I.	66	58	59	71	52	66	40	—
Nova Scotia	56	61	62	71	52	56	32	—
New Brunswick	65	61	57	71	48	54	46	—
Quebec	69	72	40	52	44	42	50	46
Ontario	62	69	48	56	51	58	41	—
Manitoba	50	72	49	53	45	62	43	—
Saskatchewan	55	56	43	58	52	61	39	—
Alberta	54	61	45	58	42	53	41	—
British Columbia	57	68	48	53	46	57	40	—
Total	62	68	46	56	47	54	44	—

[a]Asked only in Quebec in 1968.

thermometer scale.[16] The use of a similar thermometer scale to measure party leader affect in the 1968 national election study permits explicit cross-time comparisons in the reactions of the electorate.

Distributions of thermometer scale scores (Table 7.1) reveal substantial differences in levels of affect for the party leaders. In accordance with conventional wisdom, Mr. Trudeau easily outdistanced his rivals in 1974, being the only party leader to have a mean thermometer score (62) above the neutral point (50). The means for Stanfield (46), Lewis (47), and Caouette (44) all fall, albeit modestly, on the "dislike" side of the scale. Similarly, and again congruent with popular perceptions, Trudeau scored well above his counterparts in 1968. Although the average scores for Stanfield (56) and Douglas (54) were positive in this survey, they are much lower than Trudeau's score (68). The extent of Trudeau's popularity in 1968 is further evidenced by noting that only 30% of the voters accorded him a score of less than 50. Comparable percentages for Stanfield and Douglas were 47% and 52% respectively.

These data can also be viewed as evidence of the mutability in levels of affect for political figures. The notion that the popularity of political leaders is subject to potentially sharp fluctuations is, of course, the basic premise of much public opinion polling, and reports of these polls in Canada, the United States, and elsewhere have repeatedly confirmed the reality of changes in leaders' popularity, with such changes frequently occurring over relatively short time periods.[17] Limited to data drawn at two points in time six years apart, the present inquiry cannot begin to chart the full range of movement in affect levels for Trudeau, Stanfield, or the other party leaders. Still, there is substantial evidence of the reality of "net changes" in levels of affect for specific leaders in these thermometer scores. Trudeau's average score, for example, declined from 68 to 62 between 1968 and 1974 and while 30% of the electorate gave him a negative score in the former year, this figure increased to 36% in the latter. Stronger evidence of change is available in the Stanfield data, where Mr. Stanfield's mean score dropped 10 points between the two surveys. Moreover, in 1974, nearly two-thirds of the electorate (65%) gave the Conservative leader a negative affect score, a figure fully 18% more than the comparable percentage of voters who gave Stanfield a negative thermometer rating in 1968.

Generally, the thermometer scores strongly indicate that in both 1968 and 1974 the Canadian electorate had higher aggregate levels of affect for Mr. Trudeau than for Messrs. Stanfield, Lewis, Douglas, and Caouette. This conclusion can be buttressed by considering relative degrees of affect for the several party leaders at the level of individual voters. For this purpose, each respondent's thermometer ratings for all possible pairs of party leaders were subtracted from one another. The resulting scores

FIGURE 7.1
Relative Affect for Liberal, PC, and NDP Party Leaders, 1974 and 1968

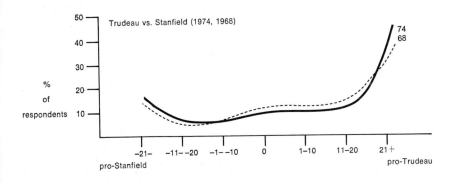

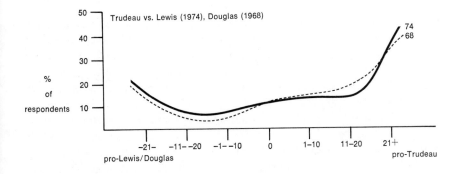

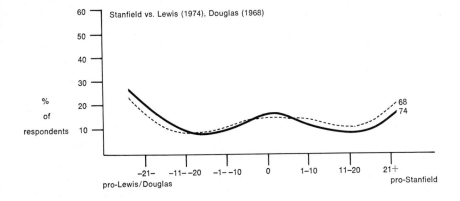

(Figure 7.1) document the relative popularity of Trudeau for most voters. Considering first the Trudeau-Stanfield comparison, 62% and 63% of the 1968 and 1974 electorates respectively gave higher thermometer scores to Trudeau than to Stanfield, and in both instances, over one-third of the electorate ranked Trudeau 21 points or more ahead of his Conservative counterpart. Trudeau also ran equally well against Lewis, Douglas, and Caouette. In the four possible comparisons, over 60% of the voters accorded higher thermometer scores to the Liberal leader.

The pattern of dominance shown by Mr. Trudeau over other party leaders is not replicated in any of the other possible leader comparisons. Perhaps most interesting, a comparison of Stanfield and Lewis in 1974 reveals that although 40% liked Stanfield better than Lewis, 42% had the opposite preference ordering. In 1968, Stanfield fares only marginally better in comparison with Douglas. Specifically, 45% of the 1968 respondents ranked Stanfield higher than Douglas, and 37% indicated the converse. In that the Conservatives had considerably more voters and party identifiers in both elections than did the NDP, these data indicate Stanfield's lack of appeal to Canadian voters.

In addition to satisfying our curiosity regarding the validity of journalistic evaluations of the relative popularity of different leaders in different sections of the country, the nature of the Canadian electoral system is such that data on reactions to party leaders in various provinces can aid in the interpretation of voting behaviour and electoral outcomes. The 1974 data displayed in Table 7.1 reveal that Mr. Trudeau's popularity relative to his rivals was a nationwide phenomenon. Indeed, in 39 of 40 possible paired comparisons across the 10 provinces, Trudeau's mean scores exceeded those of Stanfield, Lewis, and Caouette. Only in his home province of Nova Scotia did Stanfield outdistance Trudeau. Moreover, Trudeau's average thermometer rating was positive in every province but Manitoba, where his mean score was a neutral 50 points.

Second, and contrary to the Trudeau pattern, Stanfield's ratings were positive only in the three Atlantic provinces of Prince Edward Island, Nova Scotia, and New Brunswick. Similarly, Lewis had positive scores in only 5 provinces, and Caouette's scores were negative in every province save Quebec, where he registered a mean rating of 50. These data provide further evidence of Stanfield's unpopularity in 1974 in that not only did he trail Trudeau in 9 to 10 provinces, but also he ranked second only 5 times, trailing Caouette and Lewis respectively in the crucial electoral battlegrounds of Quebec and Ontario.

In 1968, Trudeau outranked other party leaders in 5 of 10 provinces, and did so by large margins in Quebec and Ontario. Further, Trudeau's scores were positive in every province. Stanfield outranked Trudeau only in the four Atlantic provinces, and as in 1974, he did not have high mean scores in either the central provinces, in the Prairies, or in B.C. The failure of Stanfield to score well in either 1974 or 1968 in the Prairie provinces is particularly interesting, given the overall strength of the Conservative party in this region in these two elections.[18] One might also note that in 1968 Mr. Douglas had somewhat greater personal popularity than did his successor Mr. Lewis in 1974. Unlike Lewis, Douglas had positive thermometer means in every province but Quebec.

Implicit in the preceding remarks is the point that affect for all party leaders declined significantly from 1968 to 1974. Indeed, in 27 of 31 instances,[19] the party leader affect scores were greater in the former year. Mr. Stanfield's popularity suffered the greatest diminution. His thermometer scores declined in all ten provinces, with the average loss being 12 points. Likewise, although Trudeau's average scores were positive in 9 of 10 provinces in 1974, these ratings declined in every province but New Brunswick and Prince Edward Island. Trudeau's average decline was 7 points. The greater popularity of Douglas in 1968, as compared to Lewis in 1974, has already been mentioned. Scores for the leader of the NDP decreased in 9 of 10 provinces in 1974, as compared to 1968, for an average loss of 9 points.

The data displayed in Table 7.1 provide a wealth of detail about levels of affect for the various party leaders in the several provinces in 1968 and 1974. These data, however, do not address the question of the degree of popularity of leaders relative to their parties, a point which is crucial for understanding the potential impact (positive or negative) of leaders on electoral choice .

Although untangling the causal linkages between levels of affect for leaders and parties is a difficult empirical question, a *prima facie* case for the potential electoral significance of party leaders will be more plausible if one can detect differences between voters' reactions to leaders and the parties they represent. To measure the electorate's level of affect for leaders versus parties, a voter's thermometer score for a particular party was subtracted from the thermometer rating given to the leader of that party. Mean party leader minus party scores for the 1974 and 1968 surveys are presented for each province, as well as Canada as a whole, in Table 7.2.

This table illustrates an intriguing pattern of similarities and differences in the positions of party leaders vis-à-vis their parties. In 1974, both the leaders of the two larger parties fared rather poorly in comparison with their parties. For the entire sample, Mr. Trudeau led the Liberal party by less than 1 point, while Mr. Stanfield trailed the PC party by 6.8 points. On a provincial basis, the data show Trudeau and Stanfield ranking behind their parties in 8 of 10 and 9 of 10 instances, respectively.

Especially noteworthy are the negative scores for Stanfield in Ontario and the Western provinces. In Ontario, Stanfield scored 8 thermometer points lower than the PC party on average, while the Western figures range from − 4.8 in Alberta and British Columbia to fully −12.8 points in Saskatchewan. In contrast, Trudeau's largest negative score is −6.2 in Nova Scotia.

Equivalent data for 1968 are sharply different. In the 1968 survey, Trudeau ranks ahead of the Liberal party in every province but New Brunswick. Similarly, Stanfield leads the PC party in five provinces, and even where the Stanfield minus PC thermometer scores are negative, these scores are substantially smaller than the equivalent figures for 1974. The extent of change in the relative degree of affect among voters for Stanfield and the PC party can be summarized by noting that between the two surveys, Stanfield's position vis-à-vis his party fell by 7.1 points for the entire country. This compares to a relative drop of only 2.4 points for Trudeau vis-à-vis the Liberal party.

Compared to Trudeau and Stanfield, the positions of the leaders of the two smaller parties are quite stable. In both 1968 and 1974, Lewis, Douglas, and Caouette tended to run well ahead of their respective parties in the minds of the electorate. This is not to say, of course, that these leaders were strongly liked in any absolute sense by the voters. Table 7.1 has already shown, on the contrary, that of these three leaders, only Mr. Douglas in 1968 had a mean thermometer score (54) above the neutral point.

In sum, the data in Table 7.2 provide additional evidence of the potential for change in the degree of affect accorded to party leaders. The scores for Trudeau and the Liberal party, and especially for Stanfield and the PC party, are cases in point. At the same time, the variations in these scores across the several provinces in each survey suggest that positions of leaders relative to their parties can vary substantially across different segments of the Canadian electorate over time.

It is reasonable to assume that voters' affect for parties as generalized political objects is related to affect for specific party leaders.[20] In Chapter Five, it has been demonstrated that, for a sizeable proportion of the electorate, partisanship is either unstable (36%) over time or inconsistent (32%) across levels of the federal system.[21] Although the inconsistency and, especially, the instability in the partisan ties of many members of the Canadian electorate renders hazardous the imputation of causality in partisanship and party leader relationships,[22] the hypothesis that the direction and intensity of partisanship is linked to levels of affect for various party leaders has considerable potential for furthering understanding of the psychological mechanisms underlying the formation of attitudes toward political leaders. To explore partisanship/party leader

TABLE 7.2

Mean 1974 and 1968 "Leader Minus Party" Thermometer Scores, by Province

		TRUDEAU −LIBERAL PARTY	STANFIELD −PC PARTY	LEWIS, DOUGLAS −NDP PARTY	CAOUETTE[a] −SC PARTY
Newfoundland	1974	−4.4	−3.3	3.1	1.6
	1968	3.0	10.4	5.9	
P.E.I.	1974	−1.7	−4.8	4.9	2.6
	1968	−3.9	−1.4	6.7	
Nova Scotia	1974	−6.2	1.7	5.1	5.3
	1968	2.3	5.9	7.7	
New Brunswick	1974	−2.7	−4.3	1.1	1.0
	1968	−1.5	5.0	8.4	
Quebec	1974	3.2	−3.8	4.0	6.3
	1968	2.3	−2.0	2.4	3.7
Ontario	1974	−0.4	−8.0	5.3	8.6
	1968	2.6	1.1	7.0	
Manitoba	1974	−4.5	−9.6	−0.9	6.8
	1968	5.3	−2.3	7.0	
Saskatchewan	1974	−0.5	−12.8	0.0	4.2
	1968	0.5	−1.9	7.1	
Alberta	1974	0.8	−4.8	3.4	−0.7
	1968	4.6	−2.3	12.7	
British Columbia	1974	−0.5	−4.8	3.4	3.6
	1968	3.4	2.8	7.8	
Canada	1974	0.2	−6.8	4.2	5.8
	1968	2.6	0.3	6.6	

[a]Asked only in Quebec in 1968.

images linkages empirically, mean party leader thermometer scores are computed for respondents having partisan ties with one of the four major parties. These score are analyzed in terms of the intensity of partisan attachments. The results of these analyses (shown in Table 7.3) are similar, in their general tenor at least, to comparable research in non-Canadian settings.[23] Specifically, the direction of partisanship has strong statistical relationships with levels of affect for party leaders.

Trudeau, for example, is given a mean score of 77 by Liberal partisans, whereas the scores accorded the Liberal leader by Conservative, NDP, and Social Credit partisans are 43, 45, and 50 respectively. Similarly, Stanfield is given a mean score of 63 by Conservative respondents. Liberals give Stanfield a mean score of only 40, and his equivalent scores for NDP (40) and Social Credit (38) partisans are also negative. Additional but virtually identical examples could be cited for Lewis and Caouette.

As might be anticipated, the relationships between party leader thermometer scores and partisanship vary with the intensity of partisan attachments. This is most notably so in the case of affect for the leader of a respondent's "own" party. To illustrate, consider again Liberal partisans' thermometer scores for Trudeau. Among "very strong" Liberals Trudeau's mean score is fully 86 points, the highest average rating accorded to any party leader by any subgroup of partisans. The Liberal leader's score drops to 76 among "fairly strong" Liberals, and to 67 for those with "weak" attachments. Monotonic patterns can also be observed among various groups of Conservative partisans in their assessments of Stanfield, and among NDP and Social Credit groups ranking Lewis and Caouette respectively.

The levels of affect which partisans have for the leaders of parties other than their own are also of interest. These affect scores do not manifest patterns comparable to those described above. Although it is generally true that those with a strong attachment to a particular party like the leaders of opposing parties less than do those with weaker partisan attachments, distinctions between respondents with "fairly strong" as opposed to "weak" partisan ties frequently do not materialize or run contrary to expectations. For example, consider levels of affect for Lewis held by Liberal partisans. Mean affect scores for Lewis among "very strong," "fairly strong," and "weak" Liberals are 41, 46, and 44. Not only are these values not significantly different, but the peak level of affect occurs for the "fairly strong" as opposed to the "weak" Liberals. While it would be tedious to recount other examples of this type of pattern, Table 7.3 provides ample evidence of the intensity of partisanship failing to relate in a statistically significant fashion with affect for leaders of other than respondents' own party.

Above, it has been demonstrated that level of affect for party leaders varies across regional and partisan subgroups in the Canadian electorate as well as over time. To provide a more adequate portrait of the range of possible variation in party leader affect, however, it is necessary to investigate how various socio-demographic groups reacted to the leaders. Relevant analyses (not shown in tabular form) are congruent with expectations based on observations of the voting tendencies of various segments of Canadian society (see Chapter Four). Although it is unnecessary to recount the results of these analyses in detail, the tenor of the findings can be indicated by noting that in both 1974 and 1968, Trudeau's thermometer scores were greatest among French Canadians and Catholics, whereas Stanfield was related most highly by Anglo-Celtic

TABLE 7.3

Mean 1974 Party Leader Thermometer Scores by Direction and Intensity of Partisanship

		TRUDEAU	STANFIELD	LEWIS	CAOUETTE
LIBERALS	N				
Very strong	(375)	86	37	41	44
Fairly strong	(547)	76	42	46	42
Weak	(248)	67	42	44	42
F=		63.9*	4.4*	2.2	0.3
All Liberal	(1170)	77	40	44	43
PROGRESSIVE CONSERVATIVES					
Very strong	(155)	34	70	42	39
Fairly strong	(254)	46	63	46	45
Weak	(135)	49	55	42	39
F=		9.7*	12.6*	2.0	1.9
All PC	(544)	43	63	44	42
NEW DEMOCRATS					
Very strong	(80)	38	36	79	37
Fairly strong	(121)	48	41	72	40
Weak	(53)	47	41	66	42
F=		3.7*	2.0	7.1*	0.5
All NDP	(254)	45	40	73	40
SOCIAL CREDIT					
Very strong	(29)	51	37	37	85
Fairly strong	(31)	55	40	35	74
Weak	(15)	38	32	30	71
F=		2.3	0.8	0.6	3.0
All SC	(75)	50	38	34	77

*Significant at .01 level.

and Protestant groups. Lewis and Douglas were ranked most highly by the Anglo-Celtic group and by those with no religious affiliations, but the range of variance was not great. Generally, socio-economic status differentials in levels of affect for various party leaders were modest. With regard to sex, age, and urban-rural cleavages in the electorate, Stanfield was rated highest by older residents and those in rural areas, but there was little evidence in the data to suggest that even in 1968, when "Trudeaumania" was supposedly an electoral phenomenon of significance, Trudeau was especially attractive to younger voters or women, the groups assumed at the time to be particularly susceptible to the Liberal appeal.[24]

More generally, in 1968 as in 1974, Trudeau was an attractive candidate among many segments of the electorate. By the same token, Mr.

Stanfield, although more popular in 1968 than 1974, failed to arouse strong enthusiasm in any particular group of voters, running behind Mr. Trudeau in virtually every socio-demographic category. This is true even among Protestants, farmers, older voters, and those of Anglo-Celtic origin, groups which gave Stanfield relatively favourable thermometer ratings in both years. There is no evidence in the present data to suggest that the Conservative leader had any *lasting* success in closing the "affect gap" between himself and Trudeau among any major sector of the electorate over the three elections in which they competed.[25] Despite Mr. Stanfield's failure to develop a level of popular affection comparable to that enjoyed by Trudeau, the analyses presented above do forcefully suggest that levels of party leader affect are variable. Affect for Trudeau and Stanfield, and for the NDP and Créditiste leaders as well, varied across major societal groups and over time. Particularly noteworthy in this regard was the decline in popularity of *all* leaders from 1968 to 1974. Trudeau was able to maintain a lead over his rivals in 1974, even though his own absolute level of affect among most groups of voters declined significantly.

PERCEPTIONS OF PARTY LEADERS

The thermometer score data on party leader affect are descriptively interesting and potentially important for understanding voting behaviour, but do not reveal the bases for voters' feelings about the party leaders. To determine *why* Canadian voters felt as they did about the several party leaders, respondents in both the 1974 and 1968 national surveys were asked a series of open-ended questions about their particular "likes" and "dislikes" for the leaders.[26] Use of these two data sets permits an analysis of how Canadians perceived various party leaders at two different points in time. Analyses employing both the 1968 and 1974 data are especially pertinent in that three of the four party leaders (Trudeau, Stanfield, and Caouette) campaigned in each election. Before discussing the results of these analyses, however, it will be useful to consider a few sample responses to the open-ended questions. Such responses can provide an indication of the types of answers encapsulated in the more abstract measures used for analytic purposes.

Ted Boutari is a 35-year-old science teacher living in Vancouver. Formerly an NDP supporter, he presently considers himself to have no partisan affiliation in either federal or provincial politics, but voted NDP in the 1974 federal election. Typical of a majority of the electorate, his party leader images contain a number of personality and stylistic comments. As the following responses indicate, however, unlike most voters, Mr. Boutari also refers to specific policies espoused by the leaders:

. . . Now we would like to ask you about your impressions of the various leaders of the federal political parties.
Is there anything in particular that you like about Mr. Trudeau?
"He is very dynamic, witty, very young person, lot of charisma. He's shown some changes in his previous attitude. Closer to the people. He has learned to talk to people."
Is there anything in particular that you dislike about Mr. Trudeau?
"He makes no commitments. Has no set policies, say about inflation."
Is there anything in particular that you like about Mr. Stanfield?
"Very knowledgeable and intelligent. Had some good ideas, like removing the Federal tax on building supplies. His idea of doing something about inflation."
Is there anything in particular that you dislike about Mr. Stanfield?
"No charisma. He's not dynamic enough, and his image is bad now."
Is there anything in particular that you like about Mr. Lewis?
"He seems very dedicated. A hard worker. He's committed to his party's doctrine and policies, and is concerned more about the average working man. He tries to get a fair shake for the working man."
Is there anything in particular that you dislike about Mr. Lewis?
"The repetition on the corporate rip-off got very tiring. And some of their national policies. Nationalizing some of these companies just isn't that easy."
Is there anything in particular that you like about Mr. Caouette?
"Seems very dedicated. But he's going against great odds."
Is there anything in particular that you dislike about Mr. Caouette?
"Some of his policies seem to be unworkable."

Mr. Boutari's willingness to offer both positive and negative comments about several party leaders is, as will be shown, characteristic of large numbers of those interviewed in 1974. A second example of this response pattern is provided by Ida McWilliams, a 48-year-old secretary of Scottish descent from Halifax, Nova Scotia, who voted Conservative in 1974. Disillusioned with the Liberal party, Mrs. McWilliams became a Conservative identifier in 1972 and now deems her attachment to the Tory party to be "fairly strong." Unlike Mr. Boutari, but typical of most of the electorate, her references to issues and policies are quite general and vague:

. . . Now, we would like to ask you about your impressions of the various leaders of the federal political parties.
Is there anything in particular that you like about Mr. Trudeau?
"I think that his impact on international affairs has been good."
Is there anything in particular that you dislike about Mr. Trudeau?
"His detachment from the problems of everyday people; his special favours to Quebec."
Anything else?
"His disregard for Commonwealth ties."
Is there anything in particular that you like about Mr. Stanfield?

"He's a sincere man, aware of the problems of ordinary people."
Anything else?
"I liked his plan for alleviating the economic situation."
Is there anything in particular that you dislike about Mr. Stanfield?
"His public image is not decisive enough."
Anything else?
"No."
Is there anything in particular that you like about Mr. Lewis?
"A nice guy. He has concern and understanding for daily problems."
Is there anything in particular that you dislike about Mr. Lewis?
"A little unrealistic in his approach to things."
Is there anything in particular that you like about Mr. Caouette?
"No."
Is there anything in particular that you dislike about Mr. Caouette?
"His oratory."

A third example of the tendency to offer both positive and negative responses to the party leader questions and to stress the leaders' personalities and styles, at the expense of specific comments on issues or policies, is found in the answers of Nicole Martin. Thirty years old, and life-long resident of Montreal, Ms. Martin is a Parti Québécois supporter in provincial politics. Federally, she is a former Liberal who now considers herself a "fairly strong" NDP identifier. Despite her Péquiste sympathies, she voted NDP in the 1974 election and was quite willing to discuss her perceptions of the federal party leaders:

[translation]
. . . *Now, we would like to ask you about your impressions of the various leaders of the federal political parties.*
Is there anything in particular that you like about Mr. Trudeau?
"His personality. He is a man with a good education and he is an intellectual."
Anything else?
"He is a very determined man."
Is there anything in particular that you dislike about Mr. Trudeau?
"His arrogance — his attitudes in discussions with journalists or with members of the Opposition."
Anything else?
"Sometimes he seems closed to different opinions. He is very hostile to the separatists."
Is there anything in particular that you like about Mr. Stanfield?
"He commands respect."
Anything else?
"He tries to speak French."
Is there anything in particular that you dislike about Mr. Stanfield?
"His lack of dynamism."
Anything else?
"No."

Is there anything in particular that you like about Mr. Lewis?
"His interest in the workers and consumers and people in general."
Anything else?
"He is a good speaker."
Is there anything in particular that you dislike about Mr. Lewis?
"I think he is not determined enough."
Anything else?
"No."
Is there anything in particular that you like about Mr. Caouette?
"A certain frankness — he says what he thinks."
Anything else?
"His sense of humour. Particularly in his opinions and comments about bills."
Is there anything in particular that you dislike about Mr. Caouette?
"I don't like the way he involves himself in provincial politics — his favouritism for certain candidates."
Anything else?
"No."

Not all respondents express both "likes" and "dislikes" about more than one party leader. Illustrative of this pattern are the responses of Jake Bixler, a 45-year-old Saskatchewan wheat farmer. Mr. Bixler follows politics "fairly closely," and although he has always been a "very strong" Conservative supporter and voted PC in 1974, his low estimation of all party leaders, including Mr. Stanfield, is quite evident:

. . . *Now, we would like to ask you about your impressions of the various leaders of the federal political parties.*
Is there anything in particular that you like about Mr. Trudeau?
"No."
Is there anything in particular that you dislike about Mr. Trudeau?
"Everything. He's never there when you want him and he doesn't care what happens in the West."
Anything else?
"He caters more to Quebec and to the industrialists."
Is there anything in particular that you like about Mr. Stanfield?
"He's a Conservative."
Anything else?
"No, he's a poor leader."
Is there anything in particular that you dislike about Mr. Stanfield?
"Not especially."
Is there anything in particular that you like about Mr. Lewis?
"Nothing, I'm just lukewarm on him."
Is there anything in particular that you dislike about Mr. Lewis?
"No."
Is there anything in particular that you like about Mr. Caouette?
"No. Lukewarm, really."
Is there anything in particular that you dislike about Mr. Caouette?
"No."

The preponderance of negative rather than positive perceptions of party leaders evident in Mr. Bixler's answers is also characteristic of the responses offered by Pat Dailey, a 21-year-old truck driver from Hamilton, Ontario. A member of the Teamsters, Mr. Dailey is single, with a Grade eleven education. Like both his parents, Dailey views himself as a "fairly strong" Liberal supporter. Since he reached the age of majority in 1971, he has voted Liberal twice. His colourful comments on the party leaders' personal characteristics convey a strength of feeling congruent with the extremely low thermometer scores he gave each of the party leaders:

. . . Now, we would like to ask you about your impressions of the various leaders of the federal political parties.
Is there anything in particular that you like about Mr. Trudeau?
"He is classy. He has a way with words."
Anything else?
"No."
Is there anything in particular that you dislike about Mr. Trudeau?
"He seems to want to mingle with the upper classes more than with the commoners."
Anything else?
"He is good for big business but not for the working class."
Is there anything in particular that you like about Mr. Stanfield?
"Not that much I like about him, but if he has anything to say he comes out with both barrels and gives it to you."
Anything else?
"Not too much."
Is there anything in particular that you dislike about Mr. Stanfield?
"I dislike the way he is always trying to back stab."
Anything else?
"That kind of a man is for the birds."
Is there anything in particular that you like about Mr. Lewis?
"He is a gutsy little buggar. He is like the baloney between the bread — he has to fight the big money."
Is there anything in particular that you dislike about Mr. Lewis?
"I think he does not use what he has got to their benefit."
Anything else?
"No."
Is there anything in particular that you like about Mr. Caouette?
"Nope."
Is there anything in particular that you dislike about Mr. Caouette?
"He is a Frenchman who wants to better Quebec, but he is mooching off the rest of Canada."
Anything else?
"He ain't got enough brains to blow his nose."

In both content and level of abstraction, the answers offered by Ed

Cusak, a PC voter in 1974, contrast sharply with those offered by Mr. Dailey. A thirty-eight-year-old, highly successful lawyer living in Toronto, Mr. Cusak describes himself as an "Independent" who is "fairly interested" in government at all levels. Raised in a home where both parents were "very strong" Conservative supporters, Mr. Cusak stated that he originally identified with the Conservative party, but abandoned this identification "when I became more mature in my thinking. . . . I like to remain flexible and vote for a party with a statesman-like leader or the better policy." Consistent with this explanation, Mr. Cusak, unlike a large majority of respondents, discussed party leaders in terms of both personality and style, as well as evaluating specific issues and policies with reference to more general ideological criteria:

. . . Now, we would like to ask you about your impressions of the various leaders of the federal political parties.
Is there anything in particular that you like about Mr. Trudeau?
"He's intelligent and he's made Canada known among other countries. Now the world knows who Canada's leader is."
Anything else?
"He's definitely a strong person and leader."
Is there anything in particular that you dislike about Mr. Trudeau?
"He's a bit pink in his thinking. The handouts of the LIP program all lead to more inflation. The amount of foolish government spending is really a cause to worry."
Is there anything in particular that you like about Mr. Stanfield?
"He's a good economist and is willing to have a meeting of minds over inflation. He's dedicated and serious in his intentions."
Anything else?
"No."
Is there anything in particular that you dislike about Mr. Stanfield?
"He has a poor public image that seems to cut down on his support. It's because of his appearance on TV by comparison with Trudeau. This does not reflect Stanfield's actual personality truthfully."
Is there anything in particular that you like about Mr. Lewis?
"He's a good speaker and very dedicated to his cause."
Anything else?
"No."
Is there anything in particular that you dislike about Mr. Lewis?
"No, I just dislike his party."
Anything else?
"No."
Is there anything in particular that you like about Mr. Caouette?
"He is forthright and says what he thinks. A hard worker."
Anything else?
"No."
Is there anything in particular that you dislike about Mr. Caouette?

"His party."
Anything else?
"No."

To provide a systematic picture of the content of party leader images across the entire electorate, voters' answers to the questions cited in the illustrative responses are collapsed into eight categories: (1) personality and personal characteristics, (2) style or approach, (3) leadership, (4) references to French Canadians, Quebec, separatism or bilingualism, (5) economic issues including inflation, (6) other issues, (7) references to groups and regions except French-Canadians and Quebec, and (8) other references. The decision to use these categories is guided by two considerations: (a) the need to present a parsimonious account of the party leader images, while at the same time preserving the basic realities of these data, and (b) the desire to evaluate the prevalence of certain 1974 campaign themes (for example inflation or leadership), in the images voters had of particular party leaders. To aid in making explicit comparisons between party leader images in 1974 and 1968, the same classification scheme was applied to both sets of party leader images. The results are displayed in Table 7.4.

The dominance of personality and stylistic references in the 1974 party leader image data is immediately evident. For all four leaders, these types of references dwarf all others, particularly with regard to positive leader images. Personality and style considerations also bulk large in the negative responses, albeit to a somewhat lesser extent. Personality and style references are particularly noticeable in Mr. Trudeau's image with fully 84% of all respondents giving this type of response when asked what they liked about the Liberal leader. Mentions of Trudeau's intelligence, frankness, energy, and speaking ability were particularly evident. It will be recalled that these types of remarks could be found in the images of Trudeau articulated by Messrs. Boutari and Cuzak and Ms. Martin quoted previously. A further appreciation of the manner in which the electorate perceived Trudeau in 1974 can be gained by considering how a few additional respondents described what they liked about him. When asked this question a 23-year-old student at York University replied:

"He's intelligent, bilingual and bicultural, dynamic." [Anything else?] "He's a good stateman and well-known abroad."

A 35-year-old secretary in Winnipeg answered:

"Terrific personality. Very quick to take advantage of a situation. Clever, adroit." [Anything else?] "Very much of a leader."

A 44-year-old housewife in Burnaby, British Columbia, responded:

TABLE 7.4

Content of Party Leader Images, 1974 and 1968

% OF RESPONDENTS MENTIONING	TRUDEAU		STANFIELD		LEWIS/DOUGLAS		CAOUETTE	
	1974	1968	1974	1968	1974	1968	1974	1968
POSITIVE IMAGES								
Personality	48	50	33	39	22	27	18	12
Style	36	25	12	16	19	26	21	17
Leadership	12	2	3	2	4	2	2	1
Quebec, Separatism, Bilingualism	2	4	x	1	0	x	1	2
Inflation, Wage and Price Controls, and Other Economic Issues	1	x	2	1	2	x	1	x
Other Issue or Policy References	7	21	3	6	7	7	5	4
Groups and Regions Except Quebec	4	x	2	2	4	3	2	1
Other References	3	3	6	2	7	1	3	1
NEGATIVE IMAGES								
Personality	26	19	34	16	7	8	3	7
Style	17	22	24	30	10	8	8	11
Leadership	7	1	2	3	2	1	1	1
Quebec, Separatism, Bilingualism	4	x	1	1	x	x	3	2
Inflation, Wage and Price Controls, and Other Economic Issues	6	x	3	x	1	x	x	x
Other Issue or Policy References	6	7	6	7	10	13	9	9
Groups and Regions Except Quebec	6	x	2	1	2	1	3	x
Other References	7	6	6	4	6	8	5	4

x Less than 1%.

"I like his frankness. I appreciate that. He has a nice personality — a charming person."

Matters of personality and style also played a very substantial part in voters' negative reactions to Mr. Trudeau, with 43% of the 1974 sample making such references. Particularly noteworthy in these negative responses were references to Trudeau's arrogance, his proclivities to travel abroad while neglecting the business of directing the government, and his lack of concern for the ordinary man. For example, some of these themes ran through the negative comments offered about Mr. Trudeau in the answers of Mrs. McWilliams, Mr. Dailey, Mr. Bixler, and Ms. Martin. Also typical of these types of references are the comments of a 51-year-old mechanic from Lévis:

"His opportunism." [Anything else?] "His arrogance."

Trudeau's perceived indifference to social and economic problems is echoed in the remarks of a 57-year-old elementary school teacher in St. John's, Newfoundland:

"[He] doesn't seem to be serious toward the problems of the country. Doesn't act as he says he will." [Anything else?] "Not as dedicated as Mr. Stanfield, and the leader of the country needs to be dedicated."

Setting aside references to Mr. Trudeau's personality and style, the data in Table 7.6 reveal that no other dimensions of his image were particularly salient. For example, despite the Liberal's campaign efforts to make leadership an issue,[27] only 12% of the respondents made positive references to Trudeau's leadership abilities. Even the issue of inflation, which presumably could have seriously injured the Liberals' electoral fortunes in 1974,[28] did not make a particularly large impact on Trudeau's image. In this regard, the comment by a 44-year-old woman, an executive with Imperial Oil in Edmonton, that "he [Trudeau] is not curbing inflation . . . it is really getting out of hand," as well as that of Mr. Cuzak, quoted above, are atypical. In sum, only 6% of the respondents made negative comments linking Trudeau with inflation or other economic issues.

As noted previously, Stanfield's image is also largely described in terms of personality and style references. Unlike Trudeau, Lewis, or Caouette, however, Mr. Stanfield received more negative (58%) than positive (45%) personality and style comments. Of those positive personal references he did receive, a very large percentage focussed on his qualities of honesty, sincerity, and dedication to his work. The aforementioned comments of Mrs. McWilliams were typical of these references to Stanfield. A further appreciation of this facet of Stanfield's image can be gained by considering some additional responses. When asked what he liked about Stanfield, a 79-year-old pensioner from Moncton answered that:

"I think he is an honest man. He has worked very hard."

Similarly, Stanfield's honesty and competence were enthusiastically expressed by a 24-year-old computer operator in Vancouver:

"Ah, I think he's an excellent man, an honest man who, if given the opportunity, would do a very good job of running the country." [Anything else?] "Yes, I think [he is] loyal to the party."

These themes were again echoed by a 78-year-old London, Ontario, woman:

"I think he's a good down-to-earth man, and given the opportunity to be a leader, he did a good job." [Anything else?] "I like him very much."

Only relatively few respondents made other types of positive comments about Mr. Stanfield. For example, Mr. Cuzak was one of the 2% of all respondents making positive references to Stanfield's strong level of concern for the problem of inflation or his policy of wage and price controls. Similarly, the percentages of respondents in Stanfield's other positive image categories were very small. In these respects, Stanfield's image is similar to those of the other three leaders.

On the negative side, Stanfield's image is again dominated by references to personality and style, with 58% of the respondents making these kinds of references. In specific terms, Stanfield is criticized as a poor speaker in both English and French, too old, lacking dynamism, uncharismatic, and generally, for being a dull and boring personality. A 65-year-old housewife from Vancouver summed up the generalized negative feelings of many Canadians about Stanfield in the following litany of criticisms:

"His slow way of speaking — he can't hold my interest. He doesn't have interest in the people." [Anything else?] "Just don't like the man — I can't put it into words — I don't like his looks."

Despite the strongly negative tone of a majority of comments about Stanfield, it is interesting to note that only 3% of all respondents criticized the Conservative leader's approach to handling the inflation issue. Although the policy of wage and price controls was closely associated with Stanfield himself in the popular press,[29] it did not become a major component of Stanfield's personal image. As an example of comments of respondents perceiving Stanfield negatively in terms of the wage and price controls issue, those offered by a 46-year-old labourer from St. John's, Newfoundland, are typical:

"I don't like him saying he'd freeze the wages. They're bad enough now."

[Anything else?] "I don't like him because he was going to freeze wages."

Perhaps unintentionally echoing the conclusions drawn by many Conservatives after the election,[30] an 18-year-old student from Wilfrid Laurier University tersely remarked that:

"Wage and price controls were the wrong answer at the wrong time."

The images of Lewis and Caouette are similar to those of Trudeau and Stanfield in that, both positively and negatively, personality and style references are prominent. Both men were frequently described as honest and sincere, hard-working, or good speakers. In this regard, the comments of Ed Cuzak about Lewis and Caouette quoted previously were quite typical. Also representative of the favourable responses offered about Lewis were the remarks of a 48-year-old manager of a Nova Scotia pulp and paper mill:

"I like his [Lewis's] personality. He is good at talking to people. I think he's sincere and believes what he's talking about."

Regarding Caouette, a 25-year-old social worker in Quebec City stated:

"I like his frank way of speaking. Also, he injects a note of humour in Parliament." [Anything else?] "Yes, he's very courageous."

The data in Table 7.4 do indicate, however, that issue or policy references (but not inflation or wage and price controls) were mentioned with relatively greater frequency in connection with Lewis and Caouette than was true for either Trudeau or Stanfield. Many of these references were quite general. For example, when asked what he didn't like about Caouette, a 28-year-old worker from Montreal replied simply: "His policies are difficult to understand." Similarly, a 45-year-old public health nurse from Calgary commented about Lewis that "I just don't like his brand of politics." Occasionally, negative references to Lewis also assumed a distinctly ideological tone. Although the total number of such responses is not very large in absolute terms, Lewis was the only leader to solicit this type of commentary in discernible proportions. As an example, a 39-year-old medical receptionist in Vancouver described her dislike of Lewis thusly:

"He's misguided . . . Too red . . . [I] don't like his Communist tendencies."

Finally, a handful of negative references were made to Lewis's role as parliamentary leader during the 1972-74 minority government period, and a few respondents explicitly blamed the NDP leader for bringing down the government and precipitating an election.

Comparing the 1974 data with those for 1968 (Table 7.4), the predominant impression is one of cross-time similarities in the components of leader images. Most obviously, for all party leaders, positive and negative references are both cast largely in terms of personality and style. Seventy-five per cent of those interviewed in 1968 made positive personality or style references to Trudeau, compared to 84% in 1974. For Stanfield, the positive personality and style percentages are 55% in 1968 and 45% in 1974, and the data for Lewis and Douglas and Caouette are similar in tenor, even though the absolute number of respondents making references to the personality and style qualities of the leaders of the smaller parties is not as great. On the negative side, percentages of respondents referencing Trudeau's personality and style in 1968 and 1974 are 41% and 43%; for Stanfield, 46% and 58%; for Douglas-Lewis, 16% and 17%; and for Caouette, 18% and 11%. Interestingly, of the three party leaders participating in both elections, Stanfield is the only leader to manifest a sizeable increase (12%) in negative references to personality and style.

Turning to other aspects of party leader images, the data in Table 7.4 reveal some minor differences between the 1968 and 1974 responses. In 1968, for example, leadership references decline to the point where no more than 3% of the electorate made positive or negative leadership comments about any particular leader. Similarly, issue references centering on Quebec, separatism, bilingualism, or economic matters are never made about any party leader by more than 6% of those interviewed. Indeed, economic issue references, a decidedly minor theme in party leader images in 1974, are virtually non-existent in 1968. Other issue and policy references also are present in only very limited numbers in the 1968 data, although issue and policy mentions are made more frequently for the NDP and Social Credit leaders. One exception to this generalization can be found in the positive references to Trudeau in 1968, where slightly over one-fifth of the respondents made comments falling into the "other issues or policy references" category. A detailed inspection of these references suggests that they are very heterogeneous, and thus the categorization scheme is not masking any single particularly salient issue or policy component of the Trudeau image in 1968.

In addition to the emphasis on personal characteristics and style, the data on party leader images in Table 7.4 suggest that many respondents are willing to offer a variety of both *positive* and *negative* comments about the party leaders. Ascertaining the precise number of respondents with party leader images, as well as the direction (positive or negative) of these images, is important for assessing the potential impact of party leaders on electoral choice. Relevant data on this point can be obtained by summing the number of positive and negative party leader image responses made by each respondent (for each respondent a maximum of three positive and three negative responses about every party leader was coded in the 1974 survey). This type of analysis (Table 7.5) indicates that fully 94% of the respondents interviewed in 1974 made one or more codeable responses to the open-ended party leader questions. The average number of responses was 5.9. Eighty-three per cent of the respondents offered positive responses, and nearly as many (80%) made negative comments. The slight tendency to give more positive than negative answers is also suggested in that the mean number of positive and negative responses is 3.5 and 2.4 respectively. Intuitively, the volume of these comments suggests that party leaders were highly salient political figures in the minds of the electorate. There is considerable variance, however, in the frequency with which comments were offered about different party leaders. Although 89% of the electorate had an image of Trudeau, the percentage of respondents mentioning a Stanfield image drops to 77%; 59% had a codeable image of Lewis; and only 49% responded to the queries concerning Mr. Caouette. This variance in the number of respondents having an image of a particular party leader is paralleled in terms of the number of comments made. The mean number of images for each leader is Trudeau (2.2), for Stanfield (1.6), Lewis (1.2), and Caouette (0.9).

Equally interesting is the relative frequency with which *positive* as opposed to *negative* comments were given for particular leaders. Although slightly over half the respondents (54%) made negative com-

TABLE 7.5

Distribution of Images of Federal Party Leaders

	% WITH IMAGE	MEAN NO. OF IMAGES
Image of a Party Leader	94	5.9
Positive Image of a Party Leader	83	3.5
Positive Image of: Trudeau	72	1.4
Stanfield	49	0.7
Lewis	46	0.7
Caouette	38	0.6
Negative Image of a Party Leader	80	2.4
Negative Image of: Trudeau	54	0.8
Stanfield	59	0.9
Lewis	34	0.4
Caouette	25	0.3
Total Images of: Trudeau	89	2.2
Stanfield	77	1.6
Lewis	59	1.2
Caouette	49	0.9
	(1203)	*(1203)*

ments about Trudeau, fully 72% made positive remarks. The Stanfield responses are very different, with 59% of the sample offering negative comments and only 49% giving positive answers. Again, while more positive than negative responses were forthcoming for both Lewis and Caouette, the volume of these responses was far less than that for Trudeau. On the other hand, the percentage of respondents making positive comments about Lewis (45%) is nearly as high as that for Stanfield (49%), and the average number of positive responses is equal (.7). Lewis (and Caouette too), however, have far fewer negative responses than does the Conservative leader.

In summary, the findings that a large majority of Canadian voters has party leader images and that party leaders are perceived in terms of personal qualities, rather than issues or policy positions, echoes the results of earlier research on party leader images in Canada and the findings of the classic voting studies conducted in the United States and Great Britain.[31] That the Canadian party leader image data are quite similar in content to those gathered in other Western democracies does not, of course, enable one to argue that the impact of party leaders on voting behaviour in Canada is equivalent to that documented in research conducted in these other political milieus. Rather, the significance of party leaders for understanding electoral choice in Canada is a topic which must be considered within the matrix of political forces at work in this country. This topic will be addressed explicitly in Chapter Eleven. Preparatory to conducting an investigation of the electoral impact of party leader images in Canada, however, it will be useful to consider in some detail the relationships between these images and partisanship.

PARTY LEADER IMAGES AND PARTISANSHIP

In Chapter Five, it was shown that many Canadian voters do not have strong, stable party identifications and that many (18%) report different party identifications in federal as opposed to provincial politics. The potential significance of partisan instability and inconsistency in Canada for understanding voters' perceptions of parties was strongly indicated in Chapter Six, where analyses of federal and provincial party images revealed that these images were related not only to the direction and strength of partisanship, but also to the stability and consistency of these ties. Given the general importance of party leaders in Canadian politics and the salience of these figures in the minds of the electorate, it is reasonable to hypothesize that party leader images will be systematically related to partisanship in a fashion similar to that for the party image variables.

The data from the 1974 survey in Table 7.6 provide an assessment of the tendency of voters to have images of the leaders of their "own"

TABLE 7.6

Distribution of Images of Own and Other Party Leaders

	% WITH IMAGE	MEAN NO. OF IMAGES
Image of Leader of Own Party	89	2.2
Positive Image of Leader of Own Party	83	1.6
Negative Image of Leader of Own Party	43	0.6
Image of Leader(s) of Other Parties	89	3.9
Positive Image of Leader(s) of Other Parties	73	2.0
Negative Image of Leader(s) of Other Parties	76	1.9
N=	(*1006*)	(*1006*)

parties — that is, the party with which they currently identify — as opposed to having images of the leaders of the other parties. An identical percentage of respondents (89%) have images of their own *and* of other party leaders. Respondents are, however, somewhat more likely to have a positive image of their own party leader (83%), than of the leaders of other parties (73%). Substantially larger differences obtain for negative party images. Although 43% of those interviewed had negative images of the leader of their own party, 76% had negative images of leaders of other parties. In terms of the mean number of images held, respondents had approximately three times as many positive (1.6), as opposed to negative (0.6), images of their own party leader. Regarding other party leaders, however, the mean number of positive and negative images is virtually identical (1.9 vs. 2.0). These data do not suggest that those with psychological attachments to a particular party fail to perceive positive features of the images of leaders of other parties, and therefore only partially conform to traditional assumptions about the psychological functions of party identification.

The manner in which partisanship influences perceptions of party leaders can be considered in greater detail by taking into account not only the direction of partisan attachments but also their intensity, stability, and consistency. Tables 7.7 and 7.8 present data on the number of mentions (positive and negative) of the leaders of one's own and other parties in terms of the intensity and stability of federal partisanship and the directional consistency of federal and provincial partisanship. Also, in a fashion analogous to the analyses in Chapter Six, a measure of deviations from a pattern of strong, stable, and consistent partisanship

TABLE 7.7

Mentions of Leader of Own Party, by Partisanship Variables

	N	POSITIVE MENTIONS %	POSITIVE MENTIONS MEAN	NEGATIVE MENTIONS %	NEGATIVE MENTIONS MEAN	TOTAL MENTIONS %	TOTAL MENTIONS MEAN
Intensity							
Very strong	(304)	88	1.8	38	0.5	92	2.3
Fairly strong	(494)	82	1.6	42	0.6	88	2.2
Weak	(230)	76	1.3	54	0.8	87	2.1
F=			17.1*		6.7*		3.0
Stability							
Stable	(726)	81	1.5	38	0.5	88	2.1
Unstable	(418)	86	1.7	55	0.8	92	2.5
F=			4.6		24.7*		23.7*
Consistency							
Consistent	(782)	83	1.6	43	0.6	89	2.2
Inconsistent	(361)	82	1.6	45	0.7	88	2.3
F=			0.3		0.8		1.0
Federal Partisanship Deviations Index							
0	(414)	84	1.6	36	0.5	90	2.1
1	(410)	81	1.5	47	0.7	88	2.2
2	(245)	81	1.5	50	0.7	90	2.3
3	(74)	86	1.7	64	0.9	94	2.6
F=			0.8		8.0*		2.5

*Significant at the .01 level.

is constructed and employed in the analyses of the party leader image data.[32]

The data displayed in these tables confirm that party leader images are related to all of the partisanship variables. First, intensity of partisanship is related to the party leader image variables so that those with very strong partisan allegiances have more positive and fewer negative images of the leader of their own party than do those with weaker partisan attachments. However, intensity of partisanship does not have statistically significant relationships with the number of positive and negative images of leaders of *other* parties. Additionally, intensity of partisanship is not significantly related to the *total* number of images of party leaders (own party or other party) articulated.

Second, consistent with the findings in Chapter Six, there are a number of significant relationships between the stability of partisanship and party leader images. Specifically, unstable partisans are more likely to have more negative images of the leader of one's own party and to have more

TABLE 7.8

Mentions of Leaders of Other Parties, by Partisanship Variables

		POSITIVE MENTIONS		NEGATIVE MENTIONS		TOTAL MENTIONS	
		%	MEAN	%	MEAN	%	MEAN
Intensity	N						
Very strong	(304)	74	1.9	81	2.0	91	3.8
Fairly strong	(494)	75	2.1	76	1.9	91	3.9
Weak	(230)	69	2.0	70	1.8	84	3.7
F=			0.6		2.0		0.1
Stability							
Stable	(726)	70	1.8	73	1.8	87	3.5
Unstable	(418)	79	2.4	84	2.1	94	4.3
F=			15.5*		7.5*		18.1*
Consistency							
Consistent	(782)	71	1.9	76	1.9	88	3.8
Inconsistent	(361)	80	2.3	78	2.0	92	4.3
F=			8.9*		0.6		10.7*
Deviations Index							
0	(414)	71	1.8	75	1.9	89	3.5
1	(410)	71	1.9	75	1.9	88	3.7
2	(245)	80	2.4	81	2.0	91	4.4
3	(74)	84	2.5	81	2.1	96	4.7
F=			4.6*		0.7		5.3*

*Significant at the .01 level.

positive *and* negative images of the leaders of other parties. Instability of partisanship is also strongly related to the total number of images of party leaders — both of the leader of one's own party and the leaders of other parties.

Third, consistency of partisanship does not have any statistically significant relationships with the number of images of own party leader. This variable is related, however, to images of *other* party leaders. Specifically, inconsistent partisans tend to have more positive and more total images of these political figures.

Fourth, there is some evidence that the effects of deviations from a pattern of strong, stable, and consistent partisanship are cumulative. Thus, the more deviations from this pattern of partisanshp voters manifest, the more likely they are to have a negative image of the leader of their own party and a positive image of one or more leaders of other parties. Similarly, deviations from strong, stable, and consistent partisanship are associated with an increase in negative images of own party leader and positive images of other leaders. The latter of these relationships is perfectly monotonic and the former, virtually so. Also, the total number of images of other party leaders increases monotonically with increasing deviations.

The analyses of the manner in which partisanship is linked empirically with party leader images can be pressed somewhat further by examining which types of partisans have positive images of the leader of their own party, combined with negative images of leaders of other parties and

TABLE 7.9

A. Percentage of Respondents with Positive Image(s) of Leader of Own Party and Negative Image(s) of Leaders of Other Parties by Partisanship Variables

Intensity*

Very Strong	Fairly Strong	Weak
76	66	59

Stability*

Stable	Unstable
64	75

Consistency

Consistent	Inconsistent
67	69

Deviations Index

0	1	2	3
68	67	70	72

B. Percentage of Respondents with Negative Image(s) of Leader of Own Party and Positive Image(s) of Leaders of Other Parties by Partisanship Variables

Intensity*

Very Strong	Fairly Strong	Weak
31	36	43

Stability*

Stable	Unstable
30	47

Consistency

Consistent	Inconsistent
34	39

Deviations Index*

0	1	2	3
29	39	43	57

*Between group differences significant at the .01 level.

vice versa. These analyses will better enable one to detect possible "screening" or "distorting" effects of partisanship variables on party leader images.

The analyses presented in Table 7.9 indicate that intensity and stability, but not consistency, of partisanship are related to manifesting both own leader-positive, other leader-negative, and own leader-negative, other leader-positive combinations of party leader images. Considering intensity first, 76% of the "very strong," but only 59% of the "weak" partisans have positive image(s) of their own party leader and negative image(s) of other party leaders. Consistent with this finding, 43% of the latter, but only 31% of the former, partisans have the opposite pattern — that is, negative-own party leader and positive-other party leader images. As was noted in Chapter Six, this type of finding is consistent with the patterns which should obtain if intensity of partisanship is influencing the manner in which voters perceive political objects.

Interestingly, stability of partisanship is also related to the pattern of positive and negative party leader images. Consistent with data presented in Tables 7.7 and 7.8, the analyses summarized in Table 7.9 indicate that unstable partisans are more likely than their stable counterparts to manifest both the own leader-positive, other leader(s)-negative, and own leader-negative, other leader(s)-positive perceptual patterns. Thus, similar to the party image findings in Chapter Six, these analyses suggest that unstable partisans are more likely to have more leader images of *all* kinds than are those who have never changed their partisan attachments.

The last step in this analysis will be to determine if the relationships documented above persist in the presence of controls for political interest. Chapter Six has demonstrated that level of political interest is significantly and positively related to the number of federal and provincial party images articulated, and that relationships between partisanship and party images were not disturbed by controls for political interest. The former of these findings is not unexpected, in that the politically interested voter is more likely to be exposed to the kind of political information which will enrich his or her images of a variety of political objects. Further, levels of political interest are positively related to other variables, such as education, which are also likely to have important effects on the types of images which individuals develop.[33] However, the latter discovery — that is, that the relationship between party images and partisanship is sustained when controlled for level of political interest — is significant in that it suggests that the party image-partisanship relationships are not merely statistical artifacts produced by strong relationships between political interest and the partisanship variables.

Upon analysis, the relationships between political interest, partisanship, and party leader images bear a strong resemblance to the patterns de-

TABLE 7.10

Summary of Relationships Between Partisanship, Political Interest and Party Leader Image Variables (1974)

(PEARSON'S r'S. FIRST ORDER PARTIAL CONTROLLING FOR POLITICAL INTEREST SHOWN IN PARENTHESES)

	POLITICAL INTEREST INDEX	FEDERAL PARTISANSHIP DEVIATIONS INDEX	COMPONENTS OF PARTISANSHIP		
			INTENSITY	STABILITY	CONSISTENCY
Total Party Leader Images	.30*	.10*(.11*)	.05 (.01)	-.15*(-.13*)	-.08*(-.09*)
Own Party Leader	.15*	.02 (.02)	.07* (.04)	-.07*(-.05)	.01 (-.00)
Own Party Leader Positive	.18*	-.02(-.02)	.13* (.09*)	-.07*(-.05)	.01 (.01)
Own Party Leader Negative	.14*	.15*(.15*)	-.11*(-.14*)	-.15*(-.14*)	-.02 (-.02)
Other Party Leaders	.27*	.10*(.11*)	.03 (-.02)	-.13*(-.10*)	-.08*(-.09*)
Other Party Leaders Positive	.24*	.12*(.12*)	-.01 (-.06)	-.13*(-.10*)	-.10*(-.11*)
Other Party Leaders Negative	.20*	.04 (.05)	.06 (-.03)	-.08*(-.06)	-.03 (-.04)

*Significant at the .01 level.

scribed above. As documented in Table 7.10, the political interest index[34] is significantly and positively correlated with all of the party leader images variables. Moreover, most of the political interest-party leader image correlations (Table 7.10, column one) are very similar in magnitude to equivalent correlations for the party image variables (Table 6.13). More interestingly, a large majority (13 of 17) of the statistically significant correlations between the partisanship variables and the several party leader image variables remain statistically significant when controls are introduced for level of political interest, and in no instance is the sign of a correlation coefficient reversed by such a control.

CONCLUSION

The analyses presented previously have documented a number of important points regarding levels of affect for Canadian party leaders and the electorate's perceptions of these political figures. In both 1974 and 1968, affective reactions to party leaders varied sharply, with Mr. Trudeau enjoying the strongest levels of affect in both years. Trudeau's affective support was relatively strong among all segments of the electorate, but he was particularly well-liked by French Canadians, Catholics, and individuals with high socio-economic status. Also of significance was the net decline in affect levels for all party leaders from 1968 to 1974. This decline was a generalized phenomenon, cutting across all major regional, religious, ethnic, and other socio-demographic categories. Affect levels for all leaders, however, did not decline to the same extent, with increasing negative affect being particularly noticeable in Mr. Stanfield's case. These patterns of variability suggest both the potential of party leader images to influence voting choice in particular elections, and the possibility that the impact of party leader images on voting choice will vary, perhaps considerably, over time, even when the same set of leaders is present in several successive election campaigns.

The data strongly indicated tendencies for the electorate to view and evaluate party leaders in personal or stylistic, rather than in issue terms. References to presumably salient campaign issues, such as leadership, inflation, wage and price controls in 1974, or national unity in 1968 were relatively infrequent in the responses to the party leader image questions. Although one might be tempted to interpret these data as indicating a somewhat jejeune component in the electorate's images of party leaders, it is possible that many voters view party leaders' personal characteristics as suggestive of ability to deal with salient issues or to execute the business of government effectively. Cognizance of this possibility is important for analyzing how both party leaders and issues influence electoral choice. The relationship between party leader images and voting behaviour will be considered explicitly in Chapter Eleven.

Similar to analyses conducted in Chapter Six, perceptions of party leaders were shown to have a number of statistically significant relationships with the intensity, stability, and consistency of partisanship. Strong partisans tended to have more images of the leader of the party with which they felt an attachment, while those with unstable and/or inconsistent partisan ties mentioned more images of all party leaders, but particularly leaders of parties other than their own. Moreover, the partisanship-party leader image correlations persisted in the presence of statistical controls for political interest, which, by itself, has positive correlations with all of the party leader image variables. These findings suggest that the impact of party and party leader images on voting behaviour are conditioned by both partisanship *and* political interest. This is a topic of considerable theoretical significance which will be explored in Chapters Ten and Eleven.

FOOTNOTES

1. On the significance of party leaders see R. MacGregor Dawson, *The Government of Canada,* 2nd ed. (Toronto: University of Toronto Press, 1956), p. 226; John Meisel, *The Canadian General Election of 1957* (Toronto: University of Toronto Press, 1962), chaps. 3, 7, 9, 10; Peter Regenstreif, *The Diefenbaker Interlude* (Toronto: Longmans Canada, 1965); Howard A. Scarrow, "Distinguishing Between Political Parties: The Case of Canada," *Midwest Journal of Political Science,* 9 (1965), p. 75; J. Murray Beck, *Pendulum of Power* (Scarborough: Prentice-Hall, 1968), chap. 28; Gilbert R. Winham and Robert B. Cunningham, "Party Leader Images in the 1968 Federal Election," *Canadian Journal of Political Science* (1970) pp. 37-55; William P. Irvine, "An Overview of the 1974 Federal Election in Canada," in H. R. Penniman, ed., *Canada at the Polls* (Washington, D.C.: American Enterprise Institute for Public Policy Research, 1975), p. 43; Stephen Clarkson, "Pierre Trudeau and the Liberal Party: The Jockey and the Horse," in H. R. Penniman, ed., *Canada at the Polls,* chap. 3.
2. Dawson, *op. cit.* See also Paul M. Sniderman, H. D. Forbes, and Ian Melzer, "Party Loyalty and Electoral Volatility: A Study of the Canadian Party System," *Canadian Journal of Political Science* (1974), pp. 268-73.
3. Regenstreif, *op. cit.,* pp. 68-9.
4. *Ibid.,* pp. 68-9. For a more general discussion of the impact of the media on the types of electoral campaigns waged by political parties, see Leon D. Epstein, *Political Parties in Western Democracies* (New York: Praeger, 1967), chap. 9.
5. Regenstreif, *op. cit.,* pp. 68-9.
6. The question asked in 1974 is cited in Appendix B, Q. 44. Similar questions were used in the 1965 and 1968 surveys.
7. For the question used, see Appendix B, Q. 49.
8. Regenstreif, *op. cit.,* p. 72; Winham and Cunningham, *op. cit.,* p. 55.
9. Winham and Cunningham, *op. cit.,* pp. 44-6; Regenstreif, *op. cit.,* p. 71.
10. Winham and Cunningham, *op. cit.,* p. 55.

11. Angus Campbell et al., *The American Voter* (New York: Wiley, 1960), chap. 4; Donald E. Stokes, "Some Dynamic Elements of Contests for the Presidency," *American Political Science Review* (1966), pp. 19-28. See also Donald E. Stokes et al., "Components of Electoral Decision," *American Political Science Review* (1958), pp. 367-87. For a study indicating the increasing importance of different aspects of images in United States presidential elections over the period 1952-72, see Samuel A. Kirkpatrick, William Lyons, and Michael R. Fitzgerald, "Candidates, Parties, and Issues in the American Electorate: Two Decades of Change," in S. A. Kirkpatrick, ed., *American Electoral Behavior: Change and Stability* (Beverly Hills: Sage Publications, 1976), pp. 35-71.

12. Warren E. Miller and Teresa E. Levitin, *Leadership and Change: The New Politics and the American Electorate* (Cambridge, Mass.: Winthrop Publishers, 1976), chap. 7.

13. David Butler and Donald Stokes, *Political Change in Britain,* 2nd college ed. (New York: St. Martin's Press, 1966), chap. 16; Hans D. Klingemann and Franz Urban Pappi, "The 1969 Bundestag Election in the Federal Republic of Germany: An Analysis of Voting Behaviour," *Comparative Politics* (1970), pp. 523-48; Jean Charlot, "The End of Gaullism?" in H. R. Penniman, ed., *France at the Polls* (Washington, D.C.: American Enterprise Institute for Public Policy Research, 1975), chap. 3.

14. Stokes, *op. cit.*

15. Journalistic accounts of elections often place heavy emphasis on the role played by the personal characteristics of party leaders. See, for example, Donald Peacock, *Journey to Power* (Toronto: Ryerson Press, 1968), or Theodore White, *The Making of the President: 1960* (New York: Atheneum, 1961).

16. The thermometer questions used are cited in Appendix B, Q. 50.

17. See, for example, Lawrence LeDuc, "The Measurement of Public Opinion," in Penniman, ed., *Canada at the Polls,* p. 230.

18. The growing strength of the PCs in the Prairies in the 1968-74 period can be appreciated by noting that the party won 36%, 48%, and 51% of the seats in this region in 1968, 1972, and 1974 respectively.

19. The thermometer question about Mr. Caouette was asked in Quebec only in 1968.

20. See, for example, Campbell et al., *op. cit.,* chap. 6; Stokes, *op. cit.*

21. See Chapter 5, especially Tables 5.2 and 5.5.

22. That party leaders may influence voters to switch their party identifications is suggested, of course, by the finding reported in Chapter 5 (Table 5.9) that 25% of those surveyed in 1974 reporting to have changed their federal party identifications stated they did so because of the party leaders. For an argument that party leaders may have an indirect effect on partisan change via the policy positions they espouse, see Jane Jenson "Party Strategy and Party Identification: Some Patterns of Partisan Allegiance," *Canadian Journal of Political Science* (1976), pp. 27-48.

23. Campbell et al., *op. cit.,* and Stokes, *op. cit.* For more recent United States data, see David E. RePass, "Comment: Political Methodologies in Disarray: Some Alternative Interpretations of the 1972 Election," *American Political Science Review* (1976), pp. 814-31.

24. See Beck, *op. cit.,* chap. 28.

25. Data on party leader affect comparable to those for 1968 and 1974 are unavailable for 1972.

26. See Appendix B, Q. 51-54. Similar questions were asked in both surveys.
27. Clarkson, *op. cit.*
28. Clarkson, *op. cit.* See also George Perlin, "The Progressive Conservative Party in the Election of 1974," in Penniman, ed., *Canada at the Polls*, chap. 4.
29. Perlin, *op. cit.*, pp. 111-14. For an analysis of press coverage of issues in the 1974 election, see chap. 9. See also Fletcher, *op. cit.*, pp. 274-78.
30. See, for example, the analysis in Perlin, *op. cit.*, pp. 109-14.
31. In Canadian studies, Winham, Cunningham, and Regenstreif found that voters emphasize the personal characteristics of party leaders. Winham and Cunningham, *op. cit.*, pp. 40-42; Regenstreif, *The Diefenbaker Interlude*, pp. 72-3. Similarly, Butler and Stokes, after examining British party leader image data, concluded: "At each round of interviews the vast majority of the positive and negative themes spontaneously associated with the Conservative and Labour leaders were personal, rather than ones whose content was supplied by the goals which the leaders were seen as the instrument for achieving." In their studies, an average of fully 85% of the party leader references are to personal characteristics. Butler and Stokes, *op. cit.*, p. 238. United States data also document that personal references bulk large in party leader image data. See Campbell et al., *op. cit.*, p. 54, and RePass, *op. cit.*, pp. 822-23.
32. See Appendix B for construction of this measure.
33. Educational level has statistically significant relationships with all of the party leader image variables employed in this chapter, except the number of images of the leader of one's own party.
34. On the construction of the political interest index, see Appendix B, Q. 1-3.

Chapter Eight

Issues in Canadian Politics

Elections take place in a context of policy debate, where party leaders and candidates make pronouncements about their stands on the issues of the day. They make promises, criticize their opponents, and define the issues of importance. Early studies of voting, however, revealed that many voters were poorly informed about parties and candidates, cared little about issue differences, and made their decisions well in advance of the election or even the campaign.[1] In keeping with these observations, models of electoral decision-making developed which place little emphasis on issues and instead stressed the impact of candidates, leaders, and particularly the political party.[2] These models of electoral choice have been debated both on methodological grounds[3] and with reference to possible limitations imposed by space and time.[4] Several recent studies have documented increases in the conceptualization, coherence, and impact of issues on voting,[5] and although these controversies are not yet settled, it is clear that the role played by issues in shaping electoral choice and electoral outcomes cannot be ignored. This is of particular note in Canada, because to date little attention has been directed toward the analysis of the electoral effects of issues.[6] By exploring in detail some of the issue perceptions of the 1974 electorate, the present chapter will lay the foundation for assessing the impact of issues on voting behaviour and electoral outcomes.

It is helpful to consider the *conditions* under which issues might theoretically be of importance in elections. There are two conditions which must be met if an issue is to have an impact either on individual behaviour or on electoral outcomes.[7] First, there must be a link developed between the issue and the voters. The issue must be *salient* to voters — that is, they must have an opinion on it and they must consider the issue

243

to be of some importance. The more voters who perceive and develop strong impressions of an issue, the greater is the potential for the issue to have an influence on changing the relative strength of the parties. A second requirement is that the issues must be *linked with partisan controversy*. An issue can have little influence on individual choice or election outcomes if all the parties are thought to have the same position on the issue. If, however, parties are perceived as having different positions on an issue, then voters can make judgments regarding which party is closest to their personal position on an issue, and a basis is thereby established for making electoral decisions with reference to individual issue preferences. Depending upon the nature of these judgments, issue preferences may reinforce existing partisan predispositions or constitute forces acting to weaken or even change such predispositions.

A third condition is necessary for an issue to affect electoral outcomes, namely opinion must be strongly skewed in a single direction. At the extreme, such an issue becomes a *valence* issue, one for which there is a high level of agreement of opinion on its resolution. In contrast, an issue where substantial proportions of the electorate assume different positions cannot have a decisive effect on the distribution of party support. Voters' movement back and forth between parties, in reaction to judgments about the relative congruence between the parties' and their own personal positions on such issues, can often be expected to cancel or "wash out" the electoral effects of these *position* issues. Thus, only if an issue has valence properties will it be one of maximum potential for influencing electoral outcomes.[8]

The conditions adumbrated above provide a means of assessing the potential importance of issues in any particular electoral context. The 1974 Election Study examined four issues in detail — foreign investment, bilingualism, majority government, and inflation. Analysis of these four issues in terms of these conditions indicates differences in the potential effects of several types of issues on electoral results and illustrates sources of variation in such effects. Such analyses also "set the stage" for studying the effects of issues on voting behaviour in 1974 and the manner in which issues influenced the outcome of this election.

Basic data on the four issues to be examined in detail and on other issues is shown in Figure 8.1. When queried concerning which issue or issues were "most important" to them personally in the 1974 election, "inflation" responses constituted the dominant theme.[9] All together, nearly 60% of the respondents mentioning an issue cited inflation, and a further 11% made reference to the related theme of wage and price controls. In addition to these two issues, a broad range of other issues was specified by smaller minorities of respondents, with no single issue being referred to by more than 9% of the electorate. The limits of issue orientation among the 1974 electorate are suggested by the fact that 30% did not delineate an important issue.

Indicative of potential variability in the electoral impact of issues is the finding that the "party closest on most important issue" responses differed widely across issues. Illustratively, whereas a minority of respondents citing inflation (39%) judged the Liberals were closest to them on this issue, of those referring to majority government or leadership, approximately three-quarters stated that Liberals were closest. As Figure 8.1 shows, many other examples of this type of pattern are in evidence. An assessment of the electoral import of these responses will require a considerably more refined analysis, but at a minimum it is evident that issue perceptions are subject to substantial variance. Further elucidation of the nature and electoral potential of issues can be achieved by considering the four specific issues of foreign investment, bilingualism, majority government, and inflation.

THE ISSUE OF FOREIGN INVESTMENT

The question of investment by foreigners in the Canadian economy has been a point of lively dispute for the past fifteen years. It has, however, a much longer history, going back to Canada's origins as an independent state. Out of Confederation and the implementation of Sir John A. Macdonald's National Policy for economic development emerged the foreign investment issue.[10] Thus, it has been of more or less importance for over a century, and the question of the control of the economy by non-Canadians again surfaced in federal politics in the first half of the 1960s. Since then it has occupied the attention of federal and provincial politicians, as well as large numbers of interest group activists and the media.[11] This issue has evoked regulatory policy responses, such as the Foreign Investment Review Agency, to screen take-overs of Canadian firms by non-Canadian interests. More generally, foreign investment is part of a larger complex of issues with political ramifications observable not only in the economy, but also in cultural activities, the universities, and publishing and broadcasting among others.

It was in this atmosphere that the 1974 study examined the salience and importance of this issue. This examination found, in brief, that foreign investment is an issue which does not seem to attract a great deal of mass attention, nor does it have a clearly agreed upon meaning for the electorate. There are large discrepancies in the way that it is conceptualized; it evokes few and very diverse prescriptions for policy action; and individuals differ a great deal in their evaluation of this issue. Foreign investment therefore is classified as an issue with little potential for influence in the 1974 election.

FIGURE 8.1
Issues in the 1974 Election

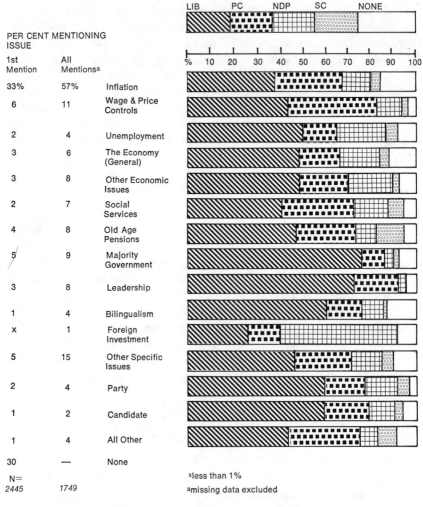

N=
2445   1749

ˣless than 1%
ᵃmissing data excluded

Respondents' attitudes toward the foreign investment issue were examined in detail by means of a combination of open-ended and closed-ended questions.[12] Using these questions it is possible to identify several different dimensions of this issue. The first of these is the general salience of the issue for the electorate. In terms of its visibility, one-quarter of the sample could give no answer at all when they were asked what foreign investment meant to them (see Table 8.1a). A further 13% responded in a

TABLE 8.1

Panel a: Some Descriptions of the Meaning of Foreign Investment (percentages)

	TOTAL SAMPLE	MISSING DATA EXCLUDED
General reference to one country investing in another	12%	19%
General reference to foreigners investing in Canada	12	19
References to foreigners investing in Canada in — Natural resources	3	5
— Manufacturing	1	2
— Other and combinations	1	2
Reference to U.S. investing in Canada in — General reference	13	21
— Natural resources	2	3
— Manufacturing	2	3
Other specific countries investing in Canada	1	2
Multinational corporations investing in Canada	1	2
Foreign trade	3	5
Canada investing abroad; Canadian foreign aid	11	17
Missing data — no answer	24	—
— no codeable definition	13	—
N=	*(1241)*	*(779)*

Panel b: Evaluations of Foreign Investment in Canada

Completely Positive	28%
Qualified Positive	28
Neutral	2
Qualified Negative	15
Completely Negative	27
N=	*(820)*[a]

[a]Includes only those respondents referring to foreign investment *in Canada*.

fashion such that we were unable to extract any meaningful content. They answered, but their words did not indicate what was actually meant by the term foreign investment. These two groups make up 37% of the sample. In other words, well over one-third of this representative group of Canadians had no views on foreign investment — the term had little salience for them.

A further indication of the poorly developed link of the issue to the voters is seen in the range of meaning attached to the term. As Table 8.1 shows, of those who could and did answer the question, a substantial number defined foreign investment as non-Canadian involvement in the Canadian economy. Sixty per cent of the answers would fall into such a characterization. A further 19% described the issue very generally as investment by one country in another, without mentioning any relevance to the Canadian situation. They saw it in the most general of terms. It is interesting to note that only 17% of the sample made any reference at all to the involvement of *Americans* in Canada. This is despite the fact that most of the popular and partisan discussion of this question for the past fifteen years has focussed quite specifically on American investment and the economic, political, and cultural implications of Canada's proximity to the United States.

A substantial number of responses took a very different approach. Five per cent of the answers described foreign investment in terms which were more appropriate descriptions of foreign trade (Table 8.1). They focussed on the exchange of goods between countries, rather than the movement of capital. Finally, and most surprisingly, another 18% of the answers described foreign investment as investment by *Canadians* in other countries or as Canadian foreign aid. In these instances, Canada was seen as the source rather than the recipient of the investment. If those who described foreign investment in terms of trade are combined with those who use the term to mean Canada investing abroad, almost one-quarter of the answers differed substantially in their characterization from the way that the term is used in day-to-day political discourse. Both the high level of non-response and the unconventional nature of some answers indicate foreign investment as an issue with *low salience* for the electorate.

The reported importance of this issue in the 1974 election confirms this judgment about its salience. When all respondents were asked to define the issue most important for them in 1974, only 1% of all references were to foreign investment, most of these being "second mentions" (Figure 8.1). As an election issue it clearly did not attract much attention.

Other dimensions of the answers to the questions on foreign investment are relevant here. Only 16% of those who answered the question included any reference to *domination* of one country by another resulting from foreign investment. Those answers which did include a component refering to domination tended to see foreign investment in terms of American activity in Canada. However, the overwhelming impression to emerge is that little sense of domination exists at all. The respondents were not fearful of the impact of foreign investment, at least as they responded to our questioning.

They also had little sense of a need to do anything about foreign investment. There were few references to actions which needed to be taken in the way of controlling, restricting, or altering the direction of this investment. Over half the answers contained no prescriptive statement at all, and of those who did make recommendations for action to deal with foreign investment, the vast majority were of the most general types, e.g., "something should be done" or "the government should do something to restrict foreign investment." Only 13% mentioned specific programmes or proposed future policy. Only one person mentioned the agency developed to monitor foreign investment, FIRA.

The *evaluations* of the issue that emerged from these answers were more positive than negative (Table 8.1b). Fifty-six per cent of the responses could be classified as positive, half of these being strongly positive. Of the negative evaluations of foreign investment, 27% were strongly negative and 15% were more qualified in their opposition. These answers do not present a picture of high levels of agreement about the source of the issue, the steps needed to resolve the question, or even whether a problem can be said to exist. Not only was this not a salient issue, but also it was not one which could qualify as having valence properties.

TABLE 8.2

Relationship Between Party Seen as Closest to Respondents' Own Position on Foreign Investment and Direction of Federal Partisanship (diagonal percentages)

PARTISANSHIP

PARTY CLOSEST ON FOREIGN INVESTMENT	LIBERAL	PROGRESSIVE CONSERVATIVE	NDP	SOCIAL CREDIT
Liberal	40	5	2	1
Progressive Conservative	2	12	1	0
NDP	6	3	9	0
Social Credit	1	1	0	1
None	9	5	2	0
				100%

V=.51*   (N=*588*)

*Significant at .01.

Some aspects of the perception of foreign investment are related to characteristics of individual respondents, but an examination of these patterns does not lead to any alteration in the original assessment. Those with higher education and higher income tended to see the issue more in terms of American influence, while those with lower education and income described it in more general terms as "foreigners investing in Canada." Anglophones also described the issue with reference to the United States more than did francophones. There was, however, little difference between groups in their evaluation of the issue — a statistically significant difference does not exist across language and income categories and only a very weak relationship to education is observable.

Further analysis (Table 8.2) shows that over 60% of those partisans selecting a party closest to them on foreign investment chose their own party. A further 16% selected the "no party closest" option, and approximately one partisan in five designated a party other than their own. Of the partisans not selecting their own party, 9% chose the NDP, 8% chose the Liberals, with the remainder being approximately equally divided between the PCs and Social Credit. Overall, the patterning in the data suggests that no one party gained a large net advantage in the evaluations of party closest on foreign investment over and above that associated with the distribution of partisanship in the electorate.

The conclusion which can be drawn from this examination of the way that the electorate sees the foreign investment issue is that there was much disagreement as to its meaning, which seems to follow from the low salience of the issue and its lack of importance for the electorate. There is also little evidence of any agreement on common goals or evaluations of the issue. For the future, sharp increases in salience and greater agreement on evaluation and goals would have to occur before it could be predicted that foreign investment might be a potentially influential electoral issue.

THE ISSUE OF BILINGUALISM

Bilingualism is an issue with quite different characteristics than foreign investment, and it was perceived very differently by the electorate. The relations between Canada's two founding cultures, the English and the French, have, since the mid-1960s and the years after the Royal Commission on Bilingualism and Biculturalism, been closely linked to the question of language policy.[13] A major thrust of the federal government action, under the leadership first of Prime Minister Pearson and then Prime Minister Trudeau, has been the development of bilingualism, particularly in the federal public service. This policy of encouraging a wider use of both official languages within the apparatus of the federal state has evoked varying responses. There has been considerable opposition among anglophones to the initiatives of the federal government and some resentment toward francophones (see Chapter One). The issue has become even more complicated recently by the actions of the provincial governments in Quebec which have taken steps to preserve and expand the use of French in the province. At the time of the 1974 federal election, the Liberal government of Robert Bourassa had just recently introduced Bill 22, language legislation designed to support and encourage a wider use of French in the economic and cultural life of Quebec.

In this atmosphere of concern over language use, language rights, and the political influence of linguistic groups, the 1974 Election Study investigated various aspects of the issue of bilingualism. As with foreign investment, the purpose of this investigation was to elicit the several dimensions of the issue in the minds of the electorate.[14]

The first of these dimensions is the content of the term — that is, what people think bilingualism means or "think of when it is mentioned."

TABLE 8.3

Panel a: Some Descriptions of the Meaning of Bilingualism (percentages)

	TOTAL SAMPLE	MISSING DATA EXCLUDED
Language or linguistic ability generally	15%	18%
Speaking two languages generally	9	11
Speaking English and French	26	31
Speaking French, for anglophones	14	15
Speaking English, for francophones	2	2
Learning English or French for schools, job, and for travel	12	14
Language legislation	4	4
Separatism	3	4
Missing data — no answer on question	7	—
— no codeable definition	9	—
N=	*(1241)*	*(1038)*

Panel b: Prescriptions Offered Concerning Bilingualism

People should be bilingual; it's a good thing; everywhere	36%
There should be no compulsory second language	22
English or French should be taught in the schools	10
English or French should be the only language	9
English or French the primary language; other optional	9
Any language should be allowed	6
French should be used only in Quebec, or where there are substantial numbers of Francophones	5
Other	5
N=	*(896)*[a]

[a]Includes only those respondents (75% of total) mentioning a prescriptive theme in their answers on bilingualism.

These answers are displayed in Table 8.3. The first thing to note about these data is that over 90% of the respondents chose to give an answer to the open-ended question on the meaning of bilingualism. This rate of response can be compared to the first issue discussed, that of foreign investment, for which 24% of those questioned had no notion of its meaning, and to the general question on issues important in the 1974 election, for which 30% of the sample had no answer or could think of no important issues. Bilingualism, in contrast, had high visibility as an issue for Canadians and evoked both personal definitions and personal positions from respondents.

For 31% of those with usable responses, the term was defined in its specific Canadian context of speaking both English and French. A further 29% described bilingualism in more general terms of language or speaking two languages, often emphasizing *any* two. Another major grouping of responses was that of anglophones who defined bilingualism specifically as speaking French. Others saw bilingualism in instrumental terms, as something that had to be learned in school or for work or travel. The mentions of bilingualism in reference to schools also included some who thought that bilingualism should be emphasized *only* in the schools and should not be required of adults past the age of formal schooling.

Interestingly, the issue was not seen primarily in regional terms. Two-thirds of the answers contained no references to locations in which bilingualism was prevalent, absent, needed, or whatever. Of the third of the answers which contain a reference to the location of bilingualism, over half (56%) gave a general reference to Quebec. The next most frequent location reference was to the need for bilingualism everywhere in the country (24%).

Thus, widespread agreement existed on the meaning of bilingualism and the nature of the issue. Bilingualism is about language and, more importantly, it is about English and French. To a minor extent it has an instrumental connection to the individual, in that it is needed for work or travel. For a very few respondents it was related directly to policy initiatives — the Official Language Bill, Bill 22, or language policy generally.

There were few differences in the meaning of the issue for sub-groups of the electorate. Differences in conceptualization of the issue, as meaning language ability generally, or as having an instrumental impact or political content, did not appear among residents of the several provinces, different age or language groups, those with different educational levels, or between native-born and other Canadians. Within all of these groups, the meaning of the issue was similar. Thus, for most respondents, whatever their personal characteristics, a discussion of bilingualism brought to mind language relations and language ability, without direct policy content. They did, however, have views on how this issue might best be dealt with by political actors. Bilingualism was an issue which had *general salience* for Canadians, as indicated both by its visibility and by the high level of agreement on the meaning, or content, of the issue. The contrast to the foreign investment issue on this dimension is striking indeed.

The general importance of the bilingualism issue did not extend to the 1974 election. In that particular election, the question asking about important issues, as reported in Figure 8.1, produced only 1% of the sample who felt bilingualism was the most important issue, and only 4% of all issue mentions included a reference to bilingualism. While it was an issue about which people were aware, it must be classified as one of low salience in 1974. However, the generally high level of awareness and understanding might lead to an expectation of potential influence in future elections, if other conditions were to be met.

Neither was bilingualism a valence issue in terms of the distribution of prescriptive and evaluative attributes. The question did evoke prescriptive statements for about 80% of those answering the questions. The most frequent of these prescriptive proposals was the most general, seeing bilingualism as a "good thing" and something to be continued (Table 8.3b). This answer was given by 36% of the respondents. On the other hand, another 22% of the answers made the point that there should be no compulsory second language. Nine per cent stated that English or French should be the only language, and an equal number suggested that English or French should be the primary language, with the other language being optional. Several other types of prescriptions were made, both for expansion and the contraction of the area of effective bilingualism in the country. The picture that emerges is one of wide divergence.

This divergence in policy preferences is also found in the expressed evaluations of bilingualism. Although there is a heavier concentration of positive views, substantial numbers of people are found on the negative side of this continuum, in the ranks of those opposed to greater bilingualism or the way that existing policy has been implemented thus far. Of those respondents whose answers contained an evaluative dimension, 35% were strongly positive and 23% were more qualified in their support. On the negative side, 21% were strongly negative and a further 16% were qualified in their negative attitude. While these answers did reflect judgments made by the electorate about the issue, it was not one which seemed to have a close personal connection to themselves and their lives. Eighty-five per cent of the answers were phrased in systemic terms, rather than in terms directly relating to their own everyday life.

These prescriptive and evaluative aspects differed within sub-groups of the population and further point to a divergence of attitudes on this position issue. The direction of evaluation is dependent upon the language group which individuals find themselves in, as well as the province within which they live. As Table 8.4 shows, 25% of anglophone Canadians were strongly negative in their evaluation of this issue, and the total number of English-speaking respondents on the negative end of the continuum was 45%. In contrast, only 16% of all francophones could be classified as having a view critical of the issue, and some of the criticisms were that enough had not yet been done. Almost half of all francophones were strongly positive about bilingualism. When the residence of the opponents and supporters is examined, it is clear, perhaps not surprisingly, that much of the negativism was concentrated in the Western half of the country. From Ontario westward the issue was seen in more negative terms than in the East. Not surprisingly, given the linguistic distribution, Quebec residents were the most positive at 80%.[15]

Table 8.5 shows the distribution of prescriptive categories between the two language groups. Over half of the anglophones prescribed some restrictions on bilingualism, whereas fewer than a third of francophones were equally restrictive. In contrast, almost three-fifths of the francophones supported bilingualism as a general idea. In terms of province of residence, the most proposals for restriction were found in the western half of the country, in particular British Columbia (65%), Saskatchewan (70%), and Manitoba (58%). Nova Scotia was the only Atlantic pro-

TABLE 8.4

Relationship Between Evaluations of Bilingualism and Language
(column percentages)

EVALUATION	LANGUAGE ENGLISH	FRENCH
Strongly positive	31%	49%
Qualified positive	20	32
Neutral	5	3
Qualified negative	20	6
Strongly negative	25	10
N=	(761)	(269)
V=.28*		

*Significant at .01.

vince in which substantial numbers propose restrictions (57%), and Ontario approximated the percentage for the country as a whole (50%). Residents of the three Maritime provinces were high in their prescriptions for expansion of bilingualism, at approximately 25% each. Quebec had the largest number of generally approving answers (59%), and Newfoundland was next (48%).

When the connection between positions on this issue and partisanship are examined, some important and potentially influential differences emerge. This issue, much more than foreign investment, has a clear connection to the positions of the political parties as they have developed historically. Thus, those members of the electorate with a highly favourable evaluation of bilingualism selected the Liberals as the party closest to them on this issue by a margin of three to one, whereas only 26% of those with strongly negative evaluations chose this party (Table 8.6). In contrast, the percentages of respondents opting for the PCs on bilingualism rises from 6% to 26% as evaluations of bilingualism shifted from strongly positive to negative. Also, there was a strong tendency among respondents with negative evaluations to select the "no party closest" alternative. In sum, there are differences in the way the bilingualism

TABLE 8.5

Relationship Between Prescriptions about Bilingualism and Language (column percentages)

PRESCRIPTION	LANGUAGE	
	ENGLISH	FRENCH
General approval	32%	59%
Expansion	17	11
Restriction	51	30
N=	(643)	(249)
V=.25*		

*Significant at .01.

TABLE 8.6

Relationship Between Party Seen as Closest on Bilingualism and Evaluations of Bilingualism (column percentages)

PARTY CLOSEST ON BILINGUALISM	EVALUATIONS OF BILINGUALISM				
	STRONGLY POSITIVE	POSITIVE	NEUTRAL	NEGATIVE	STRONGLY NEGATIVE
Liberal	75%	62%	69%	34%	26%
Progressive Conservative	6	12	11	26	23
NDP	1	3	2	7	7
Social Credit	3	2	0	3	3
None	15	20	18	30	41
N=	(264)	(164)	(29)	(118)	(142)
V=.21*					

*Significant at .01 level.

TABLE 8.7

Relationship Between Party Seen as Closest to Respondents' Own Position on Bilingualism and Direction of Federal Partisanship (diagonal percentages)

PARTY CLOSEST ON BILINGUALISM	PARTISANSHIP			
	LIBERAL	PROGRESSIVE CONSERVATIVE	NDP	SOCIAL CREDIT
Liberal	45	6	4	1
Progressive Conservative	3	10	1	x
NDP	1	1	2	x
Social Credit	1	x	x	1
None	10	9	4	x
				100%

(N=727)

V=.42*

*Significant at .01.
x Less than 1%.

issue is conceptualized and there appears to be some potential for move-ment between parties, although this was probably not realized in 1974 because of the lack of attention paid to the issue in the election.

However, if bilingualism is to be an important issue in future elections, it must be able to transcend partisan connections. A single party must be judged as best able to deal with the issue, and be able to pull partisans of other parties away from their normal attachment and convince them to support it because of its stand on the issue. There is some evidence that the Liberal party might, in the future, be able to do just that.[16] One of the characteristics of the linkage of the bilingualism issue to political parties is that the Liberal party position on this issue was seen as closest to the preferred position of many partisans of *other* parties. As Table 8.7 shows, 18% of those partisans selected a party other than the one with which they identified. Of this 18%, nearly two-thirds (11%) favoured the Liberals, with 4%, 2%, and 1% preferring the Conserva-tives, NDP, and Social Credit respectively. Viewed otherwise, fully 75% of the Liberals saw their party as closest on bilingualism. Comparable percentages are 40% for the PCs, 17% for the NDP, and 39% for Social Credit (data not shown in tabular form).

These patterns suggest that positions on bilingualism are differentially distributed among party supporters and that political parties might gain or lose adherents depending on the positions adopted on the issue. This issue does divide the electorate and does distinguish supporters of one party from the others, but there is also a degree of support for the Liberal position which might be used to mobilize support away from the other parties if bilingualism were to develop as an important campaign issue.

The picture which emerges from this exploration of the electorate's reaction to one of the long-standing issues of Canadian politics is one of future potential, not yet realized in the 1974 election. The bilingualism issue did not satisfy the first condition for potential influence because it could not be said to have been salient in the 1974 election. However, it is an issue about which people are aware and have well-developed attitudes, and its importance could increase in other electoral contexts. It is also an issue with well-developed party-issue links. The Liberal party is frequently seen as more capable of dealing with this issue by partisans of other parties. However, both positive and negative evaluations exist and there is little agreement about proper policy directions. It was not, in 1974, a valence issue.

THE MAJORITY GOVERNMENT ISSUE

The ability of elections in a multi-party system to produce a majority in Parliament and the desirability of such majorities for proper conduct of parliamentary business is a question which has attracted much discussion in Canada.[17] Some recent elections have been conducted in an atmosphere of debate about the relative benefits of majority and minority situations. The Liberals exhort the electorate to use its vote wisely and not "waste" it on a party which cannot form the government and which may take sufficient seats to prevent *any* party from forming a government with majority support. On the other hand, the minor parties argue that they can keep the government honest by acting as its conscience and holding the threat of imminent defeat over its head.

Of the last seven federal elections since 1957, four have resulted in no party gaining a clear majority of parliamentary seats. However, the 1972 election produced an even closer result than usual. Unlike the situation of the 1960s, when the plurality party was just a few seats short of a majority, the margin between the Liberal and Conservative parties between 1972 and 1974 was very slight. As the governing party, the Liberals had to rely on the support of the NDP in Parliament. Therefore, from October 1972 until the spring of 1974, the Liberal government faced almost continual predictions of its demise. Daily reports on the confidence of the House were made and, in fact, it was the failure of the NDP to support the government on a crucial vote which finally did bring about the 1974 election. Thus, the precarious situation in Parliament and the media's almost day-by-day soundings of the mood of the House of Commons were likely to provide a context within which the issue of majority government could attract considerable attention.

It was this context which led us to investigate the issue of majority government in some detail in the 1974 Election Study, albeit with a somewhat different methodology than that used for other issues. It is possible to develop indicators of the three conditions for potential influence and to assess the majority government issue in terms of these conditions. When this is done we find that majority government meets some of the criteria but not all for potential importance as an election issue. In fact, when comparisons are made to the situation in 1965, the potential of this issue seems to be in decline. This is the case despite the already discussed parliamentary conditions of the 1972-1974 period which might have been expected to lead to an increased emphasis on the issue and its potential for impact. Instead, it seems that there may be a greater appreciation of minority governments developing, perhaps as a result of the 1972-1974 experience (Table 8.8).

The first condition appears to be met with this issue. There was some public awareness of the majority government question. In response to a number of different questions about the issue, the rate of reply was high, with no more than 10% of the sample unwilling to answer any of the questions. This is a higher rate of response than was observed for bilingualism (Table 8.3), and much higher than foreign investment evoked (Figure 8.1). However, although people were aware of the issue and willing to answer questions about it, there seems to be some evidence that its importance may be in decline. This means that it probably satisfies the first condition less completely than it did in the past.[18] Nevertheless, it remains an issue with some salience. One-quarter of the sample, when asked if they were influenced by the issue, claimed to have been a great deal or somewhat affected. When it comes to election salience, Figure 8.1 shows that, after inflation and the closely related wage and price control issues, majority government more than any other single issue was mentioned as important in the 1974 election, both as the *most* important issue and when both possible mentions are taken into account. The rate of mentioning majority government (9%) was sufficiently large to indicate the importance of this issue for a respectably large segment of the electorate.

When the distribution of opinion on the issue is explored, it is found to be less skewed than might popularly be assumed. It has usually been argued, often by partisans of a party which stands to gain from such an argument, that majority government is necessary for the proper functioning of a parliamentary system. It would seem that the Canadian population is not completely convinced by this argument and may be coming to see positive advantages in minority governments. In other words, "majority government" may be assuming the properties of a position issue as opposed to remaining a valence issue. Partisan divisions are also becoming more important.

TABLE 8.8

Attitudes Toward the Majority Government Issue, 1965 and 1974 (percentages)

(a) Would switch parties to obtain a majority, 1965-74

	1965	1974
Very likely	23%	18%
Fairly likely	25	20
Not at all likely	43	54
No opinion	9	8
N=	(2721)	(1203)

(b) Preference for majority or minority government, 1974

Majority	55%
Minority	28
Depends	12
No opinion	5
N=	(1203)

(c) Was influenced by majority government issue, 1974

A great deal	12
Somewhat	12
Not at all	67
DK	9
N=	(1203)

The evidence for this argument comes from several sources. Two interesting pieces of information are available which indicate a lack of agreement in the electorate about how to evaluate the issue. The first is a Gallup Poll which asked, in the midst of the life of the twenty-ninth Parliament, for an evaluation of minority government.[19] It found that more than half the answers were supportive of minority government. Fifty-four per cent of the people interviewed by Gallup thought that minority government had been "good for the nation." In another question asked in the 1974 Study, it was found that only slightly more than half the respondents stated an outright preference for majority governments, with 28% actually preferring a minority situation, and a further 12% of the sample placing qualifications on their answers (Table 8.8b). All these data indicate that there was a tendency on the part of some voters to see minority outcomes as desirable under some circumstances. Thus, this issue was not as highly valenced as it had been in the past. There was no widespread agreement that the parliamentary system requires a majority to function properly, and people were less willing to change their vote to attempt to bring about such a majority.

The final condition to be examined is the link between this issue and the political parties. If disagreement exists in evaluating the issue, it would seem reasonable to look for partisan bases for these evaluations. If this partisan division does not exist and if one party is seen as best able to gain a majority, then there is a possibility that the issue may realize its potential for acting as a catalyst for realignment in any election. We saw such a link in the case of bilingualism, where the Liberals could potentially gain from the fact that they were often seen as best able to deal with bilingualism.

The majority government issue is obviously one which has possibilities for the development of this kind of cross-party evaluation. Supporters of the minor parties are under constant pressure not to "waste" their vote and not to vote for a party which might "steal" the majority. The potential recipients of such an evaluation are the Liberals who have, for the past fifty years, formed the government with great regularity. With solid support from Quebec, the Liberals have been able to confine their major opponents, the Progressive Conservatives, to a position in which they cannot hope for much more than a minority victory, except under extraordinary circumstances. Therefore, it is often assumed that supporters of minor parties, if they are concerned about the majority government issue, may be induced to switch to the Liberals.

The 1974 data clearly indicate that a link to partisanship does exist and that, therefore, there does not seem to be evidence of the overriding attraction of a single party for the partisans of the others. There is a gap between the Liberals on the one hand and the partisans of the minor parties on the other. While 64% of the Liberals prefer majority governments (and 56% of the Progressive Conservatives) only 32% of the Social Crediters and 28% of the NDP feel the same way. It seems to be the case that one's position on this issue is strongly related to the direction of partisanship. Partisans of minor parties differ from those of the larger parties in seeing the advantages which accrue to their parties in minority situations.

Further evidence on the relationship between majority government and partisanship may be obtained by considering "majority government" responses regarding the most important issue(s) in 1974. Nearly four-fifths of the partisans (N=125) citing this issue were Liberals, and only 7% were minor party supporters (data not shown in tabular form). Ninety-five per cent of the Liberal partisans selected the Liberal party as closest to them on majority government, as compared to 66% of the PCs who saw their own party as closest. Seventeen per cent of the Conservatives chose the Liberals, with a further 13% taking the "no party" option. Also, 63% of the minor party partisans perceived the Liberals as closest. In evaluating the tendencies of non-Liberals to deviate from their partisanship in selecting a party closest on majority government, however, it is important to note that these respondents represent only that 9% for whom majority government was a highly salient issue in 1974.

An assessment of the potential influence of the issue of majority government is now possible. Once again, only some of the criteria have been satisfied, but this issue is of particular interest because it seems to reflect a pattern of movement away from potential influence. This is in contrast to the conclusion drawn about bilingualism, which seemed to hold out possibilities for the future if some party could successfully transform it into a valence issue. In 1974 majority government was considered salient and important by at least some voters. However, it seems to be moving away from a situation which would permit it to be characterized as a classic valence issue, and is becoming a position issue, the positions on which are tied to partisanship. Nevertheless, the majority government issue in 1974 partially meets our specified conditions, and may have been capable of exerting small effects on individual behaviour and possibly the electoral outcome. In this regard it is different than either foreign investment or bilingualism.

THE ISSUE OF INFLATION

The last issue to be examined is inflation, which provides an example of an issue which meets the requirements of both high salience and a skewed distribution of attitudes. It fails, however, to meet the third requirement, that of a link to a single party.

The 1974 election took place in a context of increasing inflation, which seemed most visible in the area of rising prices for many commodities. All parties adopted electoral strategies to play upon this economic condition. The three opposition parties were critical of the way the government had handled the economy in the past, and the Progressive Conservatives formulated a policy calling for wage and price controls. The NDP reacted sharply to the Conservative policy, making arguments about the impossibility of controlling prices and the harmful effects that wage controls could be expected to have on workers. The Liberal strategy seemed to be one of down-playing inflation, calling it a world-wide problem, and emphasizing the leadership of Prime Minister Trudeau. It was this context of controversy that lay behind the answers to the open-ended questions asking about inflation in the 1974 Election Study.[20] The electorate seemed to share the high interest of the press and parties in this issue. Looking first at general salience, there is both a very high response rate for the question asking for the meaning of the issue and much agreement on its meaning. Of all issues examined, inflation evoked the most answers and this would seem to indicate that it was an issue with extraordinarily high visibility. As Table 8.9 shows, only 5% of the respondents had no notion of the meaning of the issue and all but 8% of the sample provided a codeable definition. Many of these answers were very general, and the content was little more than a statement that inflation "is a terrible problem." Twenty per cent of the answers fall into this most general category. For much of the rest of the answers, there was a very high level of agreement about what inflation meant — rising prices. Therefore, when Canadians thought about inflation, in contrast to foreign investment, they were all thinking about the same phenomenon. For a third of those who answered the question, inflation was defined in terms of increased prices and the high cost of living. The low level of wages was mentioned much less frequently, either alone (2%) or in combination with high prices (13%). For 17% of the respondents, inflation was described as a problem of specific commodities, with food the most often mentioned. There were more cataclysmic visions of the issue, with 10% of the respondents seeing it linked to a coming depression. At the same time, 4% were more phlegmatic in their views, seeing inflation as either inevitable or linked to other factors and being a "world-wide phenomenon."

Thus, in 1974 inflation was a highly visible issue which the electorate was willing to discuss in greater or lesser detail. There was a fairly high level of agreement about the meaning of the issue. Many of the answers refer to prices generally or prices of specific commodities. In sum about two-thirds of the responses described inflation in terms of prices. When the respondents were asked how they personally were most affected by inflation, prices again were the most frequently cited factor.

TABLE 8.9

Some Descriptions of the Meaning of the Inflation Issue
(percentages)

	TOTAL SAMPLE	MISSING DATA EXCLUDED
Inflation is a problem	18%	20%
Increased prices generally	31	34
Increased wages needed	2	2
Price and wages	12	13
Increases in food, alone or in combination	13	14
Increases in other commodities	3	3
Inflation as connected to economic cataclysm, especially depression	9	10
Inflation is inevitable	4	4
Missing data — no answer on the question	5	—
— no codeable definition	3	—
N=	(1241)	(1142)

There is a good deal of *prima facie* evidence that this issue was also important in the 1974 election. When the respondents were asked to list issues important to them in the electoral campaign, inflation was at the top of the list by far. Thirty-three per cent of all respondents mentioned inflation as the most important in the campaign, and fully 57% of all references to campaign issues were to inflation (Figure 8.1). If references to wage and price controls, which were used in the campaign as a more specific version of the inflation issue, are included in the calculation, the amount of attention is even higher. Six per cent of all respondents listed controls as the most important issue, and 11% of all issue references were to these controls.

Clearly, inflation was salient and considered important in 1974. Its potential impact would be great, as most observers argued it was, if this were the only condition to be met. However, other conditions must be met if this issue is to realize its full potential.

Inflation is a classic valence issue. While it is not logically impossible to be in favour of inflation, the overwhelming direction of opinion on the question is to be opposed. We did not identify anyone in our sample who could be clearly said to favour greater inflation, and most respondents spontaneously adopted a tone of opposition to inflation. Also, there are other interesting features of the answers which indicate that the evaluation of the issue is unidirectional and there is little division about policy direction. Inflation appears to be a valence issue without any preconceived notions in the electorate regarding solutions. A party can step in and mobilize support if they can convince the people that *they* have an answer. While almost everyone could define the issue and more than 80% could describe how they were personally affected, there was little attempt to make prescriptions about solutions to the problem. Inflation resembles foreign investment in this regard. As Table 8.10 shows, only 17% of the answers included anything that could be interpreted as an explanation of the causes of inflation, and there was little agreement on those causes. For 20% of the respondents who mentioned a cause, this cause was government inaction, while for almost an equal number (18%) the problem was found in individual behaviour, whether excessive spending or too little saving. For another fifth, unions and corporations were almost equally blamed (10% and 12% respectively). Of the 17% who made prescriptive statements, by far the most common was the very general "something must be done" (32%). For 40% of the prescriptive answers specific policies were proposed, but there was divergence in what they should be. For 15% the solution was wage and price controls, while the rest called for different policies.

Therefore, inflation was considered to be an important and a highly

TABLE 8.10

Reported Causes of Inflation and Prescriptions for Dealing with It
(percentages)

A: CAUSES

Companies and their actions	12%
Unions and their activities	10
Unions and companies together	3
Government — action	6
— inaction	20
Combinations of unions, companies, or government	11
Shortages	5
World situation	8
The spiral effect	7
Individual behaviour	18
N=	(*213*)ª

ªIncludes only those respondents (17%) mentioning the theme "causes" in their responses.

B: PRESCRIPTIONS

General reference to need for action	32%
Need for government action	20
Specific government action	16
Wage and price control recommendation	15
Other specific policy	9
Change in individual behaviour needed	7
N=	(*206*)ᵇ

ᵇIncludes only those respondents (17%) mentioning the theme "prescriptions" in their responses.

visible issue, but it did not have well-developed programmatic content, nor did it evoke prescriptive comment. It was thus open to mobilization by an enterprising political party. It is probable that the Progressive Conservatives attempted just such mobilization with their wage and price control proposals. However, that kind of programme is one likely to split the electorate into "for" and "against" groupings in a way that destroys the potential of a valence issue. Opinion must be consolidated in a single direction, rather than divided, if it is to mobilize large numbers of voters behind a single party. Inflation fails to meet one of our conditions because no party is seen as best able to deal with the issue. Thus, although the issue meets the first two conditions, it fails the third.

This is seen when we examine the relationship between partisanship and party closest on inflation. The relationship is very strong (V=.63), with 79% selecting their own party (Table 8.11). Eighty-two per cent of the Liberal partisans chose their party as closest on inflation. Com-

TABLE 8.11

Relationship Between Party Seen as Closest to Respondents' Own Position on Inflation and Direction of Federal Partisanship (diagonal percentages)

		PARTISANSHIP		
PARTY CLOSEST ON INFLATION	LIBERAL	PROGRESSIVE CONSERVATIVE	NDP	SOCIAL CREDIT
Liberal	47	4	1	1
Progressive Conservative	5	21	2	1
NDP	3	1	9	x
Social Credit	2	x	0	2
None	x	x	0	0
				100%

V=.63* (N=*698*)

* Significant at .01.

x Less than 1%.

parable percentages for the Conservatives, New Democrats, and Social Credit are 79%, 74%, and 63% respectively (data not shown in tabular form). Overall, 20% chose a party other than their own, and less than 1% stated no party was closest. Significantly, this 20% divides very equally between the major parties, with 8% selecting the PCs and 6% the Liberals. Taken together, these data suggest that perceptions of parties' ability to deal with inflation were closely correlated to partisan attachments, with deviations from partisanship manifesting little net advantage to any party. Clearly, the inflation issue could, and probably did, cause some voters to choose the party they did.[21] However, because of the kind of issue it was, or more precisely, the kind of issue it was *not,* it did not bring about a wholesale realignment of party support in that election.

THE USE OF ISSUES TO CONCEPTUALIZE POLITICS

We will proceed at this juncture to a consideration of the way that *individuals* rather than the *electorate as whole* respond to campaign issues. Here, the focus will be on the extent to which issues are used by people to conceptualize, or describe, electoral and partisan politics. The voter, confronted with the need to make a decision at the polls or even to think about and evaluate politics between elections, may have a number of possible ways of organizing the political world. One of the most important and most often used mechanisms to provide guidance out of chaos is the political party. Attachments to parties, maintained from one election to the next, are used by some voters as cues to be-

266 Political Choice in Canada

haviour and also as a means of processing the mass of data which flows from the complexity of politics. However, unless partisan attachments constitute overwhelmingly powerful cueing and screening mechanisms, issues in specific electoral campaigns, as well as the party leaders and local candidates contesting particular elections, must be considered potentially important electoral influences. Individual voters may be more or less concerned with such factors. Here, we will examine the characteristics of those respondents to our study who have developed a view of the political world composed in whole or in part of issue concerns. Once this characterization is developed it is possible to consider the potential impact of issues for individuals. Little issue effect can exist if the political world is not described or viewed with reference to issues. The greater the willingness to think of and discuss elections in issue terms, the greater the possibility that positions on those issues will have an effect on electoral choice and outcomes. The importance of considering and analysing issue orientations is that issues are among the most changeable of the possible foci of electoral attention. The salience of particular issues can vary dramatically over time and party stances often change in relation to the same issue. Therefore, if the electorate is relying upon issues for its evaluation of the several political actors, as well as its more general conceptualization of politics, these evaluations are potentially unstable and may lead to fluctuations in individual behaviour and perhaps electoral outcomes.

The conceptualization of politics in terms of issues will be established here by the concept of issue orientation. An orientation to issues is considered to exist if respondents are willing to engage in discussion and description of various aspects of politics by referring to issues. Two measures are developed to indicate this notion of issue orientation. The first of these is derived from the questions asking for reports of important issues in the 1974 campaign.[22] If respondents do not mention issues, this is taken to mean that they do not conceptualize politics in terms of issues and controversies over issues, whereas the reverse is the inference drawn from the answer which mentions two issues. The sample is divided quite evenly on this measure, with 30% mentioning no issues, 33% mentioning one, and 37% giving two. The second indicator is derived from the answers to questions asking for party images. In Chapter Six it was reported that 61% of the respondents to these questions gave policy concerns or issues as the content of party image.[23] Images of this type can be taken as an indication that the respondents see the political world at least partially in terms of issues and that the political party to some extent becomes the embodiment of issue positions. These two indicators provide measures of the degree to which issues are used in the voters' conceptualization of the election and of political parties more generally.

TABLE 8.12

Relationship Between Issue Orientation and Political Participation

FEDERAL PARTICIPATION SCALE	ELECTORAL ISSUE ORIENTATION % MENTIONING TWO IMPORTANT CAMPAIGN ISSUES	ISSUE ORIENTED PARTY IMAGES MENTION OF ISSUES IN PARTY IMAGES	
N=		MEAN	%
Low: 0 (92)	11	0.5	26
1 (367)	23	0.9	49
2 (414)	36	1.5	64
3 (240)	45	1.6	70
High: 4 (91)	56	1.6	72

$$Tau_c = .26^* \qquad F = 21.1^*$$

*Significant at .01 level.

TABLE 8.13

Relationship Between Issue Orientation and a Composite Measure of Political Interest

INTEREST	% MENTIONING TWO OR MORE IMPORTANT ISSUES	PARTY IMAGES THAT ARE ISSUES MEAN	%
Low	23	0.9	52
Medium	39	1.5	64
High	49	1.7	71

$$V = .28^* \qquad F = 56.8^*$$

*Significant at .01 level.

The potential for issue impact, and in particular the flexibility that might result from the inherent variability of issues, will be explored in two ways. The first will be to examine the issue orientations of those people who have high levels of political interest and participation, and the second will be to specify relationships between issue orientations and the nature of partisan ties. If those with high levels of interest and participation rely more on issues to describe their political world, and also if weak, unstable, and inconsistent partisanship is correlated with the existence of issue orientations, then it might be expected that the potential for electoral change and volatility exists. If issues are to do more than reinforce existing interpretations of politics, they must have some link to those portions of the electorate which are politically active and likely to be changeable.

Looking first at the relationship between issue orientation and political participation, Table 8.12 clearly demonstrates that participation in federal politics is associated positively with the perception of important issues in the 1974 election and with the development of party images containing policy content. The relationship for both indicators is strongly monotonic. Of those who are classified as inactive in federal politics,[24] only 11% could think of two campaign issues important to them. Fully five times more of those respondents who are classified as very active in federal politics mentioned two issues. Thus, those people who participate in politics are very much more likely to be issue oriented.[25]

In the same way, the number of party images which contain issue content and participation in federal elections rapidly increase together. Only a quarter of the respondents who have a history of inactivity in federal politics supplied party images with issue content, whereas almost three-quarters of the two most active groups composed their images in terms of issues. Similarly, the mean number of party images which are issues increases rapidly as the score on the participation scale increases.[26]

Turning to the relationship between interest in politics and issue orientation, a similar pattern emerges.[27] The per cent of the respondents who mention two or more important issues increases dramatically as interest in politics rises. As Table 8.13 shows, almost 50% of those respondents who are classified as highly interested mentioned two issues which were important in the 1974 campaign. Less than 25% of those with a low score on the interest measure did the same. Similarly, the tendency to have issue components in party images rises with interest in politics. The per cent having an issue related party image and the mean number of such issue-images increases monotonically. Both indicators of issue orientation give the same picture of the relationship between an issue related conceptualization of politics and participation and interest in politics. Thus, the first condition for the potentiality of issue impact, the perceived salience and importance of issues, is met precisely by those groups in the electorate who are most likely to be active in and attentive to politics.

However, attention to issues cannot lead to electoral change if it merely reinforces predispositions in the direction of choice which arises from already existing partisanship. There must be a combination of issue orientation with a willingness to support different parties in accordance with the changes in the positions taken by those parties on matters of current political controversy. The exploration of this question requires an examination of the relationship between issue-orientation and partisan characteristics of the respondents. Table 8.14 shows these relationships. Of those people who have three deviations in their partisanship, almost half identify two issues important to them in the election, whereas only a third of the strong, stable, and consistent partisans do the same. The other indicator of issue orientation, the tendency to mention issues as the content of party images, operates in the same manner. Of the three components of partisanship, stability is the one which relates most strongly with issue orientation.[28] In summary, then, voters who are in-

TABLE 8.14

Relationship Between Issue Orientation and Partisanship

DEVIATIONS FROM STRONG, STABLE, CONSISTENT PARTISANSHIP		% MENTIONING TWO IMPORTANT CAMPAIGN ISSUES	ISSUES MENTIONED IN PARTY IMAGES	
N=			MEAN	%
0	(850)	34	1.3	61
1	(797)	32	1.3	58
2	(459)	37	1.4	62
3	(142)	47	2.0	70
		Tau$_c$=.02		F=10.0*

COMPONENTS
OF PARTISANSHIP

INTENSITY

Very strong	(629)	38	1.3	63
Fairly strong	(927)	37	1.4	66
Weak	(423)	34	1.4	58
		Tau$_c$= −.05		F=1.2

STABILITY

Stable	(1474)	31	1.2	57
Unstable	(775)	42	1.6	68
		Tau$_c$=.14*		F=45.0*

CONSISTENCY

Inconsistent	(680)	33	1.3	58
Consistent	(1568)	39	1.5	65
		Tau$_c$=.07*		F=11.5*

*Significant at .01 level.

terested and involved in politics, as well as those who are unstable or inconsistent partisans, are more likely to manifest issue orientations.

CONCLUSION

We began this chapter by specifying three conditions which must be met if an issue is to have important effects on both voting behaviour and electoral outcomes. These were: *salience, a link to parties,* and *a skewed distribution of opinion.* Upon examination of four specific issues — foreign investment, bilingualism, majority government, and inflation — it was found that although some of these issues met one or two of these conditions, none clearly met all three. In the case of foreign investment, it was of low salience, not linked to parties in a fashion which would suggest significant effects on the 1974 electoral outcome over and above those which could be accounted for in terms of partisan attachments,[29] and not possessed of a skewed distribution. Bilingualism, in contrast, was highly salient to the population, somewhat linked with parties, but voters took sharply divergent positions on the issue. It was also not perceived to be important in the electoral context of 1974. Majority government was salient to a modest proportion of the 1974 electorate, somewhat linked to parties, but the skewness of its distribution has been declining in the period since 1965. Inflation was of very high salience, possessed of a skewed distribution, but not valenced in favour of any party. Therefore, none of these four issues can be considered to have had the potential to exert a critical and widespread effect in the 1974 election.

Canadians vary in the extent to which they use these or other issues to conceptualize politics. There are strong relationships between interest in politics, political participation, and orientation to issues. More modest relationships were found between stability and consistency of partisanship and issue orientation. These findings suggest that the potential significance of issues may be more important for some particular segments of the electorate than others, namely those of high political interest and unstable or inconsistent partisanship. An adequate measure of issue influence therefore will require a categorization of the electorate which simultaneously takes into account patterns of both partisanship and political interest.

FOOTNOTES

1. See especially Paul Lazarsfeld, Bernard Berelson, and Hazel Gaudet, *The People's Choice* (New York: Duell, Sloan & Pearce, 1944); Bernard Berelson, Paul Lazarsfeld, and William McPhee, *Voting* (Chicago: University of Chicago Press, 1954); Norman Nie, Sidney Verba, and John Petrocik, *The Changing American Voter* (Cambridge, Mass.: Harvard University Press, 1976), chap. 2.

2. See, for example, Angus Campbell et al., *The American Voter* (New York: Wiley, 1960). In a summary of the findings of the several studies of The Survey Research Centre team of Campbell, Converse, Miller, and Stokes with regard to issues and their importance, Converse writes, ". . . it [the issue variable] was rather widely outweighed by sheer party loyalty in any direct confrontations involving predictive capacity." Phillip Converse, "Public Opinion and Voting Behaviour," in F. Greenstein and N. Polsby, *Nongovernmental Politics, The Handbook of Political Science,* IV (Reading, Mass: Addison-Wesley, 1975), p. 117.

3. These arguments are summarized in, among other places, Gerald Pomper, "From Confusion to Clarity: Issues and American Voters, 1968," *American Political Science Review,* 66 (1972), pp. 415-28.

4. Among the most important works making this argument are N. Nie et al., *The Changing American Voter*; and Richard A. Brody and Benjamin Page, "The Assessment of Policy Voting," *American Political Science Review,* 66 (1972), pp. 450-58.

5. Interest in the possible effects of issues on electoral choice has been especially high in the United States, and a considerable volume of literature has appeared. See, for example, David E. Repass, "Issue Salience and Party Choice," *American Political Science Review*, 65 (1971), pp. 389-400; G. Pomper, "From Confusion to Clarity"; Richard W. Boyd, "Popular Control of Public Policy: A Normal Vote Analysis of the 1968 Election," *American Political Science Review*, 66 (1972), pp. 429-49; R. Brody and B. Page, "The Assessment of Policy Voting"; John Kessel, "Comment: The Issues in Issue Voting," *American Political Science Review*, 66 (1972), pp. 459-65; John E. Jackson, "Issues, Party Choices, and Presidential Votes," *American Journal of Political Science*, 19 (1975), pp. 161-86; N. Nie et al., *The Changing American Voter, passim;* A Miller, et al., "A Majority Party in Disarray: Policy Polarization in the 1972 Election," *American Political Science Review*, 70 (1976), pp. 832-49; Samuel A. Kirkpatrick et al., "Candidates, Parties and Issues in the American Electorate," in S. A. Kirkpatrick, ed., *American Electoral Behaviour: Change and Stability,* (Beverly Hills: Sage Publication, 1976), pp. 35-72; Warren E. Miller, Teresa E. Levitin, *Leadership and Change: The New Politics and the American Electorate* (Cambridge: Winthrop Publishers, 1976). For a recent critique of several of these studies, see Michael Margolis, "From Confusion to Confusion: Issues and the American Voter (1956-1972)," *American Political Science Review*, 71 (1977), pp. 31-43. For British studies see Butler and Stokes, *Political Change in Britain*, and James E. Alt, Bo Sarlvik, and Ivor Crewe, "Partisanship and Policy Choice: Issue Preferences in the British Electorate, February 1974," *British Journal of Political Science*, 6 (1976), pp. 273-91.

6. For a review of relevant literature see M. Pinard and R. Hamilton, "The Independence Issue and the Polarization of the Electorate: The 1973 Quebec Election," *Canadian Journal of Political Science*, X (June 1977), pp. 215-60 and especially pp. 223-24.

7. See D. Butler and D. Stokes, *op. cit.* (New York: St. Martin, 1971), pp. 166-95; Brody and Page, *op. cit.*, p. 455.

8. For a discussion of valence and position issues see Butler and Stokes, *op. cit.,* pp. 176-78.

9. See Appendix B, Q. 23 and Q. 24.

10. See T. Naylor, *A History of Canadian Business,* 1 and 2 (Toronto: Lorimer, 1976).

11. See *inter alia*, Paul Pross, *Interest Groups in Canadian Politics* (Toronto: McGraw-Hill Ryerson, 1976); G. Stevenson, "Foreign Direct Investment and the Provinces: A Study of Elite Attitudes," *Canadian Journal of Political Science*, VII (December 1974); and Government of Canada, *Foreign Direct Investment in Canada* (The Gray Report), (Ottawa, 1972).

12. See Appendix B, Q. 26.

13. See the *Royal Commission on Bilingualism and Biculturalism* (Ottawa: Queen's Printer, 1965); David Kwavnick, ed., *The Tremblay Report: Report of the Royal Commission of Inquiry on Constitutional Problems* (Toronto: McClelland & Stewart, 1973).

14. See Appendix B. Q. 25.

15. The residential differences produce a Cramers V=.19, which is significant at .01.

16. For an argument about how the Liberal Party has used the strategy in

the past, see J. Jenson, "Aspects of Partisan Change: Class Relations and the Canadian Party System," paper presented to the Conference on Political Change in Canada, University of Saskatchewan, March 1977.

17. Much of the argument and data for this section are drawn from two sources. See Lawrence LeDuc, "Political Behaviour and the Issue of Majority Government in Two Federal Elections," *Canadian Journal of Political Science*, X (June 1977), pp. 311-39; and Jon Pammett et al., "The Perception and Impact of Issues in the 1974 Federal Election," *Canadian Journal of Political Science*, X (March 1977), pp. 116-21.

18. For example, the percentage of the national samples who reported that they were "not at all" likely to switch parties in order to form a majority government rose from 43% in 1965 to 54% in 1974.

19. This particular question was: "Canada has had a number of minority governments in Ottawa during the past ten years or so — that is, a Parliament in which the party in power has no clear majority over all other parties. On the whole, in your opinion, do you think that a minority government is good or bad for the nation?" C.I.P.O., *The Gallup Report*, April 25, 1973.

20. See Appendix B, Q. 27.

21. See the discussion and references in Chapter Five.

22. See Appendix B, Q. 23 and Q. 24.

23. See Chapter Six, Table 6.11.

24. See Appendix B, Q. 10.

25. This pattern is maintained, even when education is controlled. Therefore, it is not the result of differing participation rates among educational groups.

26. A control for education does not diminish the pattern of this relationship.

27. See Appendix B, Q. 1 and Q. 2 for the construction of the composite political interest measure.

28. This observation is congruent with the results of analyses presented in Chapter Five, where it was shown that unstable partisans, particularly those with strong partisan attachments, are more likely than those with stable partisan ties to conceptualize "party reasons" for voting in issue terms. See Chapter Five, Table 5.10.

29. It is, of course, possible that partisan attachments were reinforced or modified in response to judgments regarding parties' issue positions. That issues can have such effects has already been suggested by data presented in Chapter Five (Table 5.9). To the extent that this occurred, the impact of issues on *individual* voting behaviour would be increased. The effect of issues on electoral choice at the individual level in 1974 will be considered in Chapter Eleven.

III.
ELECTIONS AND POLITICAL CHOICE

Chapter Nine

Electoral Campaigns

The ability of electoral campaigns to influence election outcomes has long been a contentious issue. It has sometimes been argued that such campaigns rarely sway many people from the positions they held at the outset, and that their main function has been to reinforce previously established positions.[1] People may pay attention to campaign stimuli which reinforce their prior beliefs, and dismiss the rest of the campaign rhetoric as "electioneering." On the other hand, close political observers can point to a number of instances where, at least on the face of it, the actual campaign did seem to make a substantial difference.[2]

Part of the difficulty in assessing the impact of the campaign stems from the immutability of the event itself. Parties employ certain strategies, nominate candidates, are led by leaders already chosen, and that is that. We cannot vary those conditions in the nature of an experiment to see what other leaders or other strategies would have accomplished, so the study of an election campaign remains filled with tantalizing "what if" questions. What if, in the 1974 campaign, the Conservatives had been led by someone other than Mr. Stanfield, or had not attempted to promote the wage and price freeze policy? Would they have done any better? What would the effects have been for any of the parties if they had employed different advertising agencies, spent their money differently, or applied more energies to canvassing individual voters? While a few isolated experiments (none, however, in Canada) have been done on these last points,[3] the overall impact of the election campaign itself remains an intriguing puzzle.

Despite these limitations, there are two aspects of the 1974 campaign that we can explore in some detail. The first is the way the campaign was reported in the press, and the use by voters of such information.

Through a content analysis of all articles on the 1974 campaign published on selected dates by 21 major Canadian newspapers, it is possible
to portray how the campaign was presented to Canadian readers. In
addition, the interview material from the 1974 National Election Study
will tell us the use voters made of the media in order to obtain campaign
information. The second aspect of the 1974 campaign we can examine
here is the nature of contact the voters had with the parties and politicians, and the relationships of those contacts to attitudes and behaviour.

The 1974 election campaign provides a particularly valuable opportunity to examine questions of campaign impact, since it was an election
in which the campaign was thought to "count."[4] Indeed, 45% of all 1974
survey respondents who voted report that they made up their minds which
way to vote *during* the campaign period (Table 9.1), and 63% of those
switching their votes from the previous election report making their
voting decision during the campaign. Furthermore, this election was one
in which short-term factors, such as inflation and leadership, received
considerable emphasis in the rhetoric of the campaign, and in which the
campaign strategies followed by the parties were thought by many to have
been highly relevant to the election outcome. The movement recorded by

TABLE 9.1

Reported Time Period at Which 1974 Vote Decision Was Made
(percentages)

"Knew all along"	16%
"Quite a while" before the election	9
When election was called	30
5 or 6 weeks before	6
3 or 4 weeks before	11
2 weeks before	9
1 week before	12
On election day	7

(N=*932*)

the Gallup Poll in the period leading up to the election is also suggestive
of the possibility of at least a limited "campaign effect."[5]

In a sense, the 1974 campaign began with the outcome of the 1972
election only nineteen months earlier. The near defeat of the Liberal
government in that election ushered in a period of precarious minority
government, which lasted from the first meeting of Parliament after the

1972 result to the dissolution which came with the parliamentary defeat of the government over its budget in May 1974. During this period of time, the Liberal government had survived 18 votes of confidence in the House of Commons, primarily because they were supported by the New Democratic Party. Because the Liberals only enjoyed a two-seat plurality over the Conservatives, and because it was clear that NDP voting support would not continue indefinitely, the government endured numerous predictions of its impending defeat. This setting had the effect of focussing a high degree of media attention on the political arena in Ottawa, and fueling almost continual speculation regarding an election. For all the political parties it was a time of intense campaign planning for the election which could occur at any time. The generally acknowledged failure of the Liberal campaign of 1972, and the nearly equal parliamentary standing of the Liberals and Conservatives, resulted in concentrated attention on planning and strategy for the upcoming campaign. It was seen as an election either major party could win, and it was assumed that the campaign period itself would be decisive.

The 1974 campaign strategies of the Liberals and Conservatives were logical extensions of the short-term strengths and weaknesses of each. The Conservatives sought to turn to their advantage the government's lack of success in dealing with the country's most pressing economic problem — inflation.[6] While in most respects the inflation issue in 1974 was a classic example of a valence issue, the fact that the Conservative Party chose to commit itself to a proposal for the adoption of wage and price controls allowed some transformation of the issue into one where the parties could be seen to hold different positions.[7] The Liberals sought to counter this strategy by emphasizing the "issue" of leadership — meaning in this context the record in office and personal leadership qualities of Prime Minister Trudeau.[8] For many participants, the catch phrase of the campaign became "The issue is inflation, and the problem is leadership" (or vice versa). The New Democratic Party, although they had won a record number of seats in 1972, faced severe problems in running their 1974 campaign. On the one hand they felt burdened with the stigma of having sustained the Liberals in power for almost two years, and on the other, of having provoked this election. They were apprehensive, as well, that many of their supporters might feel the necessity of making a choice between the two major parties in order to elect a majority government. They were unable to duplicate their 1972 success in attacking corporate power, and so entered the inflation debate with a set of complicated economic policies which failed to capture much public attention.[9]

NEWSPAPER REPORTING OF THE CAMPAIGN

Canada's newspapers devoted substantial space to reporting the 1974

TABLE 9.2

**Subject Matter of Stories on the 1974 Election Campaign
Published by Canadian Newspapers
(percentages)**

NATIONAL EVENTS			78%
Party Leaders Electioneering		26%	
Trudeau	9%		
Stanfield	7		
Lewis	6		
Caouette	2		
General	2		
Leaders' Speeches and Press Conferences		17	
Stanfield	6%		
Trudeau	5		
Lewis	4		
Caouette	2		
Analyses of the State of the Campaign		12	
Electioneering of Other Prominent Politicians		7	
Liberals	5%		
Conservatives	2		
Analyses of Election Issues		7	
Party Announcements		3	
Party Policies		3	
Election Histories		2	
Party Histories		1	
PROVINCIAL EVENTS			4
State of Campaign in Provinces		4	
LOCAL EVENTS			18
Local Electioneering		7	
Analyses of State of Local Campaigns		7	
Local Speeches		1	
Local Election Histories		1	
Local Issues		1	
Local Party Policies		1	

N=2511 event mentions, 1836 stories. In this and the following tables, if a story referred to more than one subject, all references are included separately. The total number of mentions, which totals more than the number of stories, was percentagized to 100% in order to report the overall distribution of news.

election campaign. In the 13 dates which we sampled, 21 major Canadian newspapers published 1940 articles about the campaign, an average of 7 per issue.[10] There was, of course, substantial variance between the number of articles carried by a large paper like the Toronto *Star* (an average of 9 per issue), and that of a smaller paper like the Fredericton *Gleaner* (4 per issue). The average number of articles in the four major French-language papers was substantially higher (13 per issue) than any English language paper. Allowing for this variation, however, it would have been difficult for the Canadian newspaper reader, no matter where situated, to have escaped stories, usually including front-page ones, dealing with the campaign.

The content of these stories, detailed in Table 9.2, determined a portion of the information the Canadian public received concerning events of the 1974 campaign. We can conclude with certainty that the information was, first of all, about the *national* campaign, and secondly, concerned mainly with the *leaders* of the political parties. A full 78% of the story subjects were national in scope, as opposed to 18% concerning local races, and 4% examining the campaign within a particular province. The comings and goings of the party leaders attracted most attention, with more emphasis being placed on their campaign appearances in a context of travelling and electioneering, and less on formal speeches and press conferences. It has been a matter of some dispute within the political parties about how much is gained directly in terms of votes by the tours that party leaders increasingly spend their time making during election campaigns. Whatever the answer to that, it is clear that the leaders' tours and the speeches that are made during them are the primary source of news that is reported to the public during the campaign.

The relative obscurity of anyone other than the leaders is apparent from Table 9.3. Only 15% of the news reported during the campaign had anything to do with anyone other than the party leaders, and that figure includes all mentions of local candidates, as well as other "prominent" politicians. Indeed, the reporting of the local campaigns takes a distinctly secondary place to the leaders. In terms of the reporting of political campaigns, at any rate, those who argue that Canadian politics is dominated by the party leaders have evidence in their favour.

The emphasis placed by the press on the leaders thus serves to downplay the attention given to local constituency races, and has the consequence that the battles in the constituencies have to be fought largely in other arenas, primarily on the doorsteps and at local public meetings. A second consequence of the fixation on the party leaders is that political issues and the parties themselves are usually treated only in the context of the travels and utterances of their single important spokesmen.[11] Table 9.3 shows that 26% of the news involved analysis of the state of the campaign, and another 12% involved direct analysis of the issues, but these reports were highly coloured by what the party leaders had to say in defining the issues and where they conducted their tours.

Because the reporting of the election campaign seemed to be focussed so completely on the travels and speeches of the party leaders, the importance of their particular personalities was magnified, their family relationships became subjects of popular concern, and extreme demands were placed on them and their speech-writers to have something different and interesting to say on the same subjects several times a day. In this kind of atmosphere, the chances of poorly thought-out remarks by party

TABLE 9.3

**Focus of Stories on the 1974 Election Campaign
Published by Canadian Newspapers
(percentages)**

Party Leaders	42%
Analyses of Campaign	26
Other Politicians	15
Issues	12
Parties	5

N=2511 event mentions, 1836 stories.

leaders being taken as statements of party policy, and becoming the focus of later developments, were magnified. It is obvious, in retrospect, that this glare of attention on the party leader was particularly harmful to the Conservatives.

Stanfield's first national tour was organized around a series of press conferences in which his mettle could be publicly tested. The result was disastrous. Stanfield was questioned intensively about the details of his prices and incomes policy, and he gave answers which seemed evasive and contradictory. Pressed by the journalists, he conceded that parts of the program had not been worked out and indicated that there would be exemptions from controls for certain groups. Far from demonstrating his competence and strength, Stanfield's performance on the tour reinforced his established image.[12]

From this point forward, the Conservative Party stumbled even further into disarray by issuing a series of "clarifications" which were designed to establish what they really meant by their policy, but which succeeded in giving them the image of a rudderless party with a confused leader at the helm.

The subjects of the photographs published by newspapers during the campaign are reported in Table 9.4 and reinforce the trends noted in Table 9.2, much as a picture heightens the impact of a story. Pictures of the leaders, either alone or with their families, constituted a majority of those relating to the 1974 election. Local candidates constituted 29%, their higher total here than with news stories indicating that editors may have made special efforts to print such local pictures. All in all, though, the Canadian people were given the impression by newspapers that the 1974 campaign was a battle of the party leaders; voters could scarcely pick up a paper without reading about them or seeing their faces.

TABLE 9.4

Subject Matter of Photographs Relating to the 1974 Election Published by Canadian Newspapers
(percentages)

LEADERS (AND FAMILIES)		52%
Trudeau	19%	
Stanfield	16	
Lewis	12	
Caouette	5	
OTHER PROMINENT POLITICIANS		16
Liberal	9	
Conservative	5	
New Democrat	2	
Social Credit	1	
LOCAL CANDIDATES		29
Liberal	8	
Conservative	10	
New Democrat	6	
Social Credit	2	
Other Parties	4	
OTHER SUBJECTS		4

N=658 picture subjects, 529 pictures.

The dominant attention paid to party leaders, rather than their confrères, emerges once again from Table 9.5. The primary purpose of this table, however, is to show the relative amount of news reporting which was devoted to each of the parties. Because we are lacking any measure of column-inches, we cannot specifically speak of amount of coverage devoted to the parties; however, we are in a position to report only on the number of times each party was made the subject of a news story. Table 9.5 indicates that the Liberals were mentioned more frequently, with 40% of the total number of story subjects being devoted to them. They were followed by the Conservative Party with 30%, the New Democrats with 20%, and Social Credit with 8%. Inspection of the data in Table 9.5 documents that the Conservatives, and particularly the New Democrats, could allege with some justification that they did not receive an equal amount of coverage in the newspapers for their campaigns.

Lest it appear that we are accusing the newspapers of slanting their news coverage toward the Liberal Party, a number of points should be made. For one thing, newspapers print the news that is being made at the time, and an incumbent government, which the Liberals were, is always in a position to "make news" to a greater extent than is an opposition. During the 1974 campaign, the Liberals were able to make policy announcements which had the force of government programs rather than merely a statement of what "we would do if elected." As Stephen Clarkson notes:

> Trudeau campaigned directly before the public, letting the press follow on his heels. His speeches announcing new government programs or promising new measures were timed so as to force the media to report these initiatives while forestalling intensive grilling of either the party leader or his staff. The tactic was eminently successful. Of the ten major policy announcements made by Trudeau himself, seven were reported on the front page of the *Globe and Mail*.[13]

Thus, not only did the Liberals have government programs to announce, but they timed their announcements strategically for maximum coverage. All parties, of course, try to do this; the Liberals were successful at it.

The greater concentration on the Liberals as story subjects in 1974 manifested itself in all sections in the papers in approximately the same ratio noted in Table 9.5, leading to greater coverage for that party on the front pages, interior sections, and op-ed pages. That this phenomenon was a result of factors discussed above and not of deliberate favouritism, however, is supported by an analysis of editorials published during the campaign, which establishes that the Conservatives received more positive mentions, and more editorial endorsements, than the Liberals did.[14] One other possible explanation of the results noted in Table 9.5, that these overall figures were produced because parties which are not strong in certain areas of the country might be given slighter treatment by the papers there, is shown by examination of the regional breakdown of the

TABLE 9.5

**Newspaper Mentions of the Political Parties
During 1974 Election Campaign
(percentages)**

LIBERAL PARTY		40%
Leader[a]	22%	
Other Politicians	14	
Party	5	
CONSERVATIVE PARTY		30
Leader	17	
Other Politicians	9	
Party	4	
NEW DEMOCRATIC PARTY		20
Leader	12	
Other Politicians	4	
Party	4	
SOCIAL CREDIT PARTY		8
Leader	4	
Other Politicians	3	
Party	2	
OTHER PARTIES		3

N=4374 party subjects, 1829 stories.

[a]"Leader" category includes leaders' families, and stories which referred to both leaders and their parties.

data not to be correct. There was no discernible tendency for Quebec newspapers to devote fewer stories to the Conservative Party than papers elsewhere in the country, or for the Maritime papers to neglect the NDP. Given the concentration of coverage on the national campaign, the weakness of parties in particular regions did not affect their ability to get publicity for their campaigns.

As we have seen, the issues which were mentioned in the reporting of the campaign were usually in the context of appearances by the party leaders, although there was some analytic writing about the effects of issues on the party fortunes. The great diversity of issues stressed by the politicians during the course of the campaign, as mentioned in the press stories, is apparent from Table 9.6. While inflation and wage and price controls head the list of individual issues mentioned in the newspapers, as they do with survey respondents (see also Chapter Eight), their pre-eminence in the papers is much less marked. Papers focussed to a greater extent on the Conservatives' wage and price control policy in their reporting of the campaign than respondents did in their delineation of the most important issues to them during the campaign. The papers can also be seen from Table 9.6 to have reported a substantial amount of news about other economic issues, such as the budget, taxes, interest rates, government spending and monetary reform, issues which turned out to be much less important to individuals.

When they were not stressing the economic situation, the party leaders and others were talking about a wide variety of subjects, the full range of which is reported in the note to Table 9.6. In particular, the five issues of bilingualism, housing, agriculture, transportation, and corporate control were mentioned, in total, in almost half of the news stories involving issues written about the 1974 campaign. Yet these do not seem to have been very important in the public's list of major election issues.

Given the concentration on the issue of leadership, particularly by the Liberals,[15] it is somewhat surprising to note that it was mentioned in only 8% of all news stories which included issue mentions. Rather paradoxically, this low number may perhaps be accounted for by the very concentration of reporting on the leaders; it is difficult for a leader to directly state that he would make the best leader without appearing pompous and overbearing. Such statements had to either come by implication from the leaders' actions, or had to be made by others. In 1974, the importance of leadership was also emphasized by paid advertisements (not coded in our study) placed by the Liberal Party.

Considering the large role the issue came to assume in speculation about the outcome, the need for a majority government appears to have drawn scant mention by campaigners, as reported in the press. For instance, in its post-election analyses, the Regina *Leader-Post* stated that "Canadians have given their backing to effective majority government," and the London *Free Press* was quoted as concluding that "most Canadians appear to prefer a majority government to wage and price controls."[16] It may have been that the two major parties perceived themselves as running too closely to risk introducing the majority government issue during the campaign. For obvious reasons the NDP was not likely to bring it up, despite the fact that the NDP could claim to have had some success in influencing legislation during the previous minority parliament.

In Chapter Eight we noted the dimensions of the inflation issue in 1974, pointing out what things people associated with inflation, what they saw as the causes, what action they wished to have pursued, and the ways in

TABLE 9.6

Issues Reported in News Stories During the 1974 Campaign, Compared with "Most Important Issues" Identified by Survey Respondents (percentages)

	RESPONDENTS	NEWSPAPERS
Inflation	57	30
Wage and Price Controls	11	24
Unemployment	4	3
The Economy (general reference)	6	1
Other Economic Issues	8	21
Social Services	7	5
Old Age Pensions & Care	8	6
Majority Government	9	1
Leadership	8	8
Bilingualism	4	12
Foreign Investment	1	0
Other Specific Issues	15	72[a]
Party	4	0
Candidate	2	0
Other General	4	9
N=	*1749*	1560 stories

Note: For Survey Respondents, two mentions were coded; for newspaper stories up to three mentions were coded.

[a]Issues mentioned were the following: housing 11%; agriculture 10%; transportation 8%; corporate control 7%; energy and resources policy 4%; Leonard Jones affair 4%; patronage 3%; regional issues 2%; fishing 2%; separatism 2%; election expenses 2%; minority rights 2%; ballot spoilage 2%; foreign policy, native peoples, women's rights, the FLQ, urban problems, pollution, crown corporations, parliamentary representation, federal-provincial relations, growth of the public service, defence policy, immigration, all 1%; and a scattering of mentions for several other issues.

which they were most affected by inflation. In constructing this content analysis of the way Canadian newspapers reported the campaign, their treatment of the inflation issue was coded on these same dimensions. We can therefore compare, in Table 9.7, the public's attitudes on inflation with the image of the issue presented by the newspapers. That newspaper image we assume to be a reasonably accurate picture of the way the issue was debated by the politicians during the campaign.

Table 9.7 shows some interesting differences between what voters asso-

TABLE 9.7

Dimensions of the Inflation Issue in 1974, as Reported by Canadian Newspapers, and by Respondents to the Election Study (percentages)

	RESPONDENTS	NEWSPAPERS
(A) CONTENT OF INFLATION ANSWERS		
General References to Problem	24%	77%
Reference to Depression or Recession	9	0
Wages and Prices	50	16
Prices of Specific Commodities	17	7
N=	*1145*	464
(B) ACTION CALLED FOR ON INFLATION		
General Reference to "Action Needed"	52%	16%
Wage and Price Controls	41	60
Other Specific Action	7	23
N=	*206*	240
(C) WAY PEOPLE MOST AFFECTED		
General Reference to Rising Prices	22%	40%
General Reference to Inadequate Income	9	11
Specific Reference to Prices	69	50
N=	*1014*	129

ciated with inflation, and what the politicians emphasized during the campaign. In the things they associated with inflation, and in the ways they reported being most affected by it (panels (a) and (c) of Table 9.7), individual respondents mentioned specifics far more than generalities. People were concerned with the prices of various commodities and their precipitous rise, prices of food, clothing, housing, and fuel. Politicians, in their campaign rhetoric, were more likely to talk of "the inflation problem" in the general and the abstract, and the extent to which it was home-grown or a "world-wide phenomenon." When it came to the action proposed, the indication from Table 9.7(b) is that the above situation was reversed. The politicians offered many specific courses of action to deal with the inflation problem, featuring, but by no means confined to, wage and price controls. To the extent that they referred to this action dimension at all (and relatively few did), the public was more likely to simply have stated that "action is needed" or "something needs to be done" without promoting any specific policy.

It seems, therefore, that the public and the politicians were at least somewhat out of synchronization in their thinking on the inflation issue during the 1974 campaign. The public conceived of inflation in specific terms of rising prices of commodities, but possessed little concrete opinion about specific action, governmental or otherwise, required to deal with it. Conversely, the inflation issue was seen by the politicians, in general terms, as a societal problem, and they proposed a number of specific solutions to deal with it. Possibly, the speeches they were making contained both general analyses of the inflation problem and specific references to price rises, and the reports emphasized the former instead of the latter. It is also possible that politicians may have tended to generalize their remarks on inflation so as not to needlessly offend part of their audiences, for example producers who might perceive themselves as being blamed for inflationary pressures.

It seems clear that the Conservative strategy of promoting a specific solution to the inflation problem fell directly onto a mass public which had little experience in thinking about or evaluating specific solutions to the problems of rising prices. The wage and price control plank was attractive to some voters, repugnant to others, but seemingly ignored in its specifics by most. The Conservative fumbling of details of the proposal likely contributed to the negative image of the party and its leader. The Liberal strategy of promoting a general competence to deal with inflation was much more in keeping with the scope of public perceptions and attitudes.

PUBLIC ATTENTION TO THE NEWS MEDIA

Having seen how newspapers reported the 1974 campaign, we may proceed to examine whether public exposure to the messages conveyed by newspapers, television, and radio about the election was widespread and related to attitudes and behaviour. In the widest sense, of course, it is almost impossible to conceive of the media *not* having an important impact, since a large part of the information received by all voters came through these intermediaries. Additionally, such information was likely to arrive in the household on a daily basis, as opposed to the necessarily sporadic arrival of even the most dedicated party canvassers.

Table 9.8 shows, as have other studies, that the public seems to pay somewhat more attention to news on television than other media.[17] Newspapers are a close second in this regard, while radio seems much less important in transferring political news to the public. Thus, 80% of the Canadian electorate reported seeing "quite a few" or "some" programs or advertisements about the 1974 election campaign on television, and 73% reported reading "quite a bit" or "something" about the campaign in the newspaper, but only 52% heard "quite a few" or "some" programs or ads on the radio about the campaign.[18] Since commercial radio in Canada provides very little political reporting outside of short news broadcasts, and since commercial radio dominates the listening habits of Canadians,[19] the last finding reported above should not be surprising. Despite the varying degrees of importance reported for the three media, attention to political reporting in all three of them is positively correlated, with Pearson r's ranging from .38 to .33. Thus, if a person pays attention to campaign reporting in one of the media, he or she will also tend to follow campaign news on others.

TABLE 9.8

Public Attention to Reports of 1974 Campaign in Three News Media (percentages)

ATTENTION	NEWSPAPERS	TELEVISION	RADIO
High	39%	42%	20%
Medium	34	38	32
Low	27	20	48

N=*1203*

TABLE 9.9

Attention to Media Reports of 1974 Election Campaign, by Selected Demographic Variables (Pearson r)

	NEWSPAPERS	TELEVISION	RADIO
Education	.26*	.00	.07*
Age	.08*	.14*	.04
Geographical Mobility	.15*	.03	.09*
Language	.19*	.04	.11*
Community Size	.08*	.03	.01
SES	.25*	.02	.05
Subjective Social Class	.22*	.07*	.09*

*Significant at .01 level.

Note: All demographics except language are arranged from low to high. Thus a positive correlation exists between higher education, age, class, SES, larger community size, and media attention. For language, a positive sign indicates a relationship between English and media attention.

What kinds of people pay attention to political and campaign news on the three news media? Table 9.9 indicates that television has the broadest appeal, cutting across education levels, language, place of residence, and social status. This is deduced from the absence of strong relationships between exposure to political news on television and those demographic variables. The only relationship of any strength with attention to television is with age, meaning that older people are more likely to spend time watching political programs on television. The importance attached to television by the public and the broad appeal it has to all sectors of the population make it the ideal medium from the point of view of political parties and politicians trying to get their messages across to the voters. It is little wonder that large blocs of party funds are spent on television advertisements during the campaign, and that the parties eagerly prepare special programs to fill the free-time slots they are allocated on the networks during the campaign period.[20]

Political news in the print medium does not have as broad an appeal as that on television. There is a statistically significant relationship between reading campaign news and every demographic variable presented in Table 9.9. Readers of political news, like newspaper readers in general, are more highly educated, of higher social status, somewhat older, more likely to be English-speaking, more geographically mobile in their residence histories, and somewhat more likely to dwell in larger cities. Newspapers therefore reach a more restricted segment of the population than does television. From the point of view of the political parties, however, it might be considered a more "attentive" public, perhaps receptive to appeals on the basis of political issues.

Those who are politically interested to begin with are more likely, of course, to pay attention to stories, programs, and advertisements about the election campaign, as is clearly shown in Table 9.10. We should note, however, that the correlation between interest and attention to the media is highest with newspapers, less strong with television, and still less with radio, though even the relationship with radio attention is by no means weak. A similar pattern may be observed with regard to political participation: the correlations between participation in federal politics and attention to the campaign in newspapers, television, and radio are .39, .31, and .26 respectively. Television and radio, being more passive media, are often able to present political news to people who are not normally politically interested because it is "what's on," and "what's on" is often watched or heard simply because people are in the mood for some viewing or listening. Political news in newspapers takes somewhat more "seeking out" and effort on the part of the reader, and thus the less interested are less inclined to pursue political news in print.[21]

Newspapers seem little different from the other media when it comes to

TABLE 9.10

Attention to Media Reports of the 1974 Election Campaign, by Selected Attitudinal and Behavioural Variables (Pearson r)

	NEWSPAPERS	TELEVISION	RADIO
Interest in Politics	.45*	.37*	.25*
Interest in 1974 Election	.50*	.39*	.27*
Intensity of Partisanship	.02	.04	.01
Stability of Partisanship	−.13*	−.15*	−.10*
Consistency of Partisanship	.00	−.04	−.03
Participation in Politics	.39*	.31*	.26*
Participation in 1974 Election	.39*	.34*	.26*
Vote Switch, 1972-74	−.01	.07	.02

*Significant at .01 level.

relationships with partisanship. The moderate negative correlation of stability of partisanship with attention to all the media presented in Table 9.10 indicates that unstable partisans are somewhat more likely to seek out political news, a finding consistent with other characteristics of unstable partisans documented earlier. Unstable partisans approach an election campaign less committed to a party and more open to casting their vote on the basis of short-term factors. It is, therefore, reasonable that they would seek out more political information in all the media in order to make up their minds. The other components of partisanship, intensity and consistency, show no significant relationship with media attention.

We have seen that most Canadians paid attention to news about the election campaign of 1974 through television programs, newspaper articles, and even radio reports. The amount of attention to these media has been seen to be related to people's interest in politics, political involvement, stability of partisanship, and personal demographic characteristics. None of this necessarily means, however, that attention to the media is related to changes in voting behaviour from one election to another. When we look in Table 9.10 we do not see a single significant relationship between paying attention to the campaign in the media and a vote switch between 1972 and 1974. Those who saw no programs or party advertisements on television and those who did not read much about the campaign in the newspapers were just about as likely to change their votes from the previous election as were those who avidly followed the campaign. It is, of course, possible that the news reaching people about the campaign had the effect in many cases of *reinforcing* previously established positions.

Nevertheless, the verdict on the impact of the campaign reaching people through the media remains open.

PUBLIC CONTACT WITH THE PARTIES

In addition to following the 1974 campaign through the communications media, Canadian voters were exposed to a variety of contacts with the parties and candidates contesting the election. These consisted of visits from party workers and sometimes from the candidates themselves — visits designed to consolidate known support and impress those whose votes might be swayed. To reinforce these contacts with voters, the parties distributed literature to most households, and often canvassed for support by means of telephone calls, particularly to those voters who had previously been visited in person and had shown some sympathy toward the party.

Respondents to the 1974 survey provided information on the type of contact they had with the parties during the campaign period. The kinds of contact fall into three categories: personal contact with party candidates, personal contact with other party workers, and literature or telephone contact. Table 9.11 shows the frequency with which such contacts were reported. A substantial majority of voters received literature or a phone call (or both) from one or more of the parties, the emphasis in the answers being on the receipt of literature (generally a small brochure). Less common were visits by party canvassers, and less common still were visits by the candidates themselves. While most of the voters received some kind of literature from at least one of the parties, two-thirds reported no personal contact at all by any party worker, and over four-fifths did not see any of the candidates in the flesh.

The Liberals and Conservatives managed to make about the same amount of contact with the voters in 1974. They were each able to get their literature into the hands of about two-thirds of the electorate, to have a party canvasser meet about one-fifth personally, and to have their candidates chat with about one-tenth. The New Democratic Party did less well in bringing its campaign to the public. They managed to reach less than half (49%) of the public with a piece of literature, 13% with a party worker, and only 5% with a candidate. This low level of reported contact with the NDP is interesting, since that party, being the most penurious of Canada's major political parties, has a long-standing reputation for making up for its lack of funds by vigorous and extensive campaigning, particularly by door-to-door canvass.[22] The NDP totals are accounted for in part by the weakness of the party's organization in Eastern Canada, particularly in Quebec. Although our sample contains only one constituency (Gaspé) in which the NDP did not run a candidate, some of their campaign efforts were token ones.[23]

TABLE 9.11

Types of Reported Contact with Three Political Parties[a] During the 1974 Election Campaign
(percentages)

	CANDIDATES	PARTY WORKERS	LITERATURE OR TELEPHONE
None	82%	67%	22%
Liberals Only	4	7	9
Conservatives Only	6	8	5
NDP Only	2	4	2
Liberals and Conservatives	3	6	16
Conservatives and NDP	0	1	3
Liberals and NDP	1	2	3
All Three Parties	2	6	41
N=	*949*	*1163*	*1154*

[a]Because of their relatively infrequent mention, contacts with the Social Credit Party and minor parties have been omitted from this table. Those who did not remember which party called have also been omitted.

We saw in Table 9.10 that attention to the campaign in the media had substantial relationships with political interest and participation, a not unexpected result in light of the fact that media attention is an activity controlled by the respondent. In other words, an individual must decide to pick up and read a paper, or to turn on and view the television set. When it comes to contact by parties, the individual has no such control, short of refusing to answer the doorbell. We would therefore expect the relationships of party contact with interest and political involvement to be much more modest, if indeed they exist at all. Table 9.12 shows that these relationships do exist, and that they are in most cases statistically significant, but that they are not nearly as strong as those noted in Table 9.10. The politically interested and involved do report more contact of all kinds with the parties, however, and it is interesting to speculate on why this is so. Part of the answer could be a selective memory — people uninterested in politics or the campaign may have simply forgotten that anyone from the parties called on them, since it would not have been a particularly meaningful encounter for them. Alternatively, the uninterested may have actually received less contact, especially if the parties concentrated on visiting known supporters.

In a similar vein, it is instructive to note that the correlations in Table 9.12 between interest, involvement, and receipt of party literature are in general substantially higher than those with personal visits by candidates

TABLE 9.12

Type of Contact Reported with the Parties, by Selected Attitudinal and Behavioural Variables (Pearson r)

	INTEREST IN POLITICS	INTEREST IN 74 ELECTION	INTEN-SITY	PARTISANSHIP STA-BILITY	CONSIS-TENCY	PARTICIPATION IN POLITICS	PARTICIPATION IN 1974 ELECTION	VOTE SWITCH 1972-74
CONTACT BY LIBERALS								
Candidate	.08*	.08*	-.01	.05	.03	.09*	.10*	.07
Party Workers	.10*	.14*	.01	.04	.04	.11*	.13*	.02
Literature	.13*	.24*	-.02	.04	.02	.20*	.21*	.01
Index of Amount of Contact[a]	.15*	.23*	.01	.06	.04	.20*	.22*	.04
CONTACT BY CONSERVATIVES								
Candidate	.05	.10*	-.01	.05	.01	.08*	.11*	.03
Party Workers	.08*	.17*	.01	.05	.04	.07*	.09*	.03
Literature	.13*	.23*	-.04	.09*	.03	.17*	.18*	.05
Index of Amount of Contact	.14*	.26*	.02	.09*	.04	.16*	.19*	.05
CONTACT BY NDP								
Candidate	.08*	.05	-.01	.09*	.01	.04	.05	.09*
Party Workers	.08*	.09*	.03	.08*	.02	.07*	.08*	.11*
Literature	.10*	.18*	.00	.06	-.02	.12*	.12*	.06
Index of Amount of Contact	.12*	.18*	.01	.10*	.00	.12*	.13*	.11*

*Significant at .01 level.

[a]The three indices for the parties are additive, scoring one point for each type of contact — personal (candidate/party worker) or other (literature, etc.) — reported. See also Appendix B, Q. 36-37.

or other party workers. It seems likely that contact in person with
workers or candidates was more memorable to all voters and therefore
reported by most people with whom it took place. Literature, on the
other hand, was likely *delivered* to most people, but read in detail only by
those with some degree of political interest, and especially by those who
were themselves more politically involved. There are few relationships of
any strength between contact with the parties and partisanship. In particular, the more intense partisans surveyed did not report any more contact
by any of the parties, including their own. If the parties really were
engaged in a strategy of maximizing contact with their own supporters, it
would seem reasonable to expect a relationship here, since some of the
intense partisans are of long-standing loyalty and presumably are known
to their parties. Stable partisans do report somewhat more contact with
the political parties, but these relationships are not strong enough to
render very persuasive the argument that the parties concentrated on
contacting their known long-standing supporters.

The question of most interest (at least, to the parties themselves) about
campaign contact is likely to be whether there is any evidence that their
campaigning had an appreciable effect on vote switching. Table 9.12 indicates that the correlations between either *kind* of contact or *amount* of
contact with the parties and a switch in vote between 1972 and 1974 are
very weak overall, and statistically significant only in the case of personal
contact by the New Democratic Party.

Table 9.13 allows us to examine the possible relationships between
contact with the various parties, and individual decisions to maintain or
change the pattern of voting behaviour demonstrated in the 1972 election. With the possible exception of those making the decision to switch
to the NDP, the relationships are seen to be much more with vote stability
than vote switching. Thus, for example, those switching to the Conservatives in 1974 were just as likely to report personal Liberal contact as
Conservative contact, though they were slightly less likely to report no
Conservative contact at all. Similarly, switchers to the Liberals were just
about as likely to have had a visit from a Conservative candidate or
worker as they were to have been visited by the Liberals, though again
they were less likely to have had no Liberal contact at all. While those
switching to the New Democratic Party do report more contact with that
party than with any other, almost as many saw a Conservative candidate
or worker as someone from the NDP.

On the other hand, those who report voting for the same party in the
two elections of 1972 and 1974 are considerably more likely to report
contact with that party than any of the others. We may again mention the
possibility that this may be due to a selective memory on the part of
those committed to a particular party, who may have been more likely to

TABLE 9.13

Reported Contact by the Parties in 1974 Campaign, by Voting Behaviour in 1972 and 1974
(row percentages)

1972-1974 VOTING PATTERN	LIBERAL CONTACT			CONSERVATIVE CONTACT			NDP CONTACT			
	NONE	LITER. ONLY	LITER. & PERSONAL	NONE	LITER. ONLY	LITER. & PERSONAL	NONE	LITER. ONLY	LITER. & PERSONAL	N
THOSE VOTING FOR THE SAME PARTY										
Liberal	24%	52	24	36%	48	16	51%	42	7	349
Conservative	32%	47	21	21%	46	32	53%	35	13	190
NDP	23%	53	24	22%	64	14	23%	47	31	72
THOSE SWITCHING										
To Liberals	19%	57	23	34%	46	21	41%	42	14	58
To Conservatives	21%	53	26	15%	59	26	40%	43	17	70
To NDP	36%	42	22	35%	33	31	32%	32	35	26
1972 NONVOTERS										
To Liberals	8%	61	31	12%	67	21	33%	55	12	25
To Conservatives	54%	30	15	28%	39	33	67%	9	24	12
NEW VOTERS IN 1974										
To Liberals	18%	48	34	34%	42	25	34%	45	20	29
To Conservatives	52%	30	18	42%	32	26	65%	26	9	14
TOTAL 1974 VOTE										
Liberal	22%	53	25	34%	48	17	48%	43	9	461
Conservative	31%	47	22	21%	48	31	51%	35	14	285
NDP	28%	50	22	26%	55	19	29%	40	31	113
Did Not Vote	46%	43	11	47%	45	9	65%	31	4	148

put visits by other parties completely out of their minds, or to the fact that parties made sure to contact those they knew to have supported them in the previous election. In either case, the visits from the party's workers may have reinforced inclinations to support that party again.

While the relationship between party contact and a switch in vote from one election to the other is negligible, new voters and 1972 non-voters display more highly differentiated patterns of party contact. Thus, 1972 non-voters who voted Liberal in 1974 report a visit from a Liberal worker or candidate at a 31% rate, while contact of a personal nature with the other parties is at least 10 points lower. Similarly, new voters, becoming eligible for the first time in 1974, are substantially more likely to report contact of all types from the party they ended up casting their first vote for than from any of the others.

The fact that voters were contacted by the political parties in the 1974 campaign did have some relationship to their eventual voting behaviour in that election. This was particularly true of personal contact by candidates or party workers. It does seem probable, however, that the effects of campaigning were concentrated among three groups in the electorate. The first was the party's own supporters from the previous campaign. Party contact could reinforce the inclinations of many of them to vote for that party again, though whether they would have wavered from that intention had the party not come to call is problematic. The second were those who had abstained from voting in the previous election. Here, a visit from a worker, or better still a candidate, may have made the difference between a vote and another abstention. Finally, new voters, searching for a party to support for the first time, may have been influenced by a visit. When it comes to those voters we label as switchers, however, there is little evidence that change of vote is related to differential campaign contact.

CONCLUSION

The question of whether or to what extent the election campaign of 1974 "counted" in producing the final result cannot be definitively answered by the evidence provided in this chapter. We are able to say, however, that exposure to the campaign, both through the communications media and personal canvassing by the parties was high. Certainly, few voters escaped the barrage of reporting about the campaigning of the party leaders. Many voters concurred with the media message that inflation was the major issue, though there is evidence that the public was concerned with somewhat different aspects of that issue than were politicians. Evidence of direct effects of media attention and party contact on changing peoples' voting preferences may be lacking, but the data suggest the presence of reinforcement effects and the importance of these contacts in mobilizing transient voters and new voters. By providing a two month warm-up to the main event, the election campaign clarified issues and allowed voters a specified period of time in which to make up their minds, and to evaluate once again the nation's politicians. It provided the backdrop to political choice in Canada.

FOOTNOTES

1. The classic statement of this position is by Bernard R. Berelson, Paul F. Lazarsfeld, and William N. McPhee, *Voting* (Chicago: University of Chicago Press, 1954). Thus, they state, on page 18: "The time of final decision, that point after which the voter does not change his intention, occurred *prior* to the campaign for most voters — and thus no real decision was made *in* the campaign in the sense of waiting to consider alternatives" (emphasis in original). The same position is maintained by British researchers Jay G. Blumler and Denis McQuail, "The Audience for Election Television," in Jeremy Turnstall, ed., *Media Sociology* (London: Constable, 1970), pp. 452-78.

2. Note, for example, the conclusions and analysis of the 1972 Canadian federal election by Peter Regenstreif, Jerome Black, and Barry Kay, in "Partisan Stability and Change in the Canadian Federal Election of 1972," paper presented to annual meeting of the Canadian Political Science Association, Montreal, 1973. Substantial movement from the time of party conventions to the election date is evident from the report on the 1968 American Presidential election by Philip E. Converse, Warren E. Miller, Jerrold G. Rusk, and Arthur C. Wolfe, "Continuity and Change in American Politics: Parties and Issues in the 1968 Election," *American Political Science Review*, 63 (1969), pp. 1083-1105.

3. For American studies of the effects of canvassing, see Ted Bartell and Sandra Bouxsein,' "The Chelsea Project: Candidate Preference, Issue Preference and Turnout Effects of Student Canvassing," *Public Opinion Quarterly*, 37 (1973), pp. 268-75; Gerald H. Kramer, "The Effects of Precinct-Level Canvassing on Voter Behaviour," *Public Opinion Quarterly*, 34 (1970), pp. 560-72; John C. Blydenburgh, "A Controlled Experiment to Measure the Effects of Personal Contact Campaigning," *Midwest Journal of Political Science*, 15 (1971), pp. 365-81.

4. Such is the clear implication of many of the articles in Howard R. Penniman, ed., *Canada at the Polls: the General Election of 1974* (Washington: American Enterprise Institute for Public Policy Research, 1975).

5. See Lawrence LeDuc, "The Measurement of Public Opinion," in Penniman, ed., *Canada at the Polls*, especially pp. 237-40.

6. For an account of the Conservative campaign see George Perlin, "The Progressive Conservative Party in the Election of 1974," in Penniman, ed., *Canada at the Polls*, pp. 57-96.

7. See the analysis of the inflation issue in Chapter Eight.

8. The Liberal strategy is described by Stephen Clarkson in "Pierre Trudeau and the Liberal Party: the Jockey and the Horse," in Penniman, ed., *Canada at the Polls*, pp. 57-96.

9. On the NDP campaign see Jo Surich, "Purists and Pragmatists: Canadian Democratic Socialism at the Crossroads," in Penniman, ed., *Canada at the Polls*, pp. 121-48.

10. The Wednesday and Saturday issues of 21 papers were obtained for the period of May 28 to July 8, 1974. Every article in these papers dealing with the 1974 campaign was then coded for content on a number of measures, many of which are reported in this chapter. Wire service articles were coded every time they appeared, regardless of duplication, since their appearance in a particular paper formed part of that paper's campaign coverage. The 21 newspapers coded were: St. John's *Evening Telegram*, Fredericton *Gleaner*, Saint John *Evening Times-Globe*, Halifax *Chronicle-Herald*, Montreal *Gazette*, *Le Soleil*, *Le Devoir*, *La Presse*, *Le Droit*, Ottawa *Journal*, Ottawa *Citizen*, Timmins *Daily Press*, Toronto *Star*, Toronto *Globe and Mail*, Winnipeg *Free Press*, Moose Jaw *Times*, Regina *Leader-Post*, Edmonton *Journal*, Calgary *Herald*, Vancouver *Province*, Vancouver *Sun*.

11. The country's news services provided detailed coverage of the leaders' activities. Arch Mackenzie, Ottawa Bureau Chief of Canadian Press, Canada's major wire service, indicates that all four of the party leaders were covered full-time during the 1974 campaign by a staff of 10 to 12 reporters in 10-day rotating shifts. CP filed two main stories a day on each leader, one at night to reach the morning papers and one day story. In addition, numerous spot-news reports were filed on any important aspect of the leaders' activities (interview, November 15, 1977). Charles Lynch, Ottawa Head of Southam News, said that news service also had a reporter travelling with each leader, on a rotating basis. These correspondents were instructed to file reflective articles every two to three days on the state of the leader's campaign. Lynch feels that the increased attention paid to leaders is a result of campaigns becoming keyed to television, which puts the focus on leaders at the expense of issues (interview, November 15, 1977). Anthony Westell, in "Reporting the Nation's Business," in G. Stuart Adam, ed., *Journalism, Communication and the Law* (Toronto: Prentice-Hall, 1976), pp. 54-69, states that it is the competitive pressure felt by papers which makes them reluctant to innovate in their coverage tactics. Pressure to "get the story" that the other papers are reporting causes them to take the same leads. (Interview, November 14, 1977. All interviews referred to were conducted by Jon Pammett.)

12. Perlin, *op. cit.*, p. 111-12.

13. Clarkson, *op. cit.*, p. 84.

14. See Ronald H. Wagenberg and Walter C. Soderlund, "The Effects of Chain Ownership on Editorial Coverage: the Case of the 1974 Canadian Federal Election," *Canadian Journal of Political Science*, 9 (1976), p. 688.

15. See Clarkson, *op. cit.*

16. Regina *Leader-Post* 9/7/74, p. 21, and 10/7/74, p. 45.

17. See *The Report of Special Senate Committee on Mass Media*, Vol. III, p. 42. A nationwide survey conducted for the Committee reports that the "most important medium" for different types of news was:

	INTERNATIONAL NEWS	CANADIAN NEWS	LOCAL NEWS
Television	56%	48%	25%
Radio	12	19	33
Newspapers	24	29	39
Magazines	6	2	0
No Answer	2	2	3

A 1972 national survey for the CBC reported that television was the most frequently chosen medium for "helping you make up your mind on an election." See Research Department, Canadian Broadcasting Corporation, *What the Canadian Public Thinks of Television and of the TV Service Provided by CBC: A Report to CBC Management*, Table 1.8, p. 17.

18. In the 1974 survey, respondents were asked directly whether newspapers, radio, or television was most important to them in getting information about politics. In reply, 41% cited television, 32% newspapers, 6% radio, and the remaining 21% combinations of the three. See Appendix B, Q. 38-41 for wording of the question.

19. All Bureau of Broadcast Measurement Reports establish the predominance of private commercial radio stations in the listening habits of Canadians.

20. The dominance of television over other media in terms of expenditures is documented by Khayyam Z. Paltiel, "Campaign Financing in Canada and its Reform," in Penniman, ed., *Canada at the Polls*, pp. 181-208, especially Tables 3, 4, and 5. Paltiel also notes that additional expenses were incurred in production costs of free-time broadcasts (personal communication).

21. Those respondents who reported that newspapers were most important to them in getting information about politics are more likely to report interest in the 1974 election and in politics generally, and report higher degrees of political participation than respondents reporting radio or television as most important to them.

22. See Surich, *op. cit.*, for a discussion of NDP campaign techniques and Paltiel, *op. cit.*, for a discussion of the party's finances in 1974.

23. This is reflected in the regional variation of the content measures. In Quebec and the Maritimes, for example, 74% and 70% respectively report no contact whatever with an NDP candidate or party workers, while in Ontario and the Western provinces, the percentages reporting no NDP contact are 41% and 43% respectively. Another predictable regional variation of the same type is the lower level of contact by Quebec voters with a PC candidate or party worker, 70% of our Quebec sample reporting no contact with that party in 1974.

Chapter Ten

A Typology of Partisanship

The portrait of the Canadian electorate that has been sketched thus far differs substantially from that which might have been drawn from an examination of electoral outcomes alone. One of the most obvious characteristics of federal elections has been the relative lack of variation in the results. In the fifteen elections since 1926, the Liberal Party has formed the government eleven times, and three of its four defeats were in one concentrated period between 1957 and 1963. If continuity in choice of the governing party is used as an indicator of electoral stability, the lack of change in federal elections is striking indeed. However, our analysis in Part II of this book suggests that stability at the aggregate level may mask important patterns of variation and movement of particular and identifiable sub-groups of the electorate.

Chapter Five has clearly shown that deviations from stable, consistent, and strong partisanship are prevalent and are strongly related to political behaviour and attitudes. It will be recalled that the reported rate of change in partisanship in the period between the 1972 and 1974 elections is fully 18%, and that 25% of all partisans report changing that tie between 1968 and 1974. Similarly high are the rates of inconsistent partisanship across levels of the federal system. The per cent of partisans who consider themselves supporters of different parties at the federal and provincial levels is 18%, while a further 23% support the same party but with different degrees of intensity. Yet, instability and inconsistency are not strongly related to the intensity of partisanship. Neither those who have unstable partisan histories nor those who are inconsistent in their support across levels are markedly less likely than stable or consistent partisans to report that their current affiliation is at least "fairly strong."

Findings such as these point to the need to consider the impact of this variability on behaviour and attitudes. As was seen in Chapters Six through Eight, deviations from strong, stable, and consistent partisanship are related (often strongly) to the nature of party images, perceptions of party leaders, and conceptualization of and reliance on issues. All of these analyses indicate that the manner in which voters relate to political parties can differ substantially, depending on their partisanship, and can lead to differences in attention paid, and importance attributed, to the several stimuli of electoral politics. For some individuals, *partisanship* may constitute little more than another short-term factor inserted into the decision process, along with issues, leaders, and candidates. Feelings about parties may be as ephemeral as these traditionally more unstable and time-bound factors, factors which vary with electoral conditions and contexts.

Previous analysis also demonstrates the importance of *political interest,* both in a specific election and in politics generally, for affecting levels of attention to and participation in politics. Those respondents with much interest in politics are more likely to be oriented toward issues, to pay attention to the electoral campaign, to collect information from several media sources, and to have been the recipients of visits and literature from several political parties.

These two factors taken together, the characteristics of partisanship and the importance of interest in politics, suggest the utility of constructing a new typology of Canadian partisans, one which will take into account the empirical observations made thus far. Such a typology can incorporate the observed differences in partisanship in Canada, as discussed in Chapter Five, as well as some of the patterns of the relationship between partisanship and political interest, which will be explored in this chapter. It may then be used subsequently to assess the relative effects of short-term and long-term components of electoral choice.

Construction of this typology requires a fuller exploration of some of the building blocks upon which it is based. The first of these are the three components of partisanship — intensity, stability, and consistency. The second is the level of political interest and involvement exhibited by these partisans. The discovery that many Canadian voters have altered their partisan attachments over time suggests that the sources of aggregate stability in Canadian election outcomes noted above need to be rethought. It is apparent that the similarity in such outcomes is not primarily a result of individual stability in partisanship and voting patterns over long periods of time. This is not to say that there is not a sizeable group of voters which consistently supports the same party; our evidence suggests that many such voters do exist. Additionally, however, it seems likely that the forces, primarily short-term in nature, which motivate vote switching and partisan change, have not acted in a unidirectional fashion. Rather, the normal pattern would seem to be one in which large numbers of voters are sufficiently "flexible" in their partisanship to be influenced by short-term factors such as leaders, local candidates, issues, or campaign-related phenomena of various kinds. These forces operate across the electorate as a whole in such a fashion, however, that countervailing trends in vote switching occur in most elections. Such patterns of change permit similar results to be produced over many elections, even while a relatively large amount of movement may occur from one election to the next at the level of individual voting behaviour.

An indication of the nature of the relationships between the intensity, stability, and consistency of partisanship and vote switching at the individual level is provided by the data in Table 10.1. These data reveal that each of the three components of partisanship is related to vote-switching in the elections of 1972 and 1974, and also to the personal voting history of respondents in previous elections. The relationships are strong and in the expected directions — that is, weak, unstable, and inconsistent partisans are all more likely to report voting for different parties than are those with strong, stable, and consistent partisan ties. That the effect of deviations from such a pattern of partisanship is cumulative is also evident in that the summary measure of partisan deviations has an impressive relationship with vote-switching. The percentage of respondents indicating a changed vote between 1972 and 1974 rises monotonically with each added deviation, from 6% to fully 65%. Similarly, the cumulative effect of deviations from strong, stable, and consistent partisanship is evidenced by the result that the per cent of the partisans who report that they have always voted for the same party declines monotonically from 82% to 15%. Thus, it is clear that individuals with weak, unstable, and/or inconsistent partisanship are much more likely to report voting for more than one party over the course of the elections in which they have participated than are those without these partisan characteristics.

DURABLE AND FLEXIBLE PARTISANS

That group of voters which reports a "very strong" or "fairly strong," stable, and consistent partisan tie will be characterized as *durable* partisans. Table 10.1 indicates that a large majority of these voters report always voting for the same party in federal elections. In contrast to the durable partisans, previous analyses (Chapter Five) have demonstrated that many Canadians hold a partisanship which can be characterized as *flexible* in nature. They are either unstable in their partisanship over time, inconsistent between the federal and provincial levels of the Canadian federal system, or weak in their intensity of partisanship. Also grouped with the flexible partisans will be those who do not hold any party identification at the federal level or define themselves as "independents." As shown in Table 10.1, these partisans are much more likely than durable

TABLE 10.1

Voting Behaviour in the 1972 and 1974 Federal Elections, and Federal Vote History, by Components of Partisanship and Summary Measure of Deviations from Strong, Stable, Consistent Partisanship

| | COMPONENTS OF PARTISANSHIP | | | | | | | | | | |
| | INTENSITY | | | STABILITY | | CONSISTENCY | | SUMMARY MEASURE OF DEVIATIONS | | | |
	VERY STRONG	FAIRLY STRONG	WEAK	STABLE	UNSTABLE	CONSISTENT	INCONSISTENT	0	1	2	3
Per cent always voting for same party (all elections)	70	55	42	70	26	63	34	82	43	26	15
		$Tau_c=.18^*$		$Tau_c=.39^*$		$Tau_c=.29^*$			$Tau_c=.53^*$		
Per cent switching (1972-1974)	10	22	41	14	38	16	41	6	24	43	65
		$Tau_c=.22^*$		$Tau_c=.25^*$		$Tau_c=.25^*$			$Tau_c=.36^*$		
(N)	(514)	(668)	(283)	(1029)	(585)	(1148)	(465)	(647)	(555)	(314)	(99)

*Significant at the .01 level.

partisans to switch their votes from one election to another. We would therefore hypothesize that this group might be more easily influenced by the types of short-term factors which are commonly stressed in campaigns — issues, leaders, and local candidate characteristics.

The argument outlined above is congruent with much of the literature on voting behaviour in that it postulates that voters' susceptibility to short-term forces is, in part at least, a function of the strength and stability of partisanship. Traditionally, however, it has been assumed that the influence of short-term forces on the voting choice of those with weaker, more ephemeral ties to party is to a certain extent offset by lower levels of political interest and involvement. The implicit assumption has been that the potential significance of short-term forces varies positively with the extent to which a voter is exposed to the stimuli surrounding a particular electoral campaign. Such exposure, in turn, is a function of level of political involvement.

Much of the literature on voting choice, as well as our previous analysis, suggests that a strong and stable link to a political party contributes to, or at least is related to, political interest and involvement, both behaviourally and attitudinally. These conclusions, however, are usually based only on an examination of the intensity component of partisanship.[1] Strong party identifiers in many countries score higher on various measures of political involvement than do weak party identifiers or independents. The stability component of partisanship has received less attention in most analyses. But in one study which does look at stability of partisanship over time in Britain, it is reported that those who had high exposure to political information were less likely to change their partisanship.[2]

The strength of the relationship between partisanship and political involvement in Canada is, of course, an empirical question. Those voters who have a deep commitment to a particular party may *not* be markedly more politically involved over time than their less committed counterparts, thereby increasing the potential importance of short-term forces in elections. Regardless of the manner in which the impact of short-term forces is influenced by levels of political involvement, however, the relationship between these forces and voting behaviour should be expected to vary according to the nature of voters' partisan ties. We shall hypothesize that the flexible partisans exhibit levels of political interest and involvement which are at least equal to, and often greater than, those with durable partisanship. This is in contrast to the more traditional assumption that voters who have a deeper commitment to a party are more likely to be politically aware and involved than those who do not. To the extent that the flexible partisans *are*, in fact, politically interested and aware, the potential significance of short-term forces in elections would be increased.

Analysis of the three separate components of partisanship in Canada

suggests that the relationships of each with political interest and involvement are *not* uniform in direction (Table 10.2). While intensity of partisanship is positively related to high interest and involvement, stability of
partisanship over time is *negatively* related. Further, there is no statistically significant relationship between consistency of partisanship across
levels of the federal system and political interest or involvement. The
differing direction of relationships between political interest and involvement and intensity of partisanship on the one hand and stability on the
other is suggestive of a number of important subtleties in the interaction
of partisanship and political interest in Canada. It is not, of course, surprising that more intense partisans should be more active and interested

TABLE 10.2

**Degree of Political Interest and Participation by Intensity,
Stability, and Consistency of Partisanship**

(column percentages)

| | INTENSITY | | | STABILITY | | CONSISTENCY | |
	VERY STRONG	FAIRLY STRONG	WEAK	STABLE	UNSTABLE	CONSISTENT	INCON-SISTENT
INTEREST							
High	40%	26%	25%	25%	35%	28%	27%
Moderate	25	30	21	25	27	25	27
Low	35	44	54	49	38	47	46
	Tau$_c$= .13*			Tau$_c$= −.12*		Tau$_c$=.01	
POLITICAL PARTICI- PATION[a]	2.2	1.9	1.6	1.8	2.1	1.9	1.9
	F=25.1*			F=29.1*		F=0.16	
N=	*629*	*927*	*423*	*1474*	*775*	*1568*	*680*

[a]Mean score on four-item participation scale. Participation items asked of half
sample only.

*Significant at .01 level.

in politics. However, the fact that stability is inversely related to interest
constitutes important evidence that persons who change their partisanship
are not primarily the less interested and less politically involved segment
of the electorate.[3]

In order to retain, for subsequent analysis, the differing effects of the
several components of partisanship in Canada and of political interest
and involvement, we have developed a typology of the electorate which

takes account of both factors. While both partisanship and political interest are complex phenomena, each is simplified here for purposes of analysis. This allows a greater degree of clarity than would otherwise be possible, when later voting behaviour in a specific election is related to the combined characteristics of partisanship and political interest. The combination of these two factors yields the typology of partisanship and political interest shown in Table 10.3.

Our characterization of the electorate involves an additional element, that of voting history in federal elections. At any point in time, the electorate can be thought of as being comprised of three groups — the *permanent electorate*, the *transient electorate, and new voters.* The portion of the Canadian electorate labelled "permanent" in Table 10.3 comprises about three-quarters of the voters. These are people who report that they always or usually vote in federal elections and that they voted in 1972 and 1974. Another 17% voted in only one of these two elections and also report that they do not always vote in federal elections. This group is designated the "transient" portion of the electorate. The final category is that of the new voters, those who were eligible to vote for the first time in the 1974 election.

This analytical typology categorizes 62% of the Canadian electorate as flexible partisans, people who deviate in some degree from consistent, stable, and strong partisanship. This suggests that a majority of the Canadian electorate, given the proper stimuli, might not be reluctant to switch both their votes and, in some instances, their partisan allegiance. The largest group in Table 10.3 is the flexible partisans who are part of the permanent electorate. They can be expected to vote every time the opportunity arises, and it might be hypothesized that they provide a ready pool of voters who can be moved by the context of the campaign, the particular issues, candidates, and leaders. Fully 18% of the electorate is composed of highly interested but flexible partisans. On the face of it, the constituency of potential vote switchers is large. The transient electorate is also interesting in this regard. By definition, transient voters are those who are only occasionally mobilized to participate by the events of elections and politics. Almost twice as many transients report a flexible as compared to a durable partisanship. They would also seem to provide a pool of potential voters sensitive to the influence of short-term forces. The final category in Table 10.3 is the new voters, those entering the electorate for the first time. They, too, report high levels of flexibility in their partisanship, and are important sources of new support for the parties. The way that flexible partisans in these three groups respond to campaign stimuli will be a major determinant of the outcome of any given election.

TABLE 10.3

A Typology of the 1974 Canadian Electorate, Based on Partisanship, Political Interest, and Vote History[a]

	THE "PERMANENT" ELECTORATE[b] (100%)[d] PARTISANSHIP		THE "TRANSIENT" ELECTORATE[c] (25%) PARTISANSHIP		THE NEW VOTERS (81%) PARTISANSHIP	
	DURABLE	FLEXIBLE	DURABLE	FLEXIBLE	DURABLE	FLEXIBLE
POLITICAL INTEREST HIGH	10.3%	15.3%	1.1%	1.9%	0.4%	1.2%
MODERATE	8.1%	13.2%	1.7%	2.6%	0.7%	0.3%
LOW	10.8%	19.3%	3.6%	6.1%	1.4%	2.0%
Totals	29.2%	47.8%	6.4%	10.6%	2.5%	3.5%

[a]Total N for all types = 2238.

[b]Persons who "always" or "usually" vote in federal elections and who voted both in 1972 and 1974.

[c]Persons who "do not always" vote in federal elections, or who did not vote in one of the 1972 or 1974 elections.

[d]Per cent of group voting in 1974.

ORIENTATIONS OF PARTISAN TYPES

The utility of the typology of partisans is dependent upon its ability to meaningfully distinguish the attitudes and behaviour of its component groups. Our typology does distinguish the political attitudes and behaviour of the respondents to the 1974 study, as indicated by several different measures of political orientations drawn from previous chapters, such as political parties, issues, and the electoral campaign. It is also possible to explore the content, timing, and result of the vote decision of the several types of partisans.

Since this characterization of partisans is based upon the personal history of individuals' links to political parties, it is to be expected that the orientations to political parties will differ across groups. There are several ways that these differences could develop. Flexibility in partisanship could lead to less attention to and involvement with political parties, and an increased concentration on other aspects of politics, even among the most involved segments of the electorate. On the other hand, the effect of flexible partisanship might be the opposite, to make people more aware of and involved with political parties. These possibilities can be explored through an examination of the images of political parties held by the several types. Within categories of political interest (Table 10.4), flexible partisans are more likely than are durable ones to have well-developed images of the parties. Although high levels of interest do heighten attention to political parties, even the low level of interest of some flexible partisans does not eliminate their ability to describe and delineate the content of their images of the parties. The greatest number of party images is held by the flexible, high-interest partisans. Even more than durable, highly interested partisans, this group can describe and discuss the several parties operating in federal politics. It is also this group which is most likely to have views about parties *other* than their own. Most of the difference between the flexible and durable partisans, within the "highly" interested category, is due to the fact that the flexible partisans have images of parties other than that with which they currently identify. The same pattern obtains for the other categories of flexible and durable partisans.

Another indicator of orientation to political parties is provided by the question asking for a second choice of party, if the preferred party was not available.[4] Table 10.4 shows that the willingness to contemplate a second choice is related to the partisan and interest characteristics of the voters. Only slightly more than half of the durable partisans indicate a willingness to vote for another party and many would rather abstain, irrespective of level of political interest. In contrast, the flexible partisans, particularly the high interest group, are more willing to express a second preference. The new voters and transients are somewhat more willing to

TABLE 10.4

Orientation to Political Parties by Partisan Types

		PARTY IMAGES (MEAN NUMBER OF IMAGES)			SECOND CHOICE PARTIES
		ALL FEDERAL PARTIES	OWN PARTY[a]	PARTY OTHER THAN OWN	(% WHO WOULD BE WILLING TO MAKE A 2ND CHOICE[b])
Durable, Low Interest	(N=241)	3.2	1.5	1.7	54
Durable, Moderate Interest	(N=181)	4.1	1.6	2.5	57
Durable, High Interest	(N=230)	4.6	1.8	2.8	55
Flexible, Low Interest	(N=432)	3.5	1.2	2.3	62
Flexible, Moderate Interest	(N=296)	4.5	1.6	2.9	66
Flexible, High Interest	(N=342)	5.5	1.7	3.8	70
Transient Voters	(N=379)	2.8	1.0	1.8	59
New Voters	(N=136)	3.2	1.1	2.1	57
Total Sample	(N=2445)	4.1	1.6	2.5	60
		F=28.4*	F=16.9*	F=25.0*	V=.14*

[a]Party identifiers only (N=2088).

[b]Voters in the 1974 election only (N=1862).

*Significant at .01 level.

make a second choice than are durable partisans, but less prepared to do so than the flexibles. From this analysis of orientations to political parties, it becomes clear that flexibility of partisanship is associated with more fully developed images of parties and a greater willingness to consider different voting alternatives.

Previous analyses have demonstrated that there is considerable attention paid to campaign issues by some portions of the electorate. In Chapter Six we discovered that a substantial number of voters have issue components in their images of political parties, and Chapter Eight showed that an orientation to issues is, in part, a function of partisan history and interest and involvement in politics. Thus, it will be useful to determine how the types of partisans delineated here differ in their attention to issues.

TABLE 10.5

Issue Orientation of Partisan Types

		% MENTIONING 2 IMPORTANT CAMPAIGN ISSUES	% MENTIONING PARTY AS MOST IMPORTANT FOR VOTE DECISION[a]	% MENTIONING AN ISSUE IN PARTY IMAGE	MEAN NO. OF IMAGES WHICH ARE ISSUES
Durable, Low Interest	(N=241)	30	38	60	1.1
Durable, Moderate Interest	(N=181)	40	46	59	1.3
Durable, High Interest	(N=230)	42	48	66	1.6
Flexible, Low Interest	(N=432)	25	32	54	1.1
Flexible, Moderate Interest	(N=296)	45	38	69	1.7
Flexible, High Interest	(N=342)	52	43	75	1.8
Transient Voters	(N=379)	31	43	55	1.0
New Voters	(N=136)	32	45	56	1.0
Total Sample	(N=2445)	37	41	62	1.3
		V=.20*	V=.10*		F=16.5*

[a]1974 voters only (N=1862).
*Significant at .01 level.

Campaign issues are among the most changeable elements of politics. Not only do economic, social, and political conditions alter and thereby influence the nature and content of issues, but also political parties manoeuvre their own policy statements so as to maximize their issue appeal. Thus, an electorate, or a portion thereof, highly attuned to issues, is likely to be an unstable and changeable electorate, one which reacts to short-term forces with vigour. Table 10.5 shows how the several types of partisans react to issues. Flexible, high-interest partisans are the most issue-oriented group of the electorate. On all the indicators, they achieve the highest score for issue orientation. Over half of them mentioned two campaign issues, and fully three-quarters described at least one of the images of the political parties in terms of issues. The next most issue-oriented group is the durable, highly interested partisans. These are less likely than the corresponding group of flexible partisans to mention issues in their answers, but their level of political interest reflects an issue-related orientation to politics. On the other hand, the flexible, low-interest partisans resemble the transient and new voters in their relatively low level of issue awareness and conceptualization of politics in terms of issues. Thus, both partisanship and political interest are important if a proper categorization of issue-orientation is to be achieved. Attention to issues and conceptualization of politics as conflict over issues is one of the first suggestions that short-term forces may be more influential in the voting decision of the flexible, high-interest group than for some others. They are, on the one hand, more attuned to issues and, on the other, most willing to think about changing their vote if the need arises.

The differing potential for political change among the partisan types is also shown by the timing of their voting decisions (Table 10.6). One-fifth of the 1974 voters replied that they made their choice during the final week of the campaign. A further 20% fixed the time of their decision two to five weeks before the election. The largest numbers of respondents who reported making their voting decision late in the campaign are concentrated among those groups most prone to switch their vote from 1972 — flexible partisans. Table 10.6 demonstrates clearly that the effect of a durable partisanship is to encourage an early decision which may not be subject to the intervening effect of the campaign. There is some relationship due to interest, but even the least interested of durable partisans are less likely to make their decisions during the campaign.

In order for a campaign-related influence on voting decisions to exist for any of these groups, the vote itself must be perceived as open to consideration (or reconsideration) at some point during the campaign. Certainly, there appears to be no real possibility of such influence for those persons whose vote is decided far in advance, or who rarely deviate from their support for their normal party in any case. For such individuals, if

TABLE 10.6
The Timing of the Electoral Decision by Partisan Types
(Voters in the 1974 Election Only)

		TIME OF DECISION (row percentages)			% WHO "WERE PRETTY SURE" WHAT VOTE WOULD BE
		6 WEEKS OR MORE BEFORE ELECTION	2-5 WEEKS BEFORE ELECTION	FINAL WEEK OF CAMPAIGN	
Durable, Low Interest	(N=109)	76%	13	11	90
Durable, Moderate Interest	(N=80)	78%	11	10	89
Durable, High Interest	(N=110)	86%	12	2	96
Flexible, Low Interest	(N=197)	46%	25	29	66
Flexible, Moderate Interest	(N=145)	54%	24	21	68
Flexible, High Interest	(N=169)	63%	19	19	68
Transient Voters	(N=48)	42%	29	29	79
New Voters	(N=52)	47%	27	27	76
Total Half Sample	(N=923)	61%	20	20	76
		V=.22*			V=.27*

*Significant at the .01 level.

they have high levels of political interest, the effects of the campaign are likely to be reinforcing. But any possible campaign effect, regardless of whether it is traceable to issues or to other short-term factors, is more likely to be genuine if the voters perceive themselves as consciously weighing alternatives and considering choices during a campaign. Given the nature of the Canadian electoral system, the voters often find themselves in the position of weighing conflicting factors — issues, party leaders, local candidates, and so forth. Since such means of resolving conflicting factors as "ticket-splitting" are not available to the Canadian voter, it is common for public opinion polls to show large numbers of "undecided" voters well into the campaign.[5] Among all 1974 voters sampled, 24% indicated in response to the survey questions that they had, at some point during the campaign, considered voting for a party other than the one that they eventually supported. But among those who were in fact most likely to switch parties in 1974 — the flexible partisans — the percentage who report having considered more than one party is substantially higher, identifying these voters as the ones most likely to be genuinely "weighing" alternative courses of behaviour. Table 10.6 shows that while fully 96% of durable, high-interest partisans knew all along for whom they would vote, just over two-thirds of flexible partisans were that certain. For the balance, as well as for transient and new voters, there had been a time when they had considered an alternative vote.[6]

Taken together, these responses serve to indicate that there are, in the Canadian electorate, voters who make their voting decisions during the course of the campaign, often late in the campaign, and who consider alternatives. This creates at least the minimum conditions which would be required for the kinds of short-term forces generated by a campaign to have any genuine effect either on individual voting behaviour or on election outcomes.

Not only do flexible partisans make their voting decision later and with greater difficulty than do durable partisans, but they also report that they consume more information during the campaign before they come to a decision (data not shown in tabular form). Much of the difference within the electorate in the amount of attention paid to the campaign is due to variations in the level of political interest, as might be expected. However, there are differences due to partisanship as well. This means that the partisan types are ranged along several points on the dimension of attention to campaign information. For example, when asked how much they read about the campaign in the newspapers, each category of flexible partisans was more likely than the category of durable partisans at the same level of interest to report that they read a great deal about the campaign. Of the flexible partisans who were highly interested, 79% report that they read a great deal, whereas 74% of the durable, high-interest group say the same. Similarly, whereas only 16% of the low interest, flexible partisans read a great deal, even fewer of those in the durable, low interest category (14%) did so.

From these observations, as well as those about the time and ease of decision, a picture can be drawn of an electorate which is divided in its reactions to the campaign. Once again, the direction of this division is such that there is evidence that the source of political change may lie more within the subgroup of flexible partisans than durable, and that the stimulus for change may come largely from issues, for at least one set of the flexible partisans, as was noted above.

Is there any evidence that these differences in attitudes and orientation and in patterns of decision-making are reflected in political behaviour? The final exploration of the utility of this division of the electorate into partisan types will look at the personal history of electoral choice of each of the eight types. Table 10.7 demonstrates that the correspondence between the 1972 and the 1974 vote is strongly related to the characteristics of partisanship of each of the types. Of the flexible partisans, one-third voted for different parties in these two elections, whereas less than 6% of the durable partisans did so. Thus, in 1974, much of the movement between parties that did occur was due to the decisions of the flexible partisans, decisions that tended to be made later in the campaign and on the basis of more information garnered from the mass media.

When the longer period of one's complete electoral history is examined, a similar pattern emerges. Fully four-fifths of the durable partisans, what-

TABLE 10.7

Vote History by Partisan Types

		% VOTING FOR DIFFERENT PARTIES IN 1972 AND 1974	% ALWAYS VOTING FOR THE SAME PARTY
Durable, Low Interest	(N=237)	8	84
Durable, Moderate Interest	(N=179)	5	81
Durable, High Interest	(N=227)	5	80
Flexible, Low Interest	(N=393)	32	31
Flexible, Moderate Interest	(N=280)	34	27
Flexible, High Interest	(N=334)	33	24
Transient Voters[a]	(N=86)	—	61
New Voters		—	—
Total Sample	(N=1808)	23	51
[a]Voters in 1974 election only.		V=.32*	V=.51*

*Significant at .01 level.

ever their level of interest, report that they have always voted for the same political party in elections since they were old enough to vote. On the other hand, more than three-quarters of the flexible partisans have voted for different parties. This is probably not surprising, given the fact that many of them may have held a different partisanship at an early period, since instability of partisanship is one of the characteristics of flexibility. It is, however, only one. More than changes in partisanship are reflected in these statistics. They also include the effects of weak partisan ties, and differences in the direction of these ties across levels of the federal system. It is obvious that flexibility of partisanship, whether due to instability, inconsistency, or lack of strength, is related to a history of different party choices, as well as being associated with several attitudes and types of behaviour, all of which suggest the potential for change in any particular election.

CONCLUSION

The observation of both high levels of inconsistency and instability in partisanship in Canada, and weak relationships between partisan inconsistency and instability on the one hand, and intensity on the other, prompted the development of a measure of partisanship which takes all these variations into account. This, in turn, was followed by a more detailed examination of these three components of partisanship and the distribution of political interest and involvement. While consistency of partisanship is not related to interest and participation, instability and intensity are related but in opposite directions. The more intense the partisan tie, the more interested the person is in politics. This is perhaps not a surprising finding, but more unexpected is the discovery that unstable partisans are also more interested in politics than are those people who have never changed their partisan attachment. Thus, the necessity of having a somewhat more subtle characterization of the electorate that takes these variations into account led to the development of a typology of partisanship and political interest. This typology distinguishes eight partisan-voter groups with varying levels of interest and voting participation. These groups differ in their orientations to political parties, in their conceptualization of parties and politics, in the timing of their vote decisions, and in their willingness to consider alternatives. The nature of these differences suggests that there exists, within certain categories of the electorate, a great deal of potential for influence from short-term campaign forces.

Given these findings, our next step will be to delineate the relative importance of both long- and short-term forces in the election of 1974 for these various groups of voters. Subsequently, categories of partisanship and political interest will be used to account for aggregate patterns of stability and change.

Although there is presently no well-grounded theory of voting in Canada, the existing scholarly literature does contain a number of empirical generalizations which are relevant to such analysis. Perhaps the most basic finding to emerge from previous inquiries is that voting in federal elections varies markedly across regional, religious, and ethnic cleavages in the electorate, and that other socio-demographic variables, particularly social class, are considerably less important.[7] This is not to say, however, that political scientists have argued that Canadian voters are simply the prisoners of long-term forces associated with ethnic, religious, or other ascriptive criteria. On the contrary, it frequently has been asserted that for many Canadians, long-term standing commitments to support a given political party are either weak or non-existent, and, hence, these voters are susceptible to short-term forces, especially those associated with the images of specific party leaders.

An emphasis on party leaders' personal characteristics and political style may result from conscious attempts on the part of the Liberal and Progressive Conservative parties to build broadly based electoral coalitions in a polity rent by deep-seated societal cleavages.[8] Potentially divisive issues are downplayed, and electoral campaigns focus instead on party leaders' personalities.[9] In a system where party loyalties are frequently weak, the consequence of such electoral strategies is that a sizable proportion of the Canadian electorate is "volatile." Lacking the anchors supplied by strong partisan allegiances, such voters are prone to switch their votes from one election to the next in response to the essentially non-programmatic campaign appeals of current party leaders.

Several observations concerning the foregoing characterization of voting in Canadian federal elections can be made. Data presented in Chapter Four has documented that region, religion, and ethnicity are significant correlates of the vote in the 1965, 1968, and 1974 elections. At the same time, however, these analyses demonstrated that the overall power of these variables to predict electoral choice is not strong, the maximum variance explained being only 11%. Investigation of the nature of partisanship in Canada (see Chapter Five) has also revealed that a majority of voters (62%) do not have strong, stable, and consistent party allegiances. Further, data presented in Chapter Seven has shown that voters' images of party leaders are heavily dominated by personality and stylistic references. Finally, party image perceptions, while containing a larger component of issue and ideological references than do the party leader image data, are focussed primarily on short-term and relatively recent political phenomena. In general terms, these data are consistent with the notion that many Canadians are susceptible to short-term electoral forces. However, one cannot ignore voters who do not manifest the characteristics adumbrated above, especially that 38% of the electorate having strong, stable, and consistent ties with a particular political party.[10] It can be expected that these voters will react to the political stimuli associated with specific elections largely in terms of their partisan attachments, and consequently, that short-term forces relating to issues, candidates, and leaders will be of lesser significance for these voters, except perhaps in terms of reinforcing existing partisan predispositions. This supposition provided the basis for the categorization of the electorate into *durable* (strong or fairly strong, stable, and consistent) and *flexible* (weak and/or unstable and/or inconsistent) partisans in this chapter.

Sensitivity to campaign-related or other short-term electoral forces is not simply a function of the nature of partisanship. In particular, it has been argued here that patterns of political interest will influence voters' exposure and attention to political stimuli. In Canada, the potential independent effect of political interest as a factor influencing the effects of short-term forces on the vote is indicated by the relatively weak correlations between the components of partisanship and political interest. It will be recalled that recognition of the possible effects of political interest prompted the decision to categorize the Canadian electorate in terms of levels of interest as well as partisanship. The utility of this categorization scheme for understanding voting choice will be explored in the analyses of the vote conducted in the next chapter.

FOOTNOTES

1. The relationship between strength of party identification and psychological and behavioural involvement in politics has been demonstrated in numerous studies. See, for example, Campbell et al., *The American Voter* (New York: Wiley, 1960), pp. 101-110; S. Verba and N. H. Nie, *Participation in America* (New York: Harper & Row, 1975), pp. 209-24. For Canadian data see R. Van Loon, "Political Participation in Canada," *Canadian Journal of Political Science,* 3 (1970), p. 391; Mike Burke, "Political Participation in Canadian National and Provincial Elections: An Analysis of Regional Effects," unpublished M.A. thesis, Department of Political Science, University of Windsor, 1976.
2. D. Butler and D. Stokes, *Political Change in Britain* (New York: St. Martin's, 1971), pp. 220-44.
3. This pattern of relationships can exist because there is only a weak correlation between reported stability and intensity of party identification. Unstable partisans are quite prone to report a strong attachment to their current party. See Table 5.6.
4. See Appendix B, Q. 47(a).
5. A Gallup poll taken at the beginning of the campaign classified as much as 34% of the electorate as "undecided." This percentage decreased steadily in subsequent polls taken during the campaign. See Lawrence LeDuc, "The Measurement of Public Opinion," in H. R. Penniman, ed.,

Canada at the Polls (Washington: American Enterprise Institute for Public Policy Research, 1975), p. 237.
6. See Appendix B, Q. 48(b).
7. For a bibliography listing most major studies, see Mildred Schwartz, "Canadian Voting Behavior," in Richard Rose, ed., *Electoral Behavior: A Comparative Handbook* (New York: The Free Press, 1974), pp. 608-17.
8. This interpretation of voting behaviour is often associated with the "brokerage" theory. The implications of this theory for understanding voting behaviour are discussed in Paul M. Sniderman, H. D. Forbes, and Ian Melzer, "Party Loyalty and Electoral Volatility: A Study of the Canadian Party System," *Canadian Journal of Political Science*, 7 (1974), pp. 268-88.
9. See, for example, Peter Regenstreif, *The Diefenbaker Interlude* (Toronto: Longmans, 1965), chap. 4.
10. As might be expected, there is some variance in the distribution of different types of partisans by province and region. It should be noted however that the fundamental characteristics of partisanship are essentially similar throughout the country. For example, the percentage of *strong, stable, consistent partisans*, distributed by province, was as follows:

Nfld.	P.E.I.	N.S.	N.B.	Que.	Ont.
62	51	48	50	39	39
	Man.	Sask.	Alta.	B.C.	
	34	37	33	25	

A more detailed regional analysis of individual components of partisanship (see Tables 5.2, 5.3, 5.5) does not disclose differences between provinces sufficient to require extensive qualification of our overall argument concerning the nature of partisanship in Canada.

Chapter Eleven

Voting Behaviour

For most Canadians, voting constitutes the only overt form of political participation. A preliminary indication of the forces affecting electoral choice may be obtained by considering the reasons offered by the voters themselves for their ballot decisions in 1974. When confronted with a question concerning reasons for their electoral choices,[1] voters offered a wide variety of responses, ranging from traditional partisan allegiance, to judgments about party leaders and campaign issues, to a number of more idiosyncratic, personal concerns.

A number of respondents mentioned that party leaders were particularly important. Consistent with the differences in party leader images documented in Chapter Seven, voters manifested sharply differing perceptions of the leaders in their explanations of electoral choices. Consider, for example, the comments offered by Bob Dale, a native Torontonian. Twenty years old, with a Grade 13 education, Dale is currently unemployed. Formerly an NDP identifier, he presently considers himself a Liberal who follows politics "fairly closely." When asked what prompted him to vote Liberal in 1974, Dale replied:

> Well, mainly the party leader. After hearing all three I decided he was very honest and intelligent and I agreed with most of the things he said. I generally speaking feel more kindly toward the Liberal Party. I like Trudeau better than Stanfield or David Lewis. I agree with his political views more and I think he is more intelligent than Stanfield.

Mr. Dale's judgment of the party leaders contrasts strongly with that of Jo-Ann Roberts, a 28-year-old high school teacher living in Charlottetown. Unlike Dale, Ms. Roberts is a Conservative partisan. She cast a Conservative vote in 1974, in part at least, because of her perceptions of the leaders of the two major parties:

All of a sudden I had a personality clash with Trudeau — I just don't
like him. I admired Stanfield for his tenacity. Also, the Conservatives
appear to be at least trying to do something about the inflation problem.

As Ms. Roberts' explication of her reasons for voting Conservative
indicates, the inflation issue, as well as judgments regarding party leaders,
played a role in her electoral decision. In this regard, she was similar to a
substantial minority of the electorate. Not all voters citing inflation, however, concluded that the Tories were best able to deal with this issue. On
the contrary, many respondents felt that the Liberals were the party most
qualified to combat inflation. Typical of this type of respondent is Dick
Handman, who is 32 years old and has a high school education. Mr.
Handman is the owner and manager of a janitorial service in Oshawa,
and is a "very strong" Liberal partisan. He pays little attention to
politics in general, but stated that he was "very interested" in the 1974
campaign. When asked why he voted Liberal, Handman answered:

I didn't believe Stanfield. He said he could control inflation — and he
can't because it's worldwide. I listened to him but Trudeau made more
sense. I suppose inflation was most important.

It is part of Canadian political folklore that a substantial number of
voters cast their ballots primarily in response to the appeals of local
candidates,[2] and indeed, a significant minority of respondents in the 1974
survey stressed the importance of the candidates running in their constituencies. As an example of this type of response, one may cite the
answer provided by Elizabeth Jacobs, a 29-year-old psychologist in British
Columbia. A "weak" Liberal partisan, Ms. Jacobs was "fairly interested"
in the 1974 election. Explaining her Liberal vote, she stated:

In this riding I felt there was no doubt Holt would get in. I feel very
strongly that it is important for women to run for office and it is also
very important that they have a strong showing at the polls. I wanted
to vote for a woman, and it happened she was Liberal, which was my
party, and also she was very good.

Similar to many of those mentioning party leaders as significant factors
in their voting decision, some of the respondents citing local candidates
combined candidate references with comments on issues. An example of
this response pattern is provided by Paul Richard, a retired brick-layer in
Trois Rivières. Mr. Richard, a life-long Liberal identifier, opted for the
Liberals in 1974. Articulating the reasons for this choice, he commented:

I especially like the Liberal candidate Mr. Lajoie. However, the most
important things for me were to have a government which would be
able to combat inflation and do something about the bilingualism question.

Although a large number of references to party leaders, local candidates, and issues were made, many voters talked about the parties themselves. Some simply stated that their ballot decision was a consequence of partisan ties and/or parties' general ideological positions, whereas others discussed the parties in terms of past performance or potential to deal with specific issues. An example of the former type of response is provided by Ed Nozanberg, the president of a small manufacturing firm in Toronto. Following a family tradition, Nozanberg is a "very strong" Conservative partisan. When queried about his decision to cast a PC ballot in 1974, Nozanberg tersely replied:

> I've always been a PC. I think Canada is turning towards socialism and I'm against it.

A substantially different type of "party" response was provided by a 38-year-old Winnipeg resident, John Bonwall. He holds a Ph.D. in geophysics and is employed as a research scientist by the Manitoba government. A self-defined political independent, Bonwall stated that he generally follows politics "very closely," was "very interested" in the 1974 campaign, and voted New Democrat in 1974. The reasoning behind his vote was as follows:

> First, there was the ineffectiveness of the Conservatives during the last Parliament. Also, one had to consider the makeshift economic policies of the Liberals to try and solve the problems facing people, and the ability of the NDP to manoeuver the Liberals into making some fairly good and important decisions.

Although the responses regarding reasons for voting in 1974 cited above cannot be considered to typify the answers provided by the entire electorate, they do provide a flavour of the diverse nature of the electorate's perceptions of their reasons for voting. The quoted responses indicate that the bases for concluding that a particular factor — for example party leader — was important can be varied and complex. To better appreciate the full range and relative frequency of responses, the "reasons for voting" are summarized in Table 11.1. These data document that "party" reasons were frequently mentioned, being offered by 41% of the respondents. Party leader and local candidate responses also constituted popular categories, being cited by 25% and 14% of the electorate respectively. Additionally, a relatively wide range of issue responses was forthcoming. Specifically, 23% referred explicitly to inflation, and a further 7% mentioned the closely related issue of wage and price controls. The relative salience of inflation and related economic matters in the minds of the electorate in 1974 is suggested by the fact that no other category of issue is cited by more than 11% of the voters. Thus, for example, 7% and 4% of the respondents mentioned majority government or bilingualism respectively as important reasons for their votes. The failure of these latter two issues to be referenced by large numbers of voters is consistent with findings presented earlier regarding the infrequency with which these issues appeared in newspaper coverage of the 1974 campaign, or were mentioned by respondents as important issues (see Table 9.6).

Although the reasons offered by the voters themselves for their electoral behaviour are both interesting and suggestive of possible avenues for further inquiry, such responses alone cannot provide an adequate portrait

TABLE 11.1

Reasons Cited for 1974 Vote
(percentages[a])

Party	41%
Leaders, Leadership	25
Local Candidates	14
Issues:	
Inflation	23
Wage and Price Controls	7
Other Economic	11
Bilingualism	4
Majority Government	7
Pensions, Health, Welfare	8
Foreign Policy	1
Miscellaneous	
Other Issues	15
Traditional Vote, Civic Duty, and Miscellaneous Other Reasons	19
N=	*(939)*

[a]Multiple response.

of the forces influencing voting behaviour in the 1974 election. To enhance understanding of these forces, more comprehensive and detailed analyses are required. Particular attention must be given to the possible impact of partisanship, party leaders, local candidates, and issues as forces affecting electoral choice in Canada. Here, the relationships of each of these possible influences with voting behaviour in 1974 will be considered in turn.

FORCES INFLUENCING VOTING BEHAVIOUR

Previous analyses have emphasized the flexibility of partisanship, documenting that substantial numbers of Canadians have weak, unstable, or inconsistent partisan ties. For these voters, partisanship may not constitute a long-term force on electoral choice. For durable partisans, however — those with strong, stable, and consistent ties to a party — partisanship is very likely an important enduring influence on the vote.

Regarding the correlation between the direction of partisanship and the vote, Table 11.2 summarizes a series of statistically impressive relationships. In all three national election studies (1965, 1968, 1974), overwhelming majorities of Canadians voted for the parties with which they identified. Illustratively, in 1974, 90%, 92%, 86%, and 87% of the Liberal, PC, NDP, and Social Credit partisans cast ballots for their parties. These strong correlations between partisanship and voting in Canada parallel findings in the United States, Great Britain, and elsewhere.[3]

Also, similar to findings in other political milieus is the relationship displayed in the first three columns of Table 11.2b. As might be anticipated, the relationship between vote and direction of partisanship is affected by the intensity of partisan attachments. Thus, although 74% of the "weak" Liberals cast a Liberal ballot in 1974, this percentage increased to 91% among the "fairly strong" Liberals and to fully 97% for the "very strong" Liberals. Similar results obtain for PC and NDP partisans. Also, analyses of the 1968 and 1965 data (not shown in tabular form) reveal that intensity of partisanship operated in a similar fashion in these years.

While the correlations between voting and the direction and intensity of partisanship are not unexpected ones, the relationships with other components of partisanship (Table 11.2b) are less familiar. Given the large numbers of unstable and inconsistent partisans in the Canadian electorate, it may be observed that both stability and consistency of partisanship influence the magnitude of the relationship. Stable and consistent partisans are more likely to vote for the federal party with which they currently identify than are those with unstable or inconsistent partisan attachments. For example, 95% of the stable Liberal partisans, as opposed to 81% of the unstable Liberals, cast a Liberal ballot in 1974. Again, 94% of the consistent, as compared to 78% of the inconsistent, Liberals voted Liberal in this election. Similar patterns hold for those identified with the other three parties. Also, these patterns obtain in both 1968 and 1965 (data not shown in tabular form). Overall, these data, similar to those on the components of partisanship presented earlier, strongly indicate that understanding the influence of partisanship on electoral choice in Canada requires that attention be given not only to the direction and intensity, but also to the stability and consistency of partisan ties. Analyses of voting behaviour to be conducted later in this chapter will demonstrate the significance of these differences in the nature of partisanship.

TABLE 11.2

Panel a

Vote by Direction of Partisanship, 1974, 1968, and 1965
(percentages of partisans of various parties voting for "own" party)

DIRECTION OF PARTISANSHIP

ELECTION	LIBERAL	PC	NDP	SC	V
1965	93	87	89	76	.83*
1968	95	88	86	65	.81*
1974	90	92	86	87	.84*

Panel b

Vote and Direction of Partisanship by Components of Partisanship, 1974
(per cent of partisans voting for "own" party)

DIRECTION OF PARTISANSHIP	VERY STRONG	FAIRLY STRONG	WEAK	STABLE	UNSTABLE	CON-SISTENT	INCON-SISTENT
		INTENSITY			STABILITY	CONSISTENCY	
Liberal	97	91	74	95	81	94	78
PC	93	92	91	93	89	93	88
NDP	99	80	75	89	81	90	73
SC	82	89	92	88	85	92	79
V =	.92*	.82*	.76*	.87*	.79*	.89*	.71*

*Significant at .01 level.

PARTY LEADERS AND LOCAL CANDIDATES

The present chapter has already sketched a picture of the effects of party leader and local candidate images on voting from the perspectives of the voters themselves. Reports of reasons for voting in 1974 indicate that party leader and local candidate images play a part in determining the electoral choices of large numbers of voters. Although suggestive, these data are not adequate for determining the actual strength of such factors as determinants of the vote. It is possible that a substantial proportion of references to the importance of leaders or candidates are primarily rationalizations of voting choices made on other bases. In particular, for some voters, current partisan attachments function so as to shape perceptions of political figures as well as determining directly the vote itself. In such instances, observed relationships between leader and candidate images and the vote would be essentially spurious, being caused by affect for parties. Such a possibility suggests the need to examine the impact of party leader and local candidate images on the vote in the presence of controls for levels of affect for various parties.[4]

Using the thermometer questions[5] regarding levels of affect for leaders, candidates, and parties, respondents were classified according to their relative affect for each leader, candidate, and party. For example, considering Liberal local candidates, if a respondent gave the Liberal candidate in his or her constituency a higher thermometer score than other local candidates, he or she was placed in a "positive" category; if the Liberal candidate's thermometer score was equal to but not greater than other candidate(s) score(s), the respondent was placed in a "neutral" category; and if the score for one or more other candidates exceeded that for the Liberal candidate, the respondent was placed in a "negative" category. Separate variables were constructed for each party leader, local candidate, and party. For different combinations of these variables (e.g., Liberal candidate and Liberal party) the percentage of voters casting a ballot for the Liberal, Progressive Conservative, or NDP parties is obtained. Inspection of these percentages provides a preliminary assessment of the influence of leaders and candidates on the vote *over and above that exercised by feelings for parties.*

The leader versus party analyses (Table 11.3) indicate that in 1974 and 1968, voting for the Liberal, PC, and NDP parties was influenced by both party and leader affect. For example, considering the pattern of Liberal voting in 1974 among voters positively disposed towards the Liberal party, the percentage voting Liberal declines from 94% of those who like Trudeau better than all other party leaders, to 77% of those who like at least one other leader as well as Trudeau, to 63% of those liking at least one other leader better than Trudeau. Exactly the same pattern is evident for respondents liking another party equally as well or better than the Liberals. Similar statements can be made about Liberal voting in 1968 and Conservative and NDP voting in both 1974 and 1968. The size and consistency of these percentage differences within all categories of party affect suggest the existence of *independent party leader effects.*

This is not to say that party leader effects are equal in magnitude to the effects exercised by party. If the data in Table 11.3 are examined in terms of percentage differences between the positive and negative cells in such a table, it is clear that the extent to which people like or dislike parties has more influence on voting than attitudes toward leaders. Using Conservative voting in 1974 as an example, among those feeling positively about Stanfield, the percentage difference across categories of affect toward the PC party is 50 points. The equivalent difference across categories of affect toward the PC leader controlling for party affect is much smaller, 13 points. Comparable percentage differences for the Liberal and NDP parties in 1974 are 69 and 31, and 67 and 32 points respectively.

TABLE 11.3

Vote by Relative Affect for Leaders and Parties, 1974 and 1968 (per cent voting for party)

PANEL A: LIBERAL VOTING

1974		ATTITUDE TOWARD LIBERAL LEADER		
		Positive	Neutral	Negative
ATTITUDE TOWARD	Positive	94	77	63
LIBERAL	Neutral	68	52	33
PARTY	Negative	25	17	5

1968		ATTITUDE TOWARD LIBERAL LEADER		
		Positive	Neutral	Negative
ATTITUDE TOWARD	Positive	94	79	52
LIBERAL	Neutral	79	46	29
PARTY	Negative	45	16	5

PANEL B: PC VOTING

1974		ATTITUDE TOWARD PC LEADER		
		Positive	Neutral	Negative
ATTITUDE TOWARD	Positive	94	95	81
PC	Neutral	86	58	46
PARTY	Negative	44	23	6

1968		ATTITUDE TOWARD PC LEADER		
		Positive	Neutral	Negative
ATTITUDE TOWARD	Positive	93	89	75
PC	Neutral	75	46	28
PARTY	Negative	33	23	6

PANEL C: NDP VOTING

1974		ATTITUDE TOWARD NDP LEADER		
		Positive	Neutral	Negative
ATTITUDE TOWARD	Positive	86	80	54
NDP	Neutral	26	25	22
PARTY	Negative	19	4	1

1968		ATTITUDE TOWARD NDP LEADER		
		Positive	Neutral	Negative
ATTITUDE TOWARD	Positive	88	60	39
NDP	Neutral	51	31	18
PARTY	Negative	8	4	1

TABLE 11.4

Vote by Relative Affect for Local Candidates and Parties, 1974 and 1968 (per cent voting for party)

PANEL A: LIBERAL VOTING

1974 ATTITUDE TOWARD LIBERAL PARTY	ATTITUDE TOWARD LIBERAL CANDIDATE		
	Positive	Neutral	Negative
Positive	97	90	74
Neutral	78	56	32
Negative	32	18	4

1968 ATTITUDE TOWARD LIBERAL PARTY	ATTITUDE TOWARD LIBERAL CANDIDATE		
	Positive	Neutral	Negative
Positive	95	88	69
Neutral	73	60	38
Negative	41	17	4

PANEL B: PC VOTING

1974 ATTITUDE TOWARD PC PARTY	ATTITUDE TOWARD PC CANDIDATE		
	Positive	Neutral	Negative
Positive	95	89	65
Neutral	88	50	22
Negative	30	8	3

1968 ATTITUDE TOWARD PC PARTY	ATTITUDE TOWARD PC CANDIDATE		
	Positive	Neutral	Negative
Positive	95	85	58
Neutral	66	34	25
Negative	34	10	3

PANEL C: NDP VOTING

1974 ATTITUDE TOWARD NDP PARTY	ATTITUDE TOWARD NDP CANDIDATE		
	Positive	Neutral	Negative
Positive	94	80	65
Neutral	54	33	8
Negative	29	6	2

1968 ATTITUDE TOWARD NDP PARTY	ATTITUDE TOWARD NDP CANDIDATE		
	Positive	Neutral	Negative
Positive	91	67	39
Neutral	64	35	10
Negative	12	5	1

Comparisons of the 1974 and 1968 analyses suggest the further point that the effects of party leader images differ over time. Thus, for example, among those positively disposed toward the Liberal party in 1974, the percentage voting Liberal increases by 31 points, depending upon whether one is favourably or unfavourably disposed towards Mr. Trudeau. The comparable percentage for 1968 is 42 points. PC and NDP voting for these two elections manifest similar patterns.

Analyses where feelings for local candidates are compared to those for parties (Table 11.4) are very similar to the leader and party analyses. Table 11.4 documents that the percentage of voters casting ballots for the Liberal, PC, and NDP parties in both 1974 and 1968 decreases monotonically as the level of relative affect for the local candidate of a given party decreases. This pattern holds within all categories of relative affect for different parties. In 1974, for example, the percentage of respondents voting NDP among individuals positively disposed toward the NDP party declines from 94% to 80% to 65% as relative affect for NDP candidates moves from relatively positive to neutral to negative. As with the party leader analyses, the influence of relative party affect appears to be greater than candidate affect. Thus, for example, if people liked the Liberal party but not the local Liberal candidate, fully 74% of them still voted Liberal, whereas if they liked the candidate but not the party, only 32% voted Liberal. Similarly, party differences exceed candidate differences by substantial amounts for the PC and NDP analyses in 1974 and for all the 1968 analyses (Table 11.4).

In sum, it appears that affect for both party leaders and local candidates influences the vote over and above the influence of feelings about parties, even though the effects of party are more important overall. Whether or not the magnitude of party leader effects varies for different types of voters remains unanswered. If the arguments regarding the effects of variations in partisanship and political interest advanced in Chapter Ten are valid, then one would expect that party leader and local candidate effects would be strongest among flexible and high interest partisans. To ascertain if this is the case, one needs to compare the influence of party leader and local candidate affect variables on voting within each category of the partisanship-political interest typology developed in Chapter Ten. To this end, Tables 11.5 and 11.6 present partial correlations between voting and party leader and local candidate thermometer scores controlling for the possible effects of feeling about parties.

To specify more precisely the magnitude of leader and candidate affect, the 1972 vote is used to estimate the potential impact of long-term forces on voting. The incidence of instability in partisanship in Canada is such that direction of partisanship cannot be assumed to provide an adequate measure of long-term forces on the vote for many voters. Past voting behaviour, while not the only alternative measure of long-term forces, has the advantage of predating the possible short-term effects of variables such as party leader or local candidate images. In effect, past vote summarizes the effects of forces acting on voters up until that point in time. Some of these forces will be genuinely long-term, whereas others are short-term forces acting in an earlier period.

A number of interesting findings emerge from the partial correlational analyses contained in Tables 11.5 and 11.6. First, inferences drawn in the simpler analyses of relative leader and candidate effects are substantiated. For the entire electorate, there are statistically significant leader effects on Liberal and PC voting (partial r's = +.23 and +.22 respectively), and significant local candidate effects on voting for all three parties (partial r's = +.22, +.33, and +.22 for Liberal, PC, and NDP voting respectively). Second, the magnitude of the partials varies considerably across partisanship-political interest types. When predicting Liberal voting, the strongest leader effects occur among durable high and flexible low interest partisans. For PC voting, the greatest leader effects obtain for flexible high interest partisans. The analyses using candidate variables are more consistent in that in predicting likelihood of voting Liberal, PC, and NDP, the strongest correlations are found among the flexible, and especially the flexible high interest, partisans. Overall, that the largest leader and candidate effects tend to be concentrated in the flexible and high interest categories is consistent with the proposition that such voters should be particularly susceptible to short-term forces.

TABLE 11.5
Vote and Party Leader Thermometers
Controlling for Party Thermometer and 1972 Vote
(partial correlation, with zero order correlations shown in parentheses)

PARTISANSHIP AND POLITICAL INTEREST TYPOLOGY	LIBERAL VOTE	PC VOTE	NDP VOTE
Durable Low	.18*(.73*)	.06 (.50*)	−.14 (.52*)
Durable Moderate	.05 (.70*)	.14 (.51*)	.02 (.49*)
Durable High	.24*(.81*)	.10 (.60*)	.01 (.46*)
Flexible Low	.21*(.51*)	.21*(.53*)	.02 (.51*)
Flexible Moderate	.20*(.56*)	.20*(.39*)	.09 (.44*)
Flexible High	.13*(.55*)	.29*(.48*)	.02 (.33*)
Transient Voters[a]	.23 (.49*)	.14 (.33*)	.18 (.60*)
New Voters[a]	.42*(.67*)	.37*(.55*)	.12 (.41*)
Total Sample	.23*(.62*)	.22*(.49*)	.05 (.46*)

[a]Control for party thermometer only.

*Significant at .01 level.

TABLE 11.6

Vote and Local Candidate Thermometers
Controlling for Party Thermometer and 1972 Vote
(partial correlation, with zero order correlations shown in parentheses)

PARTISANSHIP AND POLITICAL INTEREST TYPOLOGY	LIBERAL VOTE	PC VOTE	NDP VOTE
Durable Low	.06 (.51*)	.29*(.64*)	.14 (.61*)
Durable Moderate	.04 (.56*)	.03 (.62*)	−.03 (.54*)
Durable High	.20*(.66*)	.09 (.64*)	.00 (.64*)
Flexible Low	.25*(.46*)	.32*(.61*)	.24*(.60*)
Flexible Moderate	.29*(.47*)	.29*(.50*)	.13 (.41*)
Flexible High	.28*(.50*)	.44*(.57*)	.25*(.48*)
Transient Voters[a]	−.02 (.17)	.37*(.57*)	.06 (.63*)
New Voters[a]	.19 (.48*)	.36*(.52*)	.36*(.58*)
Total Sample	.22*(.51*)	.33*(.59*)	.22*(.55*)

[a]Control for party thermometer only.

*Significant at .01 level.

The need to control for the possible effects of long-term forces on the vote is abundantly evident. This point can be appreciated by noting the sharp differences between the zero-order and partial correlations in the several analyses displayed in Tables 11.5 and 11.6. In all instances application of controls for party affect and 1972 vote results in a precipitous decline in the correlation between leader or candidate affect and voting behaviour. For example, among durable high interest voters, the simple correlation between feelings about Stanfield and a Conservative vote is +.60. This correlation drops to +.10 when party and 1972 vote controls are applied. Comparable correlations for predicting Liberal and NDP voting among durable high-interest voters using leader affect are +.81 and +.24, and +.46 and +.01 respectively. Although all of the partial correlations decline markedly in magnitude, it is noteworthy that the extent of this decline does vary somewhat between leaders and between groups. This observation is consistent with the common sense notion that the effects of party leader images on voting vary not only by type of voter, but also according to specific party leaders competing in particular elections.

In summary, the analyses of the influence of party leader and local candidate images indicate the reality of these effects on voting in Canada.

As anticipated, within the context of a single election, the impact of leaders and candidates varies across different types of voters and from one political figure to the next. Further, comparisons of analyses for 1974 and 1968 indicate that leader and candidate effects vary over time. Finally, the reduction in leader and candidate correlations with electoral choice, when controls for party affect and long-term forces were applied, suggests, as hypothesized previously, that for many voters such correlations are partially spurious. For these voters, reactions to leaders and local candidates, as well as the vote itself in a specific election, are partially a function of previously established party loyalties and possibly other long-term political predispositions.

ISSUES

Analysis of the impact of issues on electoral choice is one of the most interesting and contentious topics in current voting behaviour research.[6] Although several theoretically important distinctions must be drawn when studying relationships between issues and voting, a primary distinction concerns the difference between the influence of issues on individual voting behaviour and the *net* impact of issues on electoral outcomes.[7] In any given election, depending on a number of factors, it is possible for issues to influence the behaviour of large numbers of voters, but for the force of issues on the overall electoral outcome to be minimal. The manner in which issues can affect electoral outcomes generally and the result of the 1974 election in particular will be considered in Chapter Twelve. Here, analysis will be restricted to considering to what extent issues influence individual electoral choice.

An initial indication that issues may play a significant role in the voting decisions of a substantial proportion of the electorate has been provided by the "reasons for voting" data cited previously. In addition to the simple and explicit issue references contained in these data, it is probable that an issue basis may underlie some responses to the effect that party, party leaders, or local candidates were especially important for the voting decision. For example, the answers of Ms. Roberts and Messrs. Handman and Bonwall suggest possible issue rationales for party leader or party responses. To investigate more systematically possible issue bases for voting decisions, respondents were asked to specify which of three factors — parties, leaders, or local candidates — was most important for their vote. Respondents were then queried regarding whether or not there was an issue basis for their choice, and if so, which issue was particularly salient.[8]

Consistent with the "reasons for voting" responses cited earlier (Table 11.1), parties were referenced more frequently than party leaders or local candidates as the "most important" factor in the voting decision in 1974, with 40% of the respondents mentioning "parties as a whole" and 33% and 27% citing party leaders and local candidates respectively[9] (Table 11.7). That issue considerations often underlie the choice of party, leader, or candidate is suggested by the data in Figure 11.1. These data show issues to be particularly salient for those choosing "party leaders" as "most important." Despite the strong tendencies for party leader images to be cast largely in personal and stylistic terms (see Chapter Seven), 58% of the "leader" respondents stated that the reasons for selecting party leaders as "most important" involved "stands on issues" rather than "personal qualities." Substantial numbers of those choosing local candidates or parties as a whole as "most important" also said that there was an issue basis for their response (48% and 43% respectively).

With respect to specific issues, inflation is cited most often, regardless of whether parties, leaders, or local candidates were considered the "most important" reason for the vote (Figure 11.1). Inflation bulks especially large among those citing "parties as a whole," with 50% of these voters mentioning that issue. Indeed, for these voters, fully 68% explicitly mentioned either inflation or wage and price controls. Other issues were referenced with considerably less frequency. Particularly noteworthy in this regard is "leadership." In keeping with the muted nature of references to this issue in press coverage of the campaign (see Chapter Nine),

TABLE 11.7
"Most Important Reason" for 1974 Vote
(row percentages)

	PARTY LEADERS	LOCAL CANDIDATES	PARTIES AS A WHOLE	(N)
Most Important	33%	27	40	(*1829*)
Second Most Important	38%	34	28	(*1735*)
Least Important	29%	39	32	(*1737*)

only 12% of those voters citing "party leaders" as "most important" gave "leadership" responses as the issue basis for their vote decision. It may be that voters conceptualize leadership as a personal quality of leaders, rather than in issue terms. In any event, the paucity of leadership references in the present data is also consistent with the relatively small number of leadership mentions in the party leader image data presented in Chapter Seven, and the "most important issue" references in Chapter Eight.

The bases for party leader, local candidate, and party as factors influencing voting choice can be explicated in more detail by using the partisanship-political interest typology. We would expect issues to be

FIGURE 11.1
"Most Important Reason" for 1974 Vote
(N=1829ᵃ)

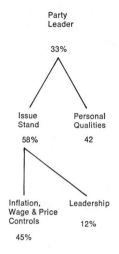

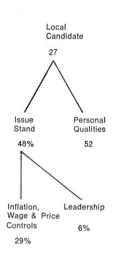

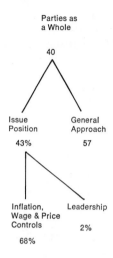

ᵃ percentages are based on subset immediately above

especially important in determining the votes of the flexible high-interest partisans. One might be tempted, therefore, to hypothesize that an issue basis for selecting party, party leaders, or local candidates would be mentioned more frequently by the flexible-high interest partisans than by other types of voters. This expectation must be tempered, however, by recognition that, in some instances at least, factors cited as influential in the voting decision are likely to be rationalizations of decisions arrived at on other grounds, or projections of personal political preferences onto parties or leaders with which voters feel a sense of psychological attachment for reasons entirely unrelated to issue positions. With reference to issues specifically, the importance and normative legitimacy ascribed to issues as an acceptable basis for electoral choice in a democratic political system suggests that large numbers of all types of voters will make issue references, but we should expect that the *independent* effects of issues on voting behaviour may be most evident for the flexible, high-interest partisans.

Overall, the party-leader-candidate question sequence shows that half of those voting in 1974 stated that there was an issue basis for their vote (data not shown in tabular form). Moreover, despite the possibility that all types of voters may rationalize their voting choices in issue terms, the frequency of issue responses is highest among the flexible high-interest partisans citing parties or leaders as the most important factor in the vote decision. Indeed, among the flexible high-interest partisans mentioning party leaders, fully two-thirds make reference to issues. However, the fact that no less than 32% of any category of voters mentioned issues suggests that more sophisticated analytic techniques will be needed to measure accurately the effect of issues on the vote.

In this regard, it was argued in Chapter Eight that a number of conditions must be met for issues to influence voting behaviour. First, voters must perceive the existence of an issue, and consider it to be a relevant and significant factor for arriving at a voting decision. Second, issues must be linked to parties; that is, voters must perceive that parties take different positions on issues, and/or parties must be perceived as differentially capable of dealing with issues in terms of criteria such as problem-solving capacity or managerial efficiency. If these conditions are not met, then it cannot be argued that an issue has influenced voters' electoral choices. For any given election, the extent to which specific issues meet these conditions will vary. Also, it is conceivable that no single issue will meet these conditions for a substantial proportion of the electorate, but rather that several issues will fulfill the conditions for small numbers of voters. In this situation, the effect of issues on individual voting choice would still be potentially great. Stated otherwise, election campaigns do not have to be dominated by one or a small number of highly salient issues for issues to have substantial impact on the behaviour of many voters.

The conditions outlined above suggest that an analysis of the impact of issues on voting in the 1974 election should begin with an appraisal of voters' issue perceptions. The reader will recall that data presented earlier has documented that 70% of the electorate were willing to state that there was an important issue in the 1974 election (Figure 8.1). In terms of the specific issues identified as "important," only inflation was mentioned by substantial numbers of voters. Thirty-three per cent of the entire electorate (or 47% of those willing to cite an issue as important) considered this issue as "most important," and all told, 57% of those mentioning issues said inflation was an important issue in 1974. Eleven per cent referred to the closely associated topic of wage and price controls. The extent to which inflation dominated issue references can be further appreciated by recalling that no other single issue was mentioned by more than 10% of the electorate. The frequency with which issues were perceived as important does not demonstrate how significant specific issues were for the electoral decisions of those voters referring to these issues. To investigate voters' perceptions of the personal significance of issues in greater detail, respondents specifying an "important" issue were requested to indicate how significant this issue was in their own voting decisions.

The data indicate that 58% of those mentioning an issue stated that this issue was "very important" for their electoral choices, and an additional 29% judged the issue cited to be "fairly important." Also, the aggregate frequency of citation of an issue was not related to reports of the personal importance of that issue. Inflation, for example, was judged a "very important" factor in voting choice by 54% of the respondents citing inflation as an election issue. "Leaders and leadership," although mentioned by far fewer voters, was designated "very important" in the vote decision by nearly three-quarters (74%) of the respondents who referenced this issue.

Finally, voters did perceive links between their issue and parties in 1974. Of that 70% of the electorate citing an important issue, fully 88% perceived a party as being "closest to them" on the issue mentioned (Figure 8.1). The data also document that the extent to which the electorate selected a party as closest to their own position on an issue varies from one issue to the next. Thus, although nearly half of those citing issues as important stated that the Liberal party was "closest," the Liberal percentage varied from a low of 23% on unemployment to a high of 73% on leaders and leadership. Given the relatively large number of voters who cited inflation as an important issue, it is worthwhile noting that the Liberals, despite their status as the government party, were judged as being the party closest by a plurality (39%) of respondents mentioning this issue. Comparable percentages for the PC, NDP, and Social Credit parties are 27%, 13%, and 3% respectively. The Conservatives, on the other hand, led the Liberals by 16% among those voters mentioning wage and price controls. Again, however, one should recall that only 11% of the electorate designated wage and price controls as an important election issue, whereas 57% cited inflation as an important issue.

The finding that the Liberals were favoured by more voters on the inflation issue than any other party might be considered surprising, given that the Liberals were the governing party and presumably would be held responsible by the electorate for Canada's perceived economic ills.[10] That this was not the case for many voters may be due to a number of factors. Perhaps, for example, the Liberals were successful in their campaign efforts to convince voters that inflation was basically a "world wide" phenomenon for which they could not be held responsible, and to the extent that any Canadian party leader could design policies and manage the economy in a way that would reduce the effects of inflation, the Liberals had the most qualified person in Mr. Trudeau. As noted previously, however, it is possible that, for a sizeable proportion of the electorate, issue perceptions and evaluations of parties' positions and competency on issues may be in large part a function of partisan predispositions. For these individuals, responses to questions regarding issue positions and judgments of parties' stands on issues will be largely rational-izations of previously established party loyalties, and/or projections of issue preferences onto parties or leaders, viewed through the lens of pre-viously established partisan attachments.

The inflation issue provides an illustration of these possibilities. As noted above, inflation was cited by a large segment of the electorate, and a substantial plurality stated that the Liberal party was "closest to them" on this issue. Despite the Liberal edge in the "party closest" on inflation responses, analysis suggests that the conclusion that inflation was a bene-ficial issue for the Liberals may be unwarranted. Table 11.8 presents a cross-tabulation of the 1974 vote, with inflation and other issues cited as "important." Also included are voters who did not perceive any important issues in the 1974 campaign. The data show that although 48% of the respondents mentioning inflation as an important issue voted Liberal, 58% citing *another* issue cast a Liberal ballot, as did 55% of the "no issue" voters.

The inference that inflation was not a Liberal issue in 1974 also is suggested by an inspection of partial correlations between voting and mentioning inflation as an important issue with controls for party affect and the 1972 vote (see Table 11.9).[11] Such correlations are computed separately for each of the partisan-political interest categories. Several points about these analyses are noteworthy. First, for the sample as a whole, the correlations are very small in magnitude, suggesting that the net impact of inflation was only marginal across the entire electorate. Second, the size of the correlations varies across the several categories of partisanship and political interest. The relationship between mentioning

TABLE 11.8

**Vote by Inflation and Other Issues, 1974
(column percentages)**

IMPORTANT ISSUES MENTIONED

1974 VOTE	INFLATION	OTHER ISSUES	NO ISSUES
Liberal	48%	58%	55%
PC	36	28	28
NDP	14	11	12
SC	2	3	6
N	(763)	(667)	(425)

V=.09*

*Significant at .01 level.

TABLE 11.9

Vote and Mention of Inflation as an Important Issue, Controlling for Party Thermometer and 1972 Vote
(partial correlation, with zero order correlations shown in parentheses)

PARTISANSHIP AND POLITICAL INTEREST TYPOLOGY	LIBERAL VOTE	PC VOTE	NDP VOTE
Durable Low	.02 (.04)	.10 (.01)	−.08 (−.04)
Durable Moderate	−.08 (−.15)	−.02 (.06)	.10 (.12)
Durable High	−.15*(−.19)*	−.03 (.14)	.18* (.08)
Flexible Low	−.06 (−.04)	−.01 (.03)	.04 (−.02)
Flexible Moderate	.01 (−.04)	.04 (.03)	.02 (.01)
Flexible High	−.14*(−.20)*	.19*(.25)*	−.09 (−.08)
Transient Voters[a]	−.07 (−.03)	−.03(−.06)	.07 (.11)
New Voters[a]	.05 (−.02)	−.13(−.05)	.14 (.16)
Total Sample	−.05 (−.09)*	.04 (.08)	.02 (.02)

*Significant at the .01 level.

[a]Control for party thermometer only.

inflation as the most important issue and voting choice is strongest for the flexible high-interest partisans in the analyses predicting Conservative voting, the partial correlation being +.19. The strongest correlations for the Liberal vote analyses are −.14 and −.15 among the flexible and durable high-interest partisans. For the NDP, the largest correlation is +.18 among the durable high-interest group. All of these correlations are statistically significant. By way of contrast, the magnitude of comparable correlations for the durable low-interest partisans are +.02, +.10, and −.08, with none of these relationships attaining statistical significance. That inflation has its strongest relationships with voting among high-interest partisans is consistent with previous arguments that these voters, particularly the flexible high-interest groups, are most apt to manifest genuine issue effects on their voting behaviour.

The direction of the relationships (as indicated by the signs of the correlations) supports the inference suggested by the data in Table 11.8 that inflation may have been an issue which worked against the Liberals. In particular, both of the statistically significant correlations between casting a Liberal ballot and citing inflation are negative, indicating that voters for whom inflation was a salient issue were *less* likely to cast a Liberal ballot than were those mentioning other issues or no issues at all.

Similarly, the statistically significant relationships between mentioning inflation and voting Conservative among flexible high-interest voters, and voting NDP for durable high-interest voters, are both positive, thereby suggesting that mentioning inflation was associated with an *increased* likelihood of voting Conservative or New Democrat among at least some types of voters.

As inflation is only one of the several issues cited as important by respondents in the survey, a more general analysis of the impact of issues in the 1974 election is desirable. Such an assessment of the influence of issues will be made, using controls for relative party affect. As in Tables 11.3 and 11.4, the dependent variables will be voting for the Liberal, Progressive Conservative, and New Democratic parties. The independent variable will be respondents' judgments regarding which party is closest to them on the issue they considered to be "most important" in the 1974 election.

Data displayed in Table 11.10 show the percentage of voters casting Liberal, PC, and NDP votes at different levels of relative party affect.[12] As in the analyses of party leader and local candidate effects considered previously, these data indicate the existence of independent issue effects. Further, a close examination of the percentages voting for each of the three parties indicates that the magnitude of issue effects varies, depending upon a voter's feelings for different parties. For example, Panel b of Table 11.10 shows the percentage of PC voters among persons favourably disposed toward the Conservative party drops from 97% of those saying

TABLE 11.10
Vote by Attitudes Towards Issues and Relative Party Affect, 1974
(percent voting for party)

PANEL A: LIBERAL VOTING

| | | PARTY CLOSEST ON ISSUES | | |
		Liberal	No Party	Other Party
1974				
ATTITUDE TOWARD	Positive	95	79	60
LIBERAL	Neutral	83	56	19
PARTY	Negative	41	2	2

| | | NET PARTY PREFERENCE ON ISSUES | | |
		Liberal	No Party	Other Party
1968				
ATTITUDE TOWARD	Positive	93	87	65
LIBERAL	Neutral	75	46	32
PARTY	Negative	39	10	6

PANEL B: PC VOTING

		PARTY CLOSEST ON ISSUES		
			No	Other
1974		PC	Party	Party
ATTITUDE TOWARD	Positive	97	96	61
PC	Neutral	90	70	25
PARTY	Negative	53	11	4

		NET PARTY PREFERENCE ON ISSUES		
			No	Other
1968		PC	Party	Party
ATTITUDE TOWARD	Positive	93	90	64
PC	Neutral	71	50	22
PARTY	Negative	41	8	5

PANEL C: NDP VOTING

		PARTY CLOSEST ON ISSUES		
			No	Other
1974		NDP	Party	Party
ATTITUDE TOWARD	Positive	94	83	50
NDP	Neutral	44	18	14
PARTY	Negative	34	5	1

		NET PARTY PREFERENCE ON ISSUES		
			No	Other
1968		NDP	Party	Party
ATTITUDE TOWARD	Positive	91	79	38
NDP	Neutral	52	25	24
PARTY	Negative	15	3	1

that the Tories were closest to them on the most important issue mentioned, to 61% among respondents citing another party as closest on the most important issue. Among those liking another party or parties equally well as the Conservatives, however, the equivalent percentages are 90% and 25%. Finally, for voters liking another party or parties better than the PCs, the relevant percentages are 53% and 4%. In each case, the decline in the PC vote suggests the significance of issues as factors influencing electoral choice. The patterns of voting for Liberal and NDP parties in 1974 are basically quite similar, as are the analogous displays of 1968 data. Thus, no matter how well parties are "liked," if they are not perceived as closest on important issues, people will be less inclined to vote for them.

Additionally, and again similar to the leader and candidate analyses, the data in Table 11.10 suggest that party effects are greater than those associated with issues. To illustrate, in 1974, among voters liking the Liberals better than other parties, the percentage voting Liberal for those stating the Liberal party was closest to them on the most important issue was 95%. Among those liking the Liberals better than other parties but favouring *another* party on the most important issue, 60% voted Liberal. However, if one looks at only those favouring the Liberals on the most important issue, 41% of those liking another party better than the Liberals cast a Liberal ballot. This type of pattern is repeated consistently in all of the 1974 and 1968 issue-voting data displayed in Table 11.10.

The influence of issues within different partisan-political interest types is analyzed in Table 11.11.[13] The matrix of partial and zero-order correlations indicates that issue effects persist for all types of voters when controls for party affect and 1972 vote are applied. Further, statistically significant issue effects are discernible within each category of the partisanship-political interest typology. Significantly, however, issue effects are consistently strongest among the flexible high-interest voters. For predicting Liberal and Conservative voting at least, issue effects are weakest among the durable low- and durable moderate-interest partisans. Such findings are consistent with the argument advanced in Chapter Ten,

TABLE 11.11

Vote and Party Closest on "Most Important Issue"
Controlling for Party Thermometer and 1972 Vote
(partial correlations, zero order correlations shown in parentheses)

PARTISANSHIP AND POLITICAL INTEREST TYPOLOGY	LIBERAL VOTE	PC VOTE	NDP VOTE
Durable Low	.30*(.65*)	.31*(.61*)	.26*(.48*)
Durable Moderate	.28*(.56*)	.20*(.67*)	.15 (.59*)
Durable High	.37*(.79*)	.39*(.79*)	.19*(.70*)
Flexible Low	.35*(.50*)	.37*(.52*)	.15 (.35*)
Flexible Moderate	.34*(.55*)	.40*(.51*)	.30*(.48*)
Flexible High	.50*(.69*)	.54*(.67*)	.34*(.52*)
Transient Voters[a]	.46*(.58*)	.47*(.56*)	.33*(.65*)
New Voters[a]	.38*(.58*)	.25*(.42*)	.29*(.45*)
Total Sample	.39*(.63*)	.42*(.61*)	.28*(.50*)

*Significant at .01 level.

[a]Control for party thermometer only.

namely, that both partisan flexibility and level of political interest will condition the influence that issues or other short-term forces exert on voting choice.

Overall, the analyses of party leader, local candidate, and issue influences on voting behaviour presented above suggest the reality of these influences and indicate that such forces vary in their impact according to the nature of partisan attachments and levels of political interest. As anticipated, the influence of leader and candidate images and issues tended to be stronger among flexible than among durable partisans, with issue effects being particularly evident for the flexible high-interest group. The conclusion that leader, candidate, and issue influences exist for various segments of the electorate is buttressed by the fact that the influence of these variables was studied in the presence of controls for both party affect and 1972 voting behaviour, to account for the possible effects of long-term influences on voting choice. Despite their consistency with theoretical expectations, however, the analyses conducted to this point cannot be said to be fully conclusive. Specifically, the impact of leaders, candidates, and issues has been examined separately, and it is possible that the force of one of these variables could be obscured by the uncontrolled influence of the others. To take account of this possibility, a comprehensive analysis of voting, including simultaneously a variety of possible long- and short-term influences on the vote is required.

VOTING: A MULTIVARIATE ANALYSIS

Although a number of techniques might be employed to ascertain the influence of several variables on voting behaviour, here multiple regression analysis is utilized.[14] Multiple regression analysis permits estimates to be made of the *independent* effects on voting behaviour of party leaders, local candidates, and issues, as well as providing an estimate of the *total* explanatory power of all of these variables taken together. In the regression analyses, 1972 vote is again employed to estimate the impact of long-term forces on voting in 1974. Also included in these analyses are party leader and local candidate affect variables, as well as a measure of the perception and salience of issues in the 1974 election.[15] These variables, along with 1972 vote, are entered into a series of regression equations predicting voting for the Liberal, Progressive Conservative, and NDP parties separately. The analyses proceed in a step-wise fashion, with 1972 vote being entered first in all instances. Leader and issue variables are entered next, and then candidate and party measures. Each regression is run twice, with the order of entry of leader and issue variables and candidate and party affect variables reversed, to permit estimates of the percentage of variance *uniquely* attributable to party leader, issue, and local candidate. The analysis also documents the existence of a number of joint effects (e.g., issue and leader) which cannot be separated by this technique. The existence of such joint effects is consistent with our earlier observation that, for some voters, references to party leaders or candidates mask issue responses, while for others, personality or party perceptions are implicit in references to individual leaders or candidates.[16]

The rationale underlying the order in which the several variables are entered into the regressions should be noted. Entry of 1972 vote first in all instances is predicated on the previously mentioned assumption that this variable provides a convenient summary of long-term forces on the vote. By entering this variable first, the individual and collective impact of the several short-term variables over and above this long-term component can be ascertained. The entry of leader and issue variables after 1972 vote, and before the local candidate measures, reflects an assumption that the former variables may influence perceptions and evaluations of candidates, but that, except in rare instances, the converse situation does not obtain. Finally, the measure of party affect is entered along with the local candidate variables to provide a convenient way of summarizing other unmeasured effects associated with the 1974 campaign not captured by other variables entered earlier. The regression analyses of Liberal, PC, and NDP voting are run separately for all types of voters, except the "transients" and the "new voters."[17] If hypotheses regarding the relative significance of long- and short-term forces for various types of voters articulated in the previous chapter are correct, then the results of the several regression analyses should vary across the different categories of partisanship and political interest. The results of the regression analyses predicting 1974 vote are presented in Figure 11.2. (A more detailed presentation of these results may be found in Appendix 11A). These data reveal that the impact of short-term forces (leaders, candidates, issues) varies sharply across the six major types of partisanship and political interest. As a predictor of Liberal, Progressive Conservative, and NDP voting, 1972 vote is far more powerful for the *durable* than for the flexible partisans. For example, for the durable low-interest partisans, the long-term component accounts for 77% of the variance in Liberal voting, and the several short-term variables for an additional 7% (Figure 11.2a). In the analysis of Liberal voting among flexible high-interest partisans, however, past vote explains only 22% of the variance, and short-term forces account for fully 41%. In predicting PC voting, among durable low-interest partisans, 1972 vote explains 68% of the variance, and short-term forces, 10%. For flexible high-interest partisans, the equivalent figures are 21% and 31% respectively. Again, the NDP data manifest exactly the same pattern.[18]

Second, the weakness of leader, candidate, and issue forces as predictors of the vote among durable partisans is a generalized phenomenon. As

FIGURE 11.2

Total Variance Explained by Long Term and Issue, Leader, and Candidate Variables, 1974 Vote

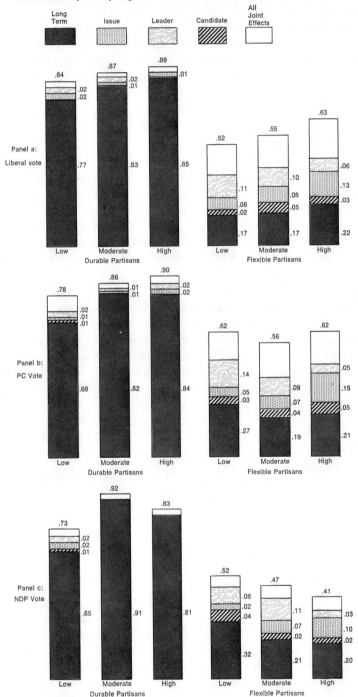

Figure 11.2 indicates, neither leader, candidate, nor issue effects uniquely explain more than 2% of the variance in voting among the durable partisans. This is true not only for the durable low- and durable moderate-interest partisans, but also for the durable high-interest group — voters who presumably might be sensitive to possible reinforcing effects of short-term forces. If such reinforcement mechanisms were at work in 1974 among the durable high-interest partisans, their effects are obscured here by the power of the long-term component.

Third, the importance of specific short-term variables varied discernibly for flexible low- and flexible high-interest groups. Generally, the data indicate that *party leader and issue effects* tend to be greater than those attributable to local candidates. Only in the analysis of NDP voting among flexible low-interest partisans are local candidate effects greater than those for issues, and local candidate effects are never larger than leader effects. A further indication of the limited explanatory power of local candidate variables is that the maximum percentage of variance uniquely attributable to these variables in any of the analyses is merely 5%.

As for the relative importance of party leaders and issues, the patterns are distinctly different for flexible low- and flexible-moderate, as opposed to flexible high-interest partisans. Among the former groups, *leader* effects are consistently greater than those for issues. Thus, for example, in analyses predicting Liberal, PC, and NDP voting among flexible low-interest partisans, the percentages of variance explained by leaders and issues are 11% and 6%, 14% and 5%, and 8% and 2% respectively. The pattern for the flexible high-interest partisans is reversed. For these voters, the explained variance in Liberal voting attributable to leaders and issues is 6% and 13%; for PC voting, 5% and 15%; and for NDP voting, 3% and 10%. The consistency of these patterns of leader and issue effects for the flexible low-, flexible moderate-, and flexible high-interest partisans, as well as the general weakness of issue effects among all groups of *durable* partisans, strongly indicate the validity of the proposition that *issue effects tend to be concentrated among flexible high-interest partisans.* Documenting substantial issue effects among a group of voters who constituted over 15% of the entire electorate in 1974 indicates the need to consider carefully the potential significance of issues for understanding electoral outcomes in Canada.

Overall, the analyses summarized in Figure 11.2 argue for the utility of the typology of partisanship and political interest developed in Chapter Ten. The sharp differences in the effects of long-term versus short-term forces, and the variable impact of specific short-term forces, are consistent with the theoretical underpinnings of this typology. To determine if these results are idiosyncratic to the 1974 election, we have replicated the

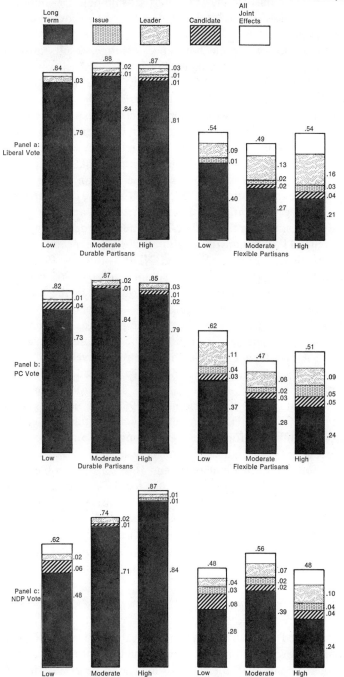

FIGURE 11.3

Total Variance Explained by Long Term and Issue, Leader, and Candidate Variables, 1968 Vote

relevant analyses, using a comparable body of data from the 1968 national election study. After constructing the partisanship-political interest typology,[19] regression analyses identical to those described above are performed using the 1968 data.

It should be noted that one would not expect *identical* results in both 1974 and 1968 analyses. Specifically, given the heavy emphasis on party leader images, particularly that of Mr. Trudeau, in the 1968 election campaign, and the minimal attention devoted to issues in that contest, one might predict relatively stronger leader effects in the 1968 data.[20] Congruent with this expectation are the analyses in Chapter Seven, which found higher levels of affect for both Trudeau and Stanfield in 1968 as compared to 1974. More generally, one might anticipate that the strength of various short-term forces would vary from one election to the next. However, it would be expected that in 1968, as well as in 1974, short-term forces would bulk largest among the flexible partisans, and that issue effects would be greatest among the flexible-high interest group.

The data in Figure 11.3 are consistent with all of these expectations. In the regressions predicting Liberal, PC, and NDP voting in 1968, the variance explained by long-term forces (as summarized by 1965 vote) is always greatest for the durable partisans.[21] For example, in the analysis of Liberal voting, the average percentage of variance explained by 1965 vote among durable partisans is 81%. For flexible partisans the comparable figure is 29%. Equivalent figures in the analyses of Conservative and NDP voting are 79% and 30%, and 68% and 30% respectively.

Also, consistent with accounts of the 1968 campaign, leader effects are shown to be relatively larger than issue effects in the 1968 analyses (Figure 11.3). For all groups of partisans in 1968, the percentage of variance in Liberal, PC, and NDP voting uniquely attributable to leaders is always greater than that for issues. Predicting tendencies to vote Liberal, the percentage of variance explained by leaders is 9% for the flexible low, 13% for the flexible moderate, and 16% for the flexible high-interest partisans. Comparable figures for issues for these three groups of voters are 1%, 2%, and 3% respectively. The patterns obtained in analyses of Progressive Conservative and New Democratic voting among all groups of flexible partisans are very similar. The consistency of these patterns again suggests the general utility of the typology of the Canadian electorate constructed in terms of patterns of partisanship and political interest.

CONCLUSION

The analyses contained in this chapter indicate the relevance of both long- and short-term forces for understanding Canadian voting behaviour. Although certain segments of the electorate appear to be almost impervious to short-term effects associated with specific party leader or local candidate images or issues, other voters do respond strongly to the stimuli generated by the presence of particular political figures and the issues surrounding a given election campaign.

More specifically, recognition of the variability and complexity of partisanship in Canada and the importance of patterns of political interest for campaign-related forces on electoral choice suggests that analyses of voting behaviour will be most rewarding when conducted within specific categories of these variables. Such analyses using 1974 and 1968 election data indicate that not only does the magnitude of short-term forces on electoral choice vary across partisan-political interest categories, but also that the impact of specific short-term forces differs for different types of voters. Of particular interest is the finding that *party leader effects are greatest for flexible low-interest voters, while issue effects are strongest among flexible high-interest voters.*

Documenting the significance of party leader effects among a large subset of the Canadian electorate is consistent with previous commentaries on the nature of electoral choice in Canada. On the other hand, that a sizeable segment of the electorate is particularly susceptible to *issue* effects is less in keeping with the tenor of most discussions of Canadian voting behaviour. The existence of a group of voters attuned to issue appeals does not imply, of course, that these or other voters will respond to the *same* issues, or that responses to given issues will be *unidirectional*. On the contrary, in 1974 at least, voters manifested a variety of issue perceptions, and electoral judgments influenced by issue concerns varied significantly. Of equal importance, comparisons of the results of parallel analyses of 1968 and 1974 data suggest that the impact of issues, party leader images, or other short-term electoral forces can differ substantially from one election to the next.

Overall, the characterization of Canadian voting behaviour developed in this chapter indicates that different segments of the Canadian public respond to various political stimuli in different ways. Clearly, the large number of what have been termed "flexible" partisans in the electorate demonstrates the potential significance of short-term factors associated with the personalities and issues present in the electoral arena at particular points in time. The importance of this large contingent of the Canadian electorate for understanding electoral outcomes and processes of political change will be examined in Chapter Twelve.

Political Choice in Canada

FOOTNOTES

1. The question is cited in Appendix B, Q. 49.

2. See, for example, John Wilson, "The Myth of Candiate Partisanship," *Journal of Canadian Studies*, 3 (1968), pp. 21-31; Robert Cunningham, "The Impact of the Local Candidate in Canadian Federal Elections," *Canadian Journal of Political Science*, 4 (1971), pp. 287-90. Both these studies argue that local candidate effects are considerably weaker than conventional wisdom would allow.

3. Data for SRC studies in the United States are summarized in Norman H. Nie et al., *The Changing American Voter* (Cambridge: Harvard University Press, 1976), p. 304. These data indicate that the correlation between party identification and the vote, although always substantial, has declined significantly since 1964. For relevant European data, see David Butler and Donald Stokes, *Political Change in Britain*, 2nd college ed. (New York: St. Martin's Press, 1976), pp. 22-8; Angus Campbell and Henry Valen, "Party Identification in Norway and the United States," in A. Campbell et al., eds., *Elections and the Political Order*, (New York: Wiley, 1966), p. 266; Jacques Thomassen, "Party Identification as a Cross-National Concept: Its Meaning in the Netherlands," in Ian Budge et al., eds., *Party Identification and Beyond* (New York: Wiley, 1976), p. 69.

4. Despite the sharp controversies over the possible effects of different variables on the vote, the need to control for possible party effects is widely recognized. See, for example, Butler and Stokes, *op. cit.*, pp. 240-44; Arthur H. Miller et al., "A Majority Party in Disarray: Policy Polarization in the 1972 Election," *American Political Science Review*, 70 (1976), pp. 753-59; David E. RePass, "Comment: Political Methodologies in Disarray: Some Alternative Interpretations of the 1972 Election," *American Political Science Review*, 70 (1976), pp. 814-31.

5. See Appendix B, Q. 50, for the form of these questions.

6. The relevant literature is cited in Footnote 5, Chapter 8.

7. See Butler and Stokes, *op. cit.*, chaps. 13 and 14.

8. The sequence of questions asked may be found in Appendix B, Q. 44.

9. In response to a very similar question on most important factors in the vote decision in 1968, 42% cited party leaders, 35% mentioned parties, and 24% referenced local candidates' or MPs' work. See John Meisel, *Working Papers on Canadian Politics*, 2nd ed. (Montreal: McGill-Queen's University Press, 1975), Appendix, Table IX.

10. Butler and Stokes argue that a sizeable proportion of the electorate do link parties, control of government, and governmental outputs. See Butler and Stokes, *op. cit.*, pp. 15-18. That similar linkages are made by many Canadian voters is a plausible assumption. Suggestive in this regard are the data that 70% and 57% of the respondents in the 1974 survey perceived that government had "a great deal" or "something" to do with their material standard of living and "general life satisfaction" respectively.

11. Those who mentioned inflation were scored 1; other respondents were scored 0. The thermometer and 1972 vote variables varied according to whether one was analyzing Liberal, PC, or NDP voting. In the analysis of Liberal voting, for example, 1972 vote was dichotomized as Liberal (scored 1) — other (scored 0), and the party thermometer scores for the Liberal party were used. For the PC vote analysis, 1972 vote was dichotomized as PC–other and the PC thermometer was used.

12. The issue variable in these analyses is constructed using responses to the "party closest" on the "most important" issue question. These responses are regrouped, depending upon whether Liberal, PC, or NDP voting is being analyzed. For example, when Liberal voting is analyzed, responses to the "party closest" question are trichotomized into "Liberal," "no party closest," and "other" parties.

13. For these analyses the "party closest" variable varies according to whether Liberal, PC, or NDP voting is being analyzed. When analyzing PC voting, for example, the dependent variable is a trichotomy with the following categories: (1) PC party mentioned as "closest" on "most important" issue, and "most important" issue is considered "very important" in the vote decision; (2) PC party mentioned as "closest" on "most important" issue, but this issue is not considered "very important" in the vote decision; (3) PC party not mentioned as "closest" on "most important" issue.

14. For example, causal modelling techniques might have been employed. See Arthur S. Goldberg, "Discerning a Causal Pattern Among Data on Voting Behavior," *American Political Science Review,* 60 (1966), pp. 913-22.

15. Variables included in the regression analyses include: (a) 1974 vote — dichotomized as Liberal–other, PC–other, NDP–other; (b) 1972 vote — dichotomized as Liberal–other, PC–other, NDP–other, according to which dependent variable is being analyzed; (c) Leaders—the standardized thermometer scores for Trudeau, Stanfield, and Lewis; (d) Issues—issue variables are entered as trichotomies: (i) Party mentioned as "closest," and issue "very important" to vote decision; (ii) Party mentioned as "closest," but issue of lesser importance to the vote; (iii) Party not mentioned as "closest" on issue or no issue cited. The issue referred to is the one cited by a respondent as the "most important" in the 1974 election. The party varies according to the party used to define the dichotomous dependent variable in the regression analysis; (e) Local candidates — the standardized thereometer scores for the Liberal, PC, and NDP candidates; (f) Parties — the standardized thermometer scores for Liberal, PC, and NDP parties.

16. See, for example, Figure 11.1. The specific joint effects documented in the regression analysis are shown in Appendix 11A. For a discussion of the method of multiple regression analysis employed here see N. Nie et al., *op. cit.,* p. 303, n. 8.

17. It is impossible to analyze the behaviour of the "transient" and "new voter" types according to this schema because of the lack of 1972 vote as a long-term baseline. The behaviour of these voters will be considered in Chapter 12.

18. The F values for short-term forces are statistically significant and larger for flexible than for durable partisans. See Appendix 11A for these statistics.

19. The partisanship-political interest typology for 1968 is identical to that constructed for 1974, except that only one measure of political interest (interest in the 1968 election) is available.

20. For a concise description of the 1968 campaign, see J. Murray Beck, *Pendulum of Power* (Scarborough: Prentice-Hall, 1968), pp. 399-419. On the significance of party leader effects in 1968, see Gilbert R. Winham and Robert B. Cunningham, "Party Leader Images in the 1968 Federal Election," *Canadian Journal of Political Science*, 3 (1970), pp. 37-55.

21. A more detailed presentation of the 1968 analyses is contained in Appendix 11B.

APPENDIX 11.A

Regression Analyses of 1974 Vote by Partisan-Political Interest Types

Dependent Variable: Liberal Vote

| | Proportion of Variance Explained for | | | | | |
| | Durable | | | Flexible | | |
	Low	Moderate	High	Low	Moderate	High
Long-term Forces						
1972 Vote (Lib.–other)	.77	.83	.85	.17	.17	.22
Short-term Forces						
Leaders (unique)	.02	.02	.00	.11	.10	.06
Issues (unique)	.02	.01	.01	.06	.08	.13
Leaders and Issues (joint)	.01	.00	.02	.09	.10	.14
Candidates (unique)	.00	.00	.00	.02	.05	.03
Party Residuals (unique)	.02	.01	.00	.04	.02	.02
Candidates and Party Residuals (joint)	.00	.00	.01	.03	.03	.03
Total Variance Explained	.84	.87	.89	.52	.55	.63
Statistical Significance of Short-term Forces						
F =	10.0*	5.2*	7.9*	27.1*	22.0*	35.4*

*Significant at the .01 level.

Regression Analyses of 1974 Vote by Partisan-Political Interest Types

Dependent Variable: Progressive Conservative Vote

| | Proportion of Variance Explained for | | | | | |
| | Durable | | | Flexible | | |
	Low	Moderate	High	Low	Moderate	High
Long-term Forces						
1972 Vote (PC–other)	.68	.82	.84	.27	.19	.21
Short-term Forces						
Leaders (unique)	.02	.01	.02	.14	.09	.05
Issues (unique)	.01	.01	.02	.05	.07	.15
Leaders and Issues (joint)	.02	.00	.01	.07	.11	.12
Candidates (unique)	.01	.00	.00	.03	.04	.05
Party Residuals (unique)	.02	.02	.01	.03	.03	.02
Candidates and Party						
Residuals (joint)	.02	.00	.00	.03	.03	.02
Total Variance Explained	.78	.86	.90	.62	.56	.62
Statistical Significance of						
Short-term Forces						
F =	10.4*	4.8*	13.1*	34.2*	21.9*	34.4*

*Significant at the .01 level.

Regression Analyses of 1974 Vote by Partisan-Political Interest Types

Dependent Variable: NDP Vote

| | Proportion of Variance Explained for | | | | | |
| | Durable | | | Flexible | | |
	Low	Moderate	High	Low	Moderate	High
Long-term Forces						
1972 Vote (NDP–other)	.65	.91	.81	.32	.21	.20
Short-term Forces						
Leaders (unique)	.02	.00	.00	.08	.11	.03
Issues (unique)	.02	.00	.00	.02	.07	.10
Leaders and Issues (joint)	.00	.00	.01	.01	.02	.02
Candidates (unique)	.01	.00	.00	.04	.02	.02
Party Residuals (unique)	.02	.00	.01	.02	.02	.01
Candidates and Party						
Residuals (joint)	.01	.01	.00	.03	.02	.03
Total Variance Explained	.73	.92	.83	.52	.47	.41
Statistical Significance of						
Short-term Forces						
F =	6.8*	2.1	2.6*	15.5*	12.8*	11.4*

*Significant at the .01 level.

APPENDIX 11.B

Regression Analyses of 1968 Vote by Partisan-Political Interest Types

Dependent Variable: Liberal Vote

| | Proportion of Variance Explained for | | | | | |
| | Durable | | | Flexible | | |
	Low	Moderate	High	Low	Moderate	High
Long-term Forces						
1965 Vote (Lib.–other)	.79	.84	.81	.40	.27	.21
Short-term Forces						
Leaders (unique)	.03	.02	.03	.09	.13	.16
Issues (unique)	.00	.00	.01	.01	.02	.03
Leaders and Issues (joint)	.02	.00	.00	.02	.02	.07
Candidates (unique)	.00	.01	.01	.00	.02	.04
Party Residuals (unique)	.01	.01	.01	.00	.01	.02
Candidates and Party						
Residuals (joint)	.00	.00	.00	.02	.02	.01
Total Variance Explained	.84	.88	.87	.54	.49	.54
Statistical Significance of						
Short-term Forces						
$F =$	2.5	7.7*	18.1*	3.8*	14.2*	36.1*

*Significant at the .01 level.

Regression Analyses of 1968 Vote by Partisan-Political Interest Types

Dependent Variable: Progressive Conservative Vote

| | Proportion of Variance Explained for | | | | | |
| | Durable | | | Flexible | | |
	Low	Moderate	High	Low	Moderate	High
Long-term Forces						
1965 Vote (PC–other)	.73	.84	.79	.37	.28	.24
Short-term Forces						
Leaders (unique)	.01	.02	.03	.11	.08	.09
Issues (unique)	.00	.00	.01	.04	.02	.05
Leaders and Issues (joint)	.01	.00	.00	.01	.00	.04
Candidates (unique)	.04	.01	.02	.03	.03	.05
Party Residuals (unique)	.01	.00	.00	.02	.02	.03
Candidates and Party						
Residuals (joint)	.02	.00	.00	.04	.02	.01
Total Variance Explained	.82	.87	.85	.62	.47	.51
Statistical Significance of						
Short-term Forces						
$F =$	4.0*	5.3*	15.6*	8.2*	11.8*	27.7*

*Significant at the .01 level.

Regression Analyses of 1968 Vote by Partisan-Political Interest Types

Dependent Variable: NDP Vote

	Proportion of Variance Explained for					
	Durable			Flexible		
	Low	Moderate	High	Low	Moderate	High
Long-term Forces						
1965 Vote (NDP–other)	.48	.71	.84	.28	.39	.24
Short-term Forces						
Leaders (unique)	.02	.02	.01	.04	.07	.10
Issues (unique)	.00	.00	.01	.03	.02	.04
Leaders and Issues (joint)	.00	.00	.00	.01	.02	.02
Candidates (unique)	.06	.01	.00	.08	.02	.04
Party Residuals (unique)	.04	.00	.00	.01	.01	.02
Candidates and Party						
Residuals (joint)	.02	.00	.01	.03	.03	.02
Total Variance Explained	.62	.74	.87	.48	.56	.48
Statistical Significance of						
Short-term Forces						
$F=$	3.0*	2.7*	9.3*	4.8*	12.7*	23.8*

*Significant at the .01 level.

Chapter Twelve

Political Choice in Canada: Stability and Change

Much of the thrust of our analysis thus far has been to demonstrate that the level of volatility in Canadian electoral behaviour is considerably higher than might be suggested by an examination of aggregate data alone, or by models of the electoral process which stress the significance of long-term forces. While the more stable elements deriving from processes of political socialization or the durability of reference groups must be recognized in any comprehensive analysis of electoral behaviour, the level of instability suggested by our foregoing analyses of partisanship, political party images, leaders, and issues is substantial. Likewise, the proportion of variance in voting choice explained by short-term factors (Chapter Eleven) for those groups of voters whose partisan attachments we have characterized as "flexible" is impressive, and it should be emphasized that flexible partisans constitute the majority of the Canadian electorate, as measured by the 1974 national sample. When the additional contributions to processes of political change of those persons who do *not* vote in all elections (transient voters) and of those who entered the electorate for the first time in 1974 (new voters) are also considered, the potential for significant variation in electoral outcomes over relatively short periods of time would indeed seem to be high. In this chapter, we shall examine the outcome of the 1974 election in this context, and consider the implications of our argument that there is considerable potential for large fluctuations in Canadian election outcomes over relatively short periods of time. The shift which took place between the 1972 and 1974 elections, separated by less than two years, is, in many respects, a case in point.

THE 1974 ELECTION

The Liberal majority victory of 1974, following upon the near defeat of

357

1972, created the impression of a substantial voter shift in favour of the Liberals, particularly at the expense of the minor parties. In all, 39 seats changed hands between the two elections, the Liberals gaining 32 seats over their 1972 total on an overall improvement of 4% in the popular vote. The NDP was seen by many as the big loser of the election, dropping 15 seats from its 1972 total of 31, but it suffered a net reduction of only about 2% in its total share of the popular vote. The Conservatives, with no appreciable change in their share of the popular vote, nevertheless suffered a net reduction of 12 seats from their 1972 total.

The overall pattern of the election result presents a montage of somewhat conflicting images. On the one hand, the shift in parliamentary seats is a substantial one, and many regional and individual constituency results display considerable volatility. But the total shift in popular vote from 1972, or indeed from other recent elections, is a modest one, producing an electoral result that might be considered "typical" by the standards of longer term patterns (Table 12.1).

These conflicting impressions reflect certain characteristics of Canadian electoral politics that we have alluded to earlier. The overall pattern is suggestive of considerable aggregate stability, which tends to ob-

TABLE 12.1

Distribution of the Vote in Eleven Federal Elections, 1945-1974
(percentages)

	1945	1949	1953	1957	1958	1962	1963	1965	1968	1972	1974
Liberal	41%	49%	49%	41%	34%	37%	41%	40%	46%	39%	43%
PC	27	30	31	39	43	37	33	32	31	35	35
NDP/CCF	16	13	11	11	9	14	14	18	17	18	15
Social Credit	4	4	5	7	2	12	12	8	4	8	5
Other	12	4	4	2	1	x	x	2	2	1	1
% Turnout	76	74	67	74	79	79	79	75	76	77	71

x less than 1%.

scure the rather considerable movement taking place in the electorate. Certainly, most observers of the 1974 campaign and election outcome hypothesized that a substantial shift of voters toward the Liberals had in fact taken place. The most common explanations advanced for this shift emphasized concern for majority government, mistrust of the Conservative position on wage and price controls, or a favourable judgment of the leadership of Prime Minister Trudeau. While each of these factors, together with others, contributed to the result, it should not be surprising in light of our previous discussion to find that virtually all such shorthand explanations of the 1974 election result contain elements of oversimplification. In our analysis in this chapter, we will demonstrate that beneath the simple aggregate differences in party support in 1974 lies a myriad of patterns of movement suggestive of anything but uni-directional shifts in the electorate, or of overall electoral stability.

The first indication of the degree of electoral change in 1974 is found in a direct comparison of respondents' 1974 vote with reports of voting behaviour in the 1972 election. A caveat is in order regarding this portion of our analysis. It must be recognized that there are limitations to the interpretations which can be drawn from a single, national, cross-section survey of the electorate with respect to patterns of temporal change. One of these relates to our ability to draw inferences about electoral change from a single national sample in an election which re-sulted in a turnover of 39 parliamentary seats. A *national* survey does not contain enough cases in any one constituency to permit analyses of behaviour at that level, and we will therefore confine our conclusions here to overall national trends.[1] Nevertheless, we recognize that particu-lar patterns of vote switching, concentrated in certain ridings, can well be decisive in a particular election and that such patterns may appear muted in a national survey. A further limitation arises from our depen-dence on respondents' recall of *past* voting behaviour, which introduces a source of error over and above normal sampling error. However, the fact that these two elections were relatively close together, coupled with the fact that the direction and magnitude of recall error can be reason-ably anticipated, will allow us to proceed.[2] Still, it is important to bear in mind that we are working with a single sample of the *1974* electorate, and not with samples of electorates as they may have actually existed at the time of past elections.

With these cautions in mind, let us examine the level of coincidence between the reports of respondents' past (1972) and present (1974) electoral behaviour. About one respondent in five, voting in the 1974 election, reported a partisan choice *different* from that of 1972. Most of this shift is accounted for by the flexible partisans who, as we have seen earlier (Table 10.7), are vastly more likely than the durable partisans to report a switching of parties across any given set of elections. In addi-tion, another 11% of our 1974 sample consisted of voters who did not vote in the 1972 election by choice (categorized in Chapter Ten as "transient" voters), or because they were new voters eligible for the first time in 1974. Over this relatively short period, then, approximately a third of the total electorate is found to be subject to change. Change in the composition of the electorate emanates from one of three specific sources: *vote switching*, which in turn is related to flexibility of partisan-

FIGURE 12.1
Stability and Change in the Canadian Electorate, 1972–74 [a]

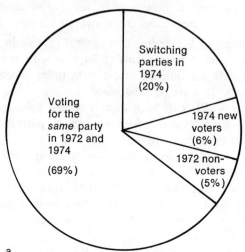

a
As per cent of those voting in the 1974 election.
N=*1885*.

ship; intermittent *non-voting*, or movement into and out of the electorate by some portion of a pool of "transient" voters; and electoral *replacement*, resulting from the death or ageing of some voters and the coming of age and entry into the electorate of others.[3] The relative strength of these several forces, as estimated from the 1974 sample, is indicated in Figure 12.1.

It is possible, of course, to emphasize either stability or change in this discussion. On the one hand, it might be argued that the choice of the *same* party by two-thirds of the electorate in two successive elections constitutes a considerable degree of electoral stability. On the other, the turnover of more than one-third in a period of less than two years might be viewed as a very considerable level of change, particularly in light of the fact that the same parties and leaders and many of the same local candidates appear in these two particular elections.[4] Even relatively small aggregate changes can be of major importance. The Liberals, after all, moved from a position of near defeat in 1972 to a parliamentary majority in 1974 with a net gain of only 4% of the total popular vote. One might imagine such a result being accounted for by a very small movement of voters in one particular direction, by a larger movement of voters in several different directions, or by some combination of circumstances between these possibilities.

There are a number of characteristics of the direction of movement of the 1974 sample (Table 12.2) which merit attention. First, and perhaps most important, is the finding that the net result of the pattern of switching from 1972 to 1974 was actually *away* from the Liberals. Half again as many voters are found to have switched from the Liberals to the Conservatives as switched from the Conservatives to the Liberals in 1974. Had the election been fought between these two groups of voters alone, the data suggest that a different result might have been obtained. Nor is the election outcome adequately explained by the movement of supporters of the minor parties toward the Liberals. Although the NDP shows a net loss of support in the sample, nearly as many respondents are found moving from the Liberals *to* the NDP as from the NDP to the Liberals (Table 12.2). Similarly, the overall magnitude of the 1972 NDP voters moving to the Conservatives is about equal to that of the NDP to Liberal shift, while a slightly smaller group of 1972 PC voters now voting NDP is found. In several ways, then, the pattern of switching displayed by those voters who supported different parties in 1972 and 1974 runs counter to expectations which might be formed on the basis of the aggregate vote patterns, or much of the post-election commentary. While it is clear that a considerable amount of switching did indeed take place, Table 12.2 fails to disclose the expected net shift to the Liberals that many observers believed had occurred. Instead, it would appear that the Liberals realized a small net *loss* of their 1972 electoral support. The pattern disclosed by Table 12.2 suggests, however, that this net loss was more than redressed by the impact of the new voters and transient voters.

TABLE 12.2

1974 Vote by Behaviour in the 1972 Election
(diagonal percentages)

1972 BEHAVIOUR

		LIBERAL	PC	NDP	SOCIAL CREDIT	DID NOT VOTE	NOT ELIGIBLE
	Liberal	39.6	4.2	2.4	0.6	3.3	3.3
1974 Vote	PC	6.3	19.9	1.7	0.4	1.5	1.3
	NDP	1.7	0.9	7.6	0.3	0.8	0.8
	Social Credit	0.6	0.1	—	2.1	0.1	0.4

100%

(N=*1791*a)

aVoters in the 1974 election only.
Other parties and spoiled ballots excluded.

These two groups, both strongly Liberal in 1974, exert an overall effect greater than the shift between the major parties *or* of 1972 supporters of minor parties toward the Liberals. Although these two groups combined comprise only 11% of the 1974 electorate, the fact that their behaviour more heavily favours a single party than does that of switchers indicates that they may have had more effect on the actual outcome of the 1974 election.

A slightly different way of looking at the success with which each of the parties held its 1972 vote, and at the behaviour of the transients and new voters, is provided by the analysis within each group shown in Table 12.3. This table indicates more directly how the supporters of each party in 1972, and the two groups of 1972 non-participants, behaved in 1974. For example, it is seen in Table 12.3 that both the Liberals and the Conservatives enjoyed about equal success in retaining their 1972 supporters (70% and 69% respectively), and that both were more successful in this regard than the NDP or Social Credit parties (54% and 49%). Our previous analysis (Table 12.2) indicated that the Liberals had lost more 1972 supporters than the Conservatives in absolute terms. However, it is also true that they held an approximately equal *proportion* of their 1972 support. Similarly, the NDP lost fewer voters in absolute terms but, since it had fewer to start with, its proportional loss of 1972 support was significantly greater than that of the two major parties.

Table 12.3 also indicates the nature of the impact of the transients and new voters. Although newly eligible voters are somewhat less likely to vote than members of the permanent electorate, their strong support for the Liberal party in 1974 is clearly seen in Table 12.3, thus indicating

TABLE 12.3

Where the 1972 Vote Went in 1974
(column percentages)

1972 BEHAVIOUR

		LIBERAL	PC	NDP	SOCIAL CREDIT	NON VOTERS	NEW VOTERS
	Liberal	70%	15%	17%	14%	28%	45%
	PC	11	69	12	9	13	17
1974 Vote	NDP	3	3	55	6	7	10
	Social Credit	1	x	—	49	1	6
	Did Not Vote	14	13	16	22	52	21
	N=	1010	517	248	80	211	131

ˣLess than 1%.

the nature of their overall impact noted earlier. The behaviour of the transient voters is particularly important because, although their effect on the result in 1974 is about equal to that of the new voters (Table 12.2), their *potential* impact on election outcomes is much greater, since transient voters move *out* of the electorate as well as *into* it. We have argued earlier (Chapter Ten) that the proportion of the electorate which votes only in *some* elections may be as much as one-sixth of the total of eligible voters. In any given election, only between one-quarter and one-third of this group may exercise their franchise (Figure 12.2). In any pair of elections, the transient group may be seen to include persons moving *into* the active electorate, as well as persons moving *out* of it, at least temporarily. Table 12.3 measures the movement of all segments of this rather sizeable group of potential participants. Of the 1972 supporters of a given party, some did not vote in 1974 (14%, 13%, and 16%, for the Liberals, Conservatives, and NDP respectively, and a slightly higher 22% for Social Credit), and thus moved out of the 1974 electorate. At the same time, slightly under half of those persons who did *not* vote in 1972 moved into the electorate. While the loss experienced by each of the parties due to 1972 supporters moving out of the electorate is approximately equal in proportional terms, the group moving into

FIGURE 12.2
The Potential and Actual Electorates in 1974

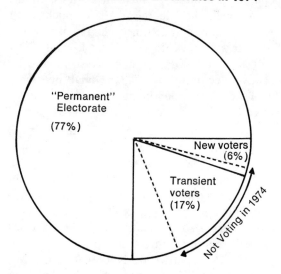

[a] As per cent of total 1974 national sample, excluding permanent non-voters and missing data. N=*2238*

the electorate is strongly Liberal and accounts for the total electoral effect of the transient voters favouring the Liberals.

There are a number of patterns not shown in Table 12.3 which should be noted, several of which relate to the cautions advanced earlier with respect to inferences drawn from national trends alone. First, although the NDP lost somewhat more of its 1972 support to the Liberals than to the Conservatives, this pattern exists only east of the Ontario-Manitoba border. In the West, the NDP defectors went primarily to the Conservatives.[5] Similarly, the Liberals and Conservatives show contrasting East-West patterns, with the Liberals maintaining their vote better in the East than in the West, and the Conservatives doing the opposite. There were four provinces in which the Liberals failed to hold more than two-thirds of their 1972 vote (Alberta, 52%; British Columbia, 52%; Newfoundland, 64%; and Manitoba, 65%), while the Conservatives failed to hold a comparable proportion in only one province (Quebec, 53%). In Ontario, the Conservatives lost proportionally more of their 1972 support than did the Liberals, although the absolute number of votes changing hands was virtually identical between the two parties.

Similar qualifications extend to the analyses of the two 1972 non-voting groups, which likewise may be subject to regional differences. Although sample size quickly places a severe limitation on a more extensive analysis of these groups by province or region, it is possible to examine the distribution of transient voters and newly eligible voters in the more populous provinces. In such an analysis, Ontario stands out as the province in which the Liberals realized much of their net gain in 1974 from the new voters and transients. In that province, 70% of the newly eligible voters sampled favoured the Liberals, 22% the Conservatives, and only 8% the NDP. Among transient voters in Ontario who entered the active electorate in 1974, the NDP does better with 25% of the vote, the Liberals are dominant with 60%, and the Conservatives received only 16%.

A return glance at Table 12.2, coupled with the realization that Ontario accounts for about one-third of the total national electorate, suggests the implications of some of these findings. The preference shown for the Liberals in 1974 by those who had not been in the active electorate in 1972, particularly in Ontario, tended to offset the loss to the Liberals contributed by those members of the permanent electorate who switched to other parties. The data from the 1974 survey do not, in summary, support the commonly held notion that it was a large scale migration of 1972 Conservative or NDP voters that best accounts for the 1974 Liberal victory. There was such a shift, nationally and in most of the provinces, but it is more than offset by a switch of 1972 Liberals away from that party. The greater contribution, caused by heavy Liberal voting in 1974, of those groups which were not in the active electorate in 1972 underscores the argument that we must consider the implications of more than one source of electoral change in any analysis of 1974 or of other elections.

The evidence indicates that the electoral effects of relatively large changes in the electorate (e.g., switching) can be offset by smaller sources of change when the latter are concentrated in a particular direction. It is not possible to determine from the 1974 study alone whether such is a common occurrence in elections in Canada. Certainly, we can easily imagine alternate sets of circumstances in elections that might produce different patterns.[6]

The 1974 data indeed suggest a number of larger questions. Is it usual for short-term forces, such as issues, leaders, or candidates, to pull groups of voters in different directions and thus produce a kind of cancelling effect in electoral outcomes? What mobilizes transient voters and causes them to enter the electorate at certain times? Are they more likely to move in a single direction, or are they sometimes subject to the same cancelling effects that have been observed here with respect to switchers? And considering the new voters that enter the electorate for the first time in each election, are there long-term forces affecting this group which might account for their strong support of the Liberals in 1974? Such a finding could have significant implications for the nature of the party system in Canada over the next generation. Or are new voters, like certain other groups in the electorate, subject to powerful short-term forces which may produce different electoral outcomes over relatively short periods of time? Most of these questions are ones that cannot be completely answered by a single survey of a particular election. But much of our foregoing analysis of partisanship, images of parties and leaders, the role of issues, etc., is relevant to such questions. We will probe the 1974 patterns further with respect to some of these larger questions, keeping the volatility and/or stability of political choice in Canada in mind.

LONG-TERM AND SHORT-TERM FORCES IN CANADIAN ELECTIONS

Most electoral change in Canada which takes place over relatively short periods of time is accounted for by the flexible partisans, transient voters, and new voters entering the electorate at a given point in time. Above we have seen that, at least in 1974, there were distinct differences in the directional movement of these several groups. The analysis of the 1974 vote undertaken in Chapter Eleven suggests the argument that the several types of voters identified in the electorate are motivated by different forces, some of which are of a long-term nature and others of

TABLE 12.4

Contribution to Electoral Change in 1974, All Partisan/Voter Types
(as per cent of total 1974 voters[a])

PARTISAN TYPES	% SWITCHING TO					% REMAINING				
	LIBERAL	PC	NDP	SC	TOTAL SWITCHING	LIBERAL	PC	NDP	SC	TOTAL REMAINING
Durable, High Interest	0.2	0.3	0.1	0.1	0.7	6.8	3.6	1.2	0.1	11.7
Durable, Moderate Interest	0.2	0.2	—	0.1	0.5	5.9	2.4	0.9	0.1	9.3
Durable, Low Interest	0.4	0.4	0.2	0.1	1.1	7.8	2.6	1.1	0.4	11.9
Flexible, Low Interest	2.6	2.4	1.0	0.3	6.3	6.6	4.7	2.0	1.1	14.4
Flexible, Moderate Interest	1.9	1.9	1.0	0.1	4.9	5.8	2.4	1.2	0.4	9.8
Flexible, High Interest	1.8	3.2	0.8	0.1	5.9	6.5	4.1	1.4	0.2	12.2
Total Switching	7.1	8.4	3.1	0.8	19.4	39.4 Total Remaining	19.8	7.8	2.3	69.3

	ENTRY/RE-ENTRY (%)				
	LIBERAL	PC	NDP	SC	TOTAL ENTRY/ RE-ENTRY
Transient Voters	2.6	1.4	0.7	0.1	4.8
New Voters	3.2	1.3	0.7	0.4	5.6
Total Entry/Re-entry	5.8	2.7	1.4	0.5	10.4

[a]N=1862 "Other" and spoiled ballots included in total, but not shown in table. Excluded groups account for a further 1% of the electorate.

which are short-term in character and therefore more volatile in their electoral effects. Specifically, the analysis indicated that issues are more important determinants of the vote for the flexible, high-interest partisans, while other short-term forces (particularly leaders and candidates) are more strongly related to the voting choice of low-interest groups.

Thus far, we have attempted to treat the long-term component of electoral behaviour in Canada only as a kind of control variable, allowing the several long-term elements affecting voting behaviour to be summarized by past voting choice. We have found, however, that this component, so defined, is the primary determinant of voting choice for the durable partisans, and a less important (although nevertheless significant) predictor for the other groups. Let us examine long-term forces more closely. At least some of the socio-demographic attributes described as weak correlates of voting behaviour in Canada in Chapter Four — for example, religion or ethnicity — are non-changing elements, at least at the individual level. Others, such as region, social class, or socioeconomic status, while more mutable, will in fact not change for most individuals or, at minimum, will do so only infrequently. These, too, might be considered as part of a long-term component of electoral behaviour, to the extent that they correlate with a partisanship that is durable for a portion of the electorate.

It has also been demonstrated, in Canada as well as in other countries, that the durability of partisanship for some voters is traceable to processes of socialization, i.e., the "inheritance" of partisan attachment, together with other reference group loyalties such as religion or ethnicity. Irvine, for example, has argued that the correlation between religion and partisanship is inherited by some voters in the same sense that religion or partisanship itself may be inherited.[7] The argument that the long-term component of electoral behaviour in Canada, particularly for durable partisans, is the product of processes of socialization across generations would be rendered more plausible if it can be shown that there is a strong relationship between the partisan attachment of voters and their parents. Such a finding would also provide at least a partial explanation of the persistence of religious, regional, and ethnic cleavages in Canadian electoral politics.

The fact that more than one-third of the electorate in 1974 report having changed their party identifications one or more times (Chapter 5) suggests that the power of inter-generational transmission of partisanship in Canada may be limited. For the entire 1974 sample, of those able to recall their parents' partisanship, 37% and 29% had the same party identification as their father and mother respectively (Table 12.5). These data also reveal that inter-generational partisan continuity varies sharply

TABLE 12.5

Intergenerational Partisan Agreement by Partisanship-Political Interest Typology

PARTISANSHIP-POLITICAL INTEREST TYPOLOGY	% AGREEING WITH FATHER'S PARTISANSHIP	% AGREEING WITH MOTHER'S PARTISANSHIP	N
Durable Low	52	43	*177*
Durable Moderate	58	54	*155*
Durable High	52	36	*202*
Flexible Low	27	21	*315*
Flexible Moderate	30	21	*246*
Flexible High	26	22	*278*
Transient Voters	37	30	*270*
New Voters	31	29	*91*
Total	37	29	*1733*

across the different partisan groups. Not surprisingly, such continuity is greater for durable than for flexible partisans. Even among durable partisans, however, only slightly more than half have the same partisanship as their father and somewhat fewer agree with their mother's partisanship. These data indicate that the long-term force of parental political socialization, at least insofar as party identification is concerned, is limited in Canada for *all* groups of voters. There is little evidence to support an interpretation of the persistence of political cleavages predicated primarily on the hypothesis that inter-generational transfer of partisanship can explain the present partisan predispositions of most voters.

A more powerful test of the ability of long-term variables to predict voting behaviour for certain of our partisan groups is provided by a series of regression analyses in which current partisanship is the dependent variable, and several essentially long-term variables, such as religious affiliation, ethnicity, region, and socio-economic status, are entered as independent variables.[8] Also entered as an independent variable is father's partisanship.[9] By entering father's partisanship into the analysis, the extent to which these variables have independent statistical effects over and above those attributable to parental socialization can be discerned. Figures 12.3 and 12.4 show the results of regression analyses of voters' partisanship in 1974 for durable and flexible partisans respectively, using father's partisanship, religious affiliation, region, and socio-economic status as independent variables.[10] As might be expected, the percentages of vari-

FIGURE 12.3

Summary of Predictive Power of Selected Long-Term Variables for Durable Partisans

(BETAS)

Panel a.

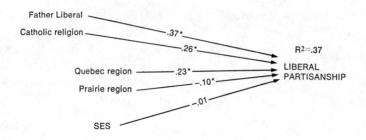

Panel b.

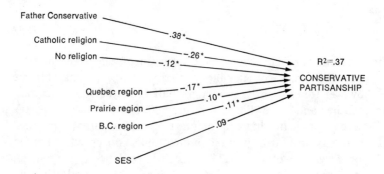

Panel c.

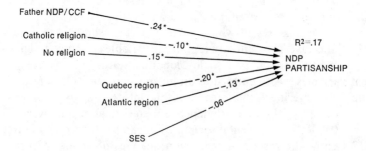

*BETA significant at .01.

FIGURE 12.4

Summary of Predictive Power of Selected Long-Term Variables for Flexible Partisans

(BETAS)

Panel a.

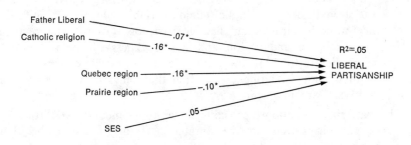

Father Liberal

Catholic religion ———— .07*

———— .16*

Quebec region ———— .16*

Prairie region ———— −.10*

.05

SES

R² = .05

LIBERAL
PARTISANSHIP

Panel b.

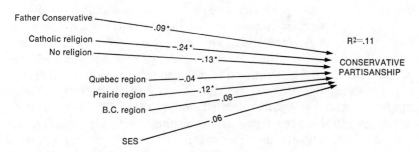

Father Conservative ———— .09*

Catholic religion ———— −.24*

No religion ———— −.13*

Quebec region ———— −.04

Prairie region ———— .12*

B.C. region ———— .08

.06

SES

R² = .11

CONSERVATIVE
PARTISANSHIP

Panel c.

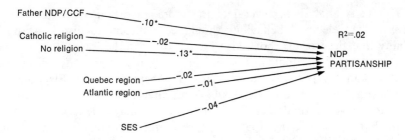

Father NDP/CCF ———— .10*

Catholic religion ———— −.02

No religion ———— .13*

Quebec region ———— −.02

Atlantic region ———— −.01

−.04

SES

R² = .02

NDP
PARTISANSHIP

*BETA significant at .01.

ance explained by such variables for durable partisans are much greater than those for flexible partisans. Even for the durable group, only approximately one-third of the variance can be explained by these long-term factors. However, several of the long-term variables continue to have statistically significant relationships with partisanship even after controls for father's partisanship have been applied. Particularly noteworthy in the analyses of Liberal and Progressive Conservative partisanship is the strength of the Catholic religion variable, which is a significant predictor for both durable and flexible partisans. Overall, the relative strength of religion and region and the weakness of socio-economic status as predictors for both the durable and the flexible groups is consistent with the long-standing observation that religion and region, but not social class, are important correlates of partisan attachment.

The pattern of relationships, coupled with the modest proportion of variance explained even for the durable partisans, demonstrates that assumptions about the nature of partisanship as a long-term force on voting choice need to be made with considerable care. For durable partisans, the rate of inter-generational agreement is such that large discontinuities in the partisan composition of the Canadian electorate could occur across a single generation. This point gains greater force if it is recalled that durable partisans constitute only 38% of the electorate, and that the rate of inter-generational agreement in partisanship for flexible partisans is only half that for the durables. All of these facts, taken in conjunction with the earlier reported finding that 36% of the respondents in the 1974 survey report changing their party identification one or more times, strongly indicates the limitations of partisanship as a long-term stable force on the vote. Such diuturnal forces, although clearly present in Canadian politics, are in summary weak determinants of partisanship, even for the durable partisans.

This brief analysis of several of the more important perennial forces in Canadian electoral behaviour should be sufficient to dispel the possibility that the various short-term factors found to be important in 1974 — issues, leaders, candidates — might constitute mere rationalizations of long-standing partisan ties for large numbers of voters. Elections in Canada are more than contests which repeatedly produce particular results reflective of fundamental patterns of long-term cleavages. On the other hand, the findings that long-term forces are relatively weak in Canada, and that short-term factors, such as issues, leaders, or candidates, are important determinants of *individual* choice by themselves tell us little about the nature of electoral outcomes. Within the range of possibilities suggested by our analysis of individual behaviour (Chapter Eleven), a number of different types of election outcomes could clearly occur. With respect to issues, it has been argued that a degree of salience must exist, and also that there must be a link to a party made by the voter before any effect on individual choice is likely to occur. Further, an issue will not affect the *outcome* of an election unless it meets both of the above conditions, and in addition exhibits a "skewness" of opinion, i.e., operates in such a way as to favour one party more than the others (see Chapter Eight). If this latter condition is not met, the issue may have a significant effect on *individual* voting choice, but an insignificant effect on the actual *outcome* of the election because approximately equal numbers of votes may be gained and lost by a particular party as a result of it.

It is possible to apply these conditions to the effect of party leaders and candidates in elections, as well as to issues. Unless leaders or candidates are salient to individual voters, it is unlikely that they, any more than issues, will be able to affect behaviour. In addition, the link to parties is automatic in the case of leaders and candidates, since each carries the party label. And finally, leaders or candidates, like issues, can affect electoral outcomes only if attitudes toward them are skewed, because a leader or candidate who gains and loses equal numbers of votes in a election will not significantly alter the fortunes of his party.

Leaders, issues, and candidates are each likely to hold a different type of significance for specific electoral outcomes, just as they have different effects on the individual voter. Their significance may also vary when measured over a period of time greater than a single election. Although leaders are normally a factor in more than one election, their personal popularity may fluctuate widely over relatively short periods of time, and it is evident that their effect is primarily short-term in nature.[11] The same argument can be advanced in the case of local candidates. While individual candidates may enjoy high personal popularity and/or a long tenure in office, their independent effects on electoral behaviour are essentially short-term. Where the appeal of a leader or candidate is merely an artifact of partisanship, or of longer term factors which correlate with partisanship, their unique effect on individual voting choice will be minimal. However, both leaders and candidates appear to have effects on individual voting choice over and above those which might be explained by long-term factors or by partisanship alone. Where such is the case, the directional impact of such effects is quite evident. Our analysis in Chapter Eleven of the specific effects of leaders and candidates demonstrated that a positive rating of a party's leader or candidate enhanced the share of the vote obtained by that party, even among those persons whose perception of the party itself was negative (Tables 11.3 and 11.4). The actual impact of leaders or candidates on electoral *outcomes* is, however, considerably less certain.[12] There is no reason to expect that, either in a particular election or over a more substantial period of time candidate effects will normally operate so as to favour a particular party. In 1974, the Conservatives appear to have enjoyed a slight advantage in overall candidate effects, but the total electoral impact of such advantage was very small (Table 12.6). It seems reasonable, then, to argue that candidate effects, even though they are of importance in individual voting choice, will generally not be critical in electoral outcomes, given that all parties will, on occasion, win or lose certain constituencies because of the strength or weakness of the particular local candidate.[13] But the circumstances where such a phenomenon operates so as to decisively favour one party more than the others will be relatively rare in a political system as large and diverse as that of Canada.

By contrast, the possible effects of the party leaders on electoral outcomes are more likely to be significant. First, the appeal of leaders, unlike that of candidates, is more likely to be national in scope, although there are, of course, important differences across regions. In 1974 all

TABLE 12.6

Summary of Electoral Effects of Leaders and Candidates, 1974
(as per cent of total 1974 voters[a])

MOST IMPORTANT FACTOR IN VOTE	LIBERAL	PC	NDP	TOTAL
a. Leader/Leadership				
% Switching to	1.3	0.3	0.2	1.8
% Remaining	7.5	1.4	0.5	10.4
New Voters/Transients	1.0	0.3	0.1	1.4
Total	9.8	2.0	0.8	13.6
b. Local Candidate				
% Switching to	0.9	1.5	0.3	2.7
% Remaining	3.2	3.9	0.7	7.8
New Voters/Transients	0.4	0.7	0.1	1.2
Total	4.5	6.1	1.1	11.7

[a]N=*1891*. Social Credit, "other," and spoiled ballots not shown in table.

indications are that the appeal of party leaders worked to the advantage of the Liberal party. Mr. Trudeau's popularity was greater than that of Mr. Stanfield and the other party leaders in every province save Nova Scotia, and among nearly all subgroups of the population (see Chapter Seven). Further, Table 12.6 indicates that, among those who assigned the most importance to the personal qualities of the party leaders in their voting decision, the effect is overwhelmingly toward the Liberals among all three groups of voters — persons remaining with the same party, those switching from another party, and those entering or re-entering the active electorate in 1974. Unlike the candidate effects which appeared to show a slight trend toward the Conservatives, the movement toward the Liberals among the more leader-oriented segment of the electorate in 1974 is large enough to be of potential significance in the outcome.

This pattern is not surprising, given the relative importance of party leaders in individual voting choice demonstrated in our multivariate analysis in Chapter Eleven, particularly for the flexible low-interest group, together with other measures demonstrating the advantage which Mr. Trudeau enjoyed in personal popularity over his opponents in 1974. It is possible, however, to suggest other patterns that might occur in other elections. Certainly, there may be circumstances in which perhaps two or more party leaders enjoy high personal popularity among certain voters, thus creating a situation in which the effects on individual voting choice are relatively high but the effect on the outcome of an election rather low because approximately equal numbers of voters are being gained and lost by each leader. Also, one might project instances in which *no* party leader is sufficiently attractive to voters, or enjoys enough of an advantage over his opponents, to affect either behaviour or outcomes.[14] Yet, the pattern shown by the 1974 data must also be a fairly common one, in which one party leader, enjoying either a permanent or temporary advantage in personal popularity, is able to significantly improve the position of his party among those groups of voters for whom party leaders are the most salient feature of the political system.

The several types of electoral situations in which issues as determinants of behaviour may also affect the outcome of an election can be conceptualized similarly. We have already noted in our previous analysis that issues differ considerably in salience and in the degree to which they are linked to parties by the electorate. In order for an issue to affect the outcome of an election, opinion must be skewed in such a way as to consistently favour a particular party (see Chapter Eight).

The issues of the 1974 election provide several examples of combinations of these conditions, all of which are undoubtedly commonplace in a number of other electoral situations. An issue, such as bilingualism, operated so as to favour the Liberals (Table 12.7), but its low salience in 1974 assures that it can have little effect on the outcome when the voters mentioning this issue are considered as a proportion of the total electorate.[15] At the other extreme is the dominant issue of the 1974 campaign — inflation — which, although mentioned as the most important issue by one-third of the total electorate, displays little in the way of a pattern which might be said to clearly affect the election outcome. Of those mentioning inflation and switching in 1974, the trend was away from the Liberals, while the pattern of those not switching favoured that party slightly. The trend of new voters and transients mentioning infla-

TABLE 12.7

Summary of Potential Electoral Effects of Four Selected Issues in 1974 (as per cent of total 1974 voters[a])

MOST IMPORTANT ISSUE	LIBERAL	PC	NDP	TOTAL
a. Inflation				
% Switching to	2.3	3.7	1.3	7.3
% Remaining	10.8	8.0	3.0	21.8
New Voters/Transients	2.0	0.8	0.8	3.6
Total	15.1	12.5	5.1	32.7
b. Wage and Price Controls				
% Switching to	0.4	0.6	0.2	1.2
% Remaining	1.7	2.2	0.9	4.8
New Voters/Transients	0.5	0.3	x	0.8
Total	2.6	3.1	1.1	6.8
c. Majority government				
% Switching to	1.0	0.5	0.1	1.6
% Remaining	3.2	0.7	x	3.9
New Voters/Transients	0.4	—	—	0.4
Total	4.6	1.2	0.1	5.9
d. Bilingualism				
% Switching to	x	x	—	0.1
% Remaining	0.8	0.2	0.1	1.1
New Voters/Transients	x	x	—	0.1
Total	0.9	0.3	0.1	1.3

[a] N=*1891*. Social Credit, other, and spoiled ballots not shown in table.

x Less than 0.1%.

tion as the most important issue also favoured the Liberals. In summary, the Liberals appear to have realized a slight advantage in the *total number of votes* associated with the inflation issue (although, as we saw in Chapter Eleven, inflation was not on balance a Liberal issue in 1974). However, it is evident that the actual electoral effects of the inflation issue in 1974 were very much less than might be suggested by the salience of the issue alone.[16] It is evident that the inflation issue in that election failed to operate as a valence issue, a shortcoming which might at first appear strange, given the potential anti-government thrust of such an issue. In other circumstances, one might well imagine the high salience of general economic issues being more explicitly transformed into votes against the government of the day. However, the interaction between attitudes toward the economy and short-term economic policies is a complex one, and the willingness of voters to affix "blame" for the ills of the economy is governed by more than a set of economic indicators.[17]

The patterns produced by the other two issues singled out in Table 12.7 are also interesting. Both of these issues have a much lower initial potential to affect the outcome of the election than does inflation, because they were salient only to relatively small proportions of the electorate. It would perhaps be mistaken to classify them as "low salience" issues, since the general pattern of issues in 1974 is one of small numbers of voters mentioning a large number of specific issues, inflation being the only one of truly high salience. (Table 8.11). By this standard, the issues of wage and price controls and majority government are mentioned as "most important" by enough respondents in 1974 to cause us to notice them, but the numbers certainly cannot be considered large.

These two issues — wage and price controls and majority government — while salient in 1974 to approximately equal proportions of the total electorate, exhibit quite different electoral effects. The wage and price controls issue, like the more general inflation issue, displays an absence of any clear directional trend. As a policy initiated by the Conservatives in the campaign, it appears to have attracted some voters to that party and repelled others. Among all three groups — the switchers, the constant supporters of one party, and the voters entering or re-entering the electorate in 1974 — the slight trend toward the Conservatives among those mentioning the wage and price controls issue is largely offset by an approximately equal number of voters moving in the opposite direction. An issue displaying these characteristics, even though it may affect individual voting choice, cannot be said to have affected the outcome of the election.

Majority government, on the other hand, displays a quite different pattern. Although not highly salient to the electorate (it is mentioned as the "most important" issue of the election by only about 6% of those voting in the 1974 contest), the majority government issue operates in favour of the Liberals, thus producing a potential electoral effect which, although small, is statistically significant and indeed higher than that exhibited by issues which are more salient generally. It is of course not surprising to find this pattern. As noted in Chapter Eight, majority government has historically been a Liberal issue, given that it has most often been the Liberal party which held the best chance of forming a majority government. In fact, it may be seen in Table 12.7 that the majority government issue in 1974 is associated primarily with Liberals *remaining* with their party, and does not appear to have generated substantial switching of votes away from the minor parties. It may, however, have *prevented* some votes from being lost by the Liberals to other parties as a result of other short-term forces. While this is clearly a speculative interpretation, it is evident that majority government, like bilingualism, exhibits the type of skewness which is essential for an issue to exert a genuine effect, however small, on the outcome of an election. To the extent that it was more salient in 1974 than was the bilingualism issue, the electoral effects are greater. An equally salient issue, such as wage and price controls, or a much more salient issue, such as inflation, do not display this essential characteristic.

Although we have attempted here to abstract from the electorate distinct issue, leader, and candidate subgroups for purposes of this analysis, it should, of course, be recognized that a number of "joint effects" may also exist. In attempting to measure pure leader or candidate effects, for example (Table 12.6), we isolated that group of voters which rated leaders (or candidates) as "most important" in their voting choice and who, in a further probe, indicated that it was the leader's (or candidate's) "personal qualities," rather than his "stand on issues," that attracted them. However, the opposite group of respondents (i.e., those who, upon mentioning leader or candidate as most important to them, also mention one or more issues) is also of some significance here.[18] While the number of possible issue combinations is too large to permit analysis of all possible subsets, two of the larger groups — those mentioning *inflation* in connection with either the leader or candidate responses — are worthy of analysis here.

Table 12.8 shows that these two groups of voters differ in small but significant ways from those mentioning "personal qualities" of leaders

TABLE 12.8

Joint Leader/Issue and Candidate/Issue Effects (Inflation)
(as per cent of total 1974 voters[a])

MOST IMPORTANT FACTOR IN VOTE	LIBERAL	PC	NDP	TOTAL
a. Leader/Issue				
% Switching to	0.3	0.5	0.1	0.9
% Remaining	2.2	1.0	0.2	3.4
New Voters/Transients	0.2	0.1	0.1	0.4
Total	2.7	1.6	0.4	4.7
b. Candidate/Issue				
% Switching	x	0.3	0.1	0.4
% Remaining	0.4	0.7	0.2	1.3
New Voters/Transients	0.1	—	0.1	0.2
Total	0.5	1.0	0.4	1.9

[a] N=*1891*. Social Credit, "other," and spoiled ballots not shown in table.

x Less than 0.1%.

or candidates (Table 12.6), *and* from those mentioning inflation as the "most important" issue (Table 12.7). The Liberals continue to enjoy an advantage within the leader/issue group, but it is much smaller than that shown for the leader/personal qualities subset (Table 12.6) and is concentrated among the non-switchers. The Conservative advantage widens in the candidate/issue group, although the total electoral effects are very small. There are indications, however, of parts of each of the patterns observed in the candidate (Table 12.6) or issue (Table 12.7) groups alone.

The several short-term forces which we have examined in the 1974 context are illustrative of a number of different types of electoral effects, some of which may vary from one election to another as the salience of issues or leaders increases or decreases, or as the advantage to a particular party changes. We have argued that local candidates, although they may affect individual voting choice, will rarely affect electoral outcomes on a national scale because of the improbability that a single party can gain an advantage in a large enough number of constituencies to truly alter the result. On the other hand, leaders, also important in individual choice, will be most likely to affect the outcome of an election in those situations where *one* leader is highly salient to voters (or where positive and negative perceptions combine), a situation which obtains in the 1974 case with Trudeau. However, we can easily imagine electoral contests where two strong leaders might exert offsetting effects, or other situations where no leader is highly salient.

On the other hand, issues cover a broader range of possibilities, and the four examined in our analysis of the 1974 outcome illustrate a number of these. An issue which is not sufficiently salient to the electorate clearly will not exert any effects on individual choice, and therefore will not affect an election outcome. Issues of modest salience, such as majority government or wage and price controls in 1974, may or may not affect the outcome of an election, depending on the ability of a single party to cause such an issue or issues to operate to its advantage. The possibility that elections are won or lost as much by aggregations of small numbers of voters who respond to *different* short-term factors as by larger numbers is a very real one, and issues such as majority government demonstrate such potential. Undoubtedly, there are other issues, both in 1974 and in other elections, which might display such a pattern, and which either singly or in concert are capable of contributing to a particular result. Further, it is evident that the potentially most important issues — those of very high salience, such as inflation — may ultimately prove in a given election to be among the least important in explaining the result. However, the potential for such an issue to operate quite differently in other electoral circumstances should not be dismissed. Finally, a number of joint effects must be considered, since leaders, candidates, and issues do not appeal to mutually exclusive categories of voters. The 1974 results, although illustrative, necessarily leave untested a number of possible combinations.

THE CHANGING ELECTORATE

We have examined the balance of long-term and short-term factors in electoral behaviour in Canada, and particularly the operation of these factors in 1974. On that occasion, about one person in five was found to have voted for a different party than that which was supported in the previous election. For some of these switchers, the change in voting choice may have caused, or been caused by, a change in partisanship, while for others the decision to switch was a function of various short-term forces specific to the election. In both instances, the type of change resulting is that often referred to as *conversion*, i.e., a change in the attitudes of voters who are already part of what we have classified earlier as the "permanent electorate." In the earlier part of this chapter, however, we have argued that a quite different type of change is also impor-

FIGURE 12.5
Electoral Replacement [a]

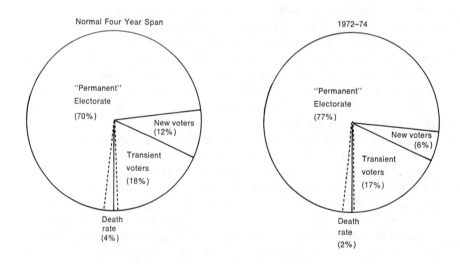

[a] Estimated from 1974 national sample and 1971 census data.
Source: *Census of Canada, 1971.*

tant in Canadian elections, i.e., that caused by voters who move into and out of the active electorate (transient voters) and by new voters entering the electorate in a given election. In fact, the evidence presented would suggest that these sources of change taken together were more important in explaining the particular outcome of the 1974 election than was the total movement within the permanent electorate. Such a source of change is of course quite different than conversion, in that it represents a change not in attitudes but in the actual composition of the electorate at a particular point in time. This type of electoral change may be referred to as *replacement*, i.e., the substitution of one group of voters for another in a particular electorate.

Although the emphasis of much of our analysis of electoral behaviour in 1974 has been on those types of change which might be classified as conversion, the importance of replacement should not be minimized, particularly when more than one election is considered. Over the short period between the 1972 and 1974 elections, we estimate that nearly one-quarter of the active electorate changed. Such change emanates from one of three sources — the turnover of non-voters, the entry of new voters, and the death of a small proportion of the total electorate. While we are dependent upon the survey data for reports of non-voting in 1974 or in previous elections, better estimates of the impact of new voters or the death of older voters can be made from census data (Figure 12.5).

As is seen in Figure 12.5, our analysis of change between the 1972 and 1974 elections in some respects underestimates the impact of electoral replacement under "normal" electoral circumstances, given the shortness of that time period. If we project a four year span between elections as "normal," the impact of new voters and of the death rate would each be about double that observed in the 1974 sample. Therefore replacement, as a potential source of change, will not normally be any less than that observed in 1974 and may in some other circumstances be much greater. Census data also indicate that although birth rates have been declining in recent years, this demographic trend has not yet been observed in the form of a reduction in the number of new voters entering the electorate. Hence, with each successive election, the absolute number of new voters entering has been larger, and the effect of this group as a percentage of the total eligible electorate has therefore been greater. Of course, participation represents an important qualification of this observation, since younger people are somewhat less likely to vote or to participate in politics than are older voters.[19] Nevertheless, it is not an overstatement of the demographic data to observe that the electorate has been getting progressively younger, and of course the addition of 18-20 year olds to the electorate in 1970 increased this proportion. In 1974, nearly one-third of

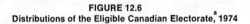

FIGURE 12.6
Distributions of the Eligible Canadian Electorate,[a] 1974

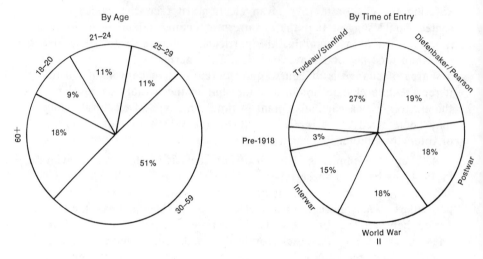

[a] Persons 18 years of age or over, estimated from 1971 census
data.
Source: *Census of Canada, 1971.*

all eligible voters were under thirty years of age (Figure 12.6), while about half of the eligible electorate was between the ages of 30 and 59.

A slightly different way of looking at these data is in terms of the time when eligible voters first entered the electorate. More than a quarter of the present electorate have entered during the Trudeau/Stanfield era (Figure 12.6). If the group entering between Diefenbaker's accession to power in 1957 and the beginning of the Trudeau/Stanfield era are added, together they comprise half of all eligible voters. Only about 18% of the total 1974 electorate consisted of voters who had been eligible to vote prior to the beginning of World War II. We refer to these "time of entry" groupings as "age cohorts" to signify the common electoral experiences of the several groups.[20]

The significance of a characterization of the Canadian electorate as a changing entity depends on additional evidence which is less obvious. We have already suggested that rates of intergenerational partisan agreement tend to be relatively low in Canada, thereby decreasing the probability that new voters entering the electorate will merely perpetuate old alignments. We have shown earlier (Chapter Five) that partisanship tends to be unstable for many voters over relatively short periods of time. Since it is often argued that conditions at the time of entry into the electorate are significant in the formation of political attitudes, each wave of new voters is likely to respond to at least some new forces, their behaviour relatively unconstrained by pre-existing societal cleavages, parental partisanship, or other long-term forces. All of the evidence previously examined — the flexibility of partisanship, the relative weakness of long-term forces, the short-term nature of party images, and the importance of leaders and issues — suggest the high potential for change in the electorate from one election to another. When we consider as well the fact that a substantial number of voters move into the electorate at a given time, the potential for fluctuation becomes quite impressive. While these changes will not necessarily produce different electoral outcomes, they cannot be ignored in any analysis of the nature of political choice in Canada.

Although the potential for change resulting from conversion and replacement combined is very high, there is little evidence that younger voters currently entering the electorate are harbingers of any fundamental realignment. The major characteristics of political choice that we have documented throughout this book would appear to be well established in nearly all age groups, and we would not, therefore, expect that Canadian politics will somehow be "different" as the result of infusions of new voters. There is a potential for such differences to develop, but there is little evidence in our data to support a contention that the nature of political choice will be altered in the near future as a result of electoral replacement. Rather, the level of volatility, already high in the electorate, is likely to remain so.

This pattern can be compared to observations which have been made about other Western countries in recent years. Several countries, the United States and Britain among them, have seen an erosion of partisanship in recent years, an erosion which appears to have been accompanied selectively by some changes in the nature of electoral behaviour and in the correlates of voting choice.[21] In the United States, for example, the most frequently observed trends in the electorate have been a weakening of partisanship, a significant increase in the number of voters defining themselves as independents, and a rise in the importance of issues as correlates of voting choice.[22] In Britain, a similar weakening of partisanship, an overall decrease in levels of participation, and significant gains by third parties have been readily noted.[23] Some of these changes have led observers of politics in those countries to predict a significant realignment or dealignment of partisan politics as an end result of the weakening of established patterns. In both countries, at least some of the observed changes have been generational in nature and have therefore been accelerated by the entry of new voters.

Although the end result in Canada may be similar, the developmental pattern is quite different. First, partisanship in Canada has not been characterized as particularly strong or stable by our measures, and there is therefore less potential for its erosion. Secondly, at least some of the

TABLE 12.9
Dimensions of Partisanship, by Age Cohorts

	TRUDEAU/ STANFIELD	DIEFENBAKER/ PEARSON	POSTWAR	WORLD WAR II	INTERWAR	PRE-1918
% With No Party Identification						
— Federal	10	13	13	12	13	6
— Provincial	12	10	13	11	9	6
% Whose Federal Partisanship Is						
— Weak*	27	23	23	20	19	17
— Unstable	30	38	33	35	30	25
— Inconsistent*	36	30	33	27	24	14
Mean Number of Deviations from Strong, Stable, Consistent Partisanship						
— Federal*	1.0	1.0	1.0	0.9	0.8	0.6
— Provincial*	0.9	0.9	0.9	0.8	0.7	0.6
% of "Flexible" Partisans	67	68	65	61	59	41
N=	542	377	365	428	305	58

*Between group differences significant at .01.

changes which have been observed in the United States in particular appear to be related to important dealigning issues in that country's politics — the Viet Nam war, Watergate, or the counter-culture of the sixties, to mention only a few.[24] Therefore, we would not expect Canadian data to show evidence of similar generational trends representative of significant discontinuities in electoral behaviour or existing partisan alignments. The six cohorts introduced earlier can provide a convenient vehicle for identifying broad generational trends if such exist.

An examination of the components of partisanship among the six age cohorts (Table 12.9) discloses only slight differences between them. Unlike the American pattern noted earlier, there is no significant increase in the number of voters without partisan attachments, nor is partisan instability higher in the younger cohorts.[25] There is a slightly larger proportion of "weak" partisans in the youngest (Trudeau/Stanfield) cohort, and a statistically significant difference between the six groups, but this observation in itself constitutes scant evidence of a potential overall weakening of partisanship. The larger number of inconsistent partisans in the younger cohorts may suggest that younger voters distinguish more clearly between the federal and provincial levels of politics, and therefore more readily accept different partisan identifications at the two levels. Overall, however, the differences between cohorts with respect to the number of deviations from a pattern of strong, stable, consistent partisanship, while statistically significant, are not large either at the federal or provincial levels. While the proportion of "flexible" partisans is slightly higher in the youngest cohorts, these overall differences are not significant. In short, the data do not constitute convincing evidence of any "erosion" of partisanship or of a potential alteration in the nature of the Canadian party system. As noted earlier, the levels of flexibility of partisanship in Canada are already quite high, and the data may be best construed as evidence that they are likely to remain so.

Just as there would appear to be only slight differences in partisanship among the six age cohorts, there is little evidence that the younger voters entering the electorate define or understand partisan politics in terms different than those which we have earlier associated with the electorate as a whole. In the data on party images, for example (Table 12.10), statistically significant differences between the cohorts appear on only two dimensions. The oldest cohorts are somewhat more likely to describe politics in pure party affect terms, and there is a tendency for issue orientation to be lower in those cohorts. There is, therefore, little evidence of a pattern which would suggest a strengthening of ideology, a rise in the level of issue awareness or issue voting, or any other impressive changes in the way that politics is conceptualized or understood by different groups of voters. Rather, it would appear more likely that the

TABLE 12.10
Dimensions of Party Images, by Age Cohorts

		TRUDEAU/ STANFIELD	DIEFENBAKER/ PEARSON	POSTWAR	WORLD WAR II	INTERWAR	PRE-1918
All Federal Party	%	85	88	88	89	88	84
Images	Mean	3.8	4.2	4.0	4.0	3.7	3.1
Leadership	%	39	38	38	37	37	32
	Mean	0.7	0.7	0.7	0.7	0.6	0.7
Policy/Issue*	%	58	67	63	63	54	41
	Mean	1.3	1.5	1.5	1.4	1.1	0.6
Ideology	%	13	16	16	15	10	12
	Mean	0.2	0.2	0.2	0.2	0.1	0.1
Area/Group	%	25	28	30	27	31	23
	Mean	0.4	0.4	0.4	0.4	0.5	0.3
Style/Performance	%	46	49	46	51	46	40
	Mean	0.9	0.8	0.8	0.8	0.8	0.6
Party*	%	31	34	32	40	40	51
	Mean	0.4	0.5	0.5	0.6	0.6	0.8
% Mentioning Two or More Issues (1974)*		35	37	39	34	32	17
N=		621	451	436	501	364	64

*Between group differences significant at .01 level.

TABLE 12.11

Level of Political Interest and Participation, by Age Cohorts

	TRUDEAU/ STANFIELD	DIEFENBAKER/ PEARSON	POSTWAR	WORLD WAR II	INTERWAR	PRE-1918
% "Very Interested" in Politics Generally*	6	10	15	20	22	25
Mean Score on Four-Item Federal Participation Scale*	1.6	1.9	2.0	2.0	1.9	1.9
Mean Score on Four-Item Political Efficacy Scale*	2.3	2.3	2.2	2.1	1.8	1.6

*Between group differences significant at .01 level.

tendency of the electorate to characterize political parties in terms of various types of short-term forces, such as issues, leaders, or performance and style, is essentially similar in all age groups.

Neither would it appear from data examined here that the nature of political choice in Canada is likely to be significantly modified by abrupt changes in levels of participation or in the response of voters to the political process. While British politics in recent years has been characterized by declining levels of turnout, there is no evidence of a similar trend in Canada (see Table 12.1). Although there are some statistically significant differences between cohorts with respect to levels of participation, there is every reason to believe that life cycle effects constitute the most logical explanation. In fact, it is evident in Table 12.11 that the participation scale exhibits the familiar curvilinear pattern, with the highest levels of overall participation being found in the middle age groups.[26] Levels of political interest are clearly lower in the youngest cohorts, but the faith of younger cohorts in the political process (as measured by the political efficacy scale) appears higher. The differences

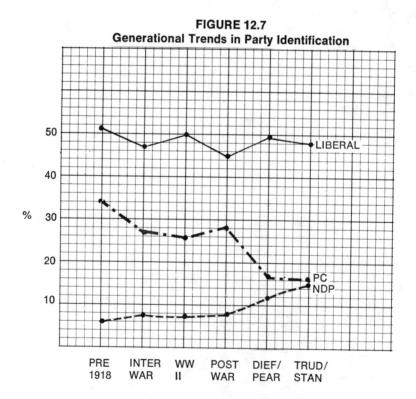

FIGURE 12.7
Generational Trends in Party Identification

between the cohorts, although statistically significant, are not large on any of these measures, and taken together they would not seem to provide evidence of the coming of future electorates which are essentially different from those of the recent past. Rather, we would expect that many of the characteristics of political choice documented in this book are likely to persist in Canada well into the future.

There are, however, some directional differences in the political orientation of the younger cohorts which are of potential significance for future election outcomes. The percentage of voters who identify themselves with the Conservative party appears to decline steadily with each successive cohort, falling to a low of 18% among the youngest (Trudeau/Stanfield era) cohort (Figure 12.7). This decline appears to be accompanied by a modest increase in the proportion of voters identifying with the NDP, which rises to a level nearly equal to that of the Conservatives in the youngest cohort. Identification with the Liberal party, on the other hand, remains relatively constant across the cohorts, and shows no sign of weakening or of growing stronger among those voters who first entered the electorate after the accession of Mr. Trudeau.

While these directional trends are worth noting, they must of course be carefully qualified. We have already noted that partisanship for many voters is unstable over relatively short periods of time, and that the level of flexibility of partisanship among Canadian voters generally is quite high. Further, we have observed in this chapter that the partisanship of younger voters tends to be weaker, whether due to normal life cycle patterns or to a gradual overall weakening of partisanship within the system. Therefore, we would not want to attempt to make projections regarding possible future election outcomes on the basis of the direction of respondent partisanship alone, given our understanding of its fundamental characteristics.

Some of the trends suggested by the analysis of direction of partisanship among the six age cohorts are corroborated by a comparison of the three national election surveys (Table 12.12). Although the time period is a relatively short one in which to measure generational trends, a similar decline in the proportion of Conservative identifiers is likewise seen across the three surveys. No significant increase in the proportion of NDP identifiers is evidenced however, suggesting that the increase in NDP support observed in our youngest cohorts is too recent a phenomenon to be seen in the nine-year comparison or, alternatively, that the NDP may lose some of its younger supporters as they grow older. Neither of these possibilities can be adequately tested in cross-section surveys alone, but the continuing strength of the Liberals is evident in both the cohort and time series comparisons.

TABLE 12.12

Direction and Intensity of Partisanship, 1974, 1968, and 1965
(as per cent of total national samples)

DIRECTION	INTENSITY	1965	1968	1974
Liberal	Very Strong	11	13	16
	Fairly Strong	20	25	23
	Weak	12	13	11
	Total	43	51	50
PC	Very Strong	7	7	7
	Fairly Strong	14	12	11
	Weak	7	7	6
	Total	28	26	24
NDP	Very Strong	4	4	4
	Fairly Strong	6	5	5
	Weak	2	2	2
	Total	12	11	11
Social Credit	Very Strong	2	2	1
	Fairly Strong	3	2	1
	Weak	1	1	1
	Total	6	5	3
No Party Identification		11	9	12
N=		*(2615)*	*(2706)*	*(2343)*

CONCLUSION

The Liberal Party has won most of the Canadian federal elections held in this century. Our analysis suggests that its success has been founded, not only on long-term stable loyalty to that party, but also on its ability to consistently turn many of the short-term factors affecting the bulk of Canadian voting decisions to its advantage. In 1974, on almost all the issues of the campaign, and with respect to leaders as well, more voters found the Liberals more to their liking than other parties.

The implication of our analysis, however, is that the pattern of Liberal dominance is more apparent than real. The composition of the electorate changes substantially at each election with infusions of newly eligible voters and mobilization of different groups of transient voters. In addition, there is a substantial amount of vote-switching from one election to the next. Since many of these switchers, transients, and new voters are motivated by the issues, party leaders, and local candidates associated with a particular election, the possibilities for dramatic election reverses, such as the Conservative victories in 1957 and 1958, are always present. These occurrences may be relatively infrequent because patterns of vote-switching often tend to be countervailing, as they were for the 1972-74 period. Given the right combination of electoral forces, however, sudden changes of the electoral fortunes of any party are quite possible.

Possibilities for large-scale electoral change are enhanced by the characteristics of the electorate's psychological attachments to political parties. A majority of Canadians are flexible in their partisanship, either because they support different parties in federal and provincial politics, because they have changed their allegiance in the past, or because they are only weakly attracted to any of the parties. Further, people evaluate the parties in ways which are easily susceptible to change and party images are dominated by references to current policies or leaders, or by the parties' recent performance in government, opposition, or the campaign itself. Reasons given for changing partisanship are consistently related to issues, policies, or leaders. Frequently such reasons involve negative references to the party being left behind, which indicates that the party favoured this time could be abandoned with the same alacrity should a different mixture of short-term factors arise. In sum, flexible partisans are open to changing their parties, and of course their votes, should any particular set of electoral circumstances make such a change appear desirable.

The popularity of political leaders is highly variable, and public attitudes toward any specific politician may warm or cool with startling rapidity. This is because the images of party leaders are dominated by impressions of their style and personality, or, less frequently, by their stands on issues of the day. The instability of leader effects is accentuated by the propensity of parties losing elections to replace their leaders in hopes that a new face will capture the public fancy, erase memories of defeat, or help disassociate the party from an unpopular policy proposal.

The nature of election issues is frequently short-term as well, with their salience largely depending on whether or not they were emphasized in the campaign. In 1974, inflation, an issue emphasized by all parties during the campaign, was the most frequently mentioned issue. In contrast, bilingualism, a relatively long-standing issue in Canadian politics and one on which most voters had opinions, was only infrequently recognized as an election issue. It is obvious that in a future campaign, the reverse may be true. In general, the relevance of an issue in a specific election is a function of its salience to groups of voters and the extent to which parties and the mass media emphasize it.

The importance of short-term factors in Canadian electoral behaviour is enhanced by the inability of social or demographic divisions in the population to manifest themselves at election time. Divisions between the sexes, age groups, rural and urban areas, or social classes have only very limited electoral significance in federal politics. Even religion and ethnicity, traditionally the deepest social cleavages in Canadian politics, are not strongly related to voting behaviour. In a sense, then, many Canadians approach electoral choice relatively free of those societal forces which might tend to "predetermine" their votes.

Neither do Canadians seem constrained by loyalties to regions of the country or levels of the federal system as they enter the polling booths. While there are certainly regional variations in aggregate electoral outcomes, there is no evidence that region or province of residence *per se* has a major impact on the way individual voters make up their minds. The proportion of flexible partisans in all regions, including Quebec, is sufficiently high to suggest that presently observed regional differences in support for various parties may be subject to substantial change in any given election. Indeed, the range of subjective perceptions of region is so complex that it is not likely to fit well with the simplification of issues and images that takes place at election time. And despite the fact that many citizens "feel closer" to one or the other level of government, they seem quite capable of distinguishing between them and making the necessary electoral choices at both. Finally, the negative feelings many Canadians manifest towards various elements of the political system may inhibit the development of long-term loyalties, and enhance the effects of short-run factors in the electoral arena.

Any Canadian election is decided by the collective behaviour of durable and flexible partisans, transients, and new voters. Durable partisans — and the electorate contains a substantial number of these — are more likely to cast ballots for "their" party, be motivated in this choice by long-term loyalty to it, and be more immune to forces of change. For such voters, short-term elements in elections, such as issues, leaders, or candidates, may very well reinforce rather than counter the effects of partisan attachment. Flexible partisans, on the other hand, who form a majority of the electorate, are more likely to contemplate alternatives and consider voting differently during an election campaign. In any specific election, the number of these people who actually do change the direction of their votes will be determined by their evaluation of issues, candidates, and leaders. Similarly, many voters who are newly eligible or re-entering the electorate after an abstention will decide their votes relatively unencumbered by long-term partisan ties. Thus, each time the nation goes to the polls, the potential for change, whether great or small, is present. Large numbers of voters from all generations respond to the short-term stimuli they encounter in the period leading up to and during the campaign. For much of the Canadian electorate, the vote decision is a matter of political choice.

FOOTNOTES

1. Within the limits possible in a national survey, some analysis of specific regional and provincial patterns in the 1974 data may be found in J. Pammett, L. LeDuc, J. Jenson, and H. Clarke, "The 1974 Federal Election: a Preliminary Report," Carleton Occasional Papers Series, No. 4, 1976.

2. See the discussion on reliability and vote report in Blair T. Weir, "The Distortion of Voter Recall," *American Journal of Political Science,* 59 (1975), pp. 53-62; and Aage R. Clausen, "Response Validity and Vote Report," *Public Opinion Quarterly,* 32 (1968-69), pp. 588-606. While the nineteen-month period between the 1972 and 1974 elections is relatively short, care must be taken not to press the analysis beyond the natural limits of data gathered at a single point in time. The use of 1972 recall is not the equivalent of the first wave of a panel study, nor a valid sample of the 1972 electorate as it then existed, neither of which are possible to fully reconstruct from cross-section data. Our use of recall here, however, is generally similar to that employed elsewhere in investigating the overall stability of voting choice in Canada within the confines of a single survey. See, for example, Mildred Schwartz, "Canadian Voting Behavior," in Richard Rose, ed., *Electoral Behavior: a Comparative Handbook* (New York: Free Press, 1974); and Paul Sniderman, H. D. Forbes, and Ian Melzer, "Party Loyalty and Electoral Volatility," *Canadian Journal of Political Science,* 7 (1974), pp. 268-88.

3. For a discussion of the importance of replacement in processes of political change, see David Butler and Donald Stokes, *Political Change in Britain* (London: Macmillan, 1969), chap. 3.

4. This would appear to be especially true, given the tendency of vote recall to *underestimate* change. See Weir, *op. cit.,* pp. 57-8.

5. The analysis here is confined primarily to a summary of national patterns. For a more detailed discussion of these regional and provincial differences, see Pammett et al., *op. cit.,* pp. 5-13.

6. A comparison with the 1965 pattern is useful here. In that national survey, the total proportion of the sample who report a switch from their recalled 1963 voting choice is somewhat smaller (14%) than in 1974, but the overall pattern of switching is more favourable to the Liberals. The two groups of voters entering or re-entering the electorate in 1965 were comparable in size to those of 1974, and were also heavily Liberal. Overall, the 1965 electorate contained a *higher* proportion of voters whose choice in 1965 was the same party as in 1963 (76%). These calculations are based on the authors' analysis of data collected by Meisel et al. following the 1965 election.

7. See the argument advanced by William Irvine in "Explaining the Religious Basis of Partisan Identity in Canada: Success on the Third Try," *Canadian Journal of Political Science,* 7 (1974), pp. 560-68.

8. Separate regression analyses are performed, predicting Liberal, PC, and NDP partisanship respectively. In these analyses, the partisanship vari-

ables are "1-0" dichotomies, i.e., Liberal–non-Liberal, PC–non-PC, NDP–non-NDP. Religious affiliation and ethnicity are entered into the regression analyses as a series of dummy variables. Categories of the religion variable are Catholic, Other, and None, with Protestant as the suppressed category. SES is measured using the Blishen index of occupations in Canada. See Appendix B, Q. 76, for a description of this measure and appropriate references.

9. In the regression analyses, father's partisanship is measured in terms of both direction and strength. If, for example, Liberal partisanship is being predicted, the categories of father's partisanship used are: (1) very strong Liberal, (2) fairly strong Liberal, (3) weak Liberal, (4) non-Liberal. These categories are scored 3, 2, 1, 0, respectively. To avoid possible multicolinearity effects, mother's partisanship is not used along with father's partisanship in the regression analyses.

10. The regressions were also run with father's partisanship, ethnicity, and religion only. This was done for two reasons: (1) possible multicolinearity effects due to the strong intercorrelations between ethnicity and region, and (2) the ambiguous status of region and socio-economic status as "long-term" forces on the vote for geographically and socially mobile segments of the electorate. A similar pattern is shown by these analyses, and the total variance explained is comparable in each instance.

11. Fluctuations in the popularity of individual leaders are evident in the thermometer measures discussed in Chapter Seven, and are commonly observed in public opinion data such as the Gallup poll. See, for example, the discussion of the fluctuations in Trudeau's popularity over the 1972-74 period in Lawrence LeDuc, "The Measurement of Public Opinion," in Howard E. Penniman, ed., *Canada at the Polls* (Washington: American Enterprise Institute, 1975), pp. 226-32.

12. The branching sequence employed earlier in Chapter Eleven (see Figure 11.1) and Appendix B, Q. 44, was used for this analysis. Specifically, those persons who choose the candidate personal qualities branch in Q. 44 were defined as the potentially candidate-oriented voters. The same procedure was used to define a potentially leader-oriented group.

13. This observation is buttressed by a parallel analysis of the 1965 study which shows that those voters who state that candidates were the "most important" element in their voting choice, or who give "candidate" answers in response to open-ended questions, divide among the parties in a pattern generally similar to that shown by the 1974 data. In 1965 however, what "candidate effect" does exist slightly favours the Liberals, and the *total* proportion of the sample giving "candidate" responses is higher in 1965. Neither of the survey questions asked in 1965, however, is perfectly comparable to the somewhat more detailed sequence (Appendix B, Q. 44) used in 1974.

14. The 1965 pattern, for example, is quite different. The per cent of that sample mentioning "leaders" in response to the party-leader-candidate sequence of questions (similar to Q. 44) or giving "leadership" responses to open-ended questions is lower than in 1974, and the parties divide much more evenly than the pattern shown in Table 12.6a. Although the overall leader effect as measured by these items also favoured the Liberals in 1965, the possible leader effects on the *outcome* of that election would appear to have been far less.

15. For each issue, the group included in the analysis consists of those persons mentioning the issue as "most important" to them personally in the 1974 election. See Appendix B, Q. 23a.

16. Because we are dealing here with relatively small percentages, considerations of sampling error are particularly important. (See the general discussion of sampling error for the 1974 study in Appendix A.) However, many of the percentages referenced in this chapter are based on the total sample N, making small differences rather more meaningful. A difference or shift, for example, of only 1% of the total electorate sample is often statistically significant at the .05 level (see Appendix A, Table A2).

17. In Britain, for example, Butler and Stokes found that although there was a relationship between the "state of the economy" and short-term swings toward or away from the governing party, there was also a tendency for economic issues to solidify perceptions of class interest. Butler and Stokes, *op. cit.,* chap. 18.

18. This group is the "stand on the issues" segment of the "leader most important" branch (see Appendix B, Q. 44, and Chapter 11, Figure 11.1).

19. For a discussion of the age-participation relationship, see Sidney Verba and Norman Nie, *Participation in America* (New York: Harper and Row, 1972), chap. 9, and Lester Milbrath, *Political Participation* (New York: Rand, McNally, 1965), pp. 134-35. For Canadian findings of a similar nature, see Rick Van Loon, "Political Participation in Canada," *Canadian Journal of Political Science,* 3 (1970), p. 389. See also Table 12.11.

20. The cohorts employed for our limited purposes here are based on time of first eligibility, which is, in turn, a function of age. The construction of these groups is shown in Appendix B, Q. 94, together with the age variable. The cohort groupings are not intended to imply any common political experiences beyond that of first eligibility. These particular groupings have been employed in an analysis of the declining significance of religion in Canadian electoral behaviour. See David Rees, "An Age Cohort Analysis of Religious Voting in Canada" (Unpublished M.A. thesis, University of Windsor).

21. See, among others, Norman Nie, Sidney Verba, and John Petrocik, *The Changing American Voter* (Cambridge: Harvard University Press, 1976); Warren Miller and Theresa Levitin, *Leadership and Change* (Cambridge: Winthrop, 1976), and Ivor Crewe, Bo Sarlvik, and James Alt, "Partisan Dealignment in Britain: 1964-74," *British Journal of Political Science,* 7 (1977), pp. 121-90.

22. Nie, Verba, and Petrocik, *op. cit.,* Chaps. 4, 10.

23. Crewe *et al., op. cit., passim.*

24. Miller and Levitin, *op cit., passim.*

25. One might expect age and stability to be inversely related, in that older voters will have had many more opportunities to alter their partisanship. However, no such relationship appears in our data. Younger cohorts are as likely to report a partisan change as are older voters, and the overall relationship is not statistically significant. This may be because of the tendency of partisan changes in the electorate to take place over relatively short periods of time in Canada, as noted earlier in Chapter Five. It is not possible in a single survey to adequately separate life cycle and generation effects, and the tendency of partisanship to strengthen with the length of time it is held is well known. See Philip Converse, "Of Time

and Partisan Stability," *Comparative Political Studies*, 2 (1969), pp. 139-71.

26. See, for example, Milbrath, *op. cit.*, pp. 134-35; Verba and Nie, *op cit.*, pp. 138-49. Voting turnout in the 1974 federal election is also slightly lower in the youngest cohorts and exhibits a pattern similar to that of the participation scale shown in Table 12.11.

APPENDIX A

Sampling Information and Methodology

The 1974 National Election Study was a single-wave, post-election survey based on a national sample of 2562 respondents. Copies of the code book and data are available from the authors or from the following data archives:

Institute for Behavioural Research
York University
Downsview, Ontario

Data Library
University of British Columbia
Vancouver, B.C.

Inter-University Consortium for Political and Social Research
The University of Michigan
Ann Arbor, Michigan

The field work was conducted by Canadian Facts, Ltd., under the direction of the authors. Approximately 90% of the interviewing was completed prior to October 1, 1974, with a maximum of four call-backs allowed per respondent. Call-backs were staggered and, in some cases, spread over a longer period in order to minimize losses of respondents due to summer vacations.

The sample design for the study was a multi-stage, stratified, cluster sample, weighted by province to allow for some systematic oversampling of the smaller provinces. A more detailed discussion of the construction and design of this sample may be found in LeDuc, Clarke, Jenson, and Pammett, "A National Sample Design," *Canadian Journal of Political Science*, 7 (1974), pp. 701-708. Weights employed in the study are shown in Table A1 below.

As the difference in sizes between weighted and unweighted samples are negligible for the total national sample, only the weighted Ns are shown in tables (italicized) in this book. Breakdowns by province, however, or analyses of single provinces, are based on unweighted N's where these occur (no italics).

TABLE A1

Sample Sizes and Weights, by Province

PROVINCE	NUMBER OF INTERVIEWS	WEIGHTS	EFFECTIVE SIZE
Prince Edward Island	97	0.125	*12*
Newfoundland	102	0.500	*51*
Nova Scotia	180	0.500	*90*
New Brunswick	134	0.500	*67*
Quebec	702	1.000	*702*
Ontario	702	1.250	*878*
Manitoba	113	1.000	*113*
Saskatchewan	101	1.000	*101*
Alberta	179	1.000	*179*
British Columbia	252	1.000	*252*
Total	2562		*2445*

Some questions in the 1974 National Election Study were asked of one of two random half-samples of 1262 or 1300 respondents only (see Appendix B). Similar weighting procedures are applied to each of the half-samples for these items.

Because sampling error for cluster samples will normally exceed that for simple random samples of comparable size, standard tables are not appropriate for use with this sample. In fact, it may be shown that the formula for simple random samples will increasingly underestimate the true sampling error as the size of the sample increases.

The following tables, based on all sample points and calculated from exact formula appropriate to the design, may be used in assigning levels of significance to the findings discussed here.

TABLE A2

Ninety-five Per Cent Confidence Limits for Percentages, by Size of Base

For Percentages

N	5 OR 95	10 OR 90	20 OR 80	30 OR 70	40 OR 60	50
100	5	7	9	11	11	12
200	4	5	7	8	8	8
400	3	4	5	6	6	6
600	2	3	4	5	5	5
800	2	3	4	4	4	4
1000	2	2	3	4	4	4
1500	2	2	3	3	3	4
2000	1	2	3	3	3	3
2500	1	2	2	3	3	3

TABLE A3

Ninety-five Per Cent Confidence Limits for Differences of Proportions, by Size of Base

	N	100	300	500	700	900	1100	1300
	100	7	6	6	5	5	5	5
	300	6	4	4	4	3	3	3
For	500	6	4	3	3	3	3	3
Percentages	700	5	4	3	3	3	3	3
About	1000	5	3	3	3	3	2	2
5-95%	1500	5	3	3	2	2	2	2
	2000	5	3	3	2	2	2	2
	2500	5	3	3	2	2	2	2
	100	14	12	11	11	11	10	10
	300	12	8	8	7	7	7	7
For	500	11	8	7	6	6	6	6
Percentages	700	11	7	6	6	6	5	5
About	1000	11	7	6	5	5	5	5
25-75%	1500	10	7	6	5	5	5	4
	2000	10	6	5	5	4	4	4
	2500	10	6	5	5	4	4	4
	100	16	13	13	12	12	12	12
	300	13	10	9	8	8	8	8
For	500	13	9	8	7	7	7	6
Percentages	700	12	8	7	7	6	6	6
About	1000	12	8	7	6	6	6	5
50%	1500	12	8	6	6	5	5	5
	2000	12	7	6	5	5	5	5
	2500	12	7	6	5	5	5	5

TABLE A4

Approximate Ninety-five Per Cent Confidence Limits for Thermometer Scale Means and Mean Differences, by Size of Base

N	MEANS	MEAN DIFFERENCE
100	5.0	3.6
200	3.5	2.6
400	2.5	1.8
600	2.0	1.4
800	1.7	1.3
1000	1.5	1.1
1500	1.3	0.9
2000	1.1	0.8
2500	1.0	0.7

Where necessary, approximations of sampling error may also be made from formulae or tables appropriate to simple random samples by taking advantage of the linear nature of the relationship between cluster variance and simple random variance. Such estimates should be multiplied by K, the ratio of cluster variance to simple random variance. For the 1974 sample, the ratio is given by the equation:

$$K = 1.1672908 + .0001526N$$

APPENDIX B

Measures and Questionnaire

The following measures have been employed in analyses throughout this book. In each instance, the questions are shown in the form that they appeared in the field questionnaire, and variables are referenced by their original question number(s). Questions or variables not referenced in the book are omitted. Items designated (*) were asked of one of two random half-samples of respondents only.

POLITICAL INTEREST

1. We have found that people sometimes don't pay too much attention to elections. How about yourself? Would you say that you were very interested in the recent *federal* election, fairly interested, slightly interested, or not at all interested in it?

VERY INTERESTED	1
FAIRLY INTERESTED	2
SLIGHTLY INTERESTED	3
NOT AT ALL INTERESTED	4
D.K.	8

2. We would also like to know whether you pay much attention to politics generally. I mean from day to day, when there isn't a big election campaign going on. Would you say that you follow politics very closely, fairly closely, or not much at all?

VERY CLOSELY	1
FAIRLY CLOSELY	2
NOT MUCH AT ALL	3
D.K.	8

The "slightly interested" and "not at all interested" categories of the general interest measure (Q.1) were combined, so that a three-point index (high-medium-low) is obtained for each item. A composite measure was then constructed as follows, to yield categories of high (+), moderate (0), and low (−) interest:

Election Interest

A question indicating primary *level* of interest was also asked.

3. Generally, would you say that you pay more attention to *federal* politics, *provincial* politics, or *local* politics?

FEDERAL	1
PROVINCIAL	2
LOCAL	3
ALL ABOUT EQUALLY	4
FEDERAL & PROVINCIAL EQ.	5
FEDERAL & LOCAL EQ.	6
PROVINCIAL & LOCAL EQ.	7
D.K.	8
N.A.	9

IMPORTANCE OF LEVELS OF GOVERNMENT

4. As far as you are concerned personally, which government is more important in affecting how you and your family get on, the one in Ottawa, the provincial government here in (NAME PROVINCE), or the local government here in (CITY, TOWNSHIP, etc.)?

FEDERAL	1
PROVINCIAL	2
LOCAL	3
ALL ABOUT EQUALLY	4
FEDERAL & PROVINCIAL EQ.	5
FEDERAL & LOCAL EQ.	6
PROVINCIAL & LOCAL EQ.	7
D.K.	8

*POLITICAL EFFICACY

9. Now, I would like to talk to you about some opinions that you hear different people giving. As I read each one, I would just like you to tell me offhand whether you strongly agree, agree, disagree, or strongly disagree.

	NO OPINION	STRONGLY AGREE	AGREE	DISAGREE	STRONGLY DISAGREE
(a) Generally, those elected to Parliament soon lose touch with the people	0	1	2	3	4
(b) I don't think that the government cares much what people like me think	0	1	2	3	4
(c) Sometimes, politics and government seem so complicated that a person like me can't really understand what's going on	0	1	2	3	4
(d) People like me don't have any say about what the government does	0	1	2	3	4
(e) So many other people vote in federal elections that it doesn't matter very much whether I vote or not	0	1	2	3	4

A Guttman scale was formed from these five questions, treating items (a) and (b) as a single composite item, and taking the responses "disagree" or "strongly disagree" as the single positive alternative for each item. The scale thus formed was as follows:

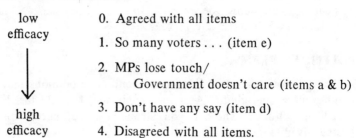

low efficacy

↓

high efficacy

0. Agreed with all items

1. So many voters . . . (item e)

2. MPs lose touch/ Government doesn't care (items a & b)

3. Don't have any say (item d)

4. Disagreed with all items.

Guttman scale coefficients of .89 (CR) and .61 (CS) were obtained for this scale. A discussion of the Political Efficacy measure may be found in Lawrence LeDuc, "Measuring the Sense of Political Efficacy in Canada," *Comparative Political Studies,* 8 (1976), pp. 490-500.

*POLITICAL PARTICIPATION

10. Some people do quite a lot in politics, while others find they haven't the time or perhaps the interest to participate in political activities. I'll read you briefly some of the things that people do, and I would like you to tell me how often *you* do each of them.

      First, please tell me how often you did each of these things in the *recent federal election* — often, sometimes, seldom, or never.

	OFTEN	SOMETIMES	SELDOM	NEVER	D.K.
(a) How often do you read about politics in the newspapers?	1	2	3	4	8
(b) Discuss politics with other people	1	2	3	4	8
(c) Try to convince friends to vote the same as you	1	2	3	4	8
(d) Work with other people in this community to try to solve some local problem	1	2	3	4	8
(e) Attend a political meeting or rally	1	2	3	4	8
(f) Contact public officials or politicians	1	2	3	4	8
(g) Spend time working for a political party or a candidate	1	2	3	4	8

11. Now, could you please tell me how often you have done any of these things *generally* in federal politics, not just in this recent election.

12. How often have you done any of these things in *provincial* politics here in (NAME PROVINCE)?

Separate Guttman scales were created for each of three levels (1974 election; federal; provincial) from the same set of four of the above items (b, c, e, and g), plus an additional item dealing with voting participation obtained from the voting sequences (questions 42a, 43a, and 72a). For purposes of obtaining the best possible set of four-item scales, items (c) and (e) were treated as a single composite item in each instance. The responses "often" or "sometimes" constitute a single positive alternative for all questions.

		1974 ELECTION	FEDERAL POLITICS	PROVINCIAL POLITICS
Low Participation	0. No Activity			
	1. Always/Usually Vote	Q43a	Q42a	Q72a
	2. Discuss Politics	Q10b	Q11b	Q12b
	3. Convince Friends/ Attend Meetings	Q10c, e	Q11c, e	Q12c, e
High Participation	4. Campaign Activity	Q10g	Q11g	Q12g
	CR=	.94	.95	.93
	CS =	.71	.77	.70

A discussion of these participation scales may be found in Mike Burke, Harold Clarke, and Lawrence LeDuc, "Federal and Provincial Political Participation: Some Substantive and Methodological Considerations," *Canadian Review of Sociology and Anthropology,* XV (1978), pp. 61-75.

REGIONAL ATTITUDES

14. Here is a blank map of Canada. It has no writing on it at all. We would like you to write in five words or phrases that you think best describe politics in Canada. You can put down anything you want and write anywhere on the map, but you can only put down five things.

The map responses were coded according to both placement and content. The distribution of frequencies for specific categories of placed and un-placed responses is shown in Appendix 1A and 1B (Chapter One). Up to five mentions were coded for each respondent.

15. (a) People often think of Canada as being divided into regions, but they don't always agree on what the regional divisions are. We would like to know if you think of Canada as being divided into regions.

YES .... ☐
NO 00
D.K. 88

[IF YES] (b) What region do you live in? ....

(c) What are the other regions of Canada? ....

(d) Any others? ....

A summary measure of regional consciousness was created by adding one point for each of the following conditions.

— Thinking of Canada in regional terms and describing "own region" (Q. 15 (a) and (b))

— Describing at least one other region of Canada (Q. 15 (c) and (d))

— Giving at least one *placed* response to the map question (Q. 14)

This produces an index as follows:

Regional Consciousness

low	0
↑	1
↓	2
high	3

16. Would you say that you feel closer to the federal government in Ottawa, or to your provincial government here in (NAME PROVINCE)?

FEDERAL 1

PROVINCIAL 2

BOTH EQUALLY 3

NEITHER 4

OTHER —————————————————

D.K. 8

17. (a) Are any *provincial* govern- YES .... ☐
       ments more powerful than NO 00
       others? NO OPINION 88

    (b) [IF YES] Which ones? _____

THERMOMETER SCALES (NATION, PROVINCE, AND REGION)

18. You will see here a drawing of a thermometer. It is called a feeling thermometer because it helps us measure people's feelings toward various things. Here is how it works. If you don't have any particular feeling about the things we are asking about, place them at the 50-degree mark. If your feelings are very warm toward a particular thing, you would give a score between 50 and 100 — the warmer your feelings, the higher the score. On the other hand, if your feelings are relatively cool toward something, you would place them between 0 and 50. The cooler your feelings, the closer the score will be to zero. If you don't know too much about any of the items mentioned, just say so and we will go on to the next one.

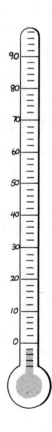

(a) First of all, we would like to know how you feel *in general* about this province of (NAME PROVINCE)?

(b) Now, as a *place to live,* could you tell me, again using the thermometer, how you feel about this province of (NAME PROVINCE)?

(c) How do you feel about the government of this province of (NAME PROVINCE)?

(d) (REFER TO REGION MENTIONED IN Q. 15 (b). IF SAME AS PROVINCE, GO TO Q. 18 (f).) How do you feel, *in general,* about this region of (NAME REGION MENTIONED IN Q. 15 (b))?

(e) Now, specifically, as a *place to live* in, how would you say you feel about this region of (NAME REGION MENTIONED IN Q. 15(b))?

(f) How do you feel, *in general,* about Canada?

(g) Now, specifically, as a country to *live* in, how would you say you feel about Canada?

(h) How do you feel about the *government* of Canada?

(i) How do you feel about *the United States*?

(j) How do you feel about *England*?

(k) How do you feel about *France*?

To correct for individual differences in the use of the thermometer scale, *standardized* thermometer scores were computed for each respondent using the mean and standard deviation of each set of scores for all objects.

This version of the thermometer scores is employed in all analyses of relationships between ratings of different objects (e.g., province and nation). In all other instances, the raw scores are used.

CANADIAN FEDERALISM

19. (a) In your opinion, are some of the provinces bearing more than their fair share of the costs of governing Canada?

YES .... ☐
NO 00
D.K. 88

    (b) [IF YES] Which provinces are these? _____

20. (a) What about benefits? Would you say that some provinces receive more than their fair share of the benefits of being part of Canada?

YES .... ☐
NO 00
D.K. 88

    (b) [IF YES] Which provinces are these?_____

21. This is a list of some things for which governments in Canada are responsible. For each one, I would like your opinion about whether the *federal* government in Ottawa or the *provincial* government here in (NAME PROVINCE) is more important in dealing with that particular item.

	NO OPINION	FEDERAL	PROVINCIAL	BOTH EQUALLY	D.K.
(a) Education	0	1	2	3	8
(b) Foreign Affairs	0	1	2	3	8
(c) Local Government	0	1	2	3	8
(d) Hospital Insurance	0	1	2	3	8
(e) Unemployment Insurance	0	1	2	3	8
(f) The Economy	0	1	2	3	8

ISSUES (GENERAL)

23. (a) Now, I would like to ask you some more specific questions about the recent *federal* election. What, in your opinion, was the *most* important issue to you, personally, in that election?

NO IMPORTANT ISSUES	00
D.K.	88

(b) How do you feel about this issue?

(c) Which party is closest to *you* on this issue?

NONE	0
LIBERALS	1
PROGRESSIVE CONSERVATIVES	2
NDP	3
SOCIAL CREDIT	4
OTHER	
D.K.	8
N.A.	9

(d) How important was that issue to you in deciding how to vote in the election?

VERY IMPORTANT	1
FAIRLY IMPORTANT	2
NOT VERY IMPORTANT	3
D.K.	8
N.A.	9

24. (a) Was there any other issue that was important to *you* in the election?

NO OTHER ISSUE	00
D.K.	88
N.A.	99

(b) How do you feel about this issue?

(c) Which party is closest to you on this issue?

NONE	0
LIBERALS	1
PROGRESSIVE CONSERVATIVES	2
NDP	3
SOCIAL CREDIT	4
OTHER	
D.K.	8
N.A.	9

(d) How important was that issue to you in deciding how to vote in the election?

VERY IMPORTANT	1
FAIRLY IMPORTANT	2
NOT VERY IMPORTANT	3
D.K.	8
N.A.	9

*BILINGUALISM

25. (a) I would like to get your opinions on an issue that has been important for some time now in Canadian politics, not just in this election. That issue is bilingualism. What do you usually think of when bilingualism is mentioned?

_____

Anything else? _____

(b) How do you feel about bilingualism? _____

NO OPINION	00
D.K.	88
N.A.	99

The bilingualism responses were coded on each of the following dimensions: LANGUAGE, PRESCRIPTION, REGIONAL/PROVINCIAL, COMPULSION, PERSONAL/IMPERSONAL, and POSITIVE/NEGATIVE. Specific content of individual responses is coded within each category.

(c) Which party is closest to you on this issue?

NONE	0
LIBERALS	1
PROGRESSIVE CONSERVATIVES	2
NDP	3
SOCIAL CREDIT	4
OTHER _____	
D.K.	8
N.A.	9

*FOREIGN INVESTMENT

26. (a) I would also like to get your opinions on an issue that has been important for some time now in Canadian politics, not just in this election. That issue is foreign investment. What do you usually think of when foreign investment is mentioned?

_____

Anything else? _____

(b) How do you feel about foreign investment? _____

NO OPINION 00

D.K. 88

N.A. 99

The foreign investment responses were coded on each of the following dimensions: INEVITABILITY, CHARACTERISTICS, DOMINATION, ACTION, and POSITIVE/NEGATIVE. Specific content of individual responses is coded within each category.

(c) Which party is closest to you on this issue?

NONE 0

LIBERALS 1

PROGRESSIVE CONSERVATIVES 2

NDP 3

SOCIAL CREDIT 4

OTHER _____

D.K. 8

N.A. 9

*INFLATION

27. (a) I would also like to get your opinions on an issue that has been discussed quite a bit in this election. That issue is inflation. What do you usually think of when inflation is mentioned?

_____

Anything else?_____

Responses to this question were coded for CONTENT, PERCEPTION OF CAUSES, and PREFERRED ACTION.

(b) How much were you personally affected by inflation over the past year or so — a great deal, some, or not much at all?

A GREAT DEAL 1

SOME 2

NOT MUCH AT ALL 3

DON'T KNOW 8

(c) (IF "SOME" OR "GREAT DEAL") In what way were you most affected?

(d) Which party is the closest to you on this issue?

LIBERALS 1
PROGRESSIVE CONSERVATIVES 2
NDP 3
SOCIAL CREDIT 4
OTHER ————————————
D.K. 8

*MAJORITY GOVERNMENT

29. (a) Before we leave the subject of issues, there is one additional question that I would like to ask you about. In recent years, the political party which has formed the government in Ottawa has frequently not had a majority of the seats in Parliament. Some people think that it is better when the government has a majority of seats in Parliament, while others feel that minority governments can accomplish more. Which do you feel is better?

MAJORITY 1
MINORITY 2
IT DEPENDS 3
D.K. 8
NO OPINION 0

(b) If you believed that one party was more likely to be able to form a majority government, but you did not ordinarily vote for that party, how likely would you be to vote for it in order to have a majority government — very likely, somewhat likely, or not at all likely?

VERY LIKELY 1
SOMEWHAT LIKELY 2
NOT AT ALL LIKELY 3
D.K. 8

(c) Did this question of majority government have a great deal, something, or nothing at all to do with the way you voted in this last election?

A GREAT DEAL 1
SOMETHING 2
NOTHING AT ALL 3
D.K. 8

PARTISANSHIP (FEDERAL)

30. (a) Thinking of *federal* politics, do you usually think
of yourself as a Liberal,
Conservative, NDP, Social
Credit, or what?

LIBERAL 1
PROGRESSIVE CONSERVATIVE 2
NDP 3
SOCIAL CREDIT 4
OTHER ——————————————
D.K. 8
INDEPENDENT OR NONE 0

(b) How strongly (PARTY
MENTIONED IN Q. 30.
(a)) do you feel — very
strongly, fairly strongly, or
not very strongly?

VERY STRONGLY 1
FAIRLY STRONGLY 2
NOT VERY STRONGLY 3
D.K. 8
N.A. 9

31.   (IF "DON'T KNOW" OR "INDEPENDENT OR NONE" IN
Q. 30. (a))

(a) Still thinking of *federal*
politics, do you generally
think of yourself as being a
little closer to one of the
parties than to the others?

YES 1
NO 2
D.K. 8
N.A. 9

(b) (IF YES) Which party is
that?

LIBERAL 1
PROGRESSIVE CONSERVATIVE 2
NDP 3
SOCIAL CREDIT 4
OTHER ——————————————
D.K. 8
N.A. 9

32. (a) Still thinking of *federal*
politics, was there ever a
time when you felt closer
to any other party?

YES 1
NO 2
D.K. 8

(b) (IF YES) Which party
was that?

LIBERAL 1
PROGRESSIVE CONSERVATIVE 2
NDP 3
SOCIAL CREDIT 4
OTHER ——————————————
D.K. 8
N.A. 9

(c) (IF PARTY NAMED) When did you change from that party?

(d) (IF YES IN Q. 32. (a) OR D.K. IN Q. 32. (b)) What was the main thing that made you change? _____

Federal partisanship is measured by INTENSITY (Q. 30(b) and STABILITY (Q. 32. (a)), as well as by DIRECTION of identification. An additional modifier, CONSISTENCY, is produced by comparing federal and provincial partisanship.

A summary measure of deviations from strong, stable, consistent partisanship was produced by counting one point for each of the three ways in which a respondent might vary from the strong, stable, consistent pattern. Thus, one point is counted for being weak or independent, one for being unstable, and one for holding a different federal and provincial partisanship or being a single level identifier. A similar measure was constructed for provincial partisanship (Q. 60-62), using the same CONSISTENCY measure and provincial INTENSITY and STABILITY components.

The categorizations of DURABLE and FLEXIBLE partisanship were created, in effect, by collapsing the summary index. A FLEXIBLE partisan, therefore, is one who deviates from the pattern of strong, stable, consistent partisanship on *any* of the three dimensions.

PARENTS FEDERAL PARTISANSHIP

33. (a) When you were growing up, did your father have any particular preference for one of the *federal* political parties here in Canada?

YES	1
NO	2
D.K.	8

(b) (IF YES) Which party was that?

LIBERAL	1
PROGRESSIVE CONSERVATIVE	2
NDP	3
SOCIAL CREDIT	4
D.K.	8
OTHER	_____
N.A.	9

(c) How strongly (PARTY MENTIONED IN Q. 33 (b)) was he then?

VERY STRONG	1
FAIRLY STRONG	2
NOT VERY STRONG	3
N.A.	9
D.K.	8

34. (a) Did your mother have any particular preference for one of the *federal* parties here in Canada?

YES	1
NO	2
D.K.	8

(b) (IF YES) Which party was that?

LIBERAL	1
PROGRESSIVE CONSERVATIVE	2
NDP	3
SOCIAL CREDIT	4
OTHER _____	
D.K.	8
N.A.	9

(c) How strongly (PARTY MENTIONED IN Q. 34 (b)) was she then?

VERY STRONG	1
FAIRLY STRONG	2
NOT VERY STRONG	3
D.K.	8
N.A.	9

35. When you were growing up, how interested were your parents in *federal* politics — very interested, somewhat interested, or not at all interested?

VERY INTERESTED	1
SOMEWHAT INTERESTED	2
NOT AT ALL INTERESTED	3
D.K.	8

*CAMPAIGN CONTACT

36. (a) During the election campaign, were you personally contacted by any of the local candidates or party workers here in this riding?

YES	1
NO	2
D.K.	8

(b) Which ones? Any others?

LIBERAL	☐
PROGRESSIVE CONSERVATIVE	☐
NDP	☐
SOCIAL CREDIT	☐
ALL CANDIDATE MENTIONS	☐
D.K.	88
N.A.	99

(c) (IF C A N D I D AT E (S)
MENTIONED IN Q. 36.
(b)) Which party was he
(were they)?

LIBERAL .... ☐
PROGRESSIVE CONSERVATIVE .... ☐
NDP .... ☐
SOCIAL CREDIT .... ☐
OTHER ————————————
D.K. 88
N.A. 99

37. (a) Were you contacted in any
other ways by the parties
during the campaign, for
example, by telephone or
by having a pamphlet left
in your mailbox?

YES 1
NO 2
D.K. 8

(b) (IF YES) Which party or
parties?

LIBERAL .... ☐
PROGRESSIVE CONSERVATIVE .... ☐
NDP .... ☐
SOCIAL CREDIT .... ☐
OTHER ————————————
D.K. 88
N.A. 99

(c) (IF YES) How did they
contact you?

MAIL 1
PHONE 2
OTHER ————————————
D.K. 8
N.A. 9

A summary index of campaign contact was created by scoring one point
for an *impersonal* contact (literature, telephone, etc.) and an additional
point for *personal* (candidate/party worker) contact. This produces a
summary measure as follows:

Campaign Contact

low   0
↑   1
high   2

*MEDIA ATTENTION

38.   During the election campaign, would you say that
you read quite a bit, something, or not much at all

QUITE A BIT 1
SOMETHING 2
NOT MUCH 3
D.K. 8

about the parties, candidates, or other aspects of the election campaign in the newspapers?

39. How about television? During the election campaign did you watch programs or advertisements about the parties or candidates or other aspects of the campaign? Would you say that you saw quite a few, some, or almost none?

QUITE A FEW 1
SOME 2
ALMOST NONE 3
D.K. 8

40. How about radio? During the election campaign did you hear programs or advertisements about the parties or candidates or other aspects of the campaign? Would you say that you heard quite a few, some, or almost none?

QUITE A FEW 1
SOME 2
ALMOST NONE 3
D.K. 8

41. Which would you say is most important to you in getting information about politics, radio, television, or the newspapers?

RADIO 1
TELEVISION 2
NEWSPAPERS 3
RADIO & TELEVISION 4
RADIO & NEWSPAPERS 5
TELEVISION & NEWSPAPERS 6
ALL EQUALLY 7
D.K. 8
NONE ARE IMPORTANT 0

VOTING BEHAVIOUR

42. (a) In *federal* elections since you have been old enough to vote in Canada, including the one held this July, would you say that you have voted in all of them, most of them, some of them, or none of them?

ALL 1
MOST 2
SOME 3
NONE 4
NOT ELIGIBLE BEFORE 5
D.K. 8

(b) Have you always voted for the same party in *federal* elections, or have you voted for different parties?

SAME	1
DIFFERENT	2
D.K.	8
N.A.	9

(c) (IF SAME) Which party is that?

LIBERAL	1
PROGRESSIVE CONSERVATIVE	2
NDP	3
SOCIAL CREDIT	4
OTHER ————————	
D.K.	8
N.A.	9

(d) (IF DIFFERENT IN Q. 42 (b)) Did you vote for different parties out of choice, or because some parties did not contest the election in your province or constituency?

CHOICE	1
DID NOT CONTEST	2
D.K.	8
N.A.	9

43. (a) Now, thinking about this year's July *federal* election, we find that a lot of people weren't able to vote because they were away, or had some other reasons for not voting. How about you? Did you vote this time, or did something happen to keep you from voting?

VOTED	1
DID NOT VOTE	2
D.K.	8
N.A.	9

(b) (IF VOTED) For which party did you vote?

LIBERAL	1
PROGRESSIVE CONSERVATIVE	2
NDP	3
SOCIAL CREDIT	4
OTHER ————————	5
D.K.	8
N.A.	9

(IF "NONE" IN Q. 42 (a) OR "DID NOT VOTE" IN Q. 43 (a), ASK QUESTIONS 43 (c) AND (d).)

(c) Was there any particular reason why you didn't vote in the July election? _____

(d) If you had voted, who would you have voted for?

LIBERAL 1
PROGRESSIVE CONSERVATIVE 2
NDP 3
SOCIAL CREDIT 4
OTHER ————————— 5
D.K. 8
N.A. 9

PARTY, LEADER, CANDIDATE INFLUENCES

44. (a) In deciding how you would vote in the recent July election, which was the *most* important to you: the *party leaders*, the *candidates* here in this constituency, or the *parties* taken as a whole?

(b) Which would you say was the next most important?

(c) Which would you say was least important?

	PARTY LEADERS	CANDIDATES	THE PARTIES	D.K.	N.A.
(a) Most important	1	2	3	8	9
(b) Next most important	1	2	3	8	9
(c) Least important	1	2	3	8	9

(d) (IF PARTY LEADER OR CANDIDATE MENTIONED AS MOST IMPORTANT IN Q. 44 (a)) When you say that (PARTY LEADER OR CANDIDATE) was the *most* important to you, are you thinking of his personal qualities, or his stand on certain issues?

STAND ON ISSUES 1
PERSONAL QUALITIES 2
D.K. 8
N.A. 9

(e) (IF STAND ON ISSUES) Which issues are you thinking of specifically?

(f) (IF PARTY MENTIONED AS MOST IMPORTANT IN Q. 44 (a)) When you say that party was the *most* important to you, are you thinking of the party's general approach to government or its position on certain issues?

POSITION ON ISSUES	1
GENERAL APPROACH	2
D.K.	8
N.A.	9

(g) (IF POSITION ON ISSUES) Which issues are you thinking of specifically?

PAST VOTING BEHAVIOUR

45. (a) The last *federal* election before the one in July was in October 1972. Do you remember for sure whether or not you voted in that election?

VOTED	1
DIDN'T VOTE	2
NOT ELIGIBLE	3
DON'T REMEMBER	8

(b) (IF VOTED IN 1972) Which party did you vote for?

LIBERAL	1
PROGRESSIVE CONSERVATIVE	2
NDP	3
SOCIAL CREDIT	4
OTHER _____	5
DON'T REMEMBER/D.K.	8
N.A.	9

VOTING DECISION (SECOND CHOICE)

47. (a) If, for some reason, you had been unable to vote for the *federal* party that you most preferred in the recent election, which other federal party would you have voted for?

WOULD NOT VOTE	0
LIBERAL	1
PROGRESSIVE CONSERVATIVE	2
NDP	3
SOCIAL CREDIT	4
OTHER _____	5
D.K.	8

(b) Which of the *federal* parties would you *least* want to vote for?

LIBERAL 1

PROGRESSIVE CONSERVATIVE 2

NDP 3

SOCIAL CREDIT 4

OTHER ————————————— 5

D.K. 8

*VOTING DECISION (TIME)

48. (a) As you know, the election was held on July 8, 1974. Can you remember exactly when you decided how you were going to vote? (INTERVIEWER: PROBE FOR APPROXIMATE DATE WITHIN WEEKS BEFORE THE ELECTION — ONE WEEK, TWO WEEKS, ETC.)

(b) Were you pretty sure all along which party you were going to vote for, or was there any point when you thought you might vote for a different party?

SURE ALL ALONG 1

CONSIDERED OTHER 2

D.K. 8

(c) Which party was that?

LIBERAL 1

PROGRESSIVE CONSERVATIVE 2

NDP 3

SOCIAL CREDIT 4

OTHER —————————————

D.K. 8

N.A. 9

*VOTING DECISION (REASONS)

49. We have asked you a lot of questions about reasons why you might have decided how to vote. Sometimes, however, in asking all these questions, researchers can lose track of what was *really* important to people. So, could you take a moment to think over all the reasons why you decided to vote the way you did, and just briefly tell me the things that were *most* important to you?

THERMOMETER SCORES (LEADERS, CANDIDATES, PARTIES)

(See Note on Standardized Scores, Q. 18)

50. There are many aspects of political parties which strike Canadians in different ways. We would like to get your feelings toward some of these aspects of our parties. We are interested to see how you liked the *leaders, the party's candidate in your riding in the last election,* and *the party as a whole.* We will use the feeling thermometer again for these questions.

   (a) Let's start with the Liberals. How much do you like their leader, Mr. Trudeau? Where would you place him on the thermometer?

   (b) How much did you like your local Liberal candidate in the recent federal election?

   (c) And, finally, how would you rate the Liberal Party, taken as a whole?

   (d) Now, the Progressive Conservatives. How much do you like their leader, Mr. Stanfield? Where would you place him on the thermometer?

   (e) How much did you like your local Progressive Conservative candidate in the recent federal election?

   (f) And, finally, how would you rate the Progressive Conservative Party, taken as a whole?

   (g) How about the NDP? How much do you like their leader, Mr. David Lewis? Where would you place him on the thermometer?

   (h) [IF NDP HAD LOCAL CANDIDATE IN THIS RIDING] How much did you like your local NDP candidate in the recent federal election?

   (i) And, finally, how would you rate the NDP Party taken as a whole?

   (j) How about Social Credit? How much do you like their leader, Mr. Caouette? Where would you place him on the thermometer?

   (k) (IF SOCIAL CREDIT HAD LOCAL CANDIDATE IN THIS RIDING) How much did you like your local Social Credit candidate in the recent federal election?

   (l) And, finally, how would you rate the Social Credit Party, taken as a whole?

*PARTY LEADER IMAGES

Now, we would like to ask you about your impressions of the various leaders of the *federal* political parties.

51. (a) Is there anything in particular that you *like* about Mr. Trudeau?

_____

Anything else? _____

(b) Is there anything in particular that you *dislike* about Mr. Trudeau?

_____

Anything else? _____

52. (a) Is there anything in particular that you *like* about Mr. Stanfield?

_____

Anything else? _____

(b) Is there anything in particular that you *dislike* about Mr. Stanfield?

_____

Anything else? _____

53. (a) Is there anything in particular that you *like* about Mr. Lewis?

_____

Anything else? _____

(b) Is there anything in particular that you *dislike* about Mr. Lewis?

_____

Anything else? _____

54. (a) Is there anything in particular that you *like* about Mr. Caouette?

_____

Anything else? _____

(b) Is there anything in particular that you *dislike* about Mr. Caouette?

_____

Anything else? _____

PARTY IMAGES (FEDERAL)

Now, I would like to ask you what you personally think are the good and bad points about political parties at the *federal* level in Canada.

55. (a) Is there anything in particular that you *like* about the *federal* Liberal Party?

_____

Anything else? _____

(b) Is there anything in particular that you *dislike* about the *federal* Liberal Party?

Anything else? _____

56. (a) Is there anything in particular that you *like* about the *federal* Progressive Conservative Party?

Anything else? _____

(b) Is there anything in particular that you *dislike* about the *federal* Progressive Party?

Anything else? _____

57. (a) Is there anything in particular that you *like* about the *federal* NDP?

(b) Is there anything in particular that you *dislike* about the *federal* NDP?

Anything else? _____

58. (a) Is there anything in particular that you *like* about the *federal* Social Credit Party?

Anything else? _____

(b) Is there anything in particular that you *dislike* about the *federal* Social Credit Party?

Anything else? _____

A number of constructed measures were employed in analysis of the federal and provincial party image questions. First, the mean number of images held (or the mean number of specific types of images) was calculated for each respondent. Since a maximum of two responses for each question were coded for each respondent, the maximum number of federal images possible is 16, and the mean number of mentions may be thought of in terms of this maximum.

The content codes for the party image variables were grouped into six categories: POLICY/ISSUE, STYLE/PERFORMANCE, LEADER/ LEADERSHIP, GENERAL, AREA/GROUP, and IDEOLOGY. This categorization is employed for images of both federal and provincial parties.

PARTISANSHIP (PROVINCIAL)

The provincial partisanship variables were constructed in the same manner as the federal measures (see Q. 30-32).

60. (a) We've been talking about how you feel about parties at the federal level — that is, at the national level. Now, let's talk about *provincial* politics here in (NAME PROVINCE).

Thinking of *provincial* politics here in (NAME PROVINCE), generally speaking, do you usually think of yourself as a Liberal, Conservative, NDP, Social Credit, or what?

(NOTE: IN QUEBEC SAY:) Liberal, Parti Québécois, Social Credit, Union Nationale, or what?

LIBERAL	1
PROGRESSIVE CONSERVATIVE	2
NDP	3
SOCIAL CREDIT	4
OTHER _____	
UNION NATIONALE	6
PARTI QUEBECOIS	7
D.K.	8
INDEPENDENT	0

(b) How strong (PARTY MENTIONED IN Q. 60-62)) do you generally feel — very strongly, fairly strongly, or not very strongly?

VERY STRONGLY	1
FAIRLY STRONGLY	2
NOT VERY STRONGLY	3
D.K.	8
N.A.	9

61. (a) (IF "DON'T KNOW" OR "INDEPENDENT" IN Q. 60. (a)) Well, still thinking of provincial politics here in (NAME PROVINCE), do you generally think of yourself as a little closer to one of the parties than to the others?

YES	1
NO	2
D.K.	8
N.A.	9

(b) (IF YES) Which party is that?

LIBERAL	1
PROGRESSIVE CONSERVATIVE	2
NDP	3
SOCIAL CREDIT	4
OTHER _____	5
UNION NATIONALE	6
PARTI QUEBECOIS	7
D.K.	8
N.A.	9

62. (a) Thinking still of politics here in (NAME PROVINCE), was there ever a time when you thought of yourself as closer to any other party here in (NAME PROVINCE)?

YES 1
NO 2
D.K. 8
N.A. 9

(b) (IF YES) Which party was that?

LIBERAL 1
PROGRESSIVE CONSERVATIVE 2
NDP (INCLUDE CCF) 3
SOCIAL CREDIT 4
OTHER ———————— 5
UNION NATIONALE 6
PARTI QUEBECOIS 7
D.K. 8
N.A. 9

(c) When did you change from that party — that is, the (NAME OF PARTY MENTIONED IN Q. 62 (b))? ————————

(d) What was the main thing that made you change? ————————

PARTY IMAGES (PROVINCIAL)

Provincial and Federal party images were treated similarly in the analysis (see Q. 55-58).

Now, I would like to ask you what you personally think are the good and bad points about political parties at the *provincial* level here in (NAME PROVINCE). Let's start with the *provincial*———————— (PARTY) here in (NAME PROVINCE).

Province	Parties Asked
Nfld., P.E.I., N.S., N.B., Ont.	PC (Q. 66), Lib. (Q. 67), NDP (Q. 68)
British Columbia	NDP (Q. 68), SC (Q. 69), PC (Q. 66), Lib. (Q. 67)
Alberta	PC (Q. 66), SC (Q. 69), NDP (Q. 68), Lib. (Q. 67)
Saskatchewan	NDP (Q. 68), Lib. (Q. 67), PC (Q. 66)
Manitoba	NDP (Q. 68), PC (Q. 66), Lib. (Q. 67), SC (Q. 69)
Quebec	Lib. (Q. 67), PQ (Q. 70), SC (Q. 69), UN (Q. 71)

66. *Progressive Conservative Party* (ASKED IN ALL PROVINCES EXCEPT QUEBEC)

   (a) Is there anything in particular that you *like* about the *provincial* Progressive Conservative Party here in (NAME PROVINCE)?
   _____

   Anything else? _____

   (b) Is there anything in particular that you *dislike* about the Progressive Conservative Party? _____
   Anything else? _____

67. *Liberal Party* (ASKED IN ALL PROVINCES)
   (a) Is there anything in particular that you *like* about the *provincial* Liberal Party here in (NAME PROVINCE)? _____
   Anything else? _____

   (b) Is there anything in particular that you *dislike* about the Liberal Party? _____
   Anything else? _____

68. *NDP Party* (ASKED IN ALL PROVINCES EXCEPT QUEBEC)
   (a) Is there anything in particular that you like about the *provincial* New Democratic Party here in (NAME PROVINCE)? _____
   Anything else? _____

   (b) Is there anything in particular that you *dislike* about the NDP Party? _____
   Anything else? _____

69. *Social Credit Party* (ASKED ONLY IN ALBERTA, BRITISH COLUMBIA, MANITOBA, AND QUEBEC)
   (a) Is there anything in particular that you *like* about the *provincial* Social Credit Party here in (NAME PROVINCE)? _____
   Anything else? _____

   (b) Is there anything in particular that you *dislike* about the Social Credit Party? _____
   Anything else? _____

70. *Parti Québécois* (ASKED IN QUEBEC ONLY)
   (a) Is there anything in particular that you *like* about the Parti Québécois here in Quebec? _____
   Anything else? _____

   (b) Is there anything in particular that you *dislike* about the Parti Québécois? _____
   Anything else? _____

Union Nationale (ASKED IN QUEBEC ONLY)

71. (a) Is there anything in particular that you *like* about the Union Nationale Party in Quebec? _____
Anything else? _____

(b) Is there anything in particular that you *dislike* about the Union Nationale? _____
Anything else? _____

PROVINCIAL VOTING BEHAVIOUR

72. (a) In *provincial* elections, since you have been old enough to vote, would you say that you have voted in all of them, most of them, some of them, or none of them?

ALL	1
MOST	2
SOME	3
NONE	4
D.K.	8

(b) In *provincial* elections, have you always voted for the same party, or have you voted for different parties?

SAME	1
DIFFERENT	2
D.K.	8
N.A.	9

(c) (IF SAME PARTY) Which party is that?

LIBERAL	1
PROGRESSIVE CONSERVATIVE	2
NDP	3
SOCIAL CREDIT	4
OTHER _____	5
UNION NATIONALE	6
PARTI QUEBECOIS	7
D.K.	8
N.A.	9

DEMOGRAPHIC MEASURES
OCCUPATION, SOCIO-ECONOMIC STATUS

The following detailed occupation sequence was used to construct the Blishen measure of socio-economic status. The Blishen index ranges from 14.41 to 75.32, and is based on the 1971 census data. A discussion of the construction and use of the Blishen measure may be found in Bernard Blishen and Hugh McRoberts, "A Revised Socioeconomic Index for Occupations in Canada," *Canadian Review of Sociology and Anthropology*, 13 (1976), pp. 71-80.

The four-digit Blishen score is used in multivariate and correlation analysis. For tabular analysis, the following categorization was employed, derived from cutting points within one standard deviation (14.60) of the mean score for the entire sample (42.41). This yields four socio-economic status categories as follows:

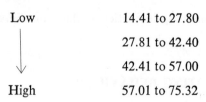

Low	14.41 to 27.80
	27.81 to 42.40
	42.41 to 57.00
High	57.01 to 75.32

76. (a) What is your occupation? (IF NO OCCUPATION, EXPLAIN WHY IN BOX BELOW.)

RECORD JOB TITLE....

_____

INTERVIEWER: IF IT IS ALREADY CLEAR THAT THE OCCUPA-TION IS NON-MANUAL, MANUAL, OR FARM-ING, GO TO (c) AS IN-DICATED.

RESPONDENT NO

OCCUPATION .... ☐
HOUSEWIFE 01
RETIRED .... 02 GO
STUDENT .... 03 TO
UNEMPLOYED .... 04 Q.
NEVER WORKED 05 77
OTHER REASONS (SPECIFY)
_____ 06

(b) (IF OCCUPATION IS *NOT* CLEAR, PROBE.) What exactly do you do?

_____

_____

(c) R E C O R D   B E L O W WHETHER OCCUPA-TION IS NON-MANUAL, MANUAL, OR FARM-ING, AND PROCEED TO QUESTION AC-CORDINGLY:

NON-MANUAL_____   MANUAL_____   FARMING_____

(IF NOT ALREADY CLEAR, ASK)

(d) Is your job an executive position or what?

EXECUTIVE —
DISTINGUISH
BETWEEN:

OWNER 1

OTHER
MANAGER.... 2

NOT
EXECUTIVE .. 3
GO TO (f)

IF OWNER OR MANAGER

(e) How many people does your company employ? —

ASK EVERYONE

(f) How many people are working under you? —————

(g) What does your company do? —
—————————
—————————

(d) Did you have any special training for your job?

YES...... 1
NO........ 2
GO TO (f)

IF YES
(e) What sort of training?

APPREN-
TICESHIP 1
SPECIAL
CLASSES 2
OTHER 3

ASK EVERYONE

(f) Does your employer regard you as a skilled person? YES.... 1
NO...... 2

(g) How many people are working under you? —————

(h) How many years experience do you have on the job?
————

(d) Do you own the farm or manage it?

OWNER 1
MANAGER 2
GO TO (f)

OTHER FARM
WORKER 3

IF FARM WORKER
(e) How many years have you been working on a farm? ——

ASK EVERYONE

(f) How many people do you have working under you or for you? —————

(g) How many acres is the farm? ——

(h) What is the main product? —————
—————————

---

77. Are you married, widowed, separated, divorced, or are you single?

MARRIED 1
WIDOWED 2
SEPARATED 3
DIVORCED 4
SINGLE 5

INTERVIEWER: CIRCLE THE CODE BELOW WHICH FITS RESPONDENT AND SEE INSTRUCTIONS IN THE BOX MARKED ***.

ALL RESPON-DENTS WITH OCCUPATION	*MALES WITHOUT OCCUPATION*	*FEMALES WITH-OUT OCCUPATION*
NOT MARRIED 1	RETIRED 2	SINGLE, RETIRED 2
MARRIED MALE 1	UNEMPLOYED 3	SINGLE,
MARRIED FEMALE 4	OTHER 6	UNEMPLOYED 3
WIDOWED FEMALE .. 5		OTHER SINGLE 6
DIVORCED FEMALE .. 5		MARRIED 4
SEPARATED FEMALE .. 5		WIDOWED,
		DIVORCED, OR
		SEPARATED 5

***INTERVIEWER: FOLLOW INSTRUCTIONS BELOW DEPENDING ON THE CODE DETERMINED ABOVE.

1. GO NOW TO Q. 79 (a)
2. ASK Q. 78 FOR RESPONDENT'S FORMER OCCUPATION
3. ASK Q. 78 FOR RESPONDENT'S REGULAR OCCUPATION
4. ASK Q. 78 FOR OCCUPATION OF RESPONDENT'S HUSBAND
5. ASK Q. 78 FOR OCCUPATION OF RESPONDENT'S FORMER HUSBAND
6. ASK Q. 78 FOR OCCUPATION OF RESPONDENT'S FATHER

78. (a) What is (was) the occupation of (PERSON SELECTED IN BOX***)

    RECORD JOB TITLE _____

    INTERVIEWER: IF THE RESPONDENT SAYS THAT THE PERSON YOU ARE ASKING ABOUT IS (OR WAS) WITHOUT AN OCCUPATION BECAUSE HE IS (OR WAS):

    1. RETIRED — ASK ABOUT THAT PERSON'S FORMER OCCUPATION.
    2. UNEMPLOYED — ASK ABOUT THAT PERSON'S REGULAR OCCUPATION.

3. ANY OTHER REASON — ASK ABOUT THAT PERSON'S FATHER'S REGULAR OCCUPATION.

INTERVIEWER: IF IT IS ALREADY CLEAR THAT THE OCCUPATION IS NON-MANUAL, MANUAL, OR FARMING — GO TO (c). IF IT IS NOT CLEAR — PROBE WITH (b).

(b) What exactly does (did) he do? _____

(c) RECORD BELOW WHETHER OCCUPATION IS NON-MANUAL, MANUAL, OR FARMING, AND PROCEED TO (d) ACCORDINGLY:

NON-MANUAL___   MANUAL___   FARMING___

(IF NOT ALREADY CLEAR, ASK.)

(d) Is (was) his job an executive position or what?	(d) Did he have any special training for his job?	(d) Does (did) he own the farm or manage it?
EXECUTIVE — DISTINGUISH BETWEEN: OWNER 1	YES.... 1 NO...... 2 GO TO (f)	OWNER .... 1 MANAGER .... 2 GO TO (f)
OTHER MANAGER 2	*IF YES* (e) What sort of training? APPRENTICE-	OTHER FARM WORKER 3
NOT EXECUTIVE .. 3 GO TO (f)	SHIP .... 1 SPECIAL CLASSES .... 2 OTHER 3	*IF FARM WORKER* (e) How many years has (had) he been working on a farm? _____
IF OWNER OR MANAGER		

(e) How many people does (did) his company employ?
_____.

ASK EVERYONE

(f) How many people are (were) working under him?
_____

(g) What does (did) his company do?
_____
_____

ASK EVERYONE

(f) Does (did) his employer regard him as a skilled person? YES.... 1 NO...... 2

(g) How many people are (were) working under him?
_____

(h) How many years experience does (did) he have on the job? _____

ASK EVERYONE

(f) How many people does (did) he have working under him or for him? _____

(g) How many acres is (was) the farm? _____

(h) What is (was) the main product?
_____
_____

EDUCATION

79. (a) How many years of school did you attend? ....Years
    (b) What is the highest grade or level of school you reached?..............

	Highest Grade or Level

(c) Did you complete high school? YES 1
NO 2
D.K. 8
N.A. 9

(d) Did you ever attend University, College, or some other post-secondary school? YES 1
NO 2
D.K. 8
N.A. 9

(e) (IF "YES") Did you obtain a degree or degrees? YES 1
NO 2
D.K. 8
N.A. 9

In multivariate and correlation analysis, the variable "years of education" (Q. 79 (a)) is used. For tabular analysis, the following categorization was employed, derived from the information contained in the entire sequence:

Grade school
Some high school
Completed high school
Some college or post secondary
College or university degree

SUBJECTIVE SOCIAL CLASS

87. (a) One hears a lot about different social classes. Do you ever think of yourself as belonging to a social class?

YES 1
NO 2
D.K. 8

(b) (IF YES) Which of the following five social classes would you say you were in: Upper class, upper-middle class, middle class, working class, or lower class?

UPPER CLASS 1
UPPER-MIDDLE CLASS 2
MIDDLE CLASS 3
WORKING CLASS 4
LOWER CLASS 5
D.K. 8
N.A. 9

(c) (IF NO OR D.K. IN Q. 87 (a)) Well, if you had to make a choice, would you say you were in the upper class, upper-middle class, middle class, working class, or lower class?

UPPER CLASS 1
UPPER-MIDDLE CLASS 2
MIDDLE CLASS 3
WORKING CLASS 4
LOWER CLASS 5
REFUSED 7
D.K. 8
N.A. 9

(d) (IF CLASS CHOSEN IN Q. 87 (b) or (c)) Some people feel they have a lot in common with other people of their own class, but others don't feel this way so much. How about you? Would you say you feel pretty close to other (*CLASS CHOSEN ABOVE*) people, or that you don't feel much closer to them than you do to people in other classes?

PRETTY CLOSE TO OWN
  CLASS 1
NOT CLOSER TO OWN CLASS 2
D.K. 8
N.A. 9

(e) On the whole, do you think that there is bound to be some conflict between different social classes, or do you think they can get along together without any conflict?

BOUND TO BE CONFLICT 1
CAN GET ALONG TOGETHER 2
D.K. 8

RELIGION

88. (a) What is your religion? (IF PROTESTANT MENTIONED, PROBE FOR SPECIFIC DENOMINATION.)

ROMAN CATHOLIC 01
UNITED CHURCH 02
ANGLICAN 03
PRESBYTERIAN 04
BAPTIST 05
LUTHERAN 06
UKRAINIAN (GREEK)
  CATHOLIC 07
GREEK ORTHODOX 08
JEWISH 09
PENTACOSTAL 10
SALVATION ARMY 11
JEHOVAH WITNESS 12
MENNONITE 13
OTHER PROTESTANT
  (SPECIFY) ——————————

ALL OTHER (SPECIFY) ——————

NONE 00

(b) About how often do you go to church (synagogue)? At least once a week, two or three times a month, once a month, a few times a year or less, never?

ONCE A WEEK 1
TWO, THREE TIMES A
  MONTH 2
ONCE A MONTH 3
FEW TIMES A YEAR OR LESS 4
NEVER 5
D.K. 8
N.A. 9

(c) Do you consider yourself a very religious person, a fairly religious person, or not very religious person?

VERY RELIGIOUS 1
FAIRLY RELIGIOUS 2
NOT VERY RELIGIOUS 3
D.K. 8
N.A. 9

MOBILITY

89. (a) In what country were you born?

CANADA	01
BRITISH ISLES	02
FRANCE	03
GERMANY	04
HUNGARY	05
ITALY	06
NETHERLANDS (HOLLAND)	07
POLAND	08
RUSSIA	09
OTHER EUROPEAN (SPECIFY)	10

UNITED STATES	11
ALL OTHER (SPECIFY)	12

(b) (IF RESPONDENT WAS BORN OUTSIDE OF CANADA, ASK) In what year did you come to live in Canada? _____

(c) How much of your life have you lived in (NAME PROVINCE)?

ALL YOUR LIFE	1
MOST OF IT	2
SOME OF IT	3
ONLY A YEAR OR SO	4
D.K.	8

(d) Have you ever lived in any other provinces?

YES	1
NO	2

(e) (IF YES) Which one(s)?

NEWFOUNDLAND	1
PRINCE EDWARD ISLAND	1
NOVA SCOTIA	1
NEW BRUNSWICK	1
QUEBEC	1
ONTARIO	1
MANITOBA	1
SASKATCHEWAN	1
ALBERTA	1
BRITISH COLUMBIA	1

A summary index of geographic mobility was constructed from the information contained in Q. 89 (d) and (e), according to the number of provinces in which respondent has lived.

Low   0. Never lived in another province.

   ↓   1. Lived in one other province.

High   2. Lived in two or more other provinces.

ETHNICITY

90. Can you tell me what ethnic or cultural group your ancestors who first came to North America belonged to? (IF NECESSARY) On the male side. (DO NOT ACCEPT CANADA OR UNITED STATES AS AN ANSWER.)

CZECKOSLOVAKIAN, SLOVAKIAN ... 01
CHINESE, JAPANESE, OTHER ORIENTAL ... 02
ENGLISH ... 03
FINNISH, ESTONIAN ... 04
FRENCH ... 05
GERMAN, AUSTRIAN ... 06
GREEK, MALTESE ... 07
HUNGARIAN ... 08
IRISH ... 09
ITALIAN ... 10
JEWISH/HEBREW ... 11
LATVIAN, LITHUANIAN ... 12
NETHERLANDS (DUTCH), BELGIAN ... 13
POLISH ... 14
SCANDINAVIAN (DANISH, ICELANDIC, NORWEGIAN, SWEDISH) ... 15
SCOTTISH ... 16
RUSSIAN ... 17
UKRAINIAN ... 18
YUGOSLAVIAN ... 19
WELSH ... 20
NATIVE INDIAN OR ESKIMO 21
OTHER (SPECIFY) _____

LANGUAGE

91. (a) What language did you first learn as a child that you still speak or understand?

ENGLISH	1
FRENCH	2
OTHER (SPECIFY) ————	3

(b) What language do you usually speak at home?

ENGLISH ONLY	1
FRENCH ONLY	2
ENGLISH AND FRENCH EQUALLY	3
ENGLISH AND OTHER EQUALLY	4
(SPECIFY) ————	
OTHER ONLY (SPECIFY) ————	5
ALL OTHER COMBINATIONS (SPECIFY) ————	

(c) Do you speak any languages other than those you have just mentioned?

YES	☐
NO	0

(d) (IF YES) Which ones?

ENGLISH	1
FRENCH	2
ENGLISH AND FRENCH	3
OTHER (SPECIFY) ————	
ALL OTHER COMBINATIONS (SPECIFY) ————	

AGE

94. What was your exact age on your last birthday? (RECORD EXACT AGE) ————

(INTERVIEWER: IF RESPONDENT REFUSES, *ESTIMATE* EXACT AGE ———— YEARS)

In addition to exact age in years (which is employed in multivariate and correlation analyses), the following two categorizations of respondent's age were used.

Age (grouped)	Age (Cohorts)
under 30	Trudeau/Stanfield era (18-27 yrs.)
30-45 yrs.	Diefenbaker/Pearson era (28-37 yrs.)
46-59 yrs.	Post World War II (38-49 yrs.)
Over 60	World War II (48-60 yrs.)
	Interwar (61-77 yrs.)
	Pre-1918 (78 yrs. or older)

97. SEX

MALE 1

FEMALE 2

98. LANGUAGE IN WHICH INTER-
VIEW WAS CONDUCTED

ENGLISH 1

FRENCH 2

OTHER (SPECIFY) ——————

LOCATION

COMMUNITY SIZE, REGION, PROVINCE
In addition to the standard province and region categorizations, the following measure of community size was employed in the analysis:

> metropolitan areas (city and suburbs)
>
> smaller cities
>
> towns
>
> rural areas

An interval scale version of this measure based on actual population size of the communities is employed in some analyses.

SUBJECT INDEX

INDEX OF AUTHORS